AF271530

COLOURS!

Edited by Didier Ottinger

Translated from French by Anne McDowall

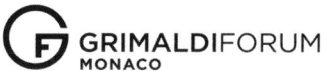 GRIMALDIFORUM MONACO

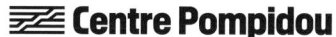 Centre Pompidou

SKIRA

Unless otherwise stated, the works reproduced
are held at the Musée National d'Art Moderne,
Centre Pompidou, Paris.

On the cover pages:

Gerhard Richter
1024 Colours (350-3), 1973,
Lacquer on canvas, 254 × 478 × 5 cm
Gift of the artist in 1984
Centre Pompidou, Paris, Musée National d'Art Moderne –
Centre de Création Industrielle

This catalogue is published on the occasion of the exhibition
"Colours! Masterpieces from the Centre Pompidou"
at the Grimaldi Forum Monaco from July 8 to August 31st 2025.

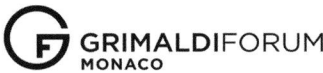 **Centre Pompidou**

GRIMALDIFORUM
MONACO

10, avenue Princesse Grace
98000 Monaco
www.grimaldiforum.com

President
Henri Fissore

General Manager
Sylvie Biancheri

Director of Cultural Events
Catherine Alestchenkoff

Director of Building
Christophe Uhring

Safety and Security Director
Philippe Martin

Director of Events
Hélène Pringault

Legal and Financial Director
Fabienne Guaitolini

Director of Communication
Dany Rubrecht

Communication Managers
Shirley Lucaccio and Cécile Valentin Musial

MONACO

Isabelle Berro-Amadeï
Acting Minister of State
Minister of Foreign Affairs
and Cooperation

Lionel Beffre
Minister of Interior

Pierre-André Chiappori
Minister of Finance and Economy

With the participation of:

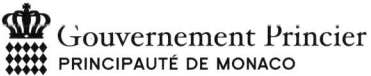 Gouvernement Princier
PRINCIPAUTÉ DE MONACO

This exhibition was made possible
with the support from:

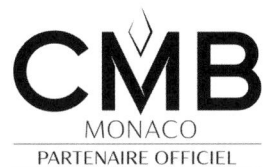 CMB
MONACO
PARTENAIRE OFFICIEL

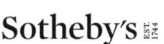 Sotheby's

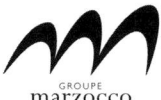 GROUPE marzocco

CENTRE NATIONAL D'ART ET DE CULTURE
GEORGES POMPIDOU

The Centre National d'Art et de Culture Georges Pompidou
is a national public establishment under the supervision
of the French Ministry of Culture (Law 75-1, 3 January 1975).

Laurent Le Bon
President, Director & CEO

Julie Narbey
Executive Director

Charlotte Bruyerre
Deputy Director

Xavier Rey
Director
Musée National d'Art Moderne –
Centre de Création Industrielle

Mathieu Potte-Bonneville
Director
Department Culture and Creation

Floriane de Saint Pierre
Chair
Amis du Centre Pompidou

MUSÉE NATIONAL D'ART MODERNE –
CENTRE DE CRÉATION INDUSTRIELLE

Xavier Rey, Director
Jeanne Brun, Deputy Director in Charge of Collections
Alexia Szumigala, Head of Collections
Raphaële Bianchi, Loans Manager
Rafaël Grynberg, Exhibition and Collections Manager
Aurélie Sahuqé, Exhibition and Collections Manager
Marie-Ange Brayer, Head Curator, Design and Industrial
Prospective Collection Department
Mathilde Vallée, Collection Manager, Design Collection
Valentina Moimas, Chief Curator, Architecture
Collection Department
Boris Hamzeian, Researcher, Architecture
Collection Department
Stéphanie Elarbi, Head of the Conservation Department
Sophie Spalek, Conservator
Bérangère Foucher, Conservator
Astrid Lorenzen, Conservator
Perrine Renaud, Photo Librarian
Éric Galliache, Framer
Sten Kimbidima, Storage Registrar

PRODUCTION DEPARTMENT

Claire Garnier, Director
Sandrine Beaujard-Vallet, Head of Artworks Management
Kim Dang, Artwork Registrar
Mariolina Cilurzo, Artwork Registrar

COMMUNICATIONS
AND DIGITAL DEPARTMENT

Geneviève Paire, Director
Marie Joly, Communication Manager
Marine Prévot, Press Attaché
Tara Benveniste, Head of Social Networks
Léa Touchaleaume, Head of Administration and Finance

ECONOMIC AND INTERNATIONAL
DEVELOPMENT DEPARTMENT

Gaële de Medeiros, Director
Élisa Vignaud, International Exhibitions Manager

PUBLISHING, LICENSING
AND RETAIL DEPARTMENT

Guillaume Grandgeorge, Director
Chloé Demey, Head of Editorial
Margot Boyer, Head and Deputy Director for Marketing and
Sales
Charlotte Lassansàa, International Rights and BtoB Manager
Héloïse Kling, International and Territorial Manager
Lauriane Pigot, Merchandising and Licensing Manager

INSTITUTE FOR RESEARCH
AND COORDINATION IN ACOUSTICS/MUSIC

Frank Madlener, Director
Emmanuelle Zoll, Cultural Programmes Director
Raphaël Bourdier, Production Manager
Roque Rivas, Composer and Sound Designer

EXHIBITION

Curator
Didier Ottinger

Guest Artists:

Alexis Dadier
Perfume Creator, Robertet

With the contribution of Charlotte Urbain
Director of Culture and Communications
Fragonard Parfumeur

Marion Mailaender
Interior Architect, Designer
Assisted by Alix Arbeille, Jeanne Facomprez
and Bela Jaffrenou

Roque Rivas
Sound Designer

Scenography and Project Management /
Grimaldi Forum Monaco
William Chatelain
Assisted by Antoine Ceunebroucke

General Coordination / Grimaldi Forum Monaco
Catherine Alestchenkoff

Cultural Executive, Education and Public
Development Manager / Grimaldi Forum Monaco
Marie Cambas

Registrar / Grimaldi Forum Monaco
Fabien Mage

Graphic Design
Philippe Brulin

Text Writing
Liv Diaz y Burgo

CATALOGUE

Editor-in-Chief
Didier Ottinger

Contributors (in order of appearance):

Didier Ottinger, Chief Curator, Deputy Director
in Charge of cultural programming at the Musée National
d'Art Moderne – Centre Pompidou
Michel Gauthier, Curator at the Musée National
d'Art Moderne – Centre Pompidou
Claire Maingon, Senior Lecturer with Habilitation in
Contemporary Art History, University of Rouen-Normandy
Alain Cueff, Art Historian and Professor at the École Nationale
Supérieure des Arts Décoratifs, Paris
Hayley Edwards-Dujardin, Art and Fashion Historian
Marie Gispert, Professor of Contemporary Art History,
University Grenoble Alpes, LARHRA
Miguel Egaña, Artist, Emeritus Professor, University Paris 1 –
Panthéon-Sorbonne
Jacques Soulillou, Doctor of Philosophy, Member of AICA
Marion Mailaender, Interior Architect, Designer
Pascal Rousseau, Professor of Contemporary Art History,
University Paris 1 – Panthéon-Sorbonne
Roque Rivas, Sound Designer
Alexis Dadier, Perfume Creator, Robertet
Marguerite Leroy, PhD Candidate in Art History – University
Paris 1 – Panthéon-Sorbonne, HiCSA

Image and Documentary Research Coordinator
Marie Cambas

Editorial Coordinator
Elsa Hougue

ÉDITIONS SKIRA

Publishing Manager
Nathalie Prat-Couadau

Editorial Coordination
Maria Notó Mora and Juliette Chambon

Editorial and Commercial Projects Manager
Irène Rodriguez

Junior editor
Roxanne Rebours

Editorial assistant
Marion Duterque (intern)

Graphic Design
Brice Tourneux

Translation from French to English
Anne McDowall

Copyediting
Timothy Stroud

Colour Separation
Litho Art

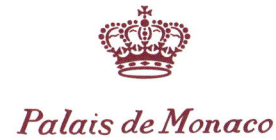

The Principality of Monaco is honoured to host, for the second time, one of the world's most prestigious museums, the Centre Pompidou, whose unique exhibition in the Espace Ravel provides a new understanding of the modern and contemporary history of colour in the arts.

The invaluable assistance of Didier Ottinger, chief curator and assistant director of the Musée National d'Art Moderne – Centre Pompidou in Paris, who is well acquainted with the excellence of the Parisian institution's collections, has made possible an exhibition that moves away from the chronological narrative of modern and contemporary art history and seeks to explore the correlations and divergences between major 20th-century works viewed through the prism of colour.

Ranging from Fauvism and Cubism to Surrealism and Abstraction, via the Écoles de Paris, and embracing, from the 1960s on, Nouveau Réalisme, Pop Art, Minimalism, Conceptual Art and the most contemporary expressions, "Colours! Masterpieces from the Centre Pompidou" excites both the eye and the mind, offering visitors a sensory and studied approach to modern chromaticism in art in all its forms – painting, sculpture and design.

The catalogue boasts contributions from some of the most highly regarded authorities in the field, making this an essential work on this historical and cultural subject. Our warmest thanks go to all the authors, and first and foremost to Didier Ottinger, the curator of this exhibition, Laurent Le Bon, president of the Centre National d'Art et de Culture Georges-Pompidou, and their teams, for taking up the challenge of this ambitious subject.

H.S.H. Prince Albert II of Monaco

Raymond Hains   *Pour le bâtiment Georges Pompidou* [*For the Georges Pompidou Building*]   1976

gelatin silver print   110.5 × 165 cm   gift of the artist, 1979, AM 1978-1

For those looking at the cityscape of Paris, the connection between the Centre Pompidou and colours is immediately apparent. Emerging from slate and zinc roofs in subtle shades of grey, the Centre Pompidou launches its bright red, blue, green and yellow pipes into the Parisian sky.

When the building first opened, some observed that its colours reflected those of Fernand Léger's paintings of 1925. Beyond this formal similarity, building and paintings share the same enthusiasm for technology, the same faith in the future.

Could the colours of the Centre Pompidou be those of the works of the Musée National d'Art Moderne housed in the building? Thirteen years after it hosted "Extra Large", an exhibition of monumental works from the Centre Pompidou collection, this is the question that the Grimaldi Forum seeks to answer, in an exhibition that considers the colours of modern art.

"Colours!" is one of the first chapters in a 'Constellation' that will see the collections – including design, which features prominently in the Monaco exhibition – presented in France and internationally in an offsite programme of exhibitions that showcase the diversity of the national collections.

In the originality of its approach and the boldness of its scenography, "Colours!" fully aligns with this vast experimental project, whose theoretical proposals and museographic innovations will enrich the Centre Pompidou once it has completed its metamorphosis.

We are grateful to H.S.H. Prince Albert II of Monaco and to the Grimaldi Forum and its teams for hosting this exhibition. Our pride in showing the history of the Centre Pompidou through the prism of its colours is magnificently matched by this Monaco setting. We gratefully acknowledge the commitment of Didier Ottinger, curator of this exhibition and deputy director in charge of cultural programming. Finally, our warmest thanks go to the Centre Pompidou teams, who have worked together to develop this major project, and to all those who have contributed to the realisation of this exhibition and its catalogue.

Laurent Le Bon
President of the Centre Pompidou

Xavier Rey
Director of the Musée National d'Art Moderne –
Centre de Création Industrielle

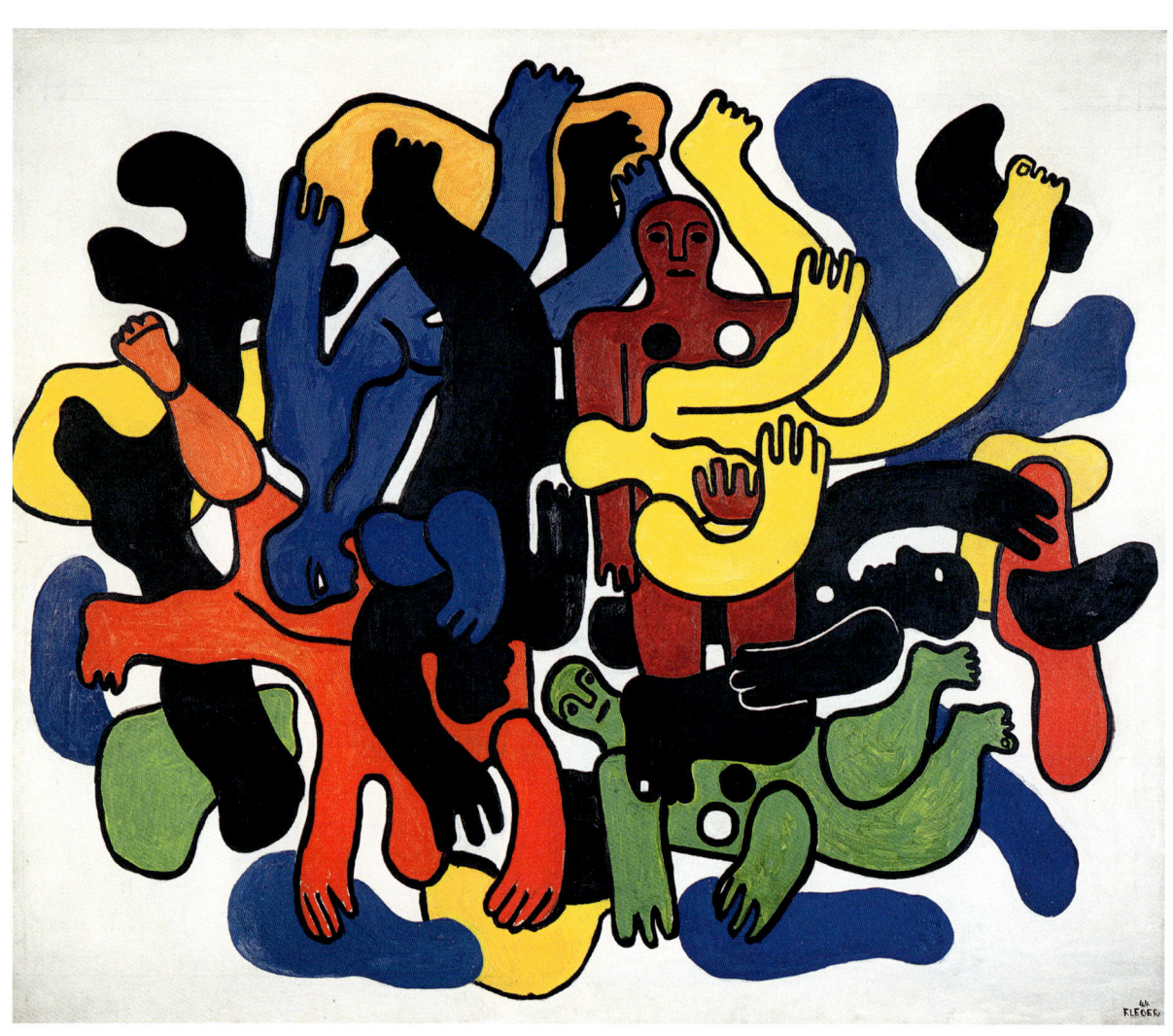

Fernand Léger   *Les Grands Plongeurs noirs* [*Large Black Divers*]   1944

oil on canvas   189 × 221 cm   dation, 1982, AM 1982-102

Didier Ottinger

MODERN GREYS

"Painting should not be exclusively retinal or visual;
it should have to do with the grey matter,
with our urge for understanding".

Marcel Duchamp

"If our grey matter was more rose-tinted,
the world would have fewer black thoughts".

Pierre Dac

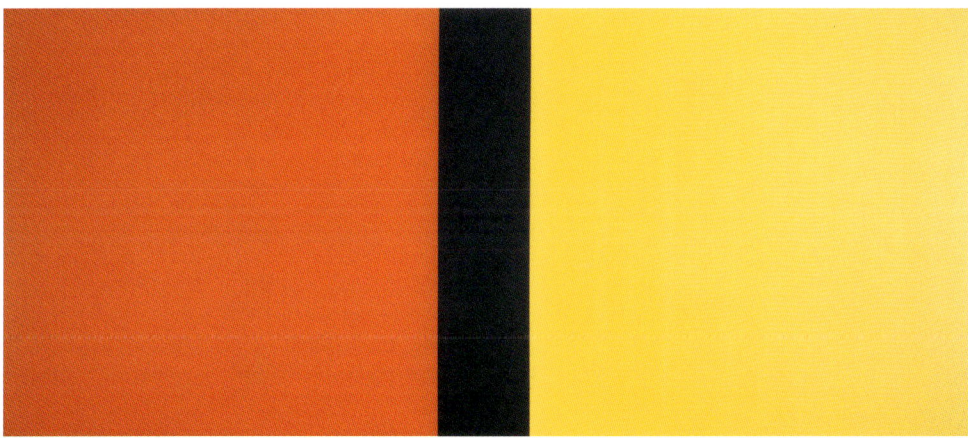

Fig.1 Barnett Newman
*Who's Afraid of Red,
Yellow and Blue IV*, 1969–70,
acrylic on canvas,
274.3 × 604.5 cm
Nationalgalerie, National
Museums, Berlin. Property
of the Verein der Freunde der
Nationalgalerie
Acquired with the support of
the Prussian Cultural Heritage
Foundation, 1982

"Who's afraid of red, yellow and blue?", wondered Barnett Newman in a painting created in 1969 (fig. 1). The question may seem strange, coming from one of the most 'progressive' figures in the art world of his time. Wasn't the avant-garde all about liberation and the celebration of colour?

Did not the efflorescence of Impressionism and its exaltation of light mark the historic triumph of emancipated colour, its 'purity' restored?

The generation that followed that of the Impressionists – Paul Signac, Camille Pissarro, Georges Seurat – brought about the fusion between artistic innovation and scientific and social progress; a fusion that gave rise to the term 'avant-garde', coined in the late 19th century by Saint-Simonian technophiles. Written in 1899, Signac's *D'Eugène Delacroix au néo-impressionnisme* [*From Eugène Delacroix to Neo-Impressionism*] was the first history of this 'avant-garde', whose attachment to colour was foundational both theoretically and practically.

For a long time, progress, of which the artistic avant-garde became a militant auxiliary, could not be conceived of independent of scientific positivism. This synthesis originated when Seurat and the Post-Impressionists decided to organise their palettes on the basis of the scientific laws of colour advanced by chemist Michel-Eugène Chevreul and physicists Ogden Rood and Hermann von Helmholtz. Modern painters' adoption of these scientific colour laws protected them from the dangers of the sort of sensualist evanescence and imprecision of which the Poussinists had accused the Rubenists, champions of colour, in the 17th century. Solidly grounded in science, the avant-garde could legitimately be associated with the march of Progress.

But colour carries within it the seeds of subjectivism, the catalyst for the capricious.

At the turn of the 20th century, František Kupka's painting was representative of the ambiguity and inner turmoil that cannot be escaped by anyone who makes colour the primary agent of their art. His work oscillates between two poles: the first, of a symbolism rooted in his background and training, and the second, of a materialistic and specific 'modern' art – in other words, one dedicated to its sole field of expression. Like his contemporaries – Wassily Kandinsky, Piet Mondrian – for whom colour was of primary importance, Kupka moved effortlessly between Newton's 'scientific' colour wheels and Johann Wolfgang von Goethe's symbolic, subjective colour.

The ambiguity inherent in colour, and its strong ties to sensualism, made it suspect in the eyes of those working to produce a form of modern art characterised by rigour and precision.

Although the virtually concomitant appearance of abstract painting and Cubism marked the advent of an art form with its own autonomy and specific laws, only Cubism, with its assertive achromatism, could come close to the objective reasoning with which modern art aspired to merge. Guillaume Apollinaire, who considered that Georges Braque's and Pablo Picasso's painting was no longer "an art of imitation, but an art of conception",[1] defined the issues surrounding the emerging Cubism. "Colour could produce sensations that disturb the space somewhat, and that is the reason I have abandoned it",[2] confessed Georges Braque, while Fernand Léger related his discovery of Braque's and Picasso's paintings thus: "... we saw, the great Delaunay and I, what the Cubists were doing. Delaunay, surprised to see their grey canvases, exclaimed 'But they're painting with cobwebs, these fellows!'"[3]

The achromatism of 'cobwebs' became a distinctive feature of Cubism at its most speculative (around 1912, during its 'analytic' phase, fig. 2). Beyond Cubism, grey soon became the hallmark of the avant-garde.

The evolution of Mondrian's art, in terms of colour, is indicative of this. In his early compositions, the Dutch painter borrowed from Fauvism, and from his compatriot Vincent van Gogh, a palette of pure colours (fig. 3) – an intensity of colour that was radically called into question in the early 1910s by his discovery of Cubism. Abandoning Fauvist lyricism in favour of Cubist speculation, he converted his painting to grey (fig. 4). When, in 1914, colour rediscovered its rightful place in his paintings, it was 'pure', as 'abstract' as his art had become. Mondrian's colour had moved from Expressionism to the 'scientific' neutrality of a colour chart.

In contrast to the colour wheels that still inspired Impressionists and Post-Impressionists, Mondrian opted for colour charts, which had become widespread from 1880 onwards, and for the objectivity of the scientific colours used in industry and decoration.[4] Significantly, his new colours fit into the geometric grid pattern that he had extrapolated from Cubist compositions.

If Mondrian's work is exemplary of the advent of modern painting in more ways than one, it is because of its systematic use of the 'grid', which epitomised the ideals and ambition of the modern project. Rosalind Krauss claims that this grid "is emblematic of the modernist ambitions of the visual arts". She adds: "The grid states the autonomy of the realm of art, [...] it is anti-natural, anti-mimetic, anti-real".[5]

FROM THE AVANT-GARDE TO MODERNISM

The transition from colour as the hallmark of the avant-garde to the grey of absolute artistic radicalism was a result of Modernism, of a theory of modern art that considers only its formal and material dimension.

This 'Modernism', which, after the Second World War, theorised the nature and development of modern art, made Cubism and its achromatism the inaugural moment of its history. A history that, after a long interruption, was being resumed. Clement Greenberg comments:

> I do not think it exaggerated to say that Pollock's 1946–1950 manner really took up Analytical Cubism from the point at which Picasso and Braque had left it when, in their collages of 1912 and 1913, they drew back from the utter abstractness for which Analytical Cubism seemed headed.[6]

Until his ideas became established, the American critic continued to drive home his theory of a transfer of the Parisian avant-garde of the 1910s to post-war New York:

> "[...] Gorky, De Kooning and Pollock [...] all three of whom set out to catch, and to some extent did catch (or at least Pollock did) some of the uncaught hares that Picasso had started".[7]

Building on the formal advances made by Cubism, the painters of the New York School put the finishing touches to a form of painting that explored the forms and techniques of its own 'self-purification', converted to 'pure visibility' and adopted an uncompromising flatness. Greenberg set the course for the new form of painting:

> It seems to be a law of modernism—thus one that applies to almost all art that remains truly alive in our time—that the conventions not essential to the viability of a medium be discarded as soon as they are recognized.[8]

The resolute reflexivity and theoretical rigour of the new American art are reflected in the achromatic

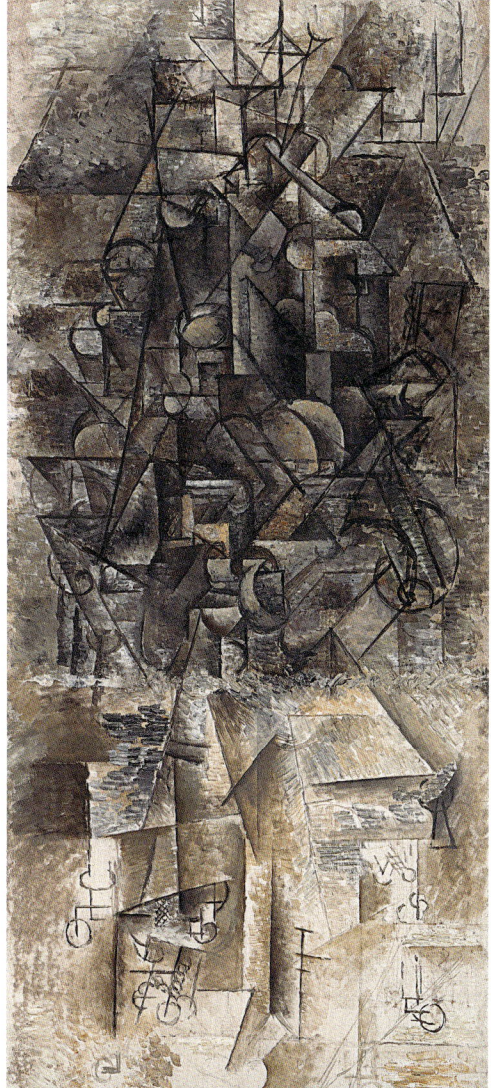

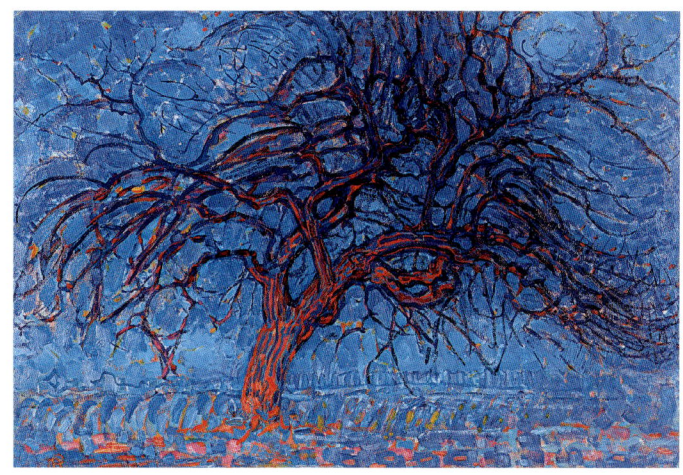

3

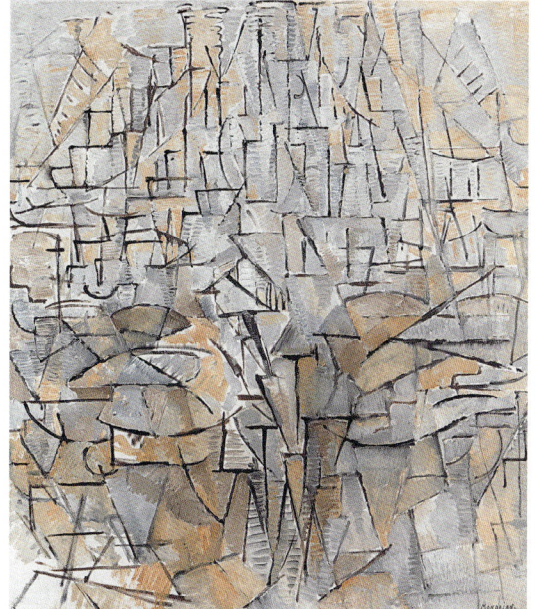

4

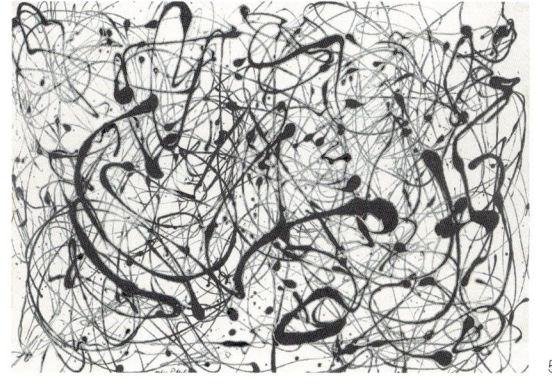

5

2

Fig. 2 Pablo Picasso
Homme à la mandoline
[*Man with a Mandolin*],
Autumn 1911,
oil on canvas, 162 × 71 cm
Musée National Picasso-Paris,
Paris. MP35

Fig. 3 Piet Mondrian
The Red Tree, 1908–10,
oil on canvas, 70 × 99 cm
Kunstmuseum Den Haag,
The Hague. 0332041

Fig. 4 Piet Mondrian
Painting no. 4 /
Composition no. VIII /
Composition 3, 1913,
oil on canvas, 95 × 80 cm
Kunstmuseum Den Haag,
The Hague. Bequest
of Salomon B. Slijper. 033431

Fig. 5 Jackson Pollock
Number 14: Gray, 1948,
enamel over gesso
on paper, 57 × 78.5 cm
Yale University Art Gallery,
New Haven. Katharine Ordway
Collection. 06520. 1980.13.74

6

7

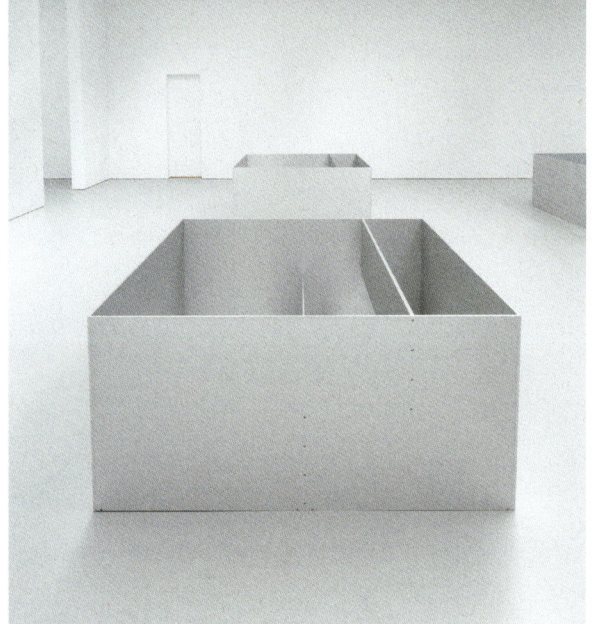

8

Fig. 6 Barnett Newman
Black Fire I, 1961,
oil on canvas, 289.5 × 213.3 cm
Private collection

Fig. 7 Agnes Martin
The Tree, 1964,
oil and pencil on canvas,
182.8 × 182.8 cm
Museum of Modern Art (MoMA),
New York. Larry Aldrich
Foundation Fund. 5.1965

Fig. 8 Installation view,
"Donald Judd"
6 May – 25 June 2011
David Zwirner Gallery, New York
Courtesy David Zwirner, Donald
Judd Art © Judd Foundation/
ADAGP, Paris, 2025

nature of the works (fig. 5). Although *Cathedral*, Jackson Pollock's first drip painting, includes a few red and blue lines, grey is the dominant tone. As Greenberg confirms:

> [...] it was only in 1950 that 'abstract expressionism' jelled as a general manifestation. And only then did two of its henceforth conspicuous features, the huge canvas and the black and white oil, become ratified.[9]

He clarifies:

> It was in 1945, or maybe even earlier, that Gorky painted black and white oils that were more than a *tour de force*. De Kooning followed suit about a year or two later. Pollock, after having produced isolated black and white pictures since 1947, did a whole show of them in 1951.[10]

As had been the case with Cubism, which had reinstated colour after a (grey) hiatus and a period of innovation,[11] Pollock's drip paintings took the easy option and were overrun with colour.

EVER MORE RADICAL, EVER GREYER

In the wake of the painters of the New York School, a new generation soon began brandishing the grey banner of radicality.

After having tried his hand in the 1930s at a style derived from Expressionism, Barnett Newman studied philosophy, opted for theory and devoted himself to teaching. His colourful paintings of the early 1950s were ignored by the art world. In the midst of prevailing indifference, he painted, from 1958 to 1966, a series of paintings devoted to the Stations of the Cross, this time using only the colour black, which became – in his large-scale drawings as in his lithographs – his colour of choice.

In 1962, the exhibition of his recent works, alongside those of De Kooning, at the Tony Smith Gallery earned him recognition from both critics and a new generation of artists. His paintings, along with those of Mark Rothko, marked the end of Abstract Expressionism in favour of 'colour-field painting', in which colour becomes the object, the primary subject.

For the painters that were then discovering Newman, however, it was his black paintings (and the white ones) that opened the way for new advances (fig. 6).

The exhibitions organised by the Jewish Museum in New York, in 1963, and, the following year, by the Wadsworth Atheneum Museum of Art in Hartford

had a profound influence on the generation of artists emerging in the early 1960s. The first was entitled "Black and White" and the second, "Black, White and Grey". Newman's 'black' paintings that Agnes Martin (fig. 7) and Robert Ryman discovered there would determine the form and colour with which their art would become identified.

The history of modernist art continued to be written in black and white, along with the grey into which they merge. In the early 1950s, Newman's conviction that the 'progress' of art resides in an expression of 'art for art's sake' led him to essentialise his painting. In 1953, having experimented with monochrome, he decided to confine himself to a single dark tone, bordering on black.

The paintings that Frank Stella showed at the Museum of Modern Art in New York in 1959 were also black. With them, the chapter of Abstract Expressionism definitively ended and that of Minimalism began, which, in the context of the 'artistic Darwinism' inherent to the modernist theory of art, was a logical next step.

MINIMALISM AND CONCEPTUAL ART: FIFTY SHADES OF GREY

At each stage of its development, modernist art became purer and got closer to its essence. After its 'minimalist' phase, during which it divested itself of all remaining 'non-specific' traits; after having been purged of all narrative, all phenomenological content; after having been reduced to the truth of its flatness and materiality, it was now the very process of production that was freeing itself from all human intervention, from all subjective singularity (fig. 8).

On the threshold of the essence with which it aspired to merge, art could complete its conceptual metamorphosis. As Sol LeWitt confirms:

> Conceptual art is made to engage the mind of the viewer rather than his eye or emotions. [...] Color, surface, texture, and shape only emphasize the physical aspects of the work. Anything that calls attention to and interests the viewer in this physicality is a deterrent to our understanding of the idea and is used as an expressive device.[12]

Conceptual art, which derived from the Cubist 'art of conception', that of Joseph Kosuth and On Kawara, was naturally achromatic. Denys Riout notes that, before becoming dematerialised and conceptual, the paintings that Kosuth produced were "achromatic",[13] while those of Lawrence Weiner were "devoid of defined colours".[14]

GREY CLOUDS LOOM OVER
THE HORIZON OF POST-MODERNISM

A contemporary of Minimalism, Pop Art was at odds with the former's values in every way, sharing with it only its taste for grey. The black and grey by means of which Frank Stella moved beyond expressionist lyricism is mirrored by the white of Robert Rauschenberg's monochromes from the early 1950s. The white of his canvases echoes the silence through which John Cage wished to make space for a world no longer refined through the filter of art, "the White Paintings [are] airports for the lights, shadows, and particles",[15] commented Cage. White is the colour of deliberate omission, that of the egotism of abstract expressionist painters. Rauschenberg's erasure of a drawing by De Kooning in 1954 is the most accomplished example of this step forward.

Jasper Johns, who, alongside Rauschenberg, rehabilitated the figure of Marcel Duchamp, heralded the return of the real in the shadow of the readymade. It was Johns' loyalty to grey that dictated the exhibition that the Art Institute of Chicago and the Metropolitan Museum of Art in New York devoted to his work in 2008:

> The color gray—ranging from warm to cool, light to dark, stringent to lush—has been a singular and unparalleled preoccupation for the artist.[16]

The word 'gray' appears three times in *Jubilee* (1959, fig. 9), one of his key paintings, of which he produced a grey version alongside his coloured version. He also affirmed:

> The encaustic paintings were done in gray because to me this suggested a different kind of literal quality that was unmoved and unmovable by coloration and thus avoided all of the emotional and dramatic quality of color.[17]

Grey impressed itself on Jasper Johns when he wanted to affirm, in Duchamp's shadow, the reflective, 'conceptual' nature of his works. Naturally, it was in grey that he painted his cast of a *Light Bulb*, in 1958.

Although Andy Warhol borrowed from Jasper Johns his practice of turning some of his images grey – Marilyn, Mao, the 'Car Crash' series, Elvis – his grey was reinterpreted in silver, in a sign of the times.

FROM GREY TO GRAU

Gerhard Richter's work follows on from the early pop art of Johns and Rauschenberg. Like them, he took on Marcel Duchamp's notion of 'detachment' and his stance of 'indifference'. Richter said he was aiming for

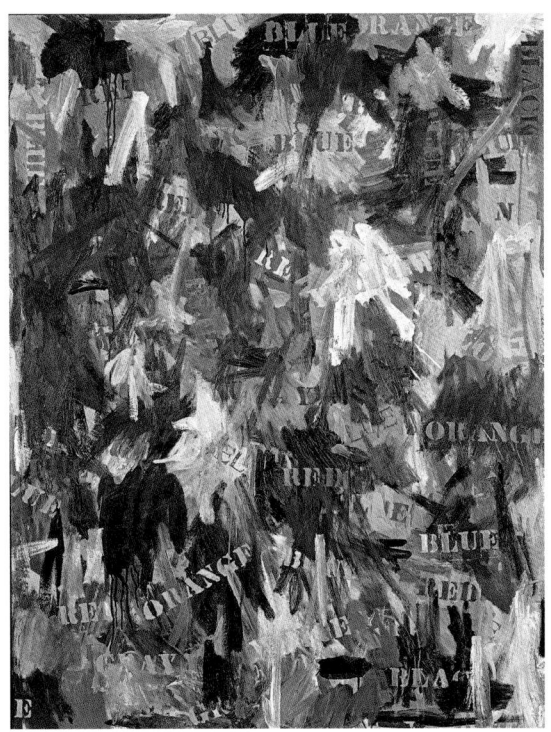

Fig. 9 Jasper Johns, *Jubilee*, 1959, oil and collage on canvas, 152.4 × 111.8 cm
Private collection

"beautiful meaninglessness".[18] From 1966, he decided that "pictures must be made according to a recipe"[19] that refutes all subjectivity, all personal style.

The entry of his art into its 'reasoning' phase, the conceptual approach that led to him adopting methods and motifs that he developed like a pre-established plan, constituted a set of movements that occurred simultaneously with the appearance of grey in his paintings. Begun in 1967, the 'Graue Bilder' [Grey Paintings] series resurfaced sporadically throughout Gerhard Richter's career; it comprises 130 paintings. Grey is for him "the welcome and only possible equivalent for indifference, noncommitment, absence of opinion, absence of shape".[20]

Although early Pop Art – and its direct filiation – remains attached to an achromatism characteristic of the avant-garde, it is significant that it is systematically associated by Johns and Richter with the 'abstract' polychromy of colour charts (fig. 10).

For the contemporary artists of Pop Art, grey had been stripped of the significance that Modernism had given it. For an art form that had embraced the appropriationism inherited from Duchamp, grey had become a gimmick, the subject of quotation (ironic? nostalgic?), like the grid, that other modernist attribute. In the Pop Art toolbox, grey was an object 'appropriated' from the real world, like an industrial colour chart, a comic frame, a stock of anonymous photos, or a packet of washing powder.

The desymbolisation and demythification that Pop Art inherited from Duchamp purged grey of the heroism and the radicality that Modernism had invested it with.

Pop Art was the herald of a break in the order of values in art, referred to as being 'postmodern'. It was not until the mid-1970s that this revolution became established as a global phenomenon. With, or under the impact of, the first oil crisis, companies in the West were forced to reconsider the ceaseless development on which their growth was based. Utopic dreams dissolved, teleological narratives were terminated: the 'Darwinian' model of art, with its vision of progress that discredited the past, soon began to affect art theory. The ideal of a 'purity', the principle of innovation, and the irreversibility of progress that underpinned the modern project gave way to eclecticism and citing the past. The eye, riveted on the rearview mirror, saw the emergence of a world freed from the hierarchy of forms and now open to all permutations.

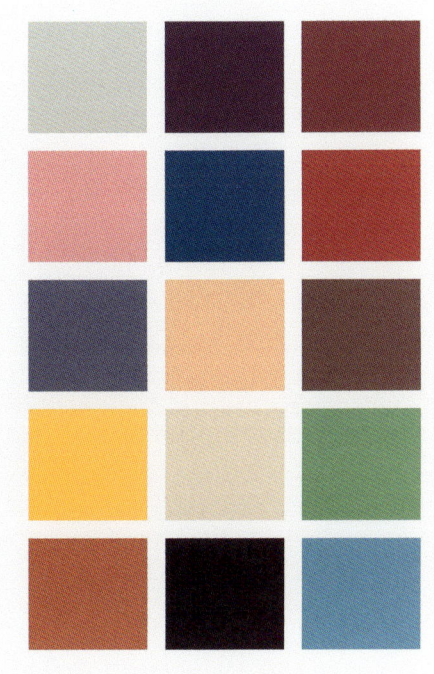

Fig. 10 Gerhard Richter, *Fifteen Colours (138)*, 1966, enamel on canvas, 200 × 130 cm

ONWARDS TO A MEDIOCRE WORLD!

It is the job of the avant-garde to open the way to the future, to herald a world that has not yet arrived. Modernism – the driving force of this avant-garde – had from this point of view achieved its aim, which was, as its works had presaged, to bring about the advent of a grey world. This is confirmed by the philosopher Peter Sloterdijk, who, in the work he devoted to this colour, claims it is the decisive colour value of the present time.[21] His diagnosis is supported by Cath Sleeman, a data study specialist, who carried out an analysis of the collections of everyday objects (seven thousand clocks, typewriters, scales, telephones, etc.) held in a number of British science museums. She concluded: "Our preliminary analysis suggests that everyday objects may have become a little greyer and a little squarer over time".[22]

In his novel *Les Couleurs invisibles* [*Invisible Colours*], designer Jean-Gabriel Causse makes the same observation. Considering our everyday objects, our cars – three-quarters of which are white, grey or black, in France, at least – our interiors, influenced by 'Japandi' (a mix of Japanese and Scandinavian) minimalism, he too concludes by noting the historic triumph of the 'cobwebs' of Braque and Picasso's Cubist paintings.

In 2000, contemporary grisaille was the inspiration behind Scottish artist David Batchelor's work *Chromophobia*,[23] in which he addresses a distrust of colour in the West, exemplified by modern intellectuals: "evidence of chromophobia in the West can be found as far back as Aristotle, for whom the suppression of colour was the price to be paid for bailing art out from a more general Platonic iconophobia".[24] Batchelor evokes the assimilation by the Ancient Greeks of colour as a *pharmakon* ('poison' or 'venom'). For Batchelor, 'chromophobia' is due to the fact that colour is "other to the higher values of Western culture".[25] Colour, considered superficial or trivial, is incompatible with a modernism that has turned art into a speculative, essentially 'conceptual', adventure: "To this day, there remains a belief, often unspoken perhaps but equally often unquestioned, that seriousness in art and culture is a black-and-white issue, that depth is measured only in shades of grey".[26]

The paradox of grey, which for Batchelor is the sign of an inclination towards the "higher concerns of the mind",[27] and for Sloterdijk, the colour of "dehierarchisation and desymbolisation".[28] In the philosopher's view, Richter and his paintings "have helped ensure that the metaphysical loquacity of iconic objects, such as Malevich's *Black Square* (1915), is rendered silent in the archives of art history".[29] Continuing, he likens the triumph of a generalised grey to the advent of a disseminated power, of a diffuse authority:

> The gray character appears to be the effect of a tendency towards the average and the mediocre that avoids the resolute *Sic et non*[30] as far as possible. This imperturbable and non-radical attitude, which diverges from extremes and is averse to decision is generally called 'lukewarm'; it is often associated with a preference for a private and non-political life.[31]

A world whose emergence Pier Paolo Pasolini had already foreseen: "an inexpressive world lacking in particularities and cultural diversification; a perfectly standardised world".[32]

MONOCHROMES

After the key moment of his discovery of Cubism, Mondrian's painting became dedicated to 'abstract' colour, applied in meticulous flat tints. The grid pattern of his paintings juxtaposes monochromes destined to become the only authentically modern form of coloured painting. As art historian Benjamin Buchloh points out: "Between 1919 and 1921, in the context of postcubist painting, monochromy became one of the most important reductivist pictorial strategies of the historical avant-garde".[33]

Painters' palettes could once again reflect the richness of colour wheels. But that did not account for Modernist chromophobia!

From the exhibition "0,10" held in 1915 in Petrograd (now Saint Petersburg), history remembers the presentation by Kazimir Malevich of the first 'monochrome' (a 'black square' floating on a white background). The genealogy of *la couleur seule*[34] (colour alone) fluctuates between Malevich's *Quadrangle* and his *White on White*, painted in 1918.[35] It disregards the red monochrome that he also exhibited in the "0,10" exhibition. Did this ostracism stem from the single colour of the work, from the overwhelming symbolism of its colour? Was it a reaction to its title – *Painterly Realism of a Peasant Woman in Two Dimensions* – which evokes, albeit ironically, a figuration banned by the avant-garde? In his study devoted to monochrome painting and to its 'archaeology', Denys Riout could only note that "the red square does not attract much attention".[36]

When, in the 1950s, the pictorial avant-garde returned to monochrome, it was from the *Black Square* that it drew inspiration. It is striking to note that Denys Riout's history of monochrome is largely based on achromatic works. Punctuating his history are Clyfford Still's "almost entirely black paintings";[37] *Abraham*, a black painting by Barnett Newman; Robert Rauschenberg's White Paintings; Ellsworth Kelly's *Black Square with Blue*; Sam Francis's *Other White*, Ad Reinhardt's black paintings; the German group Zéro, who used only white; the Dutch group Nul, also devoted to white; Piero Manzoni's 'Achromes' and Lucio Fontana's *White Manifesto*, among others.

In colour, monochrome had a hard time finding its place in the modern epic. Pierre Aubertin, a disciple of Yves Klein, used only red in his paintings. Riout noted that he would "never attain the rank of prophet or hero".[38] Klein was the only artist to have identified his work by its colour while fitting into the grand narrative of modern art, though his place remains problematic. Although the monochrome to which Klein adhered – he even called himself 'Yves le Monochrome' – was derived from modernist reduction, the meaning it gives to his works is at odds with its formalism. Symbolic and metaphysical, Klein's blue inspires a suspicion that Benjamin Buchloh describes as follows: "[…] Klein […] incorporates a reactionary petit bourgeois spirit".[39]

Klein accepted his marginalisation by the upholders of the radical avant-garde, declaring, "In no way do I consider myself an avant-garde artist". Rather provocatively, he added: "I think and believe that I am a classical artist, perhaps even one of the rare classical artists of this century".[40]

The anomaly of a colour monochrome was confirmed by the wave of chromophobia that engulfed the art of the late 1960s. Denys Riout noted: "In the late 1960s, grey made its appearance in its territory (that of monochrome) and spread throughout the following decade".[41] Gerhard Richter and Alan Charlton were the exemplary promoters of the new 'grisaille'.

The 'colour alone' of monochrome proved to be a 'non-colour'.[42] After the seminal exhibition "Monochrome Malerei" [Monochrome Painting] curated in 1960 by Udo Kultermann at the Städtisches Museum Schloss Morsbroich, in Leverkusen, exhibitions devoted to monochrome painting honoured achromatism. In 1970, the Musée d'Art et d'Industrie de Saint-Étienne devoted an exhibition to white ("Itinéraires 'Blanc'"). Two years later, the Museum of Contemporary Art of Chicago put on "White on White". In 1974, in London, the Institute of Contemporary Arts presented the exhibition "Basically White". In 1981, at the Kunsthalle, Düsseldorf paid tribute to black in "Schwarz", while Tokyo celebrated it three years later in "Black".

In the January/February 1967 issue of *Art in America*, Lucy Lippard published "The Silent Art",[43] an article devoted to monochrome and to its historical artists, such as Malevich and Rodchenko, but also to the Americans Reinhardt, Newman, Rothko and Still, and, of course, Yves Klein, in which she presented the entirely black or white canvas as the ultimate stage in monochrome painting.

In answer to the question posed by Barnett Newman, "Who's afraid of red, yellow and blue?", one response, as unexpected as it is plausible, might be: modern art itself.

1
Guillaume Apollinaire, *Les Peintres cubistes. Méditations esthétiques* (Paris: Eugène Figuière, 1913), p. 24.
2
Georges Braque, in "Braque, la peinture et nous", *Cahiers d'art*, no. 1 (October 1954), pp. 13–24, quoted in Dora Vallier, *L'Intérieur de l'art. Entretiens Avec Braque, Léger, Villon, Miro, Brancusi (1954-1960)* (Paris: Seuil, 1982), pp. 29–51 (p. 38).
3
Fernand Léger, in 'La vie fait l'œuvre de Fernand Léger', *Cahiers d'art*, no. 2 (1954), pp. 133–72, published in Dora Vallier, ibid., pp. 53–89 (p. 66).
4
On the dialectics of colour wheels and colour charts, see Ann Temkin, *Color Chart: Reinventing Color, 1950 to Today*, exh. cat., 2 March–12 May 2008, New York: Museum of Modern Art.
5
Rosalind Krauss, 'Grids', *October* 9 (1979), pp. 50–64.
6
Clement Greenberg, "'American-Type' Painting", *Art and Culture: Critical Essays* (Boston, MA: Beacon Press, 1961), p. 218.
7
Ibid., p. 212.
8
Ibid., p. 208.
9
Ibid., p. 219.
10
Ibid., p. 220.
11
The First World War brought to a halt the dynamic that Cubism had begun. Picasso was the first to call into question the movement that had been initiated by his Cubist works. From 1914, figures appeared in his works that owe nothing to Cubist tenets. The curtain that he designed for the ballet *Parade* in 1917 shows how far he had departed from Cubism. Boldness and experimentation belonged to a bygone age. It was time for a 'Return to Order', to art inspired by national traditions – classical in France, Renaissance in Italy and medieval in Germany. Symptomatic of this change of direction his art was taking, Picasso reintroduced colour into his compositions, producing the 'oxymoronic' form of a 'decorative Cubism'.
12
Sol LeWitt, "Paragraphs on Conceptual Art", *Artforum*, vol. 5, no. 10 (Summer 1967), pp. 79–83 (p. 83).
13
Denys Riout, *La Peinture monochrome* (Paris: Gallimard, Folio essais, 2006), p. 108.
14
Ibid., p. 109.
15
John Cage, "On Robert Rauschenberg, Artist, and His Work", *Silence* (Middletown, CT: Wesleyan University Press, 1961) pp. 98–108 (p. 102).
16
Jasper Johns quoted in Joseph E. Young, "Jasper Johns: An Appraisal", *Art International*, vol. 13, no. 7 (September 1969), pp. 50–56 (p. 51).
17
Ibid., p. 51.
18
Hans Ulrich Obrist (ed.), Gerhard Richter, *The Daily Practice of Painting: Writings and Interviews 1962–1993*, (Cambridge, MA: The MIT Press / London: Anthony d'Offay Gallery, 1995), pp. 79–80.
19
Ibid., p. 49.
20
Ibid., pp. 82–83.
21
Peter Sloterdijk, *Gris. Une théorie politique des couleurs* (Paris: Payot, 2023), p. 23.
22
Cath Sleeman, "Colour & Shape: Using Computer Vision to Explore the Science Museum Group Collection", *Science Museum Group Digital Lab*, 8 October 2020 online, https://lab.sciencemuseum.org.uk/colour-shape-using-computer-vision-to-explore-the-science-museum-c4b4f1cbd72c [accessed 27 November 2024].
23
David Batchelor, *Chromophobia* (London: Reaktion Books, 2000).
24
Ibid., p. 29.
25
Ibid., p. 23.
26
Ibid., p. 30.
27
Ibid., p. 29.
28
Peter Sloterdijk, *Gris. Une théorie politique des couleurs*, op. cit., p. 17.
29
Ibid., p. 262.
30
The Latin expression *sic et non* can be translated by 'yes and no'. It is used in reference to the book *Sic et Non* by the theologian and philosopher Pierre Abélard (1079–1142), father of scholasticism. The book employs the dialectical method, a disciple that enables apparent contradictions to be reconciled.
31
Sloterdijk, op. cit., p. 275.
32
Pier Paolo Pasolini, quoted in Guillaume de Sardes and Bartolomeo Pietromarchi (eds.), *Passolini en clair-obscur*, catalogue of the exhibition held at the Nouveau Musée National de Monaco, 29 March–29 September 2024 (Paris: Flammarion and Monaco: Nouveau Musée National de Monaco, 2024), p. 139.
33
Benjamin Buchloh, "The Primary Colors for the Second Time: A Paradigm Repetition of the Neo-Avant-Garde", *October*, vol. 37 (Summer 1986), p. 41.
34
Title of the exhibition that the Musée d'Art Contemporain de Lyon devoted to monochrome in 1988.
35
To Modernist theorists, the triptych exhibited by Aleksandr Rodchenko, *Pure Red*, *Pure Yellow*, *Pure Blue* (1921), which was devoid of all esoteric references and spirituality, appeared even more radical.
36
Denys Riout, *La Peinture monochrome*, op. cit., p. 50.
37
Ibid., p. 70.
38
Ibid., p. 101.
39
Benjamin Buchloh, "Formalisme et historicité, modifications de ces concepts dans l'art européen et américain depuis 1945", *Essais historiques II* (Villeurbanne: Art éditions, 1992), p. 36.
40
Yves Klein quoted by Molly Warnock, "Le classicisme d'Yves Klein", *Les Cahiers du Musée national d'art moderne*, trad. Catherine Vasseur, no. 162 (2023), p. 5.
41
Denys Riout, *La Peinture monochrome*, op. cit., p. 121.
42
From a technical point of view, black and white are not colours; they are shades.
43
Lucy Lippard, "The Silent Art", in *Art in America*, vol. 55 no. 1 (January/February 1967).

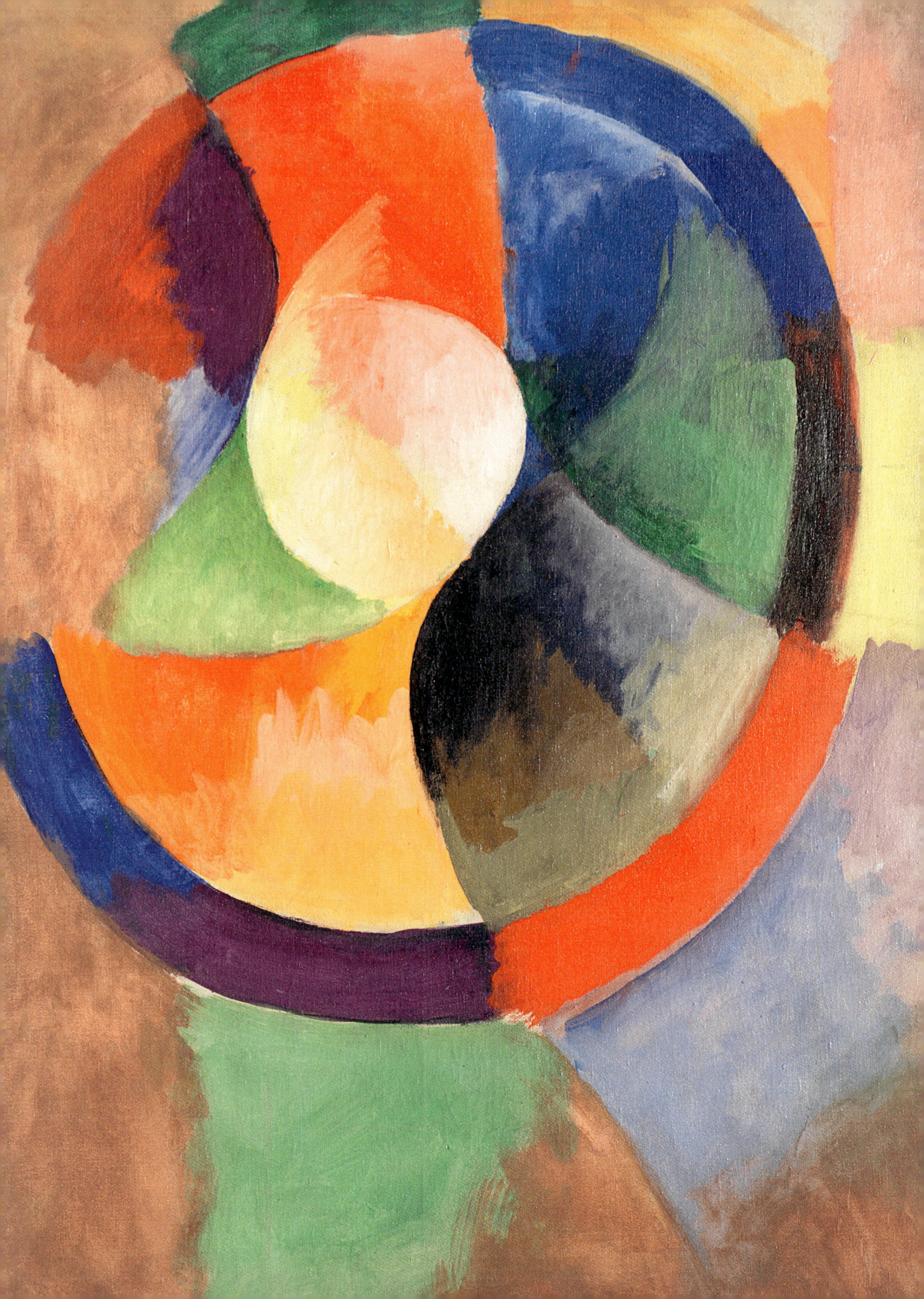

UNITED COLOURS

FROM THE COLOUR WHEEL TO THE COLOUR CHART

Didier Ottinger

It is a fact that defies all common sense that colour and its use in the modern artistic context has only very rarely been the subject of exhibitions. If we focus on those devoted to the global conception of colour (rather than to a particular colour), they can be counted on one hand.

In 1988, the Musée d'Art Contemporain in Lyon dedicated an exhibition to the only form of colour that seemed compatible with the principles of pictorial modernism: the monochrome. It was entitled: "La couleur seule, l'expérience du monochrome" [Colour Alone: The Monochrome Experience].

It was another two decades before colour was given a fresh look, in an exhibition that updated the theoretical issues surrounding its modern use. In 2008, the Museum of Modern Art in New York unveiled "Color Chart", which studied the transformation that took place around 1950 and led artists to abandon a chromaticism still influenced by their sensory experience in favour of ready-made colours issuing from the colour charts of industry, decoration and graphic design.

The scarcity of studies on modern colour prompts in me a hint of scepticism, and suggests a degree of discomfiture on the part of institutions.

In 1986, the neo-Situationist troublemakers of Présence Panchounette twisted the knife in the wound. Their exhibition, ironically entitled "Coquet, lumineux, meublé" (Stylish, Bright, Furnished), which was held at the Centre Culturel de l'Albigeois in Albi, revealed the unmentionable and shameful 'decorative' dimension of modern art, which the 'purity' and abstract idealism of its theoretical reasoning vigorously refuted.

The exhibition at the Grimaldi Forum Monaco pays tribute to these exhibitions. It opens with a look back at the transformation that took place in New York, in which the colour wheels of Isaac Newton and Johann Wolfgang von Goethe were replaced by colours made available by industry and communications. In Monaco, 'colour alone' has given rise to the creation of monochromatic and multisensory rooms, in which the old idea of 'synaesthesia' – the correlation that can exist between our different senses – is reinvented. The 'decorative' – intrinsic to the use of colour – is addressed in a series of rooms in which objects of modern design and works of art are 'installed'.

The one hundred or so masterpieces from the Centre Pompidou collection that form the core of the exhibition provide an insight into the iconographic, symbolic and cultural foundations underpinning the modern use of colour.

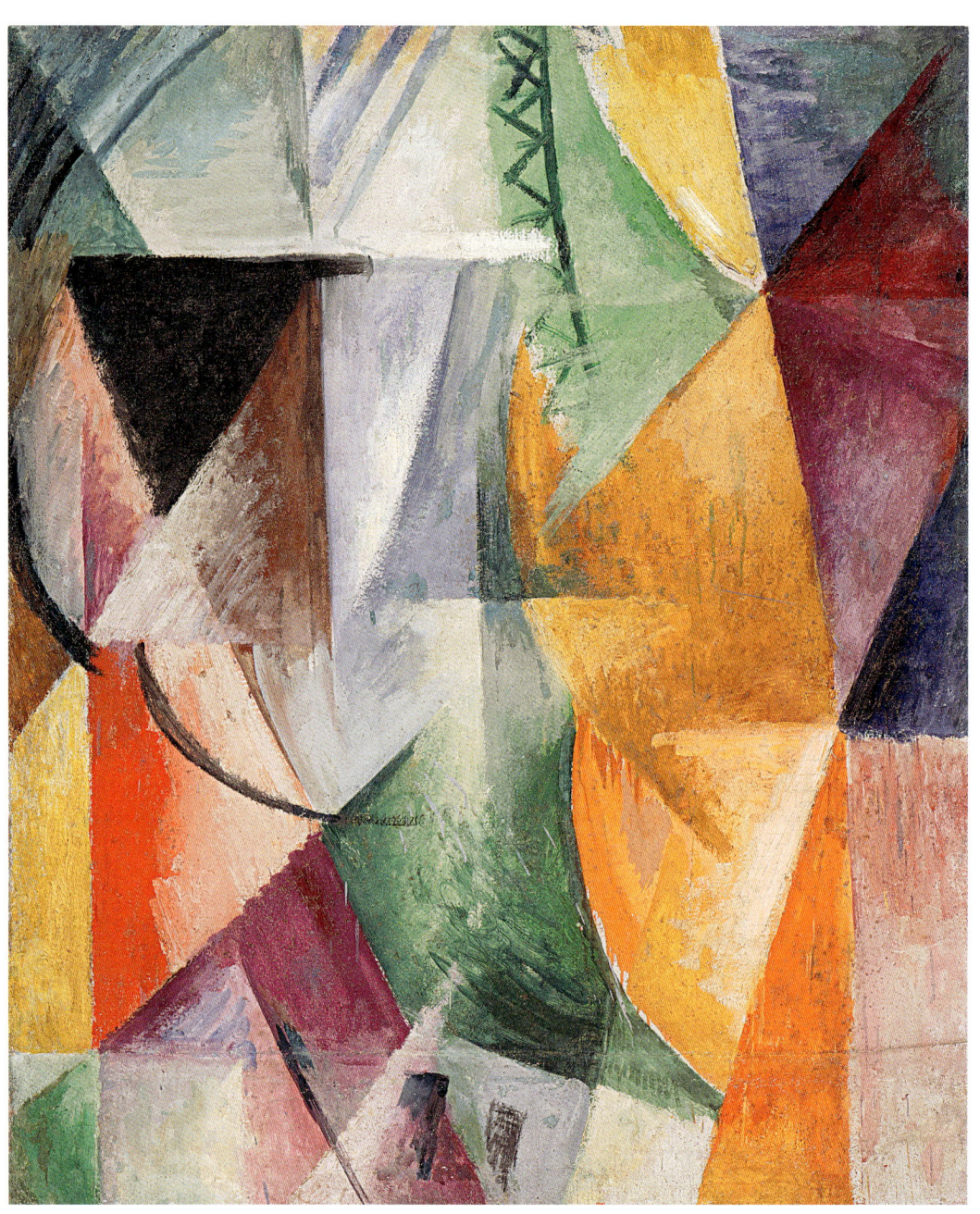

Robert Delaunay   *Une fenêtre* [*A Window*]   1912

oil on canvas   111 × 90 cm   purchase, 1950, AM 2975 P

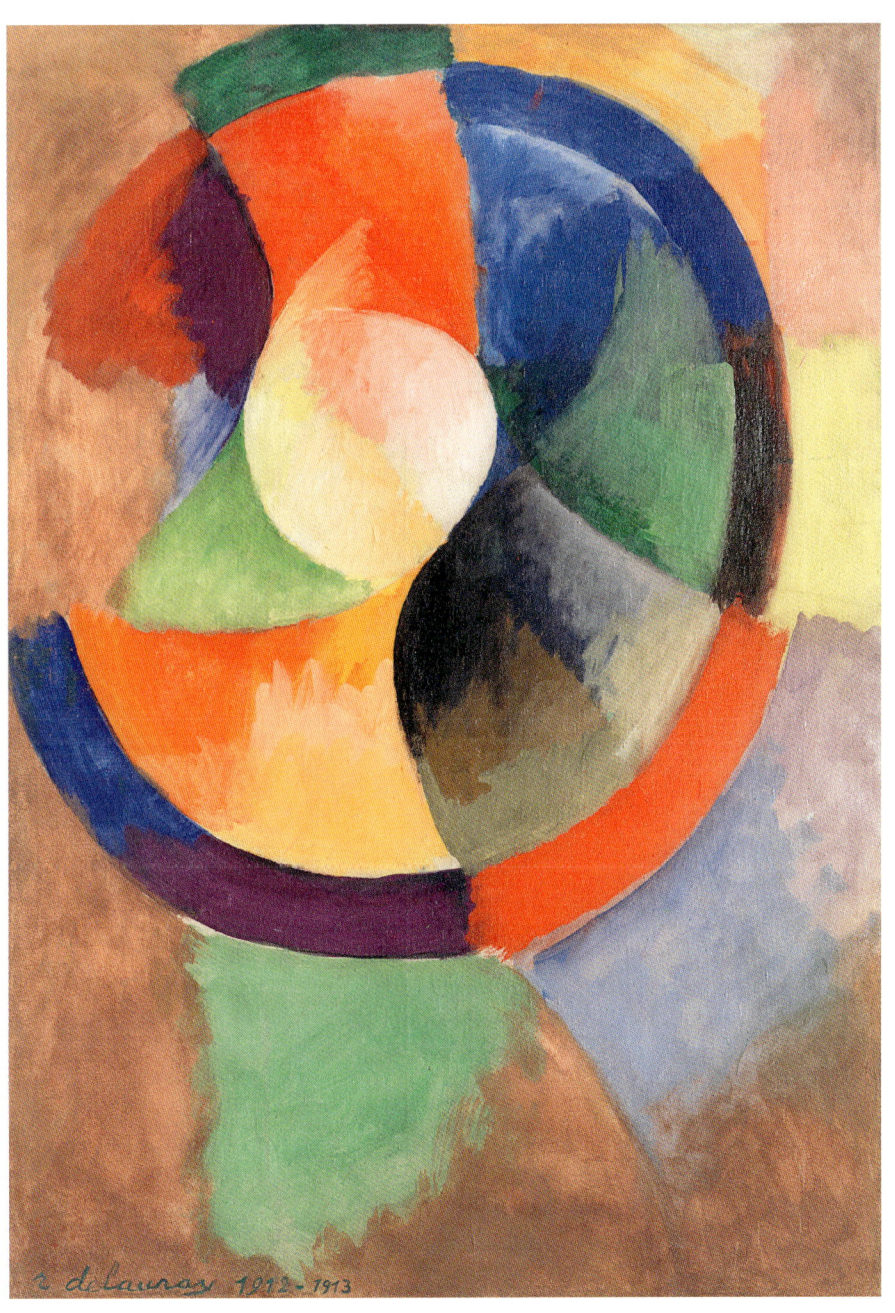

Robert Delaunay   *Formes circulaires, Soleil n° 2* [*Circular Forms, Sun no. 2*]   1912–13

glue-based distemper on canvas   100 × 68.5 cm   gift of the Société des Amis du Musée National d'Art Moderne, 1961, AM 3910 P

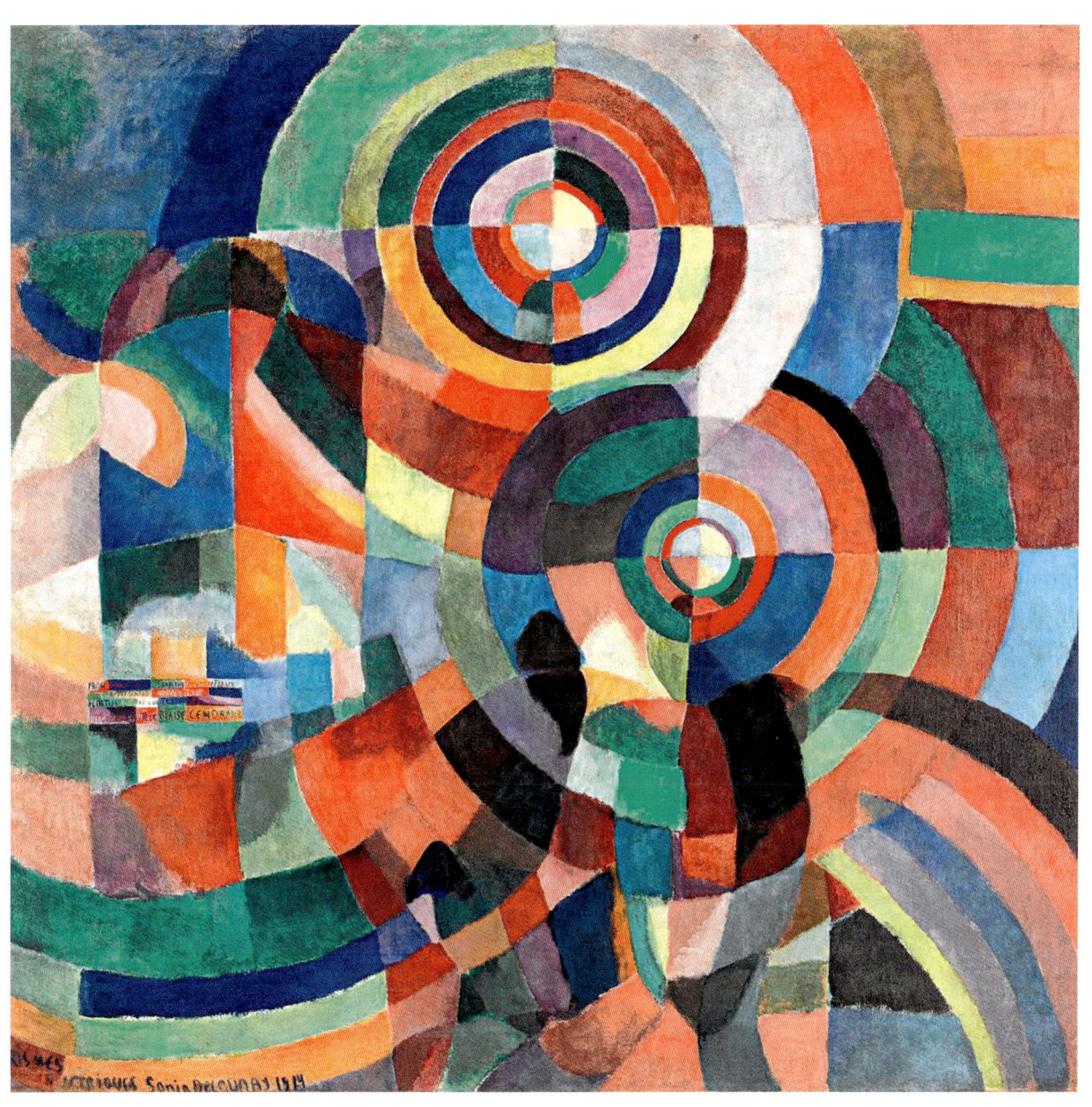

Sonia Delaunay   *Prismes électriques* [*Electric Prisms*]   1914

oil on canvas   250 × 250 cm   purchase by the French State, 1958, attribution, 1958, AM 3606 P

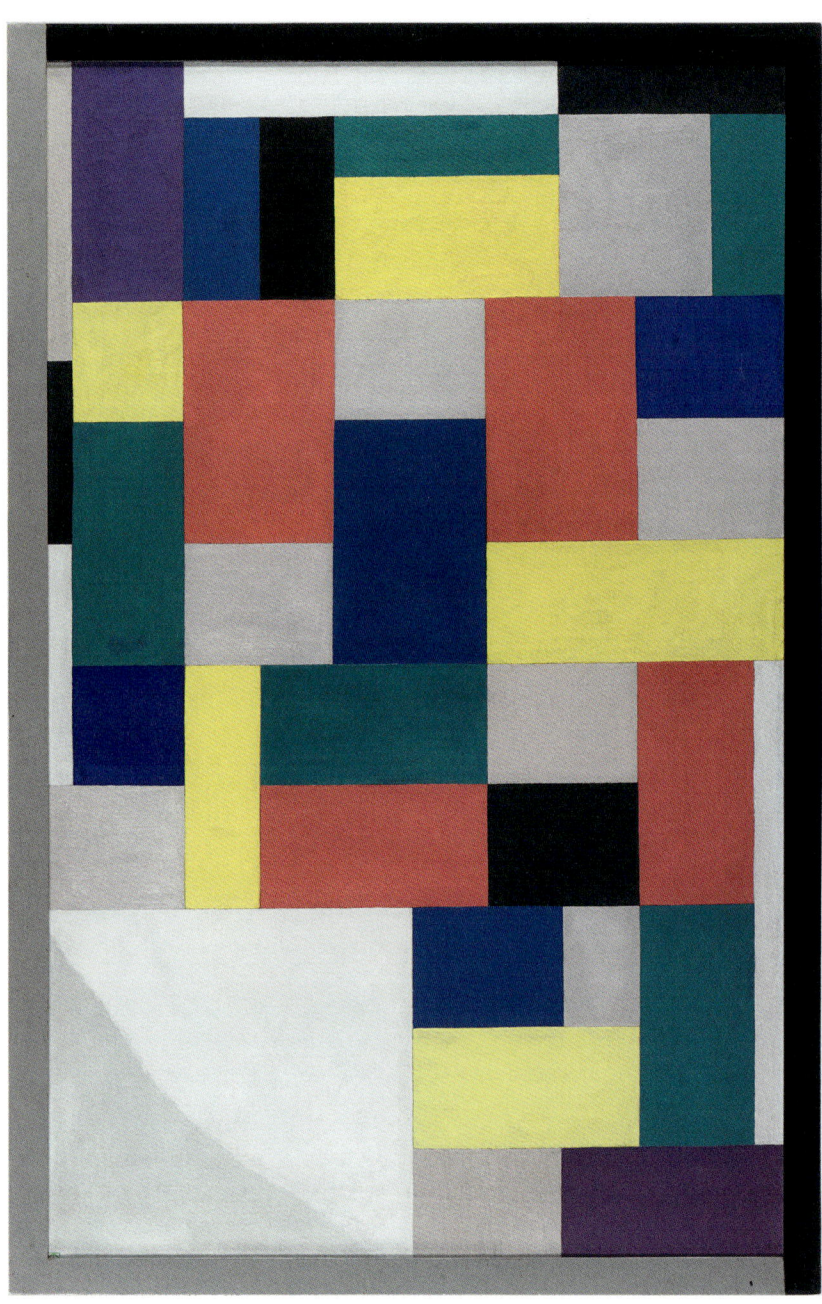

Theo Van Doesburg   *Peinture pure* [*Pure Painting*]   May 1920–7 July 1920

oil on canvas   130 × 80.5 cm   purchase, 1964, AM 4281 P

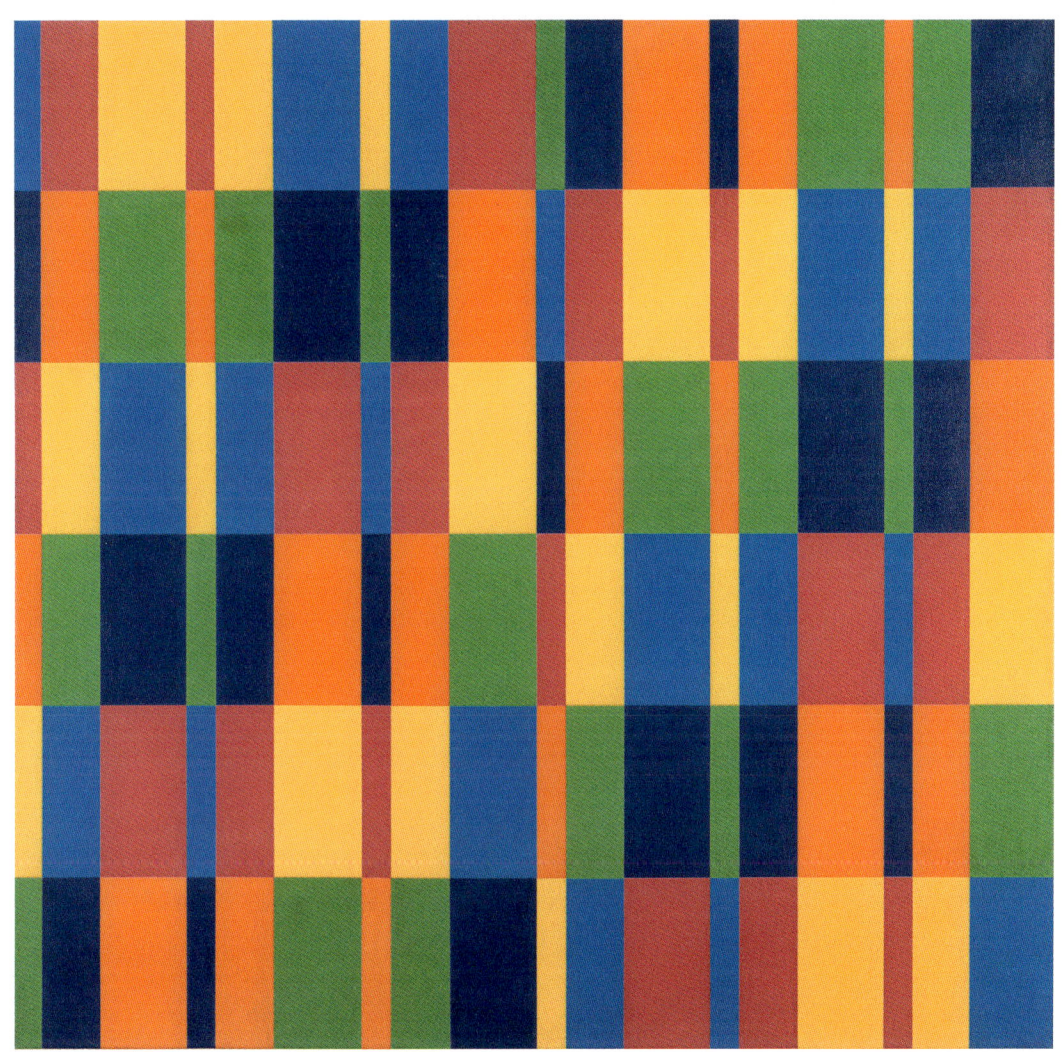

Richard-Paul Lohse   *Six Horizontal Bands, Each with Formally Identical Colour Groups*   [1950–69]

oil on canvas   126 × 126 cm   purchase, 1977, AM 1977-569

33

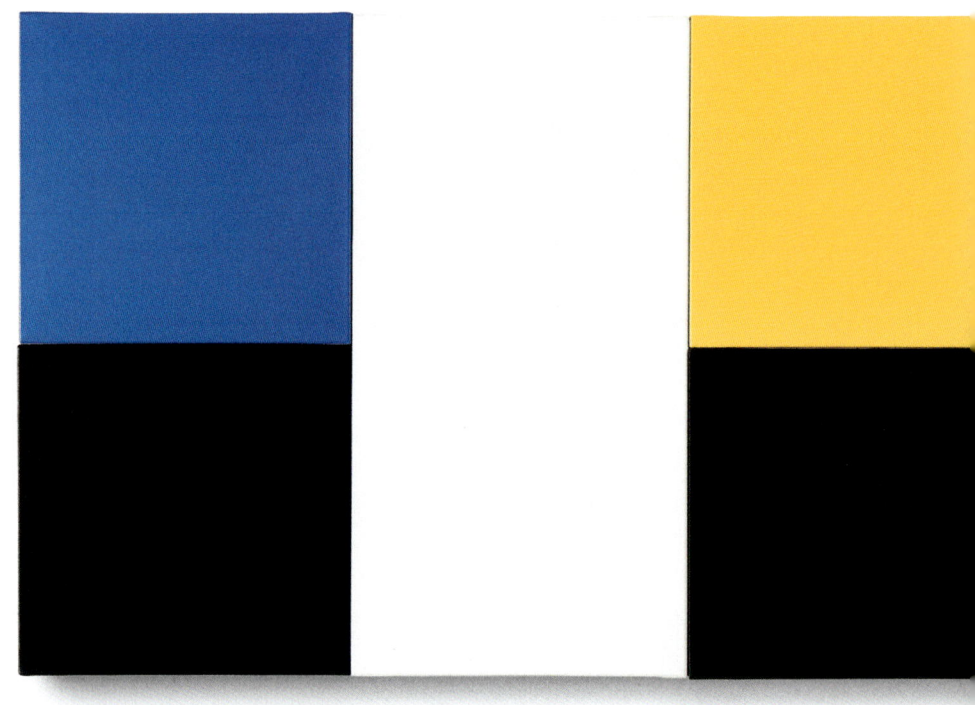

Ellsworth Kelly   *Kite II*   1952

oil on canvas, eleven joined panels   80 × 280 cm   purchase, 1987, AM 1987-560

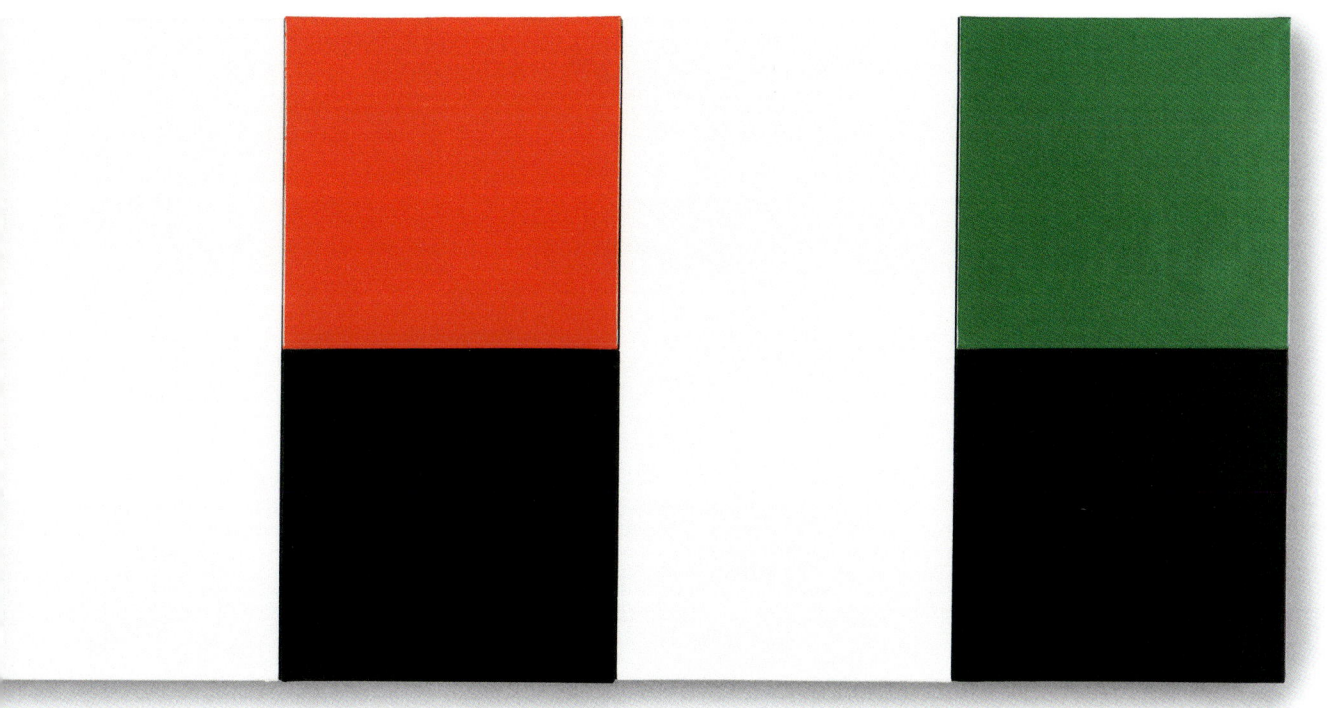

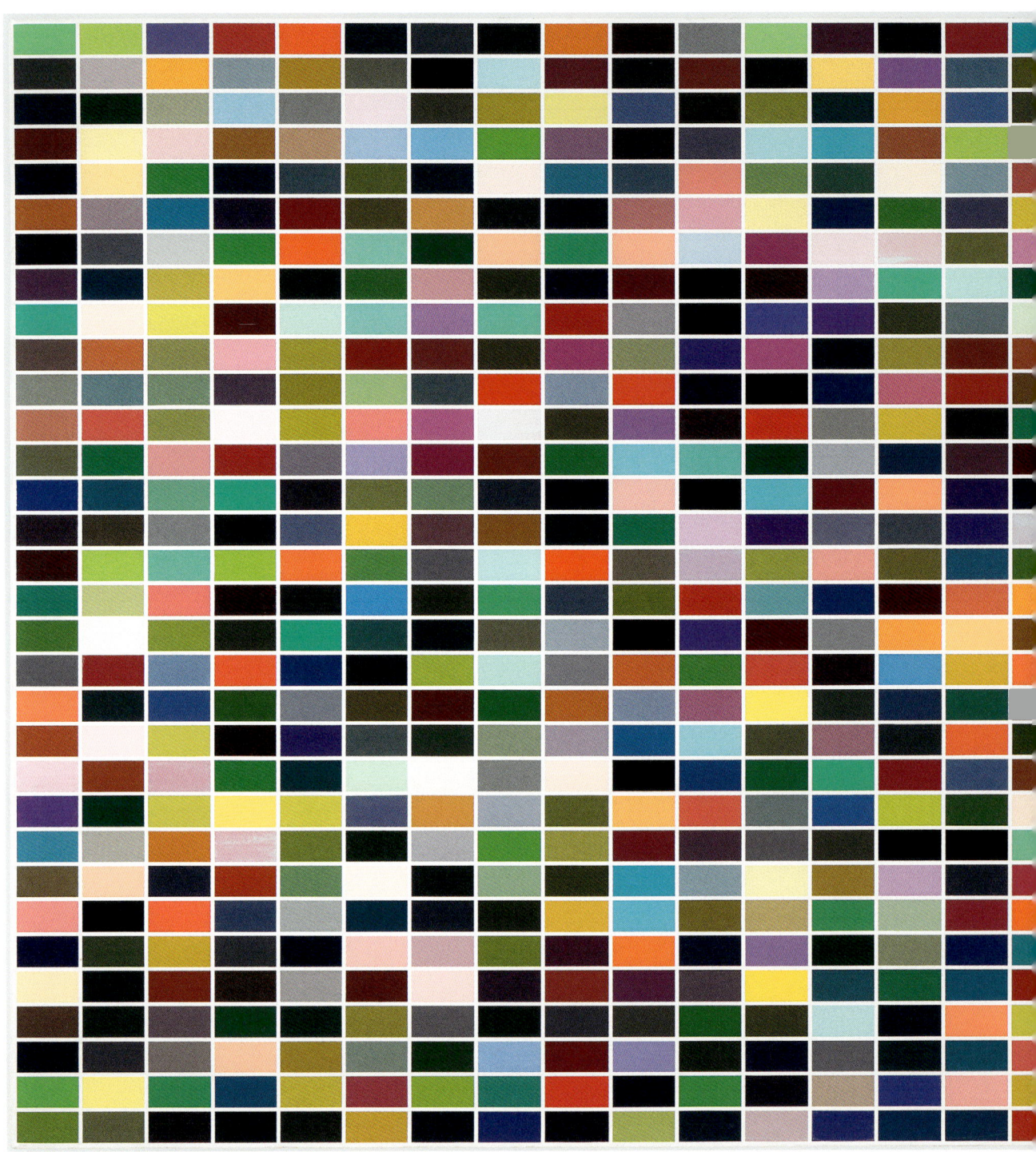

Gerhard Richter   *1024 Colours (350-3)*   1973

lacquer on canvas   254 × 478 × 5 cm   gift of the artist, 1984, AM 1984-285

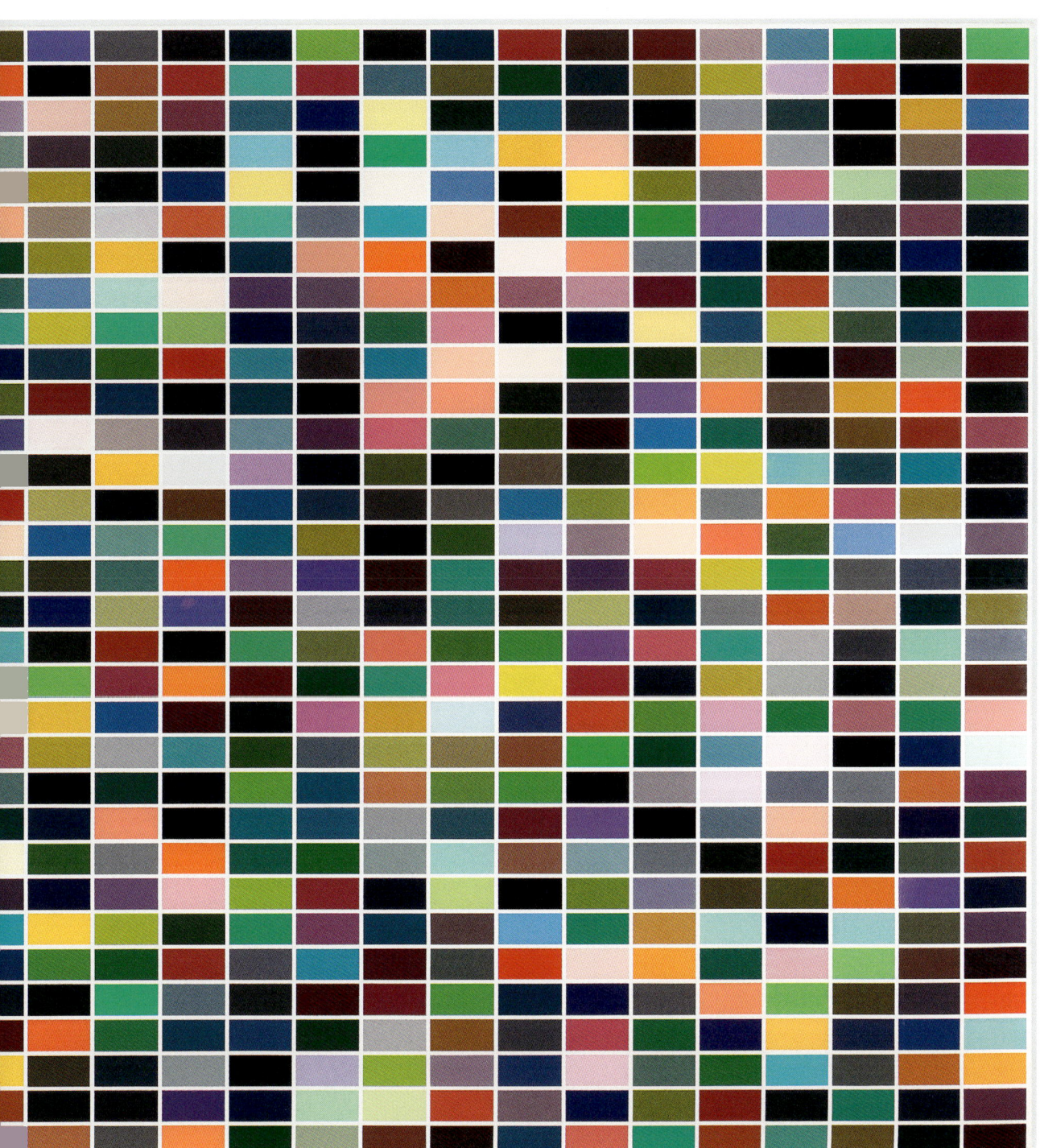

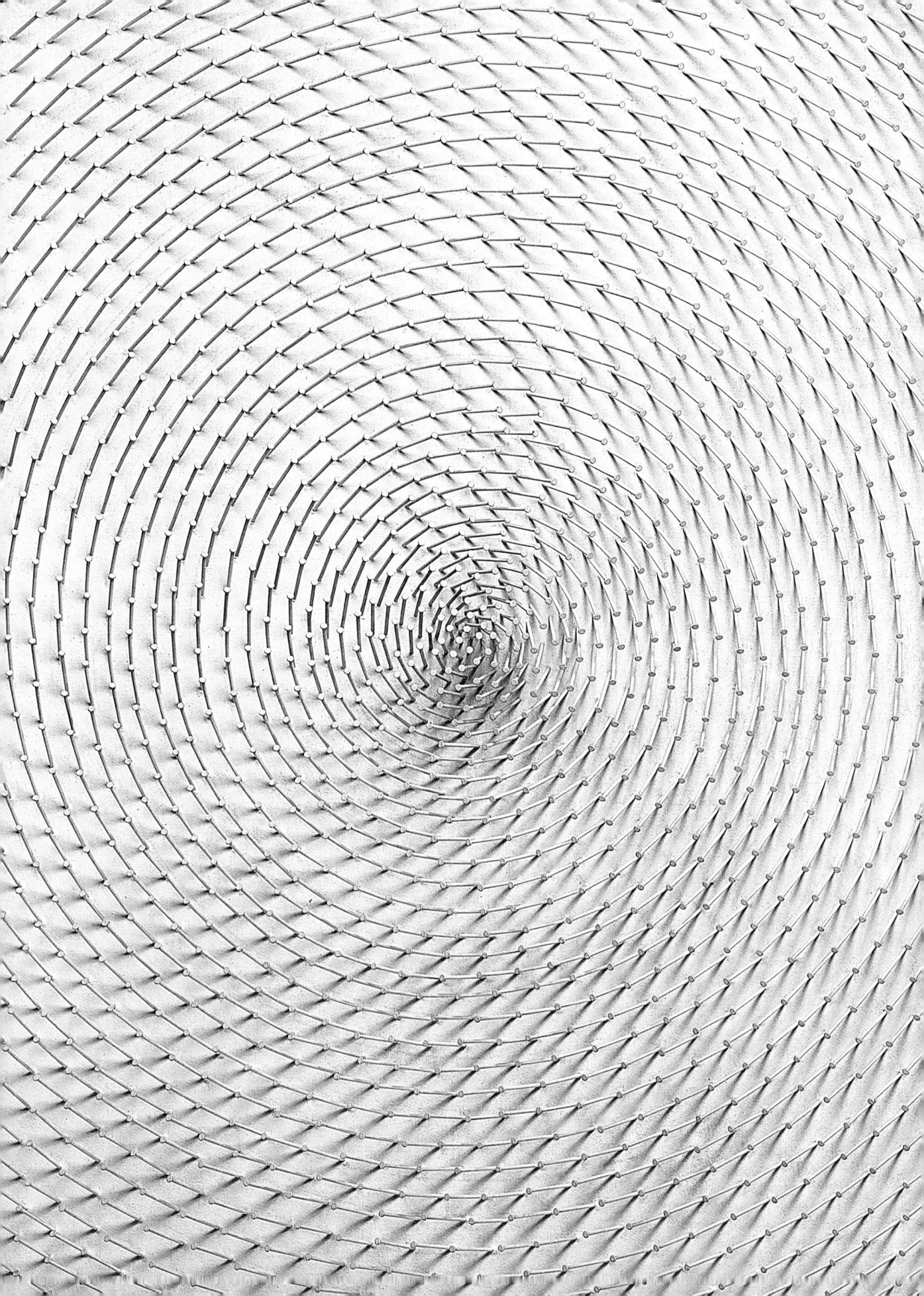

WHITE

Michel Gauthier

WHITENESS IN THE MODERN ERA

The 20th century should have been the age of liberated colour. Freed from mimetic obligation, colours could have enjoyed their new autonomy to the full. Things did not happen quite like that, however. Although colour did indeed become the sole subject of some artistic studies (from Josef Albers to Carlos Cruz-Diez), its advent as an autonomous phenomenon was thwarted by other aesthetic issues. The singular good fortune of white in the history of modernity enables us to assess it. In 1897, Stéphane Mallarmé wrote, in the preface to his poem *Un coup de dés jamais n'abolira le hasard* [*A Throw of the Dice Will Never Abolish Chance*] and in a famous and prophetic formulation, that *"les blancs [y] assument l'importance"*.[1] A few years earlier, in 1883, in a practice as literary as it was artistic, Alphonse Allais had stuck a sheet of pristine white Bristol paper on a wall of the Exposition des Arts Incohérents: *Première communion de jeunes filles chlorotiques par un temps de neige* [*First Communion of Anaemic Young Girls in the Snow*] (fig.1). It took humour and a nonsensical fabrication to spark the importance of white, an importance that would be sanctioned by the poetic modernity that Mallarmé would soon usher in. While, until the invention of the printing press, which locked it into an intimate dialogue with black alone, white had been perceived as a colour in its own right,[2] it gradually came to signify an absence of colour, a vacuum, silence, as borne out by the Mallarmé episode and the painting that was to come, which saw white ceasing to be the abundance of colour with infinite nuances that it had still been in the most radical of Monet's snowscapes, *Effet de neige à Giverny* [*Snow Effect, Giverny*] (1893, fig.3). Although the following pages are not the place for a detailed chronicle of modern whiteness, we can, at least, note some of the milestones in the artistic narrative that established this empire of white in modernity and that a memorable Harald Szeemann exhibition, held in the spring of 1966, "Weiss auf Weiss" [*White on White*], presented and explored.

Half a century earlier, Kazimir Malevich produced a series of White Paintings, of which the *White on White* of 1918 (fig.4) is the most famous. The artist wrote about these works in words that are explicit despite their grandiloquence: "I have breached the blue lampshade of colour limitations and have passed out into the white beyond. Follow me, comrade aviators, sail on into the depths. I have established the semaphores of Suprematism. I have conquered the lining of the coloured sky, I have plucked the colours and put them in the bag I have made, and tied a knot in it. Sail on! The white, free depths, eternity is before you".[3] "Colour limitations": the anti-colour bias could not be clearer. It is as if, in Suprematist

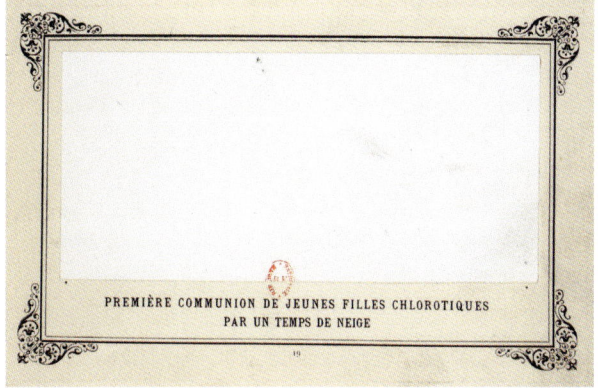

Fig.1 Alphonse Allais, *Première communion de jeunes filles chlorotiques par un temps de neige* [*First Communion of Anaemic Young Girls in The Snow*], 1883, In *Album Primo-Avrilesque* (Paris: Paul Ollendorff, 1897), p.19
Bibliothèque nationale de France, département des Livres rares, RESP-Y2-2999

thinking, cosmic aspiration could have only white as a (non)-colour, unless the achromatic impulse can find acceptable justification only in the cosmos. Malevich ventured out into white as, several decades later, cosmonauts would venture out into interplanetary space. And pictorial sputniks[4] can be only white, having distanced themselves from the blue of our low-hanging sky. Denys Riout rightly points out that Malevich seems thus to prophetically denounce the future blue monochromes of Yves Klein.[5] In other words, while the nascent non-figuration seemingly signified the promise of pure chromatic expression, Malevich was hastening to tie colours up in a bag in order to connect the pictorial space with colourless, white infinity.

From Soviet Russia to Peronist Argentina, from Kazimir Malevich to Lucio Fontana, white retained the same singular value. With its title, *White Manifesto*, the first major theoretical text endorsed by Lucio Fontana in Buenos Aires, in 1946,[6] makes white the colour of the still immaculate immensity of the aesthetic spaces yet to be conquered. White is the non-colour of the clean slate represented by revolution, and, as in Malevich's art, of the infinite, towards which the perforations and incisions would aspire that Fontana, who had left Buenos Aires for Milan, would soon make in his paintings. Fontana formulated his reflections in words similar to those of Malevich: "I make holes, infinity passes through them".[7] Certainly, the suspension of form in the pictorial field has been replaced by the slitting of the latter, but the ambition remains the same: "If I choose white, it is because … it is perhaps the purest colour, the least complicated, the easiest to understand, and because this hole is more apparent on white than on any other colour. But my feelings about the colour are

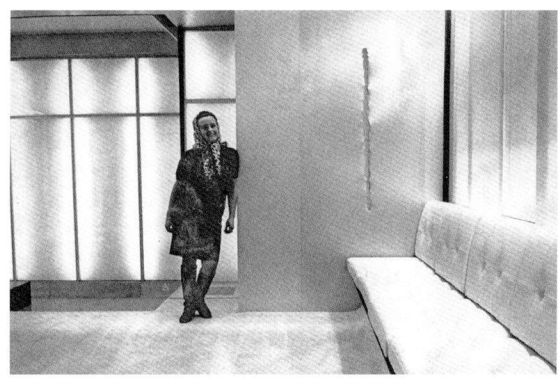

Fig. 2 *Nanda Vigo, Zero House in Milan,*
n.d. (1959/1962), photograph
ZERO Foundation, Düsseldorf. mkp.ZERO.0.VII.78_1

of no importance, white, red or yellow ..."[8] Fontana's
spatialism is not chromophilic. The *Zero House* that
Nanda Vigo created in Milan between 1959 and 1962
(fig. 2) is entirely white. One of the walls is simply a
white *Spatial Conception* by Fontana, with its vertical
spatialising slit.

This *Zero House* was an attempt to architecturally
transpose the ideals of the Zero group, founded in
1957 in Düsseldorf by Heinz Mack and Otto Piene, and
joined in 1961 by Günther Uecker, for which Fontana
was the major inspiration. Together, they affirmed:
"Zero is silence. Zero is the beginning. Zero is round.
Zero spins. Zero is the moon. The sun is Zero. Zero
is white [...]".[9] Düsseldorf's white zero is that of the
countdown before departure for the Moon and the
Sun, drawn in rings of soot by Piene, and the space
sought by Suprematist forms. But it is also the zero
of formal reduction and deflation: "Zero is Zero".[10]
In the vast galaxy moving around the Zero group,
white is the colourless colour of cosmic infinity as
well as that of the zero point of a work of art (fig. 5).
This is exemplified in the 'Achromes' series (1957–63)
by Piero Manzoni, one of the fastest meteors in
the aforesaid galaxy.

Concerning 'Achromes', Manzoni explains his use
of white impeccably: "The issue for me is to offer
a surface that is entirely white (or rather entirely
colourless, neutral) lacking any pictorial phenomenon,
any intervention unrelated to the value of the
surface; white that is neither a polar landscape, nor
an evocative or beautiful material, nor a sensation or
symbol or anything else; a white surface that is simply
a white surface (a colourless surface that is simply
a colourless surface) or rather, and better yet, that
simply *is* and that is all".[11] White, for Manzoni, was the
colour par excellence of literalism, the tautological
process; in short, of the proscription of meaning.

It is significant that Manzoni chose to call these
white works 'Achromes',[12] thus formalising the
non-chromatic quality of white in his eyes.

A few years earlier, in the United States, white had
experienced one of the most decisive shifts of its
modern life. In 1951, Robert Rauschenberg produced
his White Paintings (fig. 6): six works, comprising,
respectively, one, two, three, four, five and seven
panels, entirely and flawlessly covered with a
completely smooth layer of white paint,[13] in contrast
to his very Matterist Black Paintings of the same
period. Although the primary virtue of Rauschenberg's
white, as with Manzoni's, is its neutrality, this was
not required by the need to affirm a literal presence,
but rather to reveal the changing light and shadows
projected by the surrounding space. The neutrality
of white is not a guarantee of asemia but rather
of the work's dialogue with the close rather than
cosmic exterior. It is a long way from the white of
Suprematist infinity. However, as Branden W. Joseph
reminds us, László Moholy-Nagy had chosen to see
White on White as a surface designed to receive light
and shadow effects, in other words, as a projection
screen.[14] Regardless of the extent to which they were
influenced by Malevich, the White Paintings were the
source of inspiration for *4'33"* (1952), John Cage's
silent 'composition', as if to confirm white's modern
absence of colour. White had definitively lost its
status as a colour and become the visual equivalent
of silence. However, Rauschenberg's White Paintings
"no longer represented a return to the [Rodchenkian]
monochrome as the zero point of painting. Rather,
they demonstrated that 'there was no zero point'".[15]
A painting could never be truly empty, because the
shadows and light of its surroundings will inscribe
themselves on it. But to reveal them, it had to be white.

A decade after the White Paintings, the choice of
white was made by another American artist in a way
that, while radically different, also followed a rationale
of neutralisation. In the early 1960s, Robert Ryman
gradually eliminated every colour but white from his
palette (fig. 7). He explained his decision as follows:
"As I worked and developed the painting, I found that
I was eliminating a lot. I would put the color down, then
paint over the color, trying to get down to a few crucial
elements. It was like erasing something to put white
over it".[16] So, white seems to have been for him both
the instrument and the end of a parametric process
of reduction. White serves to erase that which is not
consubstantial with painting and defines the chromatic
condition most conducive to the manifestation of
pictorial essence: "The use of white in my paintings
came about when I realized that it doesn't interfere.
It's a neutral color that allows for a clarification of
nuances in painting. It makes other aspects of painting
visible that would not be so clear with the use of other

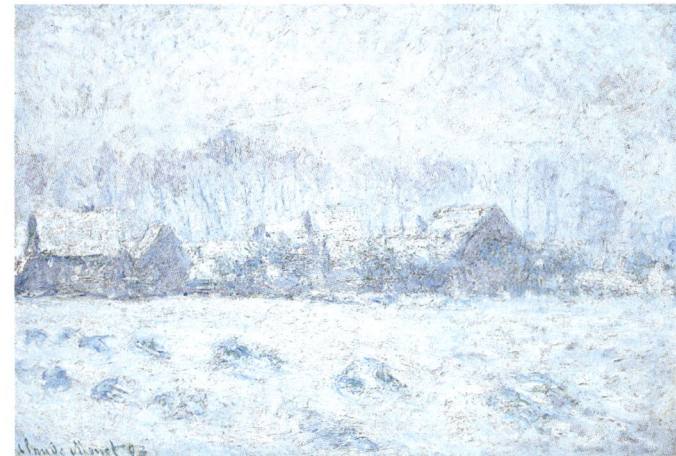

3

4

5

6

Fig. 3   Claude Monet
Effet de neige à Giverny
[*Snow Effect, Giverny*], 1893,
oil on canvas, 65.4 × 92.7 cm
Private collection

Fig. 4   Kazimir Malevich
*Suprematist Composition:
White on White*, 1918,
oil on canvas, 79.4 × 79.4 cm
Museum of Modern Art (MoMA),
New York. Acquisition confirmed
in 1999 by agreement with the
Estate of Kazimir Malevich and
made possible with funds from
the Mrs. John Hay Whitney
Bequest (by exchange) 817.1935

Fig. 5   Heinz Mack
White Rhythm, 1958, synthetic
resin on canvas, 121 × 96 cm
Private collection

Fig. 6   Robert Rauschenberg
White Painting (three panel),
1951, latex paint on canvas,
182.9 × 274.3 cm
San Francisco Museum
of Modern Art, San Francisco
Purchase through a gift of Phyllis
C. Wattis, 1998

7

Fig. 7   Robert Ryman
Chapter, 1981, oil on linen
canvas, four metal fixings,
223.5 × 213.5 cm
Centre Pompidou – Musée
National d'Art Moderne – Centre
de Création Industrielle, Paris
Purchase, 1982. AM 1981-850

Fig. 8   Harold E. Edgerton
Milk Drop Coronet, 1957,
negative, Panatomic X
and Ektacolor films
Image: 46.7 × 33.9 cm;
paper: 50.7 × 40.4 cm
Harold E. Edgerton collection
MIT Museum (Massachusetts Institute
of Technology), Cambridge, Mass.
HEE-NC-57001

Fig. 9   Jackson Pollock
White Light, 1954, oil, enamel
and aluminium paint on canvas,
122.4 × 96.9 cm
Museum of Modern Art (MoMA),
New York. The Sidney and Harriet
Janis Collection. 337.1967

Fig. 10   Mark Tansey
White on White, 1986, oil on
canvas, 198.1 × 350.5 × 1.3 cm
Walker Art Center, Minneapolis
Gift of Charles and Leslie Herman,
1991. 1991.99

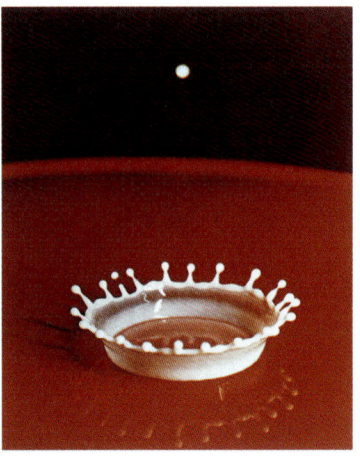

8

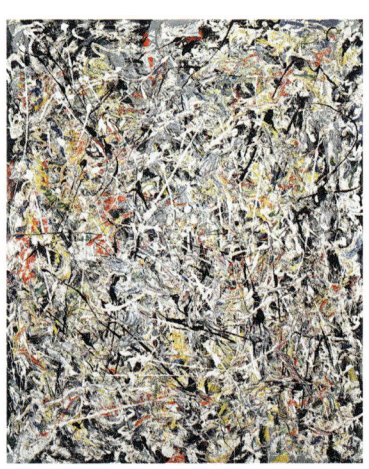

9

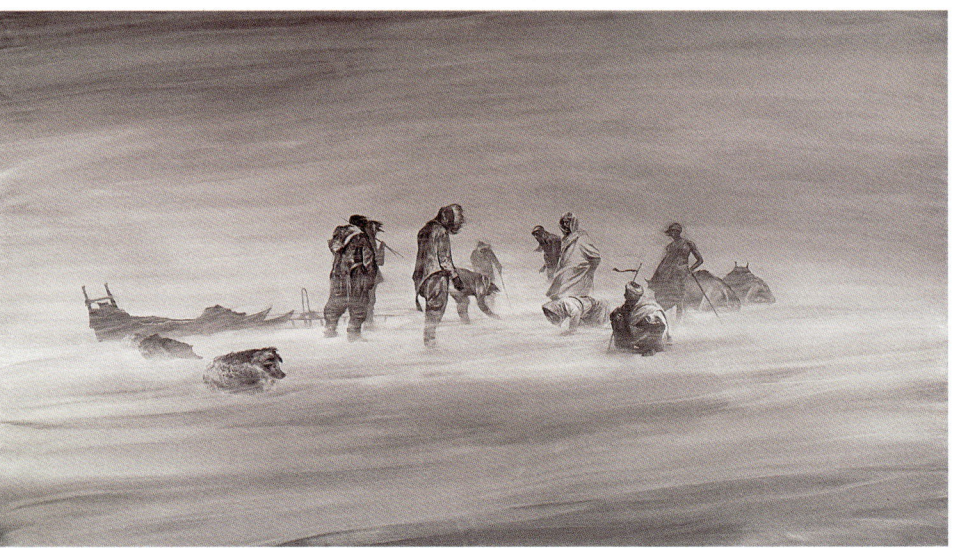

10

colors".[17] As a colour-neutralising agent, white is the ideal adjunct for revealing the variables that make up a painting (intensity and direction of the brushstroke, volume of pigment carried by the brush, tension of the support, method of fixing the painting, etc.). White was, for Ryman, the indispensable tool in his pictorial laboratory.

So, whether it is a question of the literalist manifestation of the painting as object, or of the potential screen of the painting, or of pictorial analysis, the white of modernity had numerous opportunities to proclaim its chromatic innocence.

But what of white in the Postmodern age? Two works can perhaps give us an idea. In Jack Goldstein's film *Glass of Milk* (1972), an infuriated man bangs his fist several times on a card table, on which is placed a glass of milk, a natural material if ever there were one, which, after a few splashes, finally tips over. This glass full of thick white liquid is laden with historical significance, that of the photographic experiments conducted by scientist Harold Edgerton (fig. 8), who, in the 1930s, invented stroboscopic photography and captured an image of a glass of milk smashing, and that of Alfred Hitchcock's *Suspicion* (1941) and the luminous glass of milk, possibly poisoned, that Cary Grant hands to Joan Fontaine. But it is above all a parody of action painting and the drip painting of

Jackson Pollock, whose last painting is entitled *White Light* (1954, fig. 9). The immaculate macula becomes imbued with affect, the product of an absurd fiction, and causes a breakage.[18] In other words, white was no longer what it had been for Malevich, Manzoni and Ryman. While Goldstein's film evokes Pollock, Mark Tansey's painting *White on White* (1986, fig. 10) references Malevich even more clearly. The work offers a curious image. More grey than white, it is a hybrid of bad snowy weather – which Allais had already used as a symbol for whiteness, whereas Manzoni had feared it would prevent a literal interpretation – and a sandstorm, incorporating Bedouins and Inuit in the same landscape. In the same way that Suprematist painting had combined two tones of white, the Postmodern allegory coupled hot and cold, North and South. Here, white is no longer, as it was in Malevich's work, the non-colour of the infinite spaces of the cosmic void and of metaphysical immateriality. It can be associated with a given material, or even two completely opposite ones, between which it is no longer possible to choose. Not only is white no longer the counterpart of figuration, of meaning to be deciphered, but its meaning has become complex and contradictory. It has not rediscovered its colour – the bright colour of Edgar Degas's cotton or that of Édouard Manet's piece of tulle[19] – it has instead become the melancholic symbol of lost truth.

1
With the word *blanc*, Mallarmé was referring to more than the colour white, he also meant blank spaces. Thus, to cope with this ambiguity this celebrated phrase is often translated in English as "here the *blancs* assume importance".
2
See Michel Pastoureau, *Blanc. Histoire d'une couleur* (Paris: Seuil, 2022).
3
Kazimir Malevich, "Suprematism" (in the catalogue of the 10th State exhibition "Non-Objective Creation and Suprematism", held in Moscow in 1919), in John Bowlt (ed. & trans.), *Russian Art of the Avant-Garde, Theory and Criticism, 1902–1934* (New York: Viking Press, 1976), p. 145.
4
It should be remembered that it was Malevich who gave to the word *sputnik*, which in Russian signifies 'fellow traveller', the meaning of 'artificial satellite launched into cosmic space' that it has since taken on, in a 1920

text *Suprematizm: 34 risunka* ["Suprematism: 34 Drawings"] (Forest Row, UK: Artists Bookworks, 2002).
5
Denys Riout, *La Peinture monochrome. Histoire et archéologie d'un genre* (Nîmes: Jacqueline Chambon, 1996) p. 265.
6
Inspired by Lucio Fontana, this manifesto was written by a group of young artists.
7
Enrico Crispolti, Lucio Fontana, *Lucio Fontana: Paintings, Sculptures, Drawings* (Milan: Skira, 2005), p. 27.
8
Ibid.
9
Heinz Mack, Otto Piene and Günther Uecker, untitled text originally published on a poster and in a booklet for *Zero. Der neue Idealismus, poetisches Manifest* (Berlin: Galerie Diogenes, 1963).
10
Ibid.

11
Piero Manzoni, *"La nuova concezione artistica"*, exh. cat., Azimut Gallery, Milan, January 1960.
12
As Claude Bellegarde, whose work Piero Manzoni knew, had done not long before.
13
As many of the original canvases had been recycled by the artist into other works, the series was created by Brice Marden in 1968 for an exhibition at the Castelli Gallery in New York.
14
Branden W. Joseph, *Random Order: Robert Rauschenberg and the Neo-Avant-Garde* (Cambridge [MA] and London: MIT Press, 2003), p. 36.
15
Ibid., p. 86.
16
Robert Ryman quoted in Robert Storr, *Robert Ryman* (London: Tate Gallery and New York: Museum of Modern Art, 1993), p. 16.
17
Ibid.

18
For more on this film, and, more broadly, on the image of milk in conceptual art and Postmodern photography, see Kenneth Hayes, *Milk and Melancholy* (Toronto: Prefix Press, 2008).
19
The references here are to *Le Bureau de coton à la Nouvelle-Orléans* (1873) by Edgar Degas, with its mass of white fabric, which could be a Manzoni 'Achrome', and to *Argenteuil* (1874) by Édouard Manet, and his masterly piece of tulle decorating the hat, which alone could make a magnificent painting by Raimund Girke, one of the great proponents of white in Neo-Avant-Garde painting.

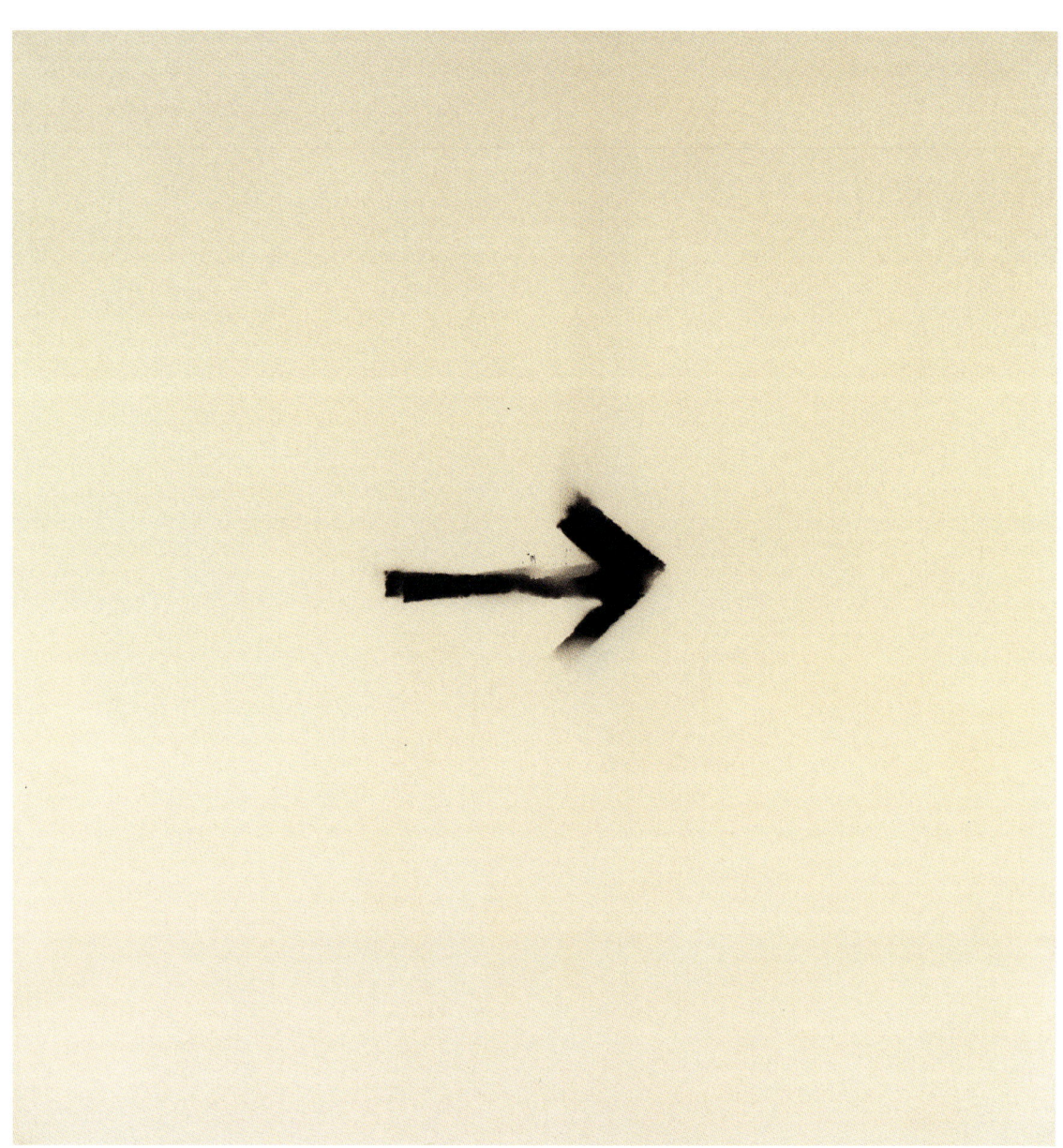

Martin Barré   *67-F-2-113x105*   1967

glycerophtalic paint and acrylic on canvas   113 × 105 cm   long-term loan by the Centre Pompidou Foundation, 2016 (promise of donation by Thea Westreich Wagner and Ethan Wagner to the Centre Pompidou Foundation)

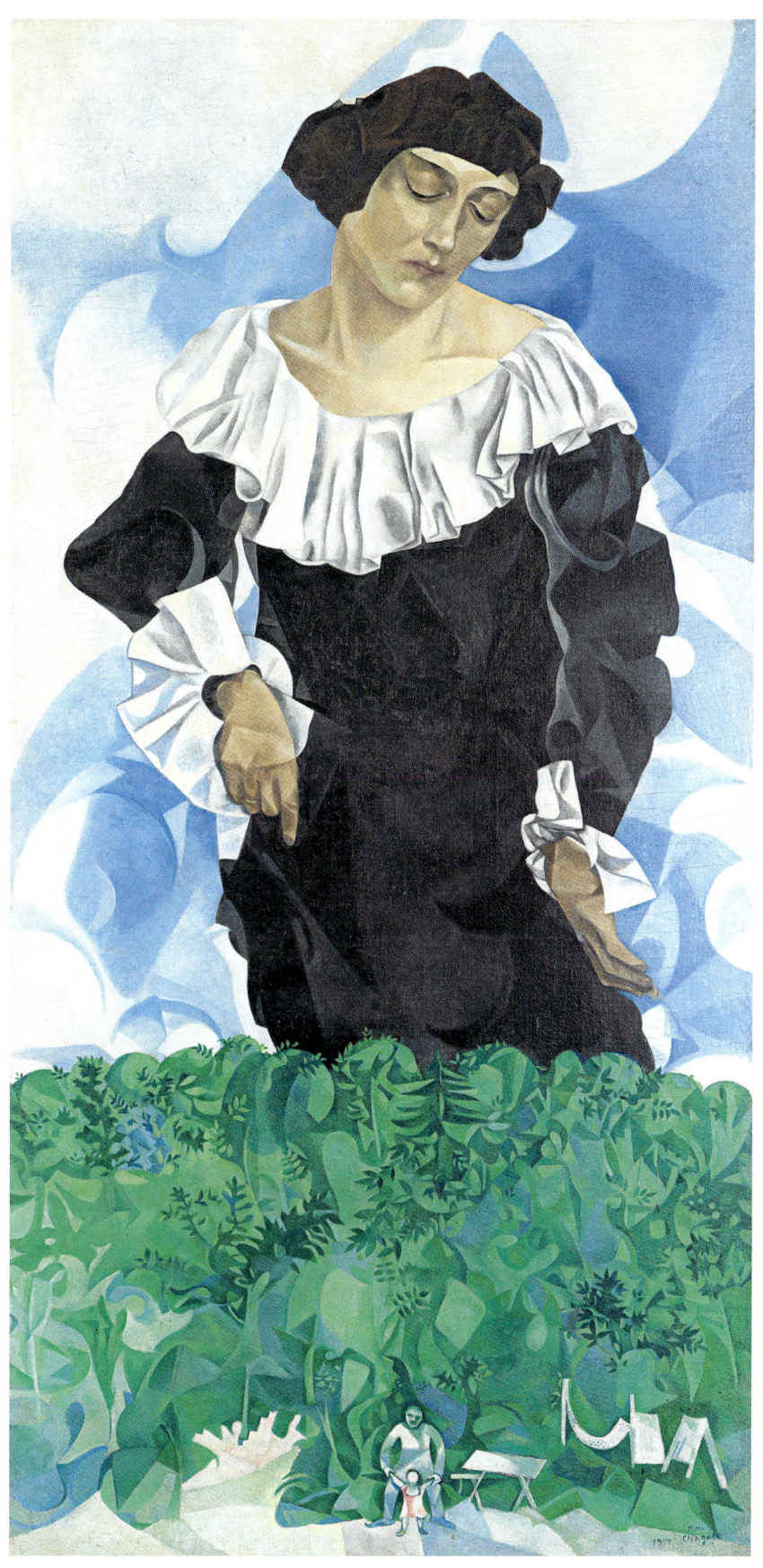

Marc Chagall   *Bella au col blanc* [*Bella with a White Collar*]   1917

oil on linen   149 × 72 cm   dation, 1988, AM 1988-61

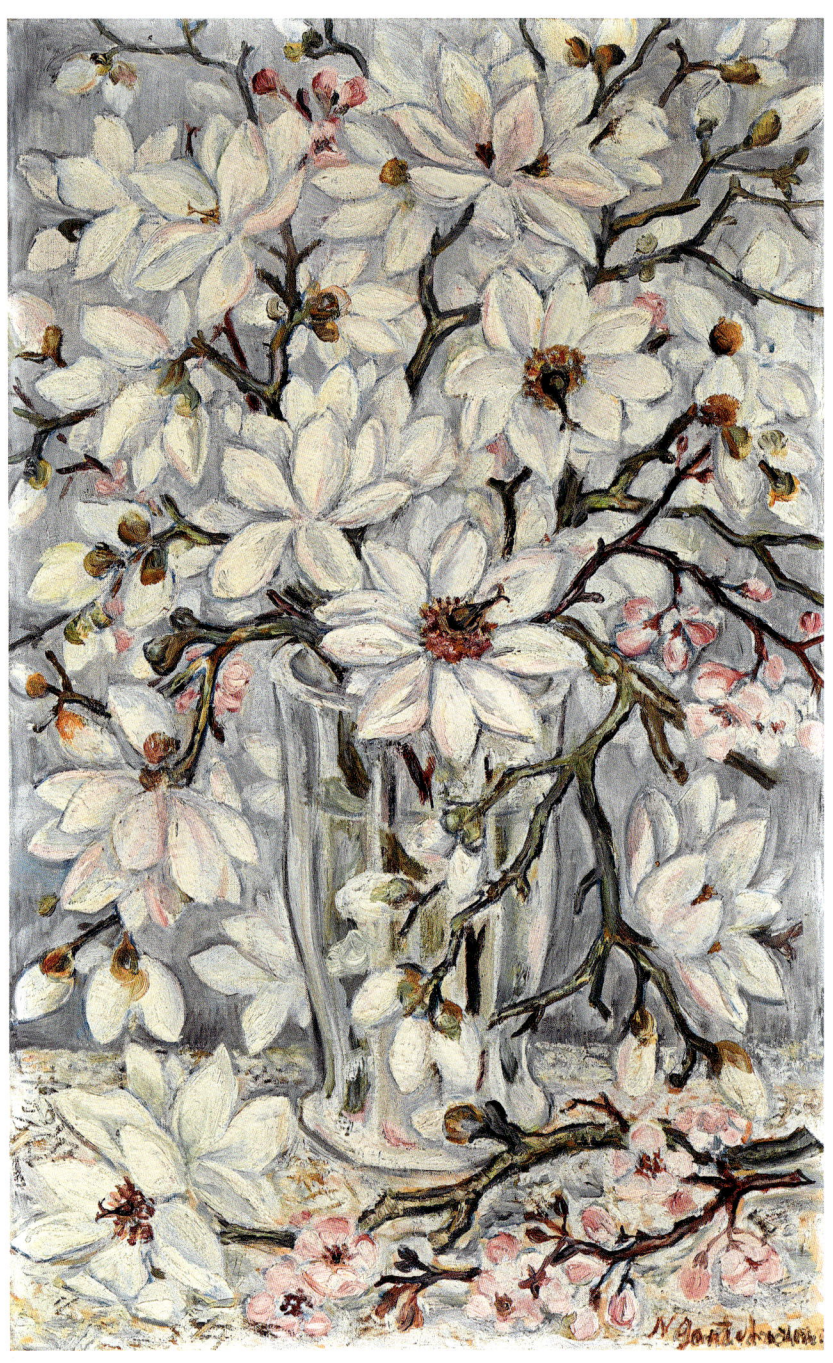

Natalia Goncharova   *Vase de fleurs blanches* [*Vase of White Flowers*]   [1930–35]

oil on canvas   60 × 37 cm   bequest of Marie Louise Rosenfeld, 2012, AM 2013-5

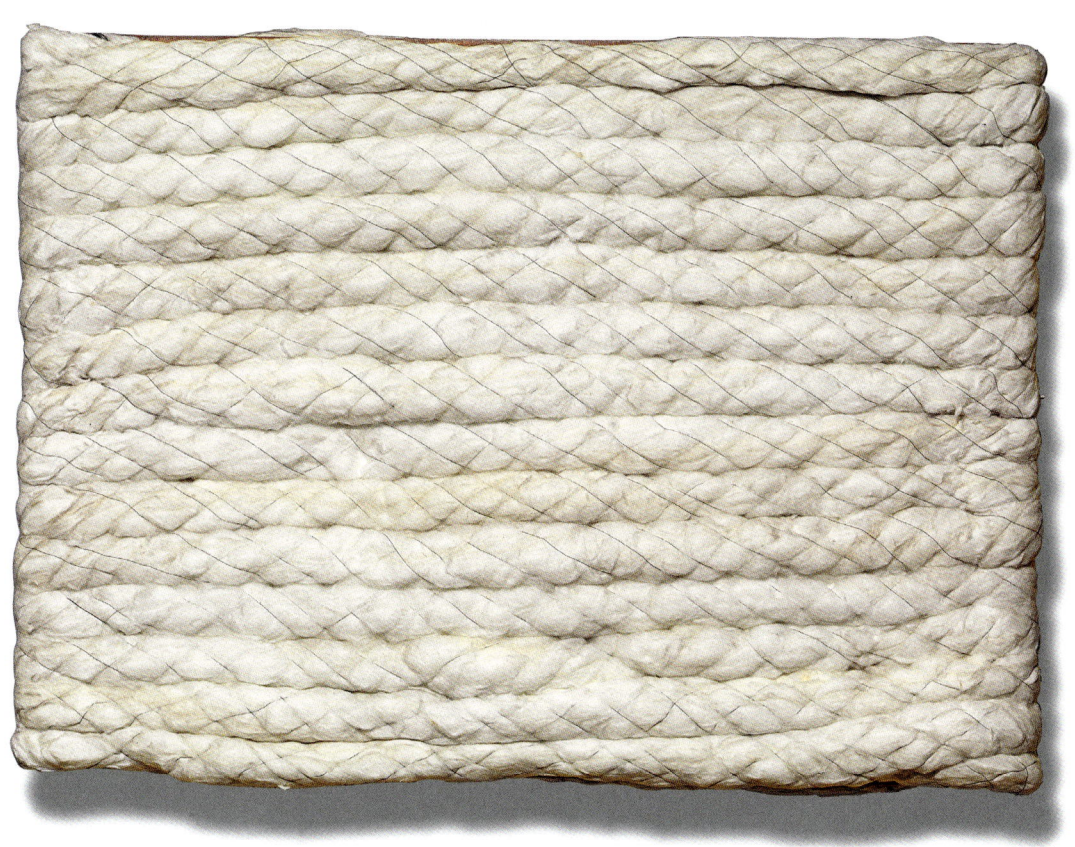

Piero Manzoni   *Achrome*   1961
fibreglass, wire, wood   51 × 66 × 13 cm   purchase, 1994, AM 1994-98

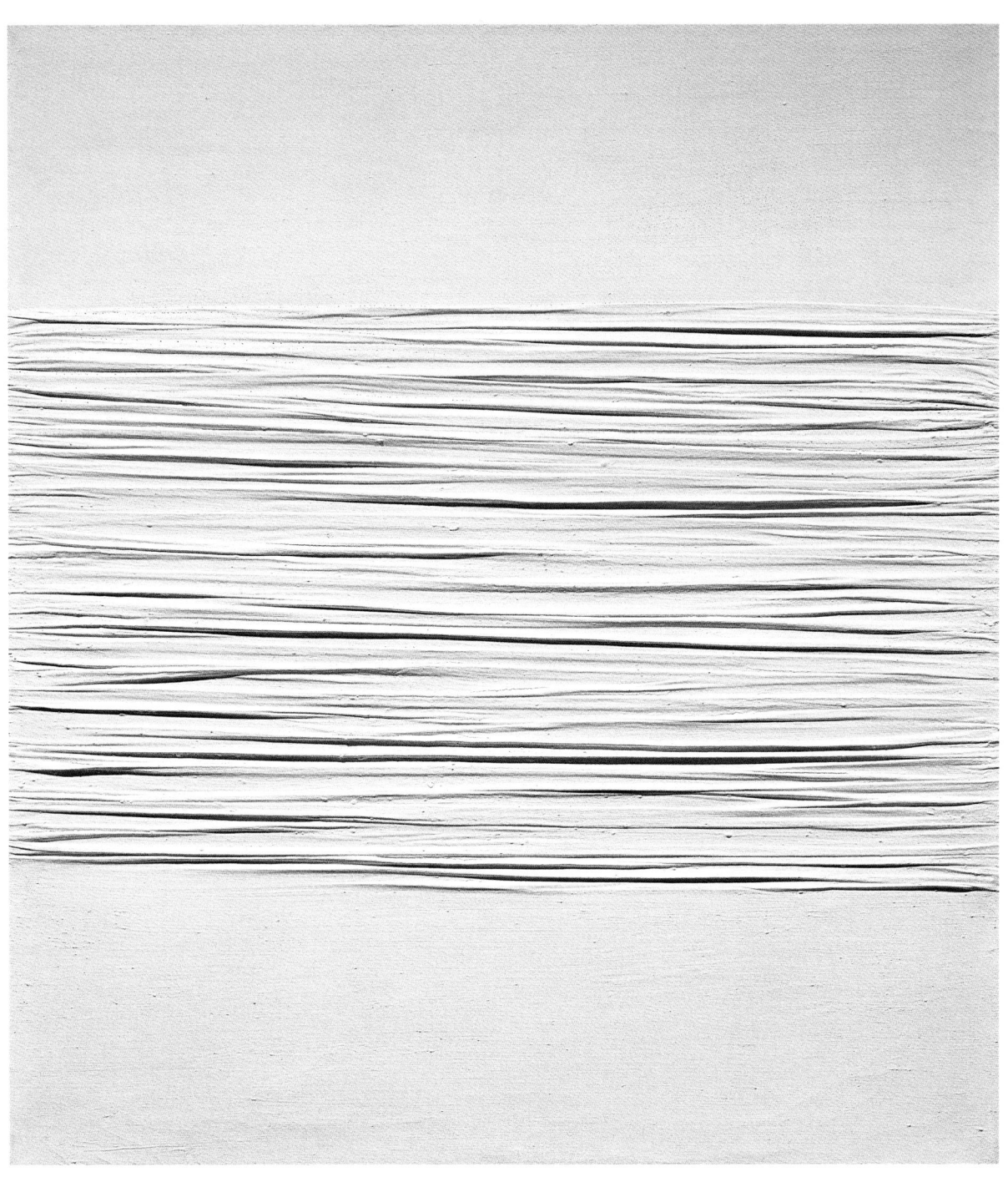

Piero Manzoni *Achrome* 1959

kaolin on pleated canvas   140 × 120.5 cm   purchase, 1981, AM 1981-36

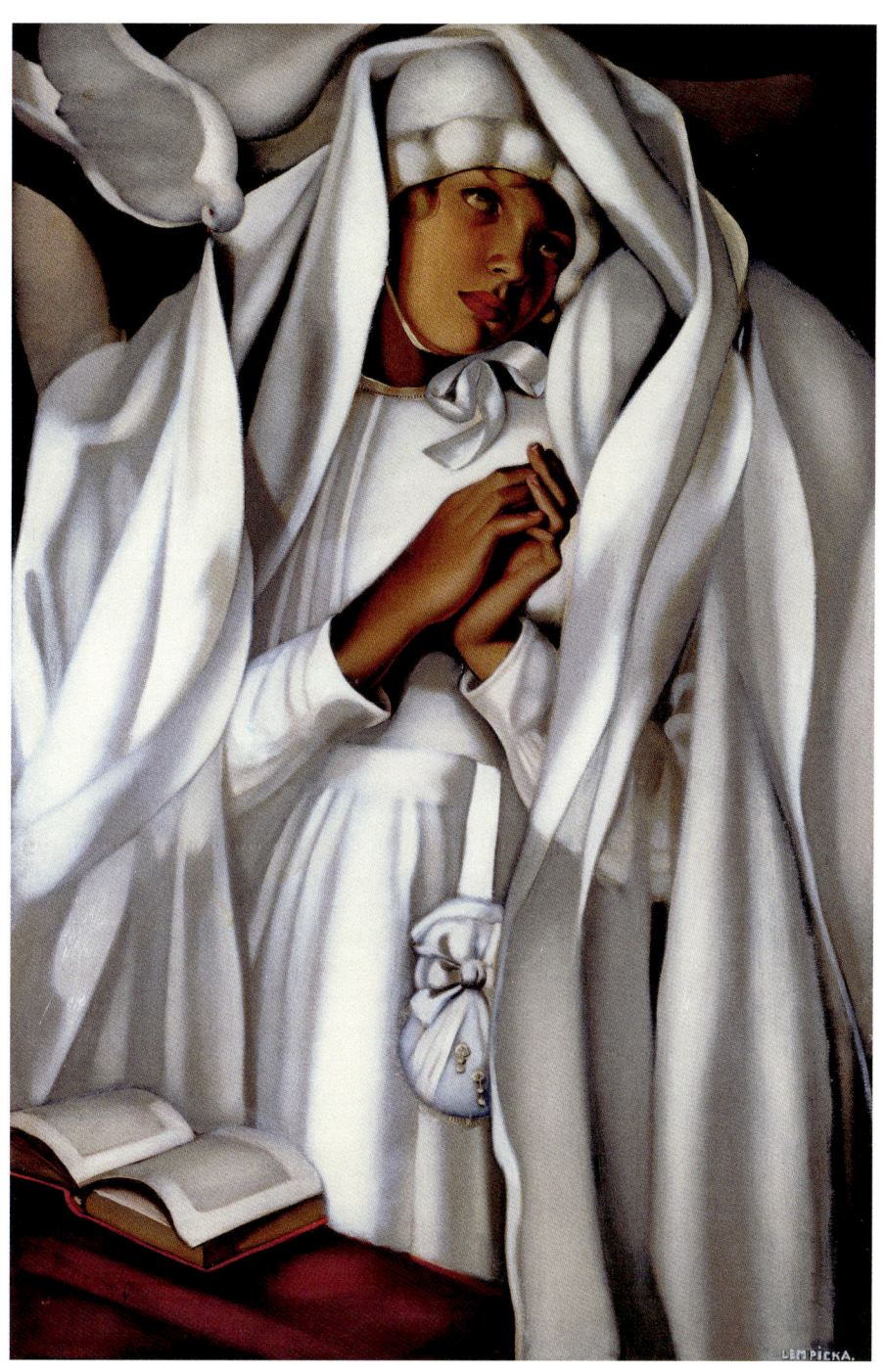

Tamara de Lempicka   *La Communiante* [*The Communicant*]   1929

oil on canvas   101 × 64.8 cm   gift of the artist, 1976, AM 1976-1134

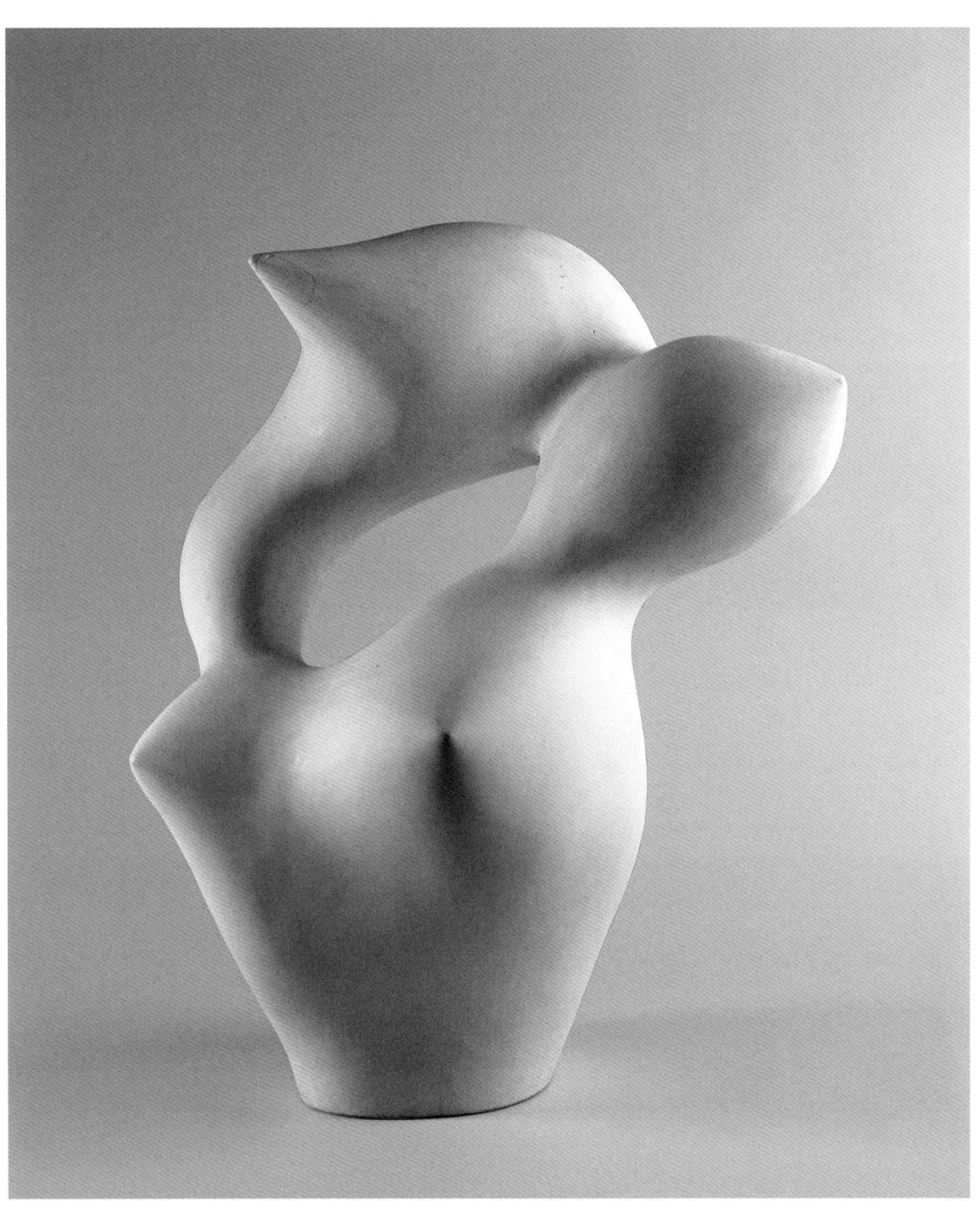

Jean Arp   *Couronne de bourgeons II* [*Crown of Buds II*]   1936

plaster   52 × 42.5 × 42 cm   confiscation by the Customs authorities, 1996, AM 2004-238

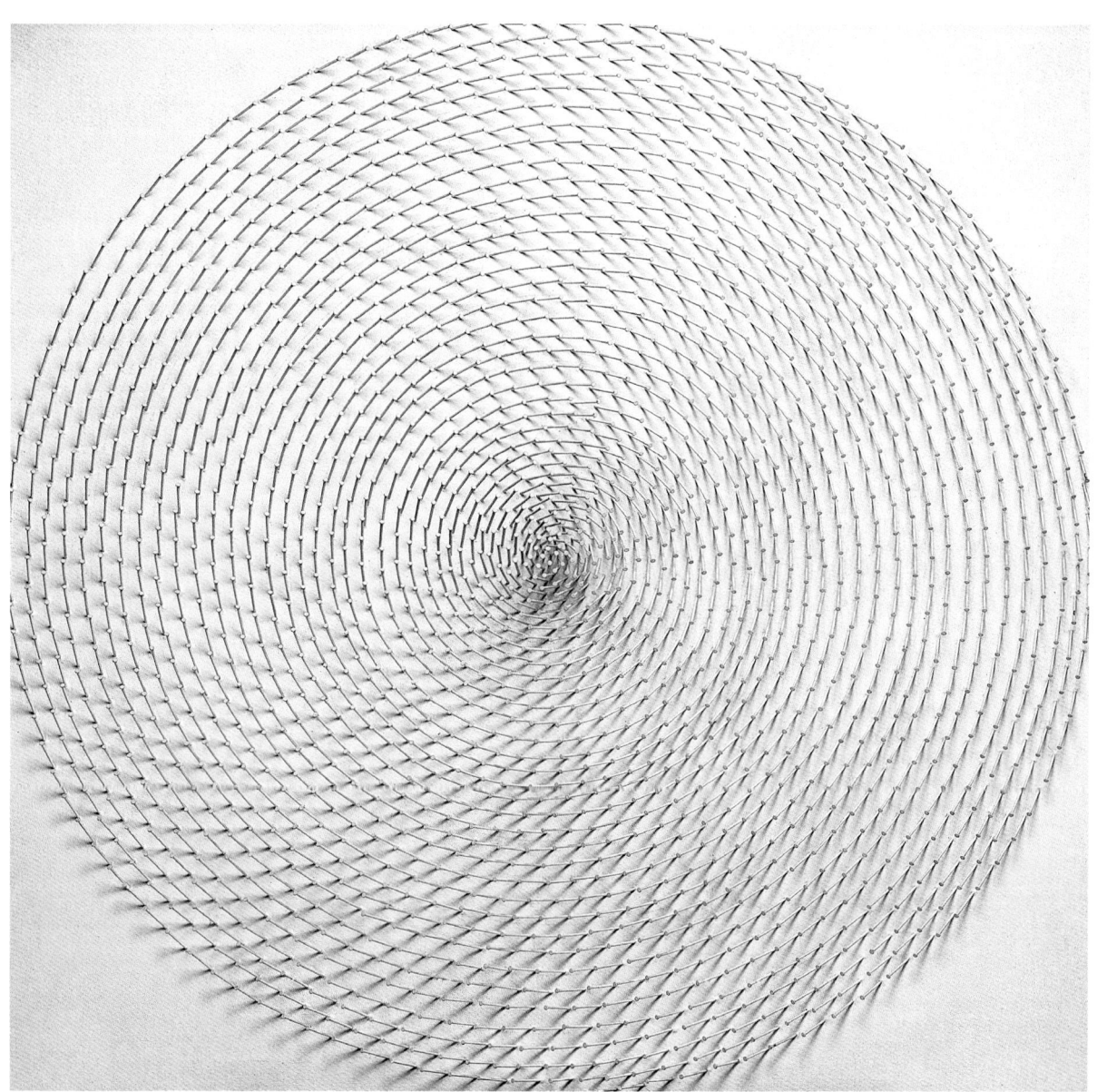

Günther Uecker   *Spiral III*   1968

oil on canvas, agglomerate, painted metal   100 × 100 cm   purchase, 2008, AM 2008-22

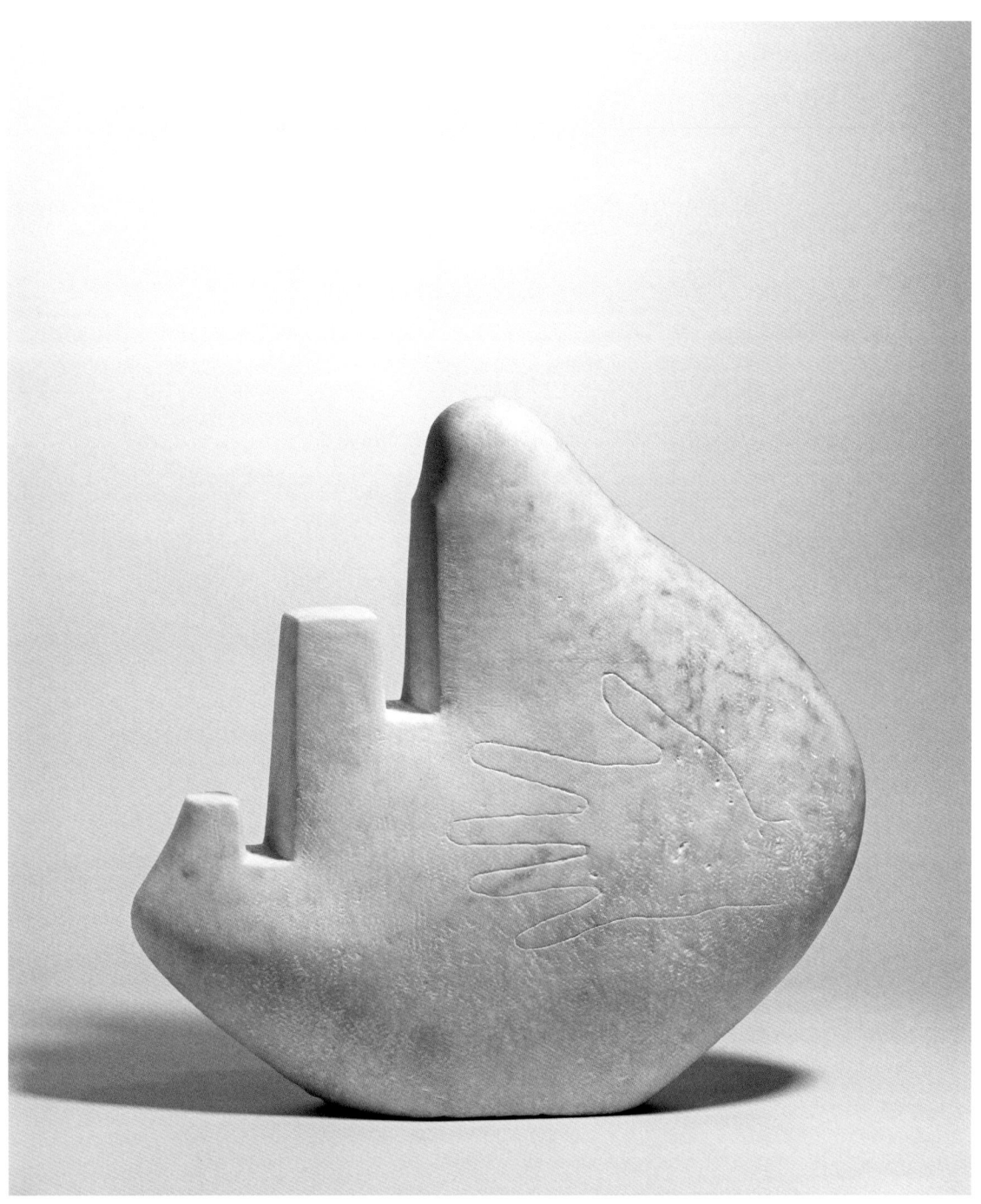

Alberto Giacometti   *Caresse* [*Caress*]   1932

white marble   47.5 × 49.5 × 16 cm   purchase, 1984, AM 1984-310

Otto Piene   *La Force pure III* [*Pure Energy III*]   1959

oil on canvas   125 × 125 × 7.3 cm   purchase, 2012, AM 2012-268

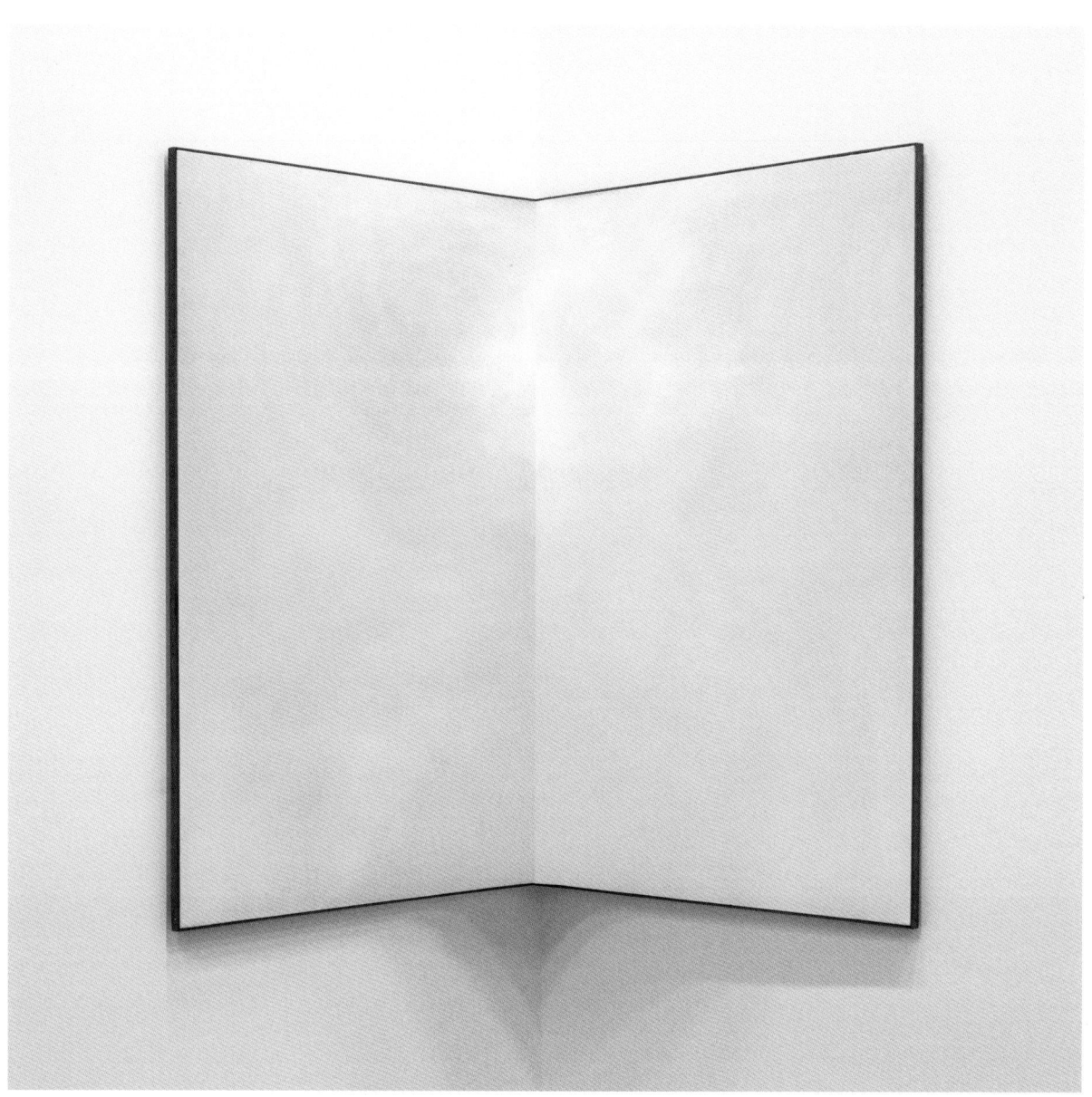

Enrico Castellani   *White Angular Surface no. 6*   1964

acrylic on canvas   149.7 × 145 × 59 cm   purchase, 1992, AM 1992-106

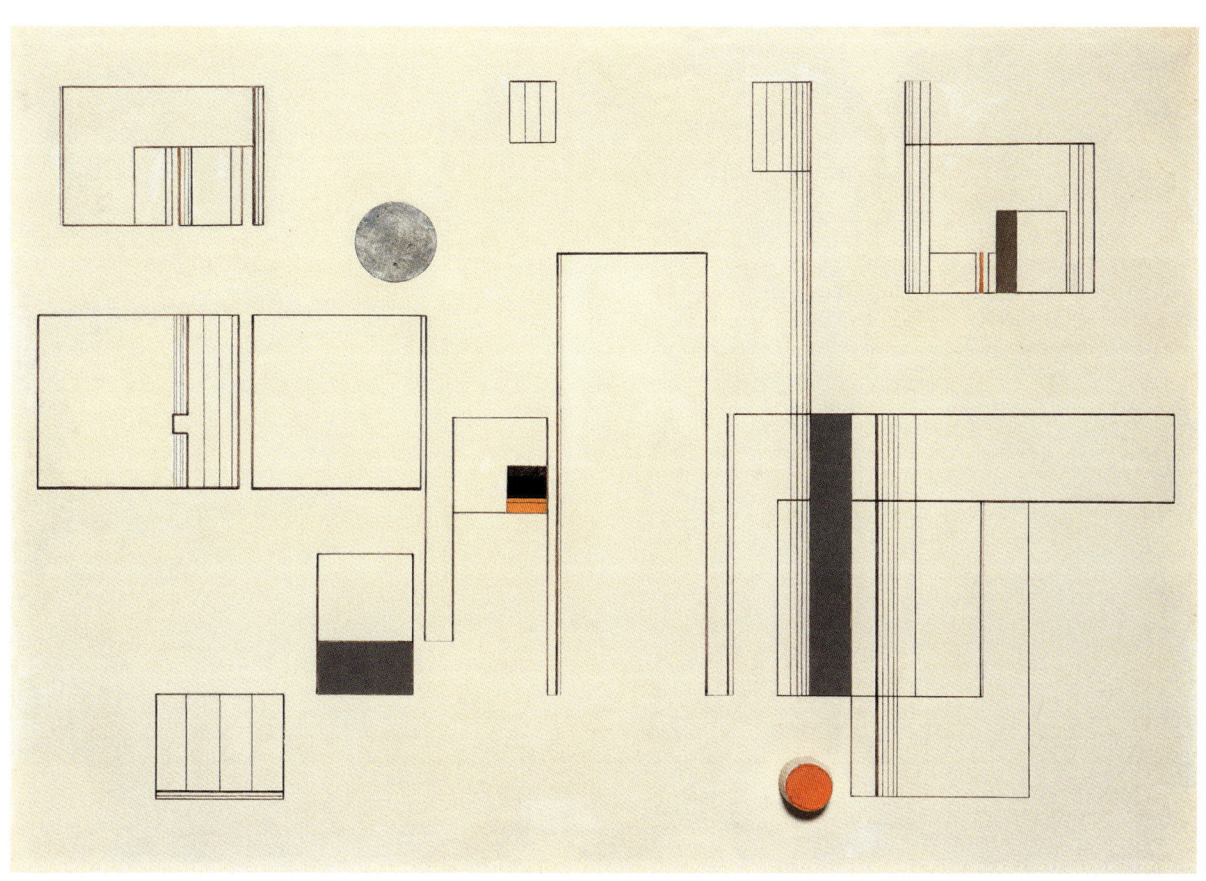

Marcelle Cahn *Abstrait linéaire* [*Linear Abstract*] 1954

vinyl paint, gouache and ink on Isorel, collage cardboard, balsa, metal 72.7 × 100 cm gift of Mr. and Mrs. Michel Seuphor, 1978, AM 1977-613

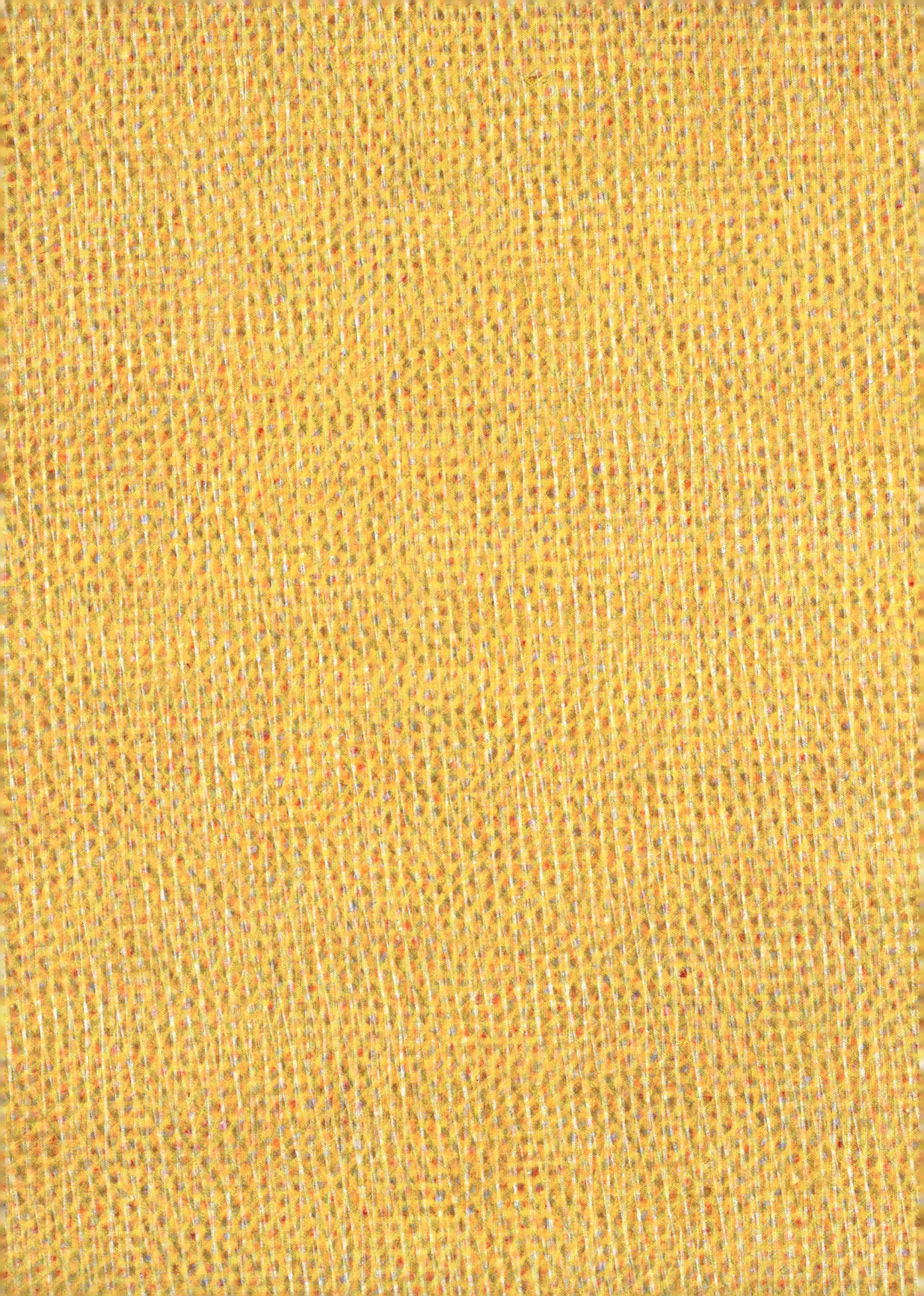

YELLOW

THE HIGH NOTE OF THE COLOUR YELLOW

Claire Maingon

French readers, at least, will be familiar with the "little patch of yellow wall"[1] that, in Marcel Proust's *The Prisoner* (1923) the writer Bergotte contemplates fondly before he dies. This motif visible in Johannes Vermeer's famous *View of Delft* (1659–60, fig.1) is not purely iconographic: it stands as a symbol for the whole, for painting itself, in the same way that Abbé Séguin's 'yellow dog' in François-René de Chateaubriand's *Vie de Rancé* does, according to Roland Barthes,[2] for the whole of literature. *A posteriori*, the modern eye sees in them revelatory signs of the autonomy of art, of its absolute ontological truth, proof that the colour yellow played a role in this epistemological revolution well after Vermeer or Chateaubriand. But let us not get ahead of ourselves and let us not forget that "every work of art is the child of its time",[3] as Wassily Kandinsky, the painter who theorised his ideas on colours and their actions on the human soul in *On the Spiritual in Art* in 1911, the time of the avant-gardes, was fond of saying.

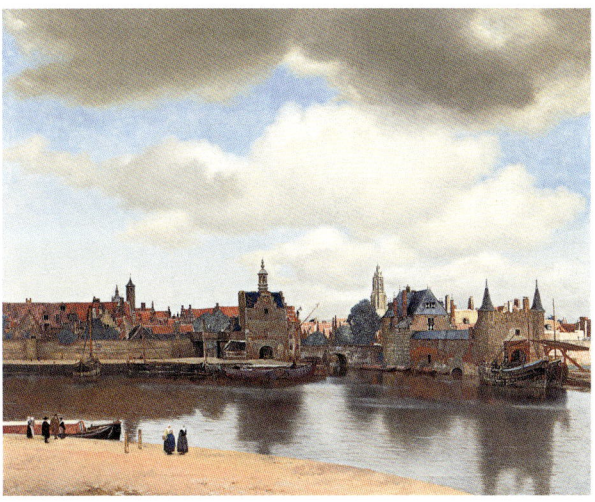

Fig.1 Johannes Vermeer
View of Delft, 1660–61, oil on canvas, 96.5 × 115.7 cm
Mauritshuis, The Hague. 92

PLEASE DRAW ME A SUN

Like Antoine de Saint-Exupéry's Little Prince, every child draws the sun as a bright yellow circle, sometimes shooting out its rays. This naive depiction can be found in popular images, in allegories of mystic ecstasies or of royal or political power, but also in modern art, like the sun that illuminates *La Vigne rouge à Arles* [*The Red Vineyard Near Arles*], painted by Vincent van Gogh in 1888. The star takes on soft or saturated hues, from the palest to the deepest yellow, verging on orange or red, depending on whether it is seen at high noon, dawn or dusk. In Claude Monet's *Impression, soleil levant* [*Impression, Sunrise*] (1872), the sun is a red signal that warms the chilly and misty atmosphere of a sleeping port and directs the viewer's eye. Edvard Munch's *The Sun* (1911–16) is a Symbolist celebration of the power of the light – white and yellow in reality – cast by this celestial or divine star.

Yellow is the colour we associate with warmth and light. Joseph Mallord William Turner made it his favourite colour, using an incredible range of yellows in his works to enhance the light – ochre yellow (natural ferric oxide), chrome yellow (lead chromate) and, probably, yellow lacquer – aided in this by the arrival of new pigments on the market, from the late 18th century. Yellow, production of which was industrialised during the 19th century, is a key colour on the palette of plein-air painters, Impressionists and Post-Impressionists, but also Fauvists and Expressionists. Van Gogh loved this colour with a passion and, during his stay in Arles, lived in the "yellow house". For him, yellow represented light, the sun, brightness.[4] The Langlois Bridge is yellow, as is the garden of Les Alyscamps. The sunflower, heliotrope flower par excellence, is the subject of a series of seven paintings that depict it as a "vegetal star",[5] the terrestrial equivalent of the sun (fig.3). A symbol of life, optimism and joy, yellow radiates in Pierre Bonnard's *L'Atelier au mimosa* [*Studio with Mimosa*] (1939–46), one of the last large-format pictures he painted at Le Cannet.

Yellow, as Paul Signac and Wassily Kandinsky mention, quoting Eugène Delacroix, symbolises the idea of "joy and plenty".[6] *La Joie de vivre* [*The Joy of Life*], which Henri Matisse painted in 1905–06, is drenched in yellow, the colour of citrus fruits and summer. "Yellow is lemon, straw, wheat, which takes on golden hues as it ripens",[7] wrote František Kupka in *La Création dans les arts plastiques* [*Creation in the Plastic Arts*], a theoretical text written between 1910 and 1913, contemporaneous with Kandinsky's thought. The beneficial effects of the sun on the soul and body are well known. By connecting a lemon to a socket fitted with a bulb of the same yellow as the Mediterranean fruit in *Capri Battery* (1985, fig.2), Joseph Beuys paid tribute to the healing and invigorating power of solar energy while he was recovering from a lung condition on the famous Italian island in the Bay of Naples, the city that has given its name to a warm, golden yellow (Naples yellow).

YELLOW QUALITIES

A colour with "a serene, gay, softly exciting character",[8] according to Johann Wolfgang von Goethe, yellow was considered by Kandinsky as a "typical earthly colour",[9] capable of becoming too aggressive if the tone is too sharp. In his view, the qualities of this colour are further enhanced in the highly spiritual and symbolic space of a triangle. It is true that, due to its chromatic power, yellow has often been used, in the history of painting, only as a form of punctuation or in isolation. With its bright yellow colour, the lemon lifts a still life or other composition in dark, black or grey tones remarkably well, as was shown by the Flemish painters of the 17th century. Revisiting the masters, Édouard Manet used a similar touch of colour in the *Portrait de Théodore Duret* (1868) as well as in a small still life (*Le Citron* [*The Lemon*], 1880, fig. 4) that presents the intensely coloured fruit as a veritable jewel.

For a long time, yellow was associated with gold, and used as a substitute for it, symbolising wealth, beauty and femininity. This lyrical and idealised use of the colour yellow is evident, too, in Marc Chagall's paintings. Yellow and gold are also closely associated in Gustav Klimt's work. Gold is the colour of idols and, by extension, of sham, caprice, ostentation and artificiality. It is not insignificant that Andy Warhol devoted the first of his silkscreen print portfolios to the blond, Hollywood-industry sex symbol Marilyn Monroe in 1967. And when Minimalist Dan Flavin began his research into the use of fluorescent lights, arranged on a dynamic diagonal, it was yellow – or more precisely the colour the closest to gold – that he chose for *The Diagonal of May 25, 1963* (1963, fig. 5), as a magnificent introduction to the series.

František Kupka also notes the positive symbolism associated with the colour yellow in Tibetan and Chinese cultures.[10] In fact, this is the sense that Piero Dorazio attributes to yellow in *Qualités jaunes* [*Yellow Qualities*] (1960), which treats the colour as a textured all-over painting. This work was painted after the artist's return from a trip to the USA, where he visited Asian art collections and fully realised the persistence of discriminatory ideologies concerning people from the Far East (fear of the infamous 'Yellow Peril'). On the one hand, *Yellow Qualities* exemplifies Dorazio's opposition to gestural painting; on the other, it pays tribute to a fetish colour in Asia, and particularly in China, where it is considered imperial and sacred.

But yellow remains an ambiguous colour, as Kupka notes. "Yellow has been the colour of infamy, the mark of bad places, the emblem of lepers and Jews", he wrote.[11] As highlighted in the work of Michel Pastoureau, since the Middle Ages, yellow has also been perceived in the West as the colour of treason, ill temper, urine, greed and vice.[12] It is no coincidence that Judas is clothed in yellow in *Kiss of Judas*, the fresco painted by Giotto di Bondone in the Scrovegni Chapel in Padua (1304–06), and in the works of Cimabue and Fra Angelico. Neither is it by chance that Paul Gauguin portrays himself juxtaposed with a yellow Christ (*Portrait de l'artiste au Christ jaune*

[*Self-Portrait with the Yellow Christ*], 1890–91, fig. 6), an archaic Christ, "piteous and barbaric",[13] evoking the painter's own isolation and suggesting, possibly, his image as a pariah (and, by extension, his place as the future Messiah of modern art). And what does the yellow star, the shameful insignia imposed on Jews during the Second World War, owe to this distant symbolic legacy? The colour is more than a chromatic punctuation mark in the *Self Portrait with Jewish Identity Card* painted by Felix Nussbaum in 1943.

Artists have known how to make use of this ambiguous symbolism, which is enhanced, of course, by the choice of a highly saturated or very sharp shade. In Georg Baselitz's work, yellow is seen as a stimulating, acidic colour that almost evokes a sense of malaise when combined with the Neo-Expressionist's familiar inverted figures. Yellow can be a Fauvist colour that disturbs, brutalizes and challenges the eye, especially when it is combined with the image of nudity, and when it is deliberately used to suggest prostitution, impurity, immorality (Sonia Delaunay, *Nu jaune* [*Yellow Nude*], 1908; Kees van Dongen, *The Spanish Shawl*, 1913). So, it is easy to understand the strange feeling evoked by *Madonna Figure* (1982), Katharina Fritsch's yellow Virgin, or the yellow halo illuminating a crucifix submerged in Andres Serrano's own urine in *Piss Christ* (1987), a work that is regularly vandalised.

IN THE YELLOW SPACE

Yellow, just as much as red or blue, has contributed to one of the major challenges of art modern: liberating art from the mimetic representation of real life. Paul Gauguin assumed a key role in this. An instance can be seen in the lesson he gave to Paul Sérusier in Pont-Aven in 1888, which resulted in the *Paysage au bois d'amour* [*Landscape at the Bois d'Amour*], later titled *Le Talisman* [*The Talisman*] (1888, fig. 7). This small Synthetic work painted using pure colours, predominantly yellow, rewrote the rules of naturalistic representation. Gauguin had invited Sérusier to interpret real life in a subjective way. This was one of the first major lessons in modern art, and led Maurice Denis (to whom *The Talisman* was offered) to reflect that "a painting, before it becomes a battle horse, a nude woman or an anecdote of any kind, is essentially a flat surface covered with colours assembled in a particular order".[14] The aim of the artist is not to punctiliously copy nature, but to express it in plastic form, to place colour at the heart of the visual experience as well as of the pictorial space.

I see in Matisse's *Le Rideau jaune* [*The Yellow Curtain*] (1915, fig. 8) – the last of the paintings the artist devoted to the theme of windows during

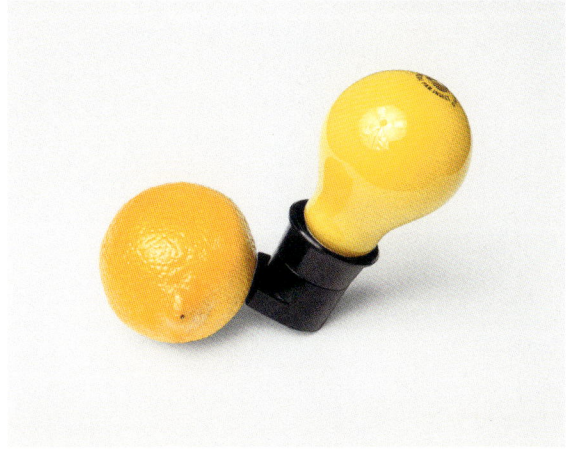

2

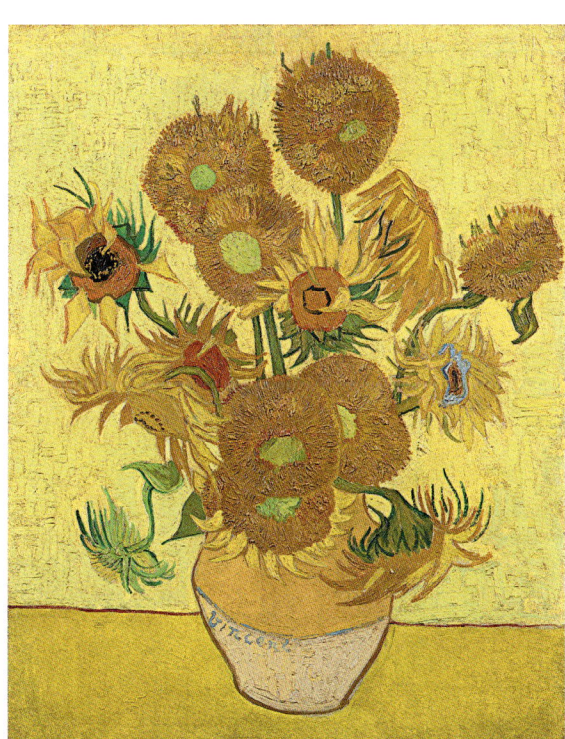

3

Fig. 2   Joseph Beuys
Capri Battery, 1985, light bulb
with plug socket, in wooden box;
lemon, 8 × 11 × 6 cm
National Galleries of Scotland,
Edinburgh. Purchased with
assistance from the National
Heritage Memorial Fund and Art
Fund, 2002. GMA 4646

Fig. 3   Vincent van Gogh
Tournesols [*Sunflowers*],
January 1889,
oil on canvas, 95 × 73 cm
Van Gogh Museum (Vincent van
Gogh Foundation), Amsterdam
s0031V1962. F0458

Fig. 4   Édouard Manet
Le Citron [*The Lemon*], 1880,
oil on canvas, 14 × 22 cm
Musée d'Orsay, Paris. Bequest of Earl
Isaac de Camondo, 1911. RF1997

Fig. 5   Dan Flavin
*The Diagonal of May 25, 1963
(to Constantin Brancusi)*,
1963, yellow fluorescent light,
244 cm long on the diagonal
David Zwirner Gallery
Courtesy of David Zwirner Gallery,
© ADAGP, Paris, 2025

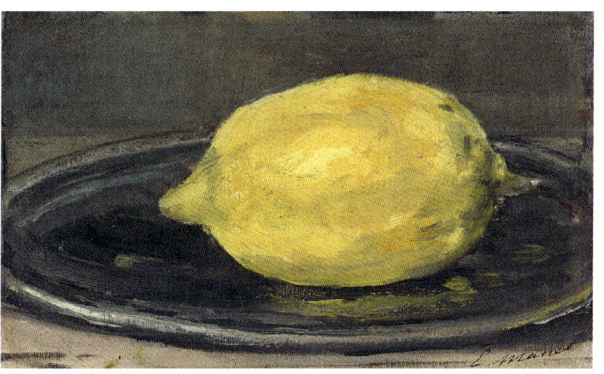

4

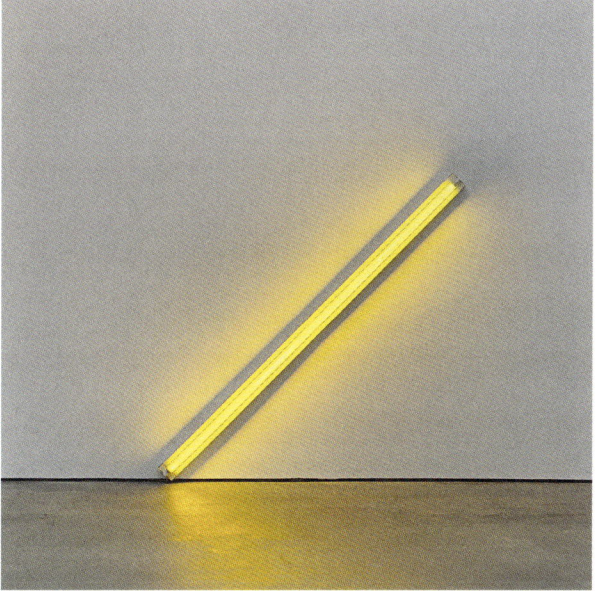

5

63

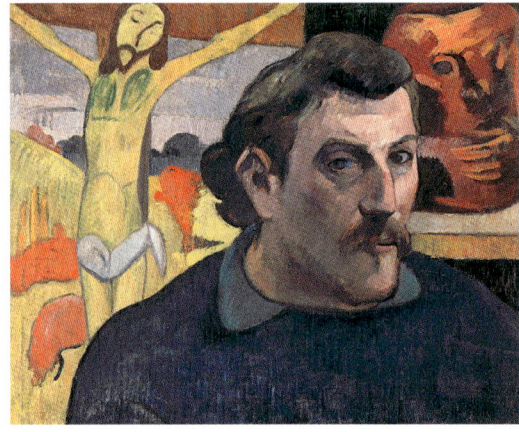

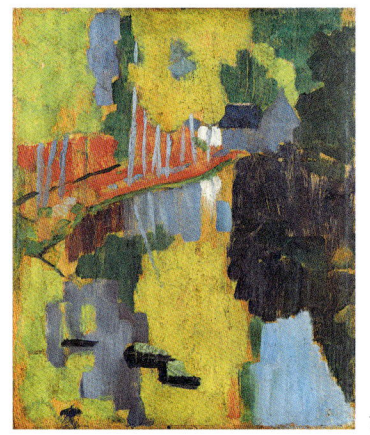

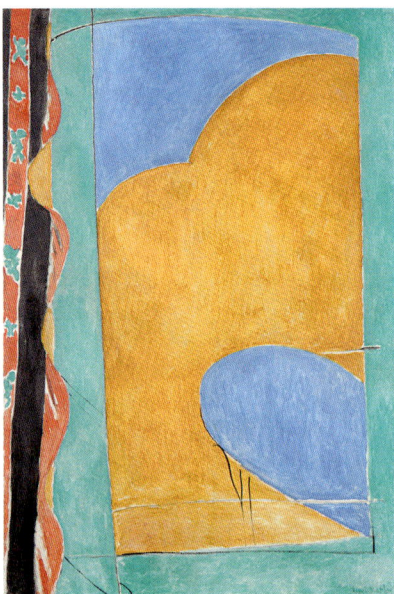

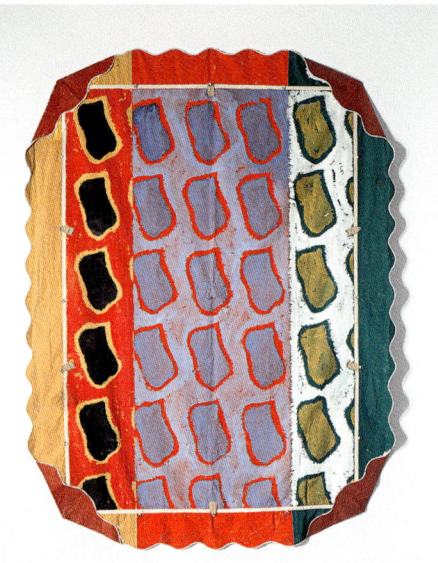

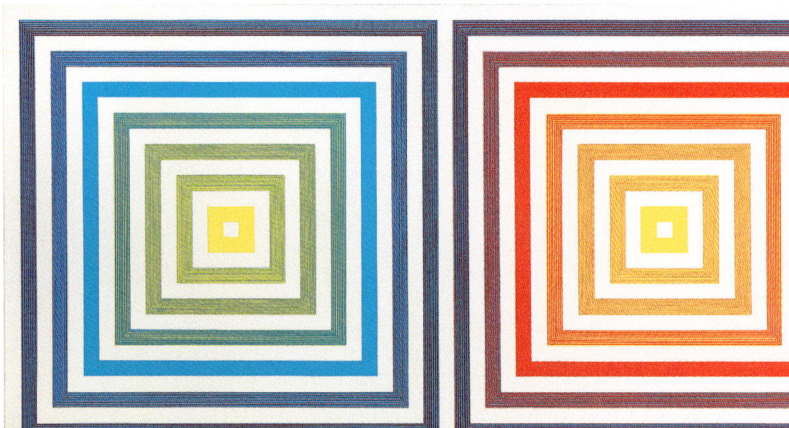

6

7

8

9

10

Fig. 6   Paul Gauguin
*Portrait de l'artiste au Christ
jaune* [*Self-Portrait with the
Yellow Christ*], 1890–91,
oil on canvas, 38 × 46 cm
Musée d'Orsay, Paris. RF 1994 2

Fig. 7   Paul Sérusier
*Le Talisman, Paysage
au bois d'amour*
[*The Talisman, Landscape
at the Bois d'Amour*], 1888,
oil on wood, 27 × 21.5 cm
Musée d'Orsay, Paris
Purchased with the generous
support of Philippe Meyer, 1985
RF1985-13

Fig. 8   Henri Matisse
*Composition (Le Rideau
jaune)* [*The Yellow Curtain
(or Composition)*], 1915,
oil on canvas, 146 × 97 cm
Museum of Modern Art (MoMA),
New York. Gift of Jo Carole
and Ronald S. Lauder; Nelson
A. Rockefeller bequest, gift of
Mr. and Mrs. William H. Weintraub,
and Mary Sisler bequest
(all by exchange). 355.1997

Fig. 9   Claude Viallat
*Hommage à Matisse
(Le Rideau jaune)* [*Homage
to Matisse (The Yellow
Curtain)*], 1992, acrylic
on tarpaulin, 340 × 250 cm
Centre Pompidou – Musée
National d'Art Moderne – Centre
de Création Industrielle, Paris
Gift of the artist in honour of
Dominique Bozo, 1994
AM 1994-139

Fig. 10   François Morellet
Du jaune au violet [*From
Yellow to Violet*], 1956,
oil on canvas, 110.3 × 215.8 cm
Centre Pompidou – Musée
National d'Art Moderne – Centre
de Création Industrielle, Paris
Purchase, 1982. AM 1982-15

the war years – another talisman of modern art. As with the famous *Porte-Fenêtre à Collioure* [*French Window at Collioure*] (1914), which magnifies black as a colour of light, Matisse here verges on abstraction without ever losing his link with reality. It is not so much the curtain that is yellow as the shape in the centre of the painting, which Matisse preferred to call *Composition*. A poetic yellow biomorphic shape, it imposes a space that is that of the painting itself. We are immersed in yellow, the only reality of the work, in the same way that we are immersed in red in *L'Atelier rouge* [*The Red Studio*] (1911). Matisse makes use of flat tints of colour like paper forms he cut out and stuck on the canvas, foreshadowing not only Nicolas de Staël's large expanses of colours (for example in his *Soleil* of 1952) but also the research of Supports/Surfaces artists such as Vincent Bioulès and Pierre Buraglio, for whom paint was a material fact in its own right. Claude Viallat, a founding member of this group, was particularly interested in the "yellow high note",[15] echoing a work by Van Gogh, *Champ de blé aux corbeaux* [*Wheatfield with Crows*] that had fascinated him in his youth. It is no coincidence that it was to Matisse's *Yellow Curtain* that Viallat chose to pay tribute in 1992 (*Hommage à Matisse [Le Rideau jaune]*, fig. 9). In Matisse's work, the space is rendered without perspective; colour had become a plastic motif. The yellow and the blue are equally intense in tone, the two adjacent complementary colours achieving a state of perfect harmony. This balance, combining poetry and reason, was explored by Matisse again in the *Intérieur jaune et bleu* [*Yellow and Blue Interior*] of 1946 and in the large stained-glass windows of the Chapelle du Rosaire de Vence. Matisse, who was very knowledgeable about colour theories, was skilled in using complementary colours for maximum contrast and harmonic expression. It is perhaps worth highlighting that Matisse's last painting, a testament if ever there was one, *Katia à la chemise jaune* [*Katia in the Yellow Shirt*] (1951), is a perfect tribute to the complementarity between the two Mediterranean colours.

No one explored the diatonic power of colours and their musicality more than Kupka. In his *La Gamme jaune* [*The Yellow Scale*] (1907), a portrait of a Baudelairean reader, Kupka – the synchronist[16] –, who was fascinated by the psychology of colours and the theory behind their harmonies, created a richness of tones in the same scale of yellow colours. This portrait, which combines warmth and coolness, is also ambiguous (are the reader's eyes closed or empty?) and includes orange and blue notes. Kupka continued his research into colour and the equivalence between painting and music in abstract form in *Ordonnance sur verticales en jaune* [*Arrangement in Yellow Verticals*] (1913). But when it comes to enhancing the power of yellow in a complex composition, nothing beats its proximity to purple, a secondary colour belonging to the family of blues, and vice versa. It is easy to understand why the Impressionists, who used purple tones to depict shadows, placed such importance on yellow in their landscapes. Furthermore, in *Du jaune au violet* [*From Yellow to Violet*] (1956, fig. 10), François Morellet presents an edifying chromatic lesson on all the retinal possibilities that offer themselves to the painter to lead from a primary colour to its secondary one, passing via either cold tones (green and blue) or warm ones (orange and red). As the adventure of modern art has unfolded, has colour not become the visual object of painting itself?

1
Marcel Proust, *The Prisoner* (1923), vol. 5 of *In Search of Lost Time* (London: Penguin Classics, 2002), p. 169.
2
Roland Barthes, *Writing Degree Zero*, trans. Annette Lavers and Colin Smith (London: Jonathan Cape, 1967).
3
Wassily Kandinsky, *On the Spiritual in Art* (New York: Solomon R. Guggenheim Foundation, 1946), p. 9.
4
"The sun dazzles me and goes to my head, a sun, a light that I can only call yellow, pale sulphur yellow, pale lemon, gold", letter from Vincent van Gogh to his brother Theo, March 1888, quoted on the website https://vangoghletters.org/vg/letters/let659/letter.html#translation

5
Gabriel-Albert Aurier, "Les isolés, Vincent Van Gogh", *Le Mercure de France*, vol. 1, no. 1 (1890), p. 28.
6
Paul Signac, *D'Eugène Delacroix au néo-impressionnisme* (Paris: Henri Floury, 1911 [1899]), quoted in Wassily Kandinsky, *On the Spiritual in Art*, op. cit., p. 27.
7
František Kupka, *La Création dans les arts plastiques*, Karl Flinker (preface), Philippe Dagen (introduction), Erika Abrams (ed.) (Paris: Cercle d'art, 1989), p. 139.
8
Herb Aach (trans. and ed.), *Goethe's Color Theory* (New York: Van Nostrand Reinhold, 1971), p. 169.
9
Wassily Kandinsky, *On the Spiritual in Art*, op. cit., p. 63.
10
František Kupka, *La Création dans les arts plastiques*, op. cit., p. 140.
11
Ibid.

12
Michel Pastoureau, *Yellow: A History of a Color* (Princeton NJ: Princeton University Press, 2019).
13
Octave Mirbeau, "Paul Gauguin", *L'Écho de Paris* (16 February 1891), quoted in Octave Mirbeau, *Des artistes* (Paris: Union générale d'édition, 1986), p. 127.
14
Maurice Denis, "Définition du néo-traditionalisme", *Art et critique* (30 August 1890), in Maurice Denis, *Du symbolisme au classicisme. Théories* (Paris: Hermann, Miroirs de l'art, 1964), p. 14.
15
Claude Viallat, *La haute note jaune*, exh. cat., Arles, Palais de Luppe, 3 July – 11 November 2007 (Arles and Saint-Étienne: Fondation Vincent van Gogh and Institut d'art contemporain, 2007).

16
Markéta Theinhardt, "*La Gamme jaune* de František Kupka: un exemple de synesthésie", Revue des études slaves, vol. 74, fascicule 1 (2002), pp. 97–103. The word 'synchronist' comes from Kupka's *Création dans les arts plastiques*, where he wrote: "Whether the sensitivity of the colourist – or synchronist – depends on the action of retinal electricity or that of the cerebral cortex, it seems to me that this activity will always be more fruitful if the general psychic state, which nourishes the motor forces, provides good-quality substances in the required quantities". František Kupka, *La Création dans les arts plastiques*, op. cit., p. 130.

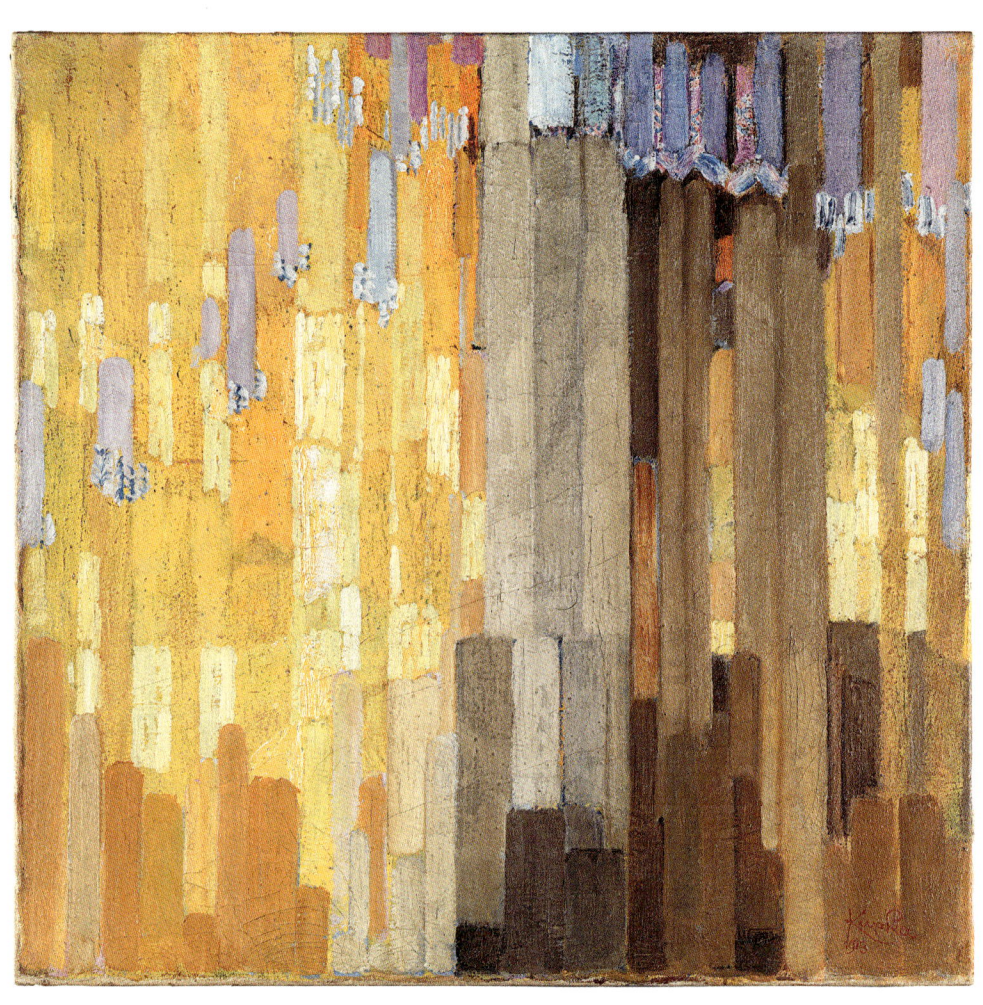

František Kupka   *Ordonnance sur verticales en jaune* [*Arrangement in Yellow Verticals*]   1913

oil on canvas   70 × 70 cm   purchase, 1957, AM 3558 P

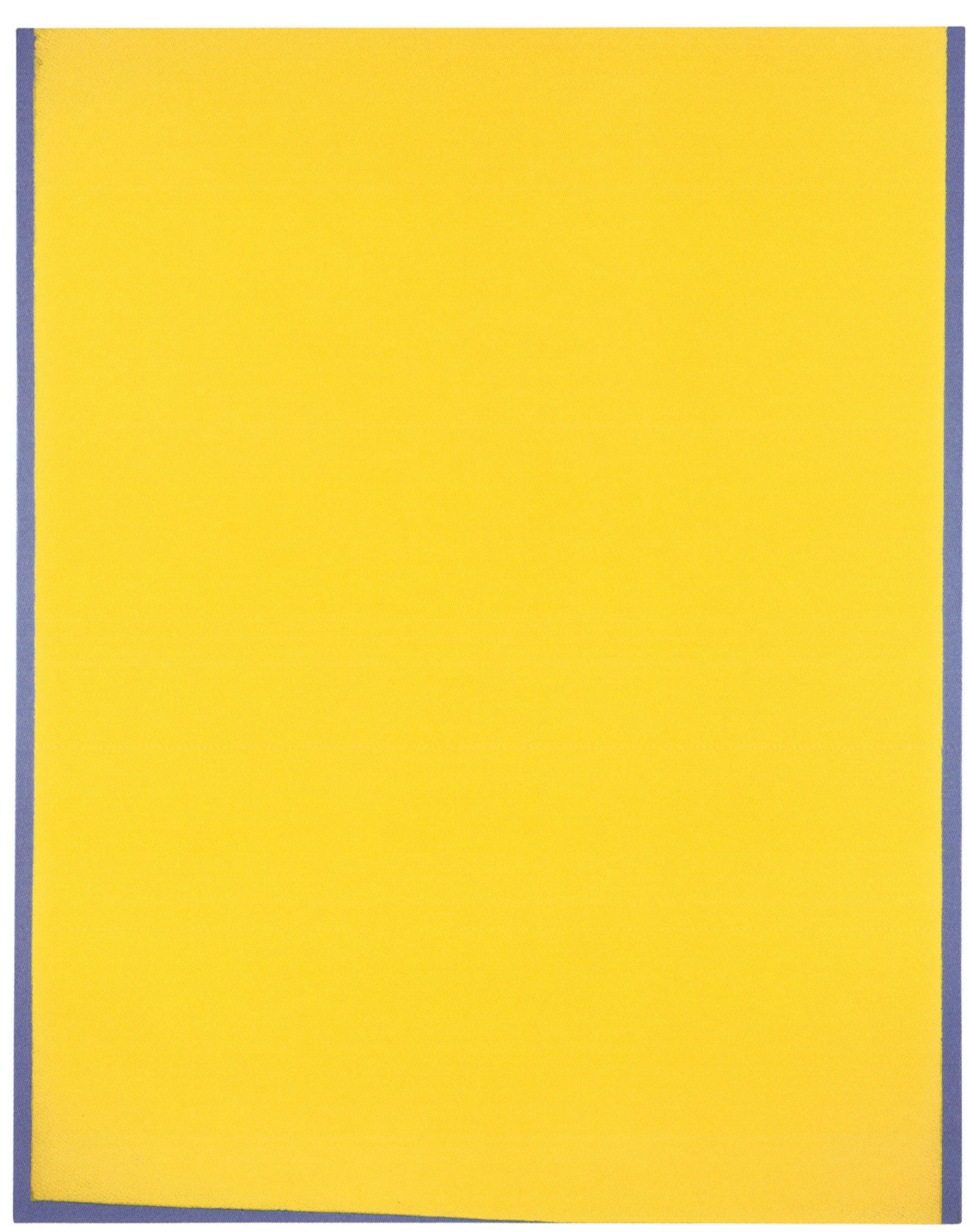

Vincent Bioulès *Sans titre* [*Untitled*] 1969

acrylic on canvas 146.7 × 114.6 × 3 cm purchase, 1998, AM 1998-118

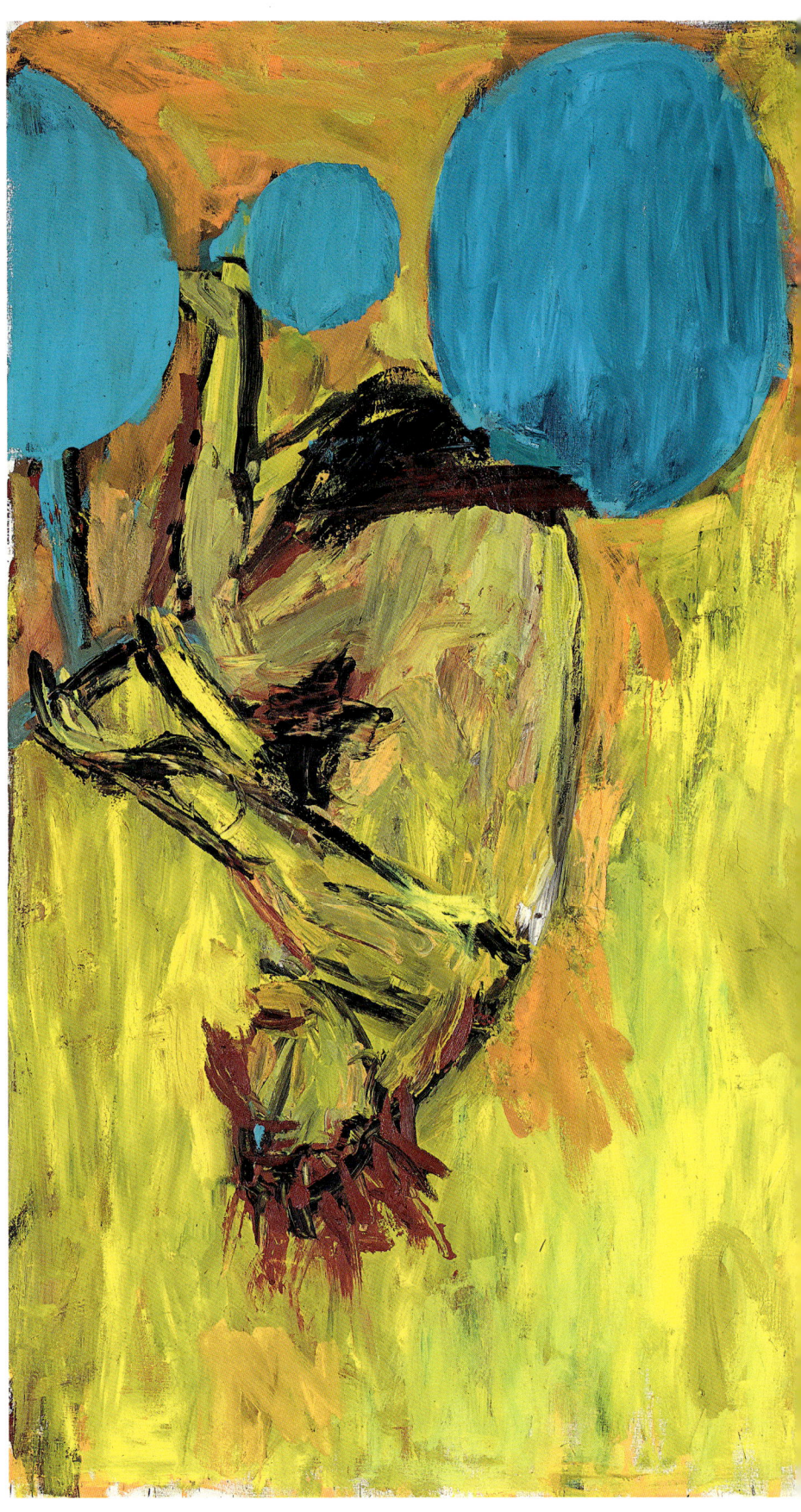

Georg Baselitz *The Girls from Olmo II* 1981

oil on canvas 250 × 249 cm purchase, 1982, AM 1982-19

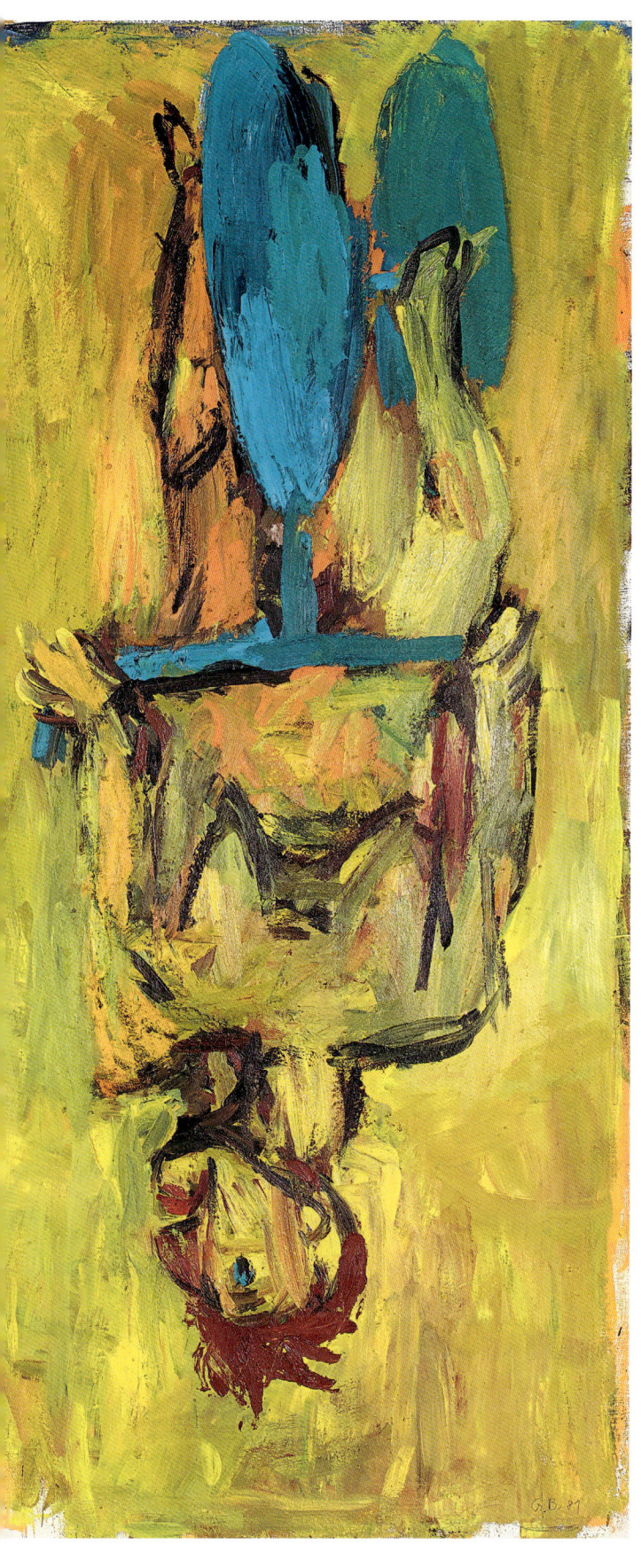

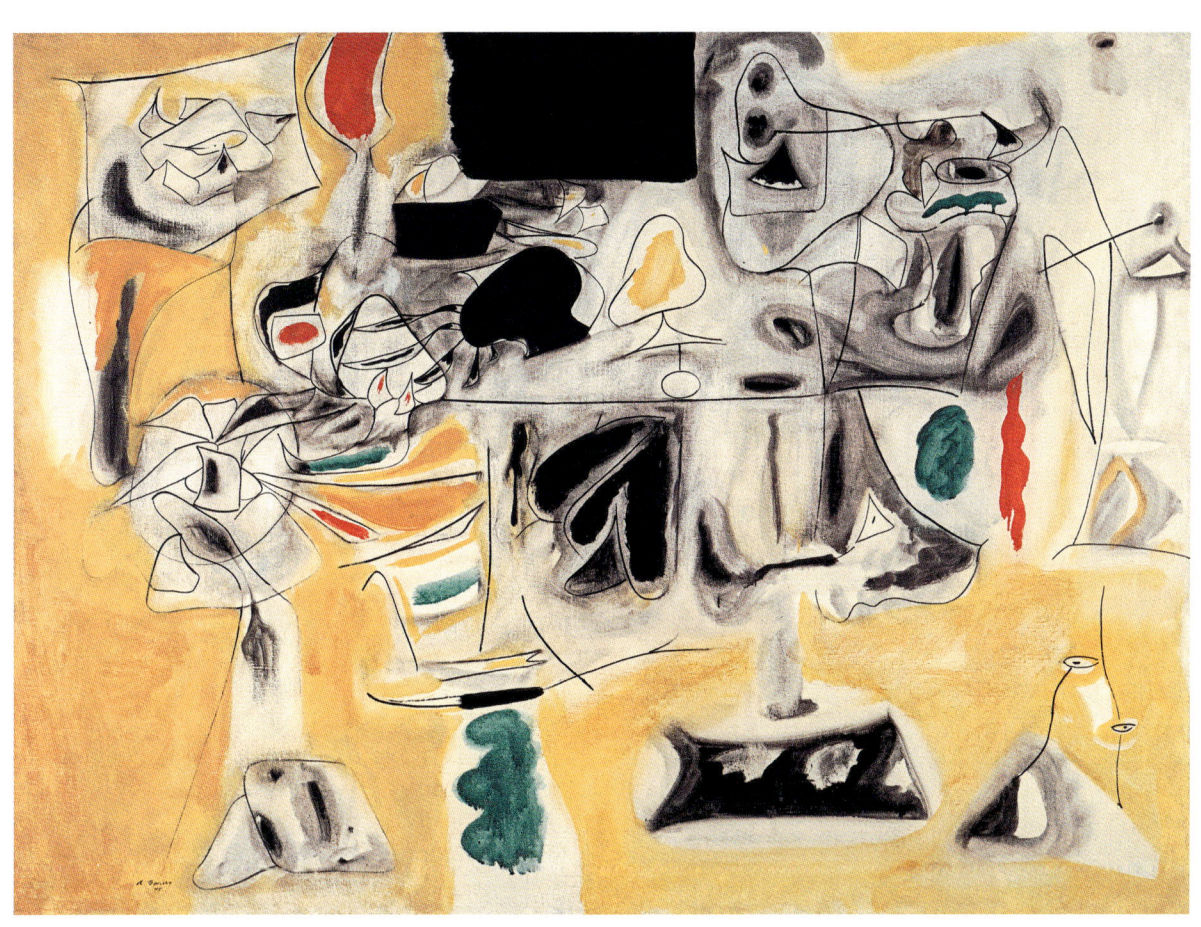

Arshile Gorky *Landscape-Table* 1945

oil on canvas   92 × 121 cm   purchase, 1971, AM 1971-151

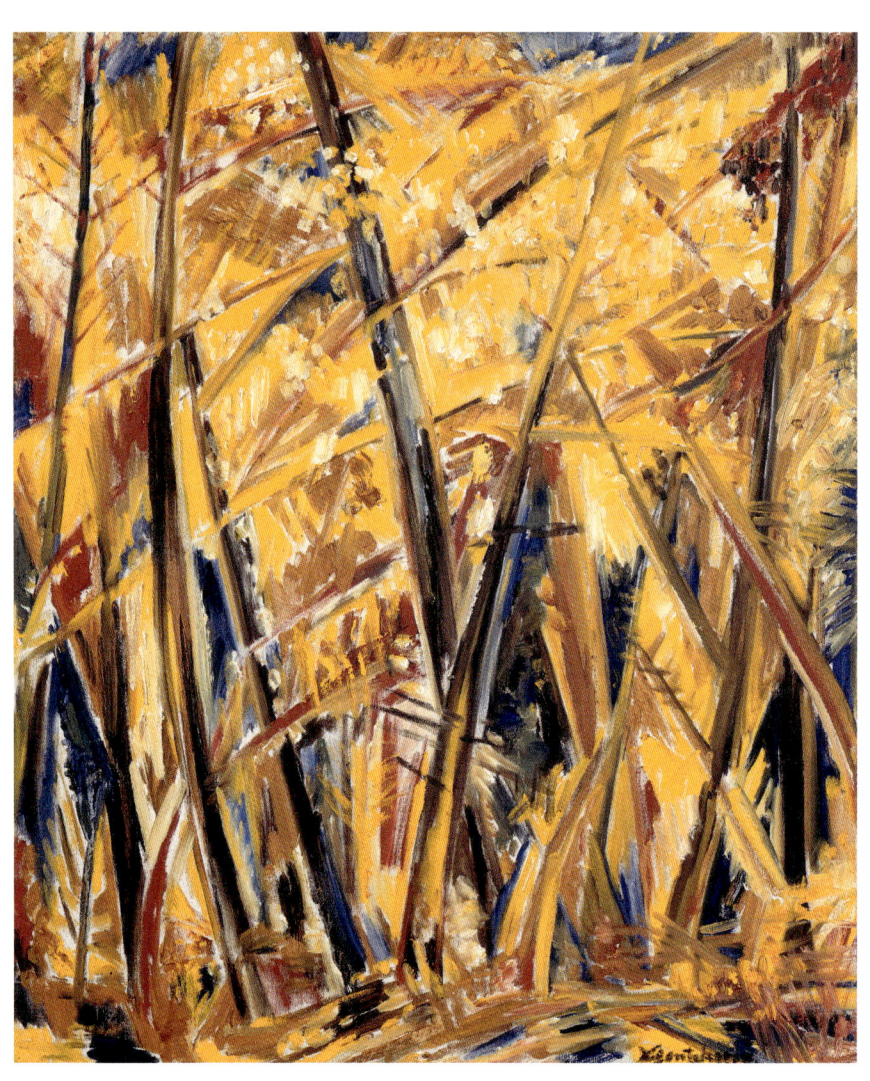

Natalia Goncharova   *Forêt d'automne* [*Autumn Forest*]   [1950]

oil on canvas   60.5 × 50.3 cm   purchase, 1960, AM 3860 P

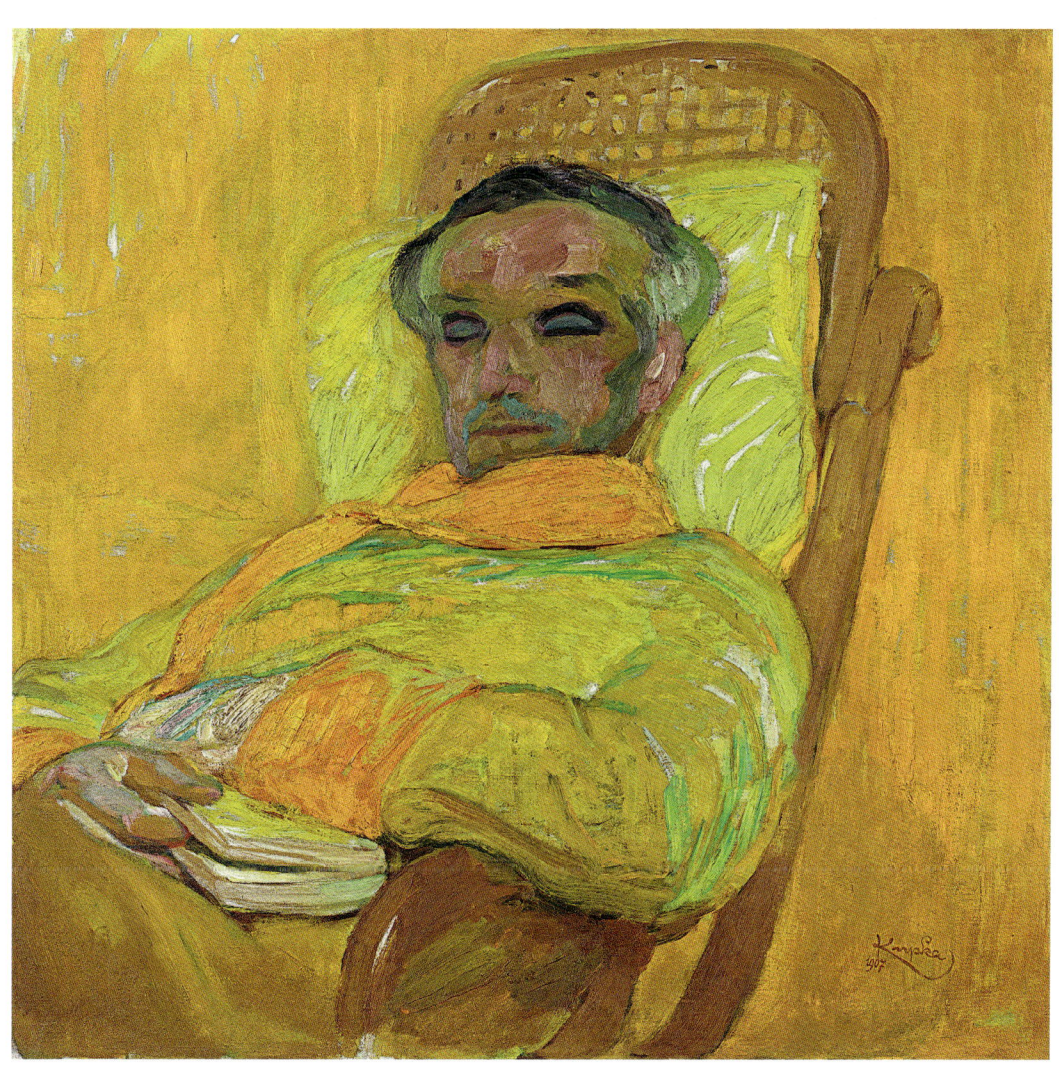

František Kupka   *La Gamme jaune* [*The Yellow Scale*]   1907

oil on canvas   79 × 79 cm   gift of Eugénie Kupka, 1963, AM 4165 P

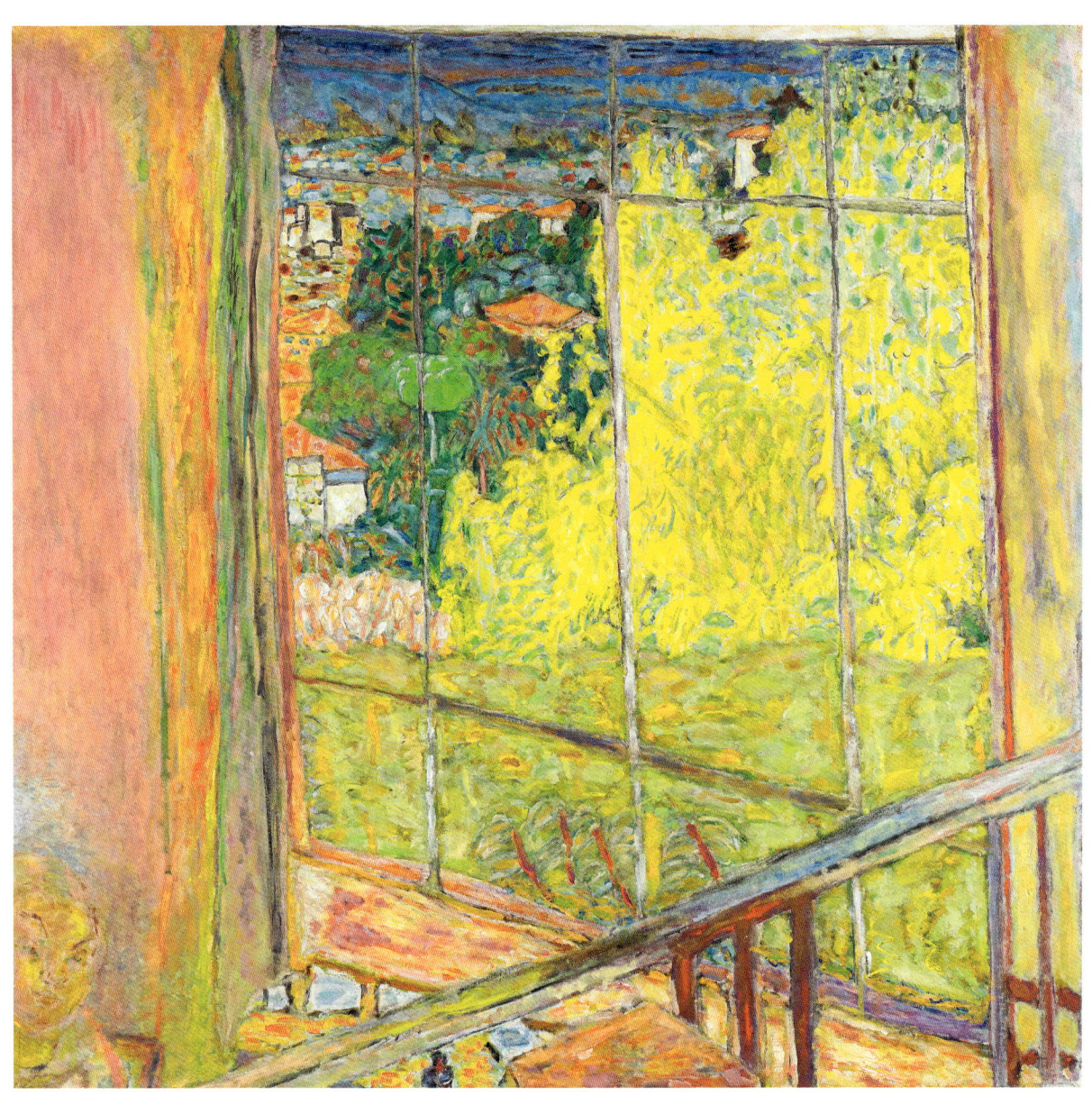

Pierre Bonnard   *L'Atelier au mimosa* [*The Studio with Mimosa*]   [Winter 1939–October 1946]

oil on canvas   127.5 × 127.5 cm   purchase, 1979, AM 1978-732

Piero Dorazio   *Qualités jaunes* [*Yellow Qualities*]   1960

oil on canvas   197 × 113.5 cm   purchase 2004, AM 2004-41

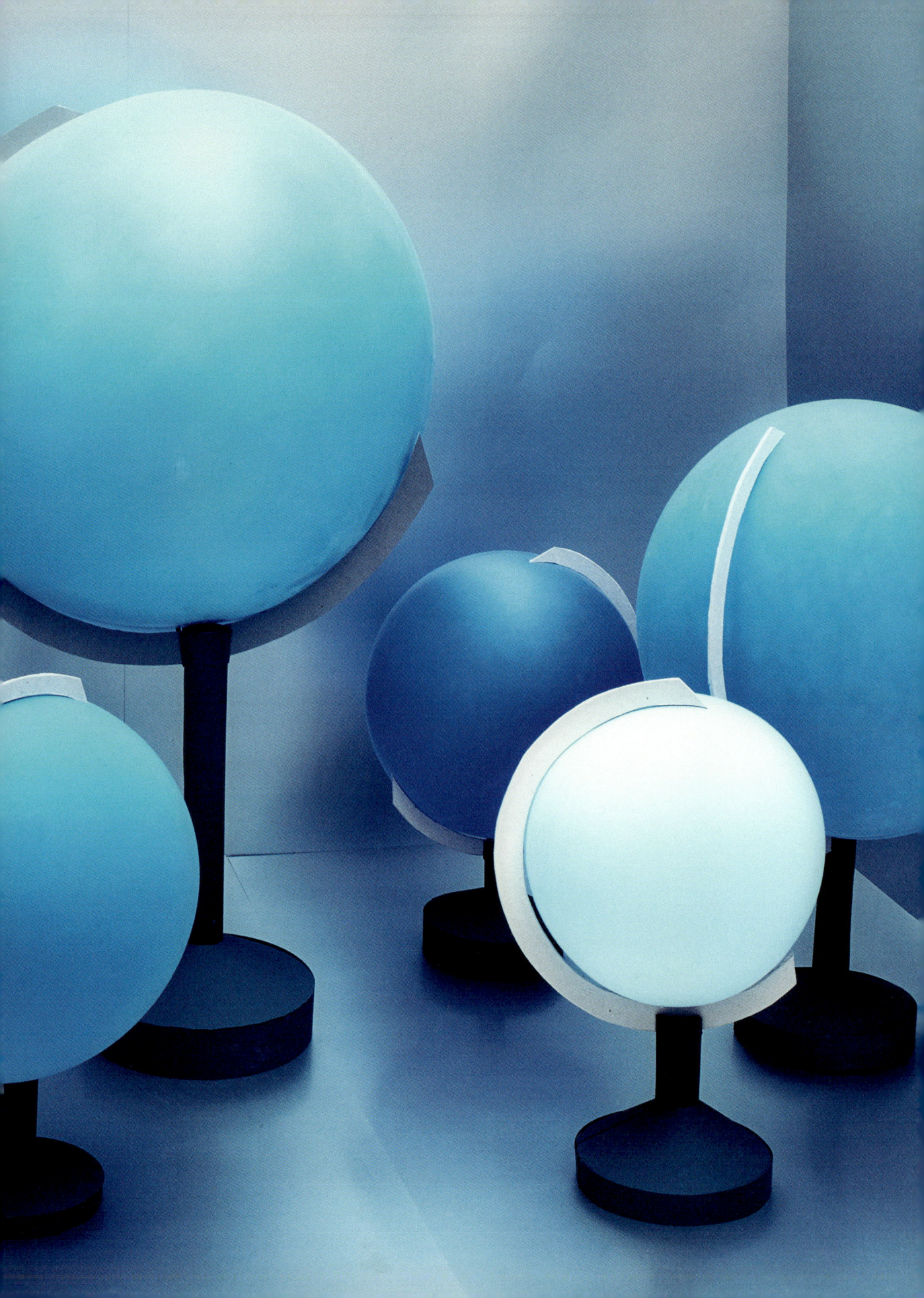

BLUE

FORMS
OF BLUE

Alain Cueff

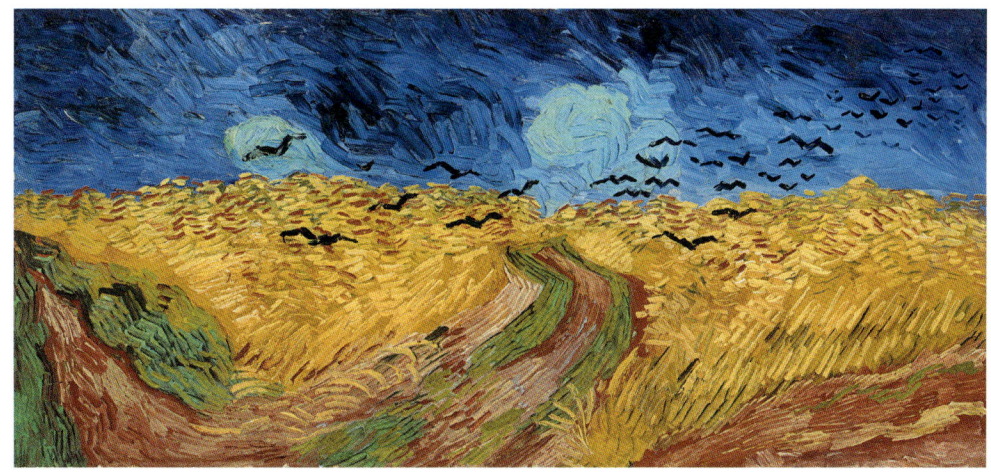

Fig. 1 Vincent van Gogh, *Champ de blé aux corbeaux* [*Wheatfield with Crows*], July 1890, oil on canvas, 50.5 × 103 cm
Van Gogh Museum (Vincent van Gogh Foundation), Amsterdam. s0149V1962. F0779

Chemically controlled, mass-produced to match an industrial colour chart, placed in boxes and aluminium tubes, reproduced without error: since the late 19th century, everything has conspired to make colour a commodity, a standardised product customised for specific uses, from watercolour to the toughest enamel, transparent or opaque, in the required viscosity. The painter no longer grinds and mixes pigments to create colours and can now replace these sensations with measuring wavelengths, from 380 to 740 nanometres, from violet to red. But was ready-made colour meant to become a simple sign, rendered arbitrary in systemic arrangements, or signifying only itself when Modernism gave way to its historical opposite, the decorative? Was it meant to lose forever its descriptive vocation and, later, its capacities for expressiveness and symbolism? The history of this mutation is as complex as it is contradictory, punctuated by theoretical promises and regrets, sometimes giving the impression that dogmatism derives its strength from the renunciations it demands as inalienable debts.

Yet, despite being subject to permutations prohibiting their complementarity and to rigid grammars that tended to condemn their topological dimension, colours – as advertising was simultaneously becoming aware – became neither indifferent nor neutral. Artists such as Barnett Newman and Ad Reinhardt, misunderstood as heralds of intransitive chromaticism, continued to imbue them with "mystical profundity".[1] Without doubt, in cultural terms, some are only of relative strength, passing everywhere as mere intermediaries, supplementary and optional, too nuanced to play a significant role. But the fundamentals have retained more or less the symbolic connotations that Leon Battista Alberti attributed to them in his *De Pictura* [*On Painting*]: "... for painters there are four true colours – as there are four elements – from which more and more other kinds of colours may be thus created. Red is the colour of fire, blue of the air, green of the water, and of the earth grey and ash."[2] Grey – versatile – lends itself to all uses; to the fire and water of red and green are added codified values that transform them into signals (negative and positive), not forgetting those that, varying from one culture to another, have relegated natural references to an almost trivial status.

As for blue – named by Alberti "*celestis seu caesius*", as if to prevent the variations of its names in Greco-Latin Antiquity[3] – it has been annexed by various urban conventions, but these have never supplanted the reference to the sky, which remains the universal archetype. Regardless of geographical, seasonal and climatic changes, it is perpetually associated with the celestial vault. The permanency of this symbolism is guaranteed by the omnipresence of the sky, but it should also be emphasised that the tension between colour as substance and colour as a property of light remains intact and immediately perceptible as far as azure is concerned. It is a tension that is shared with other colours, no doubt, but it interests us all the more here in that it is like the origin of blue's symbolic ambivalences, which were so intensified in 20th-century painting as to become contradictions. Johann Wolfgang von Goethe noted a few of them: according to him, blue's energy tends towards the negative, its purity transforming it into a "stimulating negation", offering a singular

Previous pages: Thomas Demand, *Six Globes* (detail) → page 97 spectacle torn "between excitement and repose".[4] The Romantics and their successors gave it all its poetic lustre, a symbol of both purity and melancholy. My hypothesis here is that it is precisely these fluctuations and contradictions in the perception and expression of blue that have assured its symbolic power.[5]

The tropological spectrum of blue – numerous languages share the same obscure origin (from the Medieval Latin *blavus*, from the High German *blao*) – is very wide. Embracing the sacred and the secular, blood and flowers, astonishment and fear, novelty and anger, and, in English, anxiety and exaltation, safety of investment (blue chip), conservatism and the blues, the unexpected (out of the blue), adventure (go off into the blue) and the obscene (blue movies), there is no end to the pairs of opposites in which blue finds itself – like the Latin adjective *altus*, which designates both height and depth, the sublime and the unfathomable. The French expression '*passer quelque chose au bleu*', to express the elimination or side-stepping of an undesirable reality, could be understood as the axis around which such opposing meanings extend. This semantic and poetic adaptability aptly reflects the extensive character of blue as it is seen in painting. In other words, we could say that it is essentially ambient, like the air that surrounds us and that we breathe, that envelops us and that lets us pass through it – it is the conveyor of all sensations, the emblem of all feelings on a dimension that needs to be described in detail.

While it is associated with '*joie de vivre*', a sense of abundance or exaltation in the work of Henri Matisse or Joan Miró – we will come back to them later – we cannot forget the dramatic use Vincent van Gogh made of it (in, among many other paintings, *Champ de blé aux corbeaux* [*Wheatfield with Crows*], 1890, fig. 1), when his cerulean colour is definitely an appeal to the black. This moving and menacing aspect can be found in the work of many Expressionists (Ernst Ludwig Kirchner, *The Red Tower in Halle*, 1915) and of the Futurist Luigi Russolo, in whose work it sometimes harbours hostile connotations (*Dynamism of a Car*, 1912–13). In Mark Rothko's painting, the contrast with orangey red sometimes gives blue a manifest radiance, then, from 1967 onward, it becomes above all the primer for black (*Untitled*, 1967, fig. 2). For the young Pablo Picasso, it was the primary symbol of loss. As we know, it was the grief prompted by the death of his friend Carles Casagemas that provoked his melancholic 'Blue Period',[6] in which he spread the morbid, invasive colour across the entire surface of the canvas (fig. 3). There is no glory in this washed-out hue that subjugates the figures, swallows up the depth of field and excludes anything beyond: it absorbs nothing, but makes itself the insubstantial milieu of a shipwreck. At more or less the same time, isolated on the New England coast and belonging to a very different generation, Winslow Homer (1836–1910) was meditating on his work at the end of his life and realised – *out of the blue* – that he had always refrained from painting a blue sky, whether in his oils or watercolours (fig. 4). He explained in no uncertain terms why to an astounded interlocuter: "Because it looks like the devil, that's all".[7] The *diabolos* in Biblical Greek, the one who causes division, destroys the solidarity of the elements and tears apart the continuity of the world.

However cold it might be, blue represents the openness of space; while red and yellow are warm to the eye, "we love to contemplate blue, not because it advances to us, but because it draws us after it", wrote Goethe.[8] Kazimir Malevich rebelled against this attraction in 1919 in his manifesto *Suprematism*. His aim was to consider the programmatic imperatives of an art freed from the notion of beauty and every emotional quality in favour of a revolutionary philosophical system. The standard for this reform was *White on White*, painted the previous year: a triumph of "white free depths".[9] The text comments on it unambiguously: defeated by the Suprematist system, "I have breached the blue lampshade of color limitations and have passed into the white beyond".[10] Malevich was intent on crossing the final frontiers and breaking through the last layers of the atmosphere, but above all on overcoming any special feelings evoked by "the blue lampshade" of the sky – animated by nuances too subtle, too fleeting, uncertain and disquieting – to ensure the symbolic departure of the new humanity into the limitless.

Infinity equated with emptiness or nothingness as conceived by Malevich is the antithesis of paradise, whether it be the lost paradise of the Bible and John Milton or an idealised one built on modern syncretic values. The intransigeance of Kazimir Malevich and Aleksandr Rodchenko, with his 1921 triptych *Pure Red, Pure Yellow, Pure Blue*, was countered by the spiritualism of Wassily Kandinsky and the hedonism of Henri Matisse. In the work of the former, we find the same diagnosis of a transition from blue to white: "Rising toward the light, a movement little suited to it, it takes on an indifferent character, growing more distant to men like the high, light blue of the sky. The lighter it is the weaker it becomes until it achieves a silent repose by becoming white".[11] And while deep blue, "the typical heavenly colour", "beckons man into the infinite", it is in order to arouse in him "a longing for purity and the supersensuous".[12] Despite this appraisal, however, blue is not a colour he frequently used in his work: the Fauvist-influenced *Murnau, Landscape with Tower*, in 1908, is partially in keeping with his definition. In *Sky Blue*, painted in 1940, a tribute to Joan Miró's 'Constellations', which he had seen in March

2

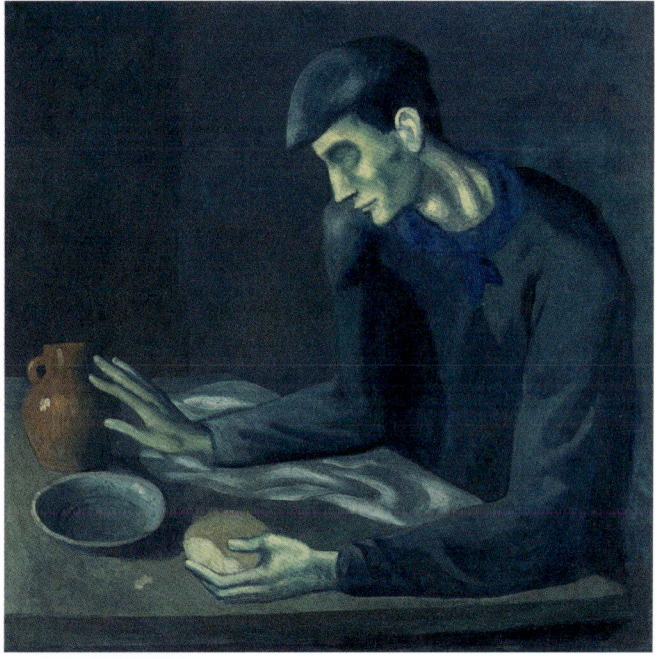

3

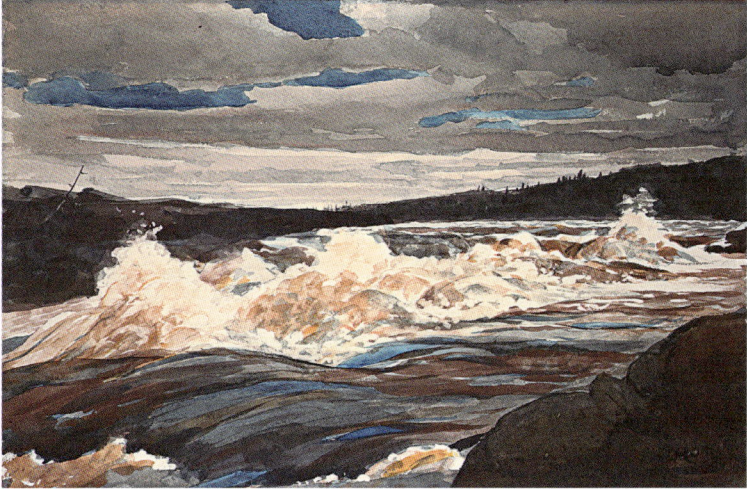

4

Fig. 2 Mark Rothko
Untitled, 1967, acrylic,
watercolour paper mounted
on hardboard, 61 × 45.9 cm
Kate Rothko Prizel collection

Fig. 3 Pablo Picasso
Le Repas de l'aveugle
[*The Blind Man's Meal*], 1903,
oil on canvas, 95.3 × 94.6 cm
The Metropolitan Museum of Art,
New York. Purchase, Mr. and Mrs.
Ira Haupt Gift, 1950. 50.188

Fig. 4 Winslow Homer
*Grand Discharge,
Lake St. John, Province of
Quebec*, c. 1902, watercolour
over graphite pencil
on paper, 35.6 × 53.4 cm
Museum of Fine Arts, Boston
From the Estate of Henry
O. Underwood, bequest
of Francis W. Davis. 1978.345

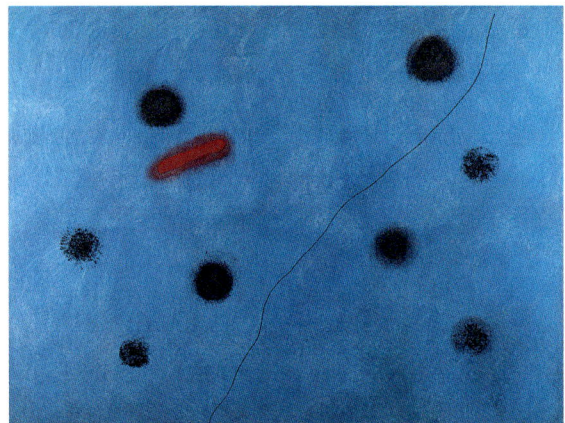

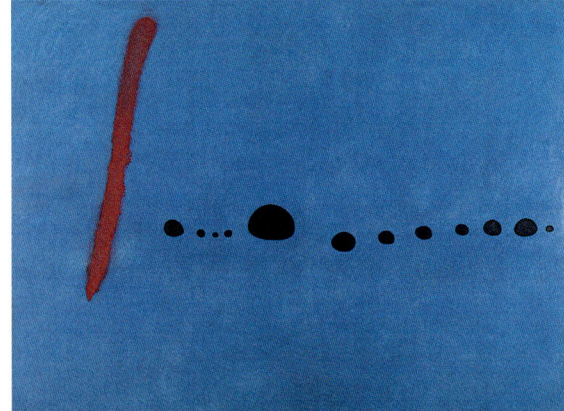

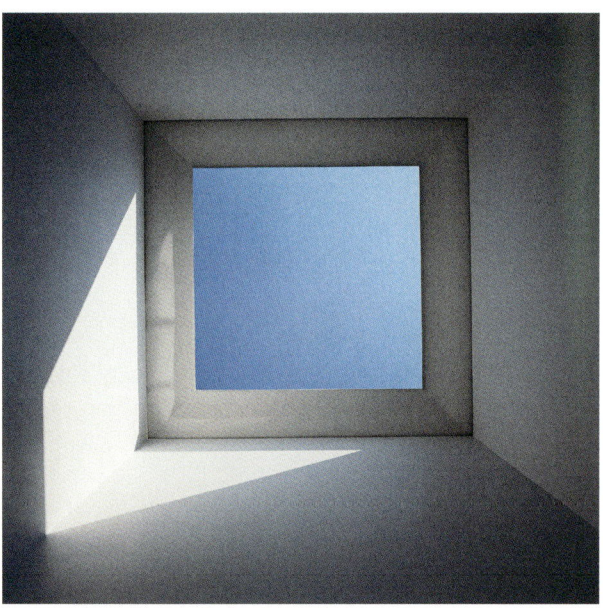

8

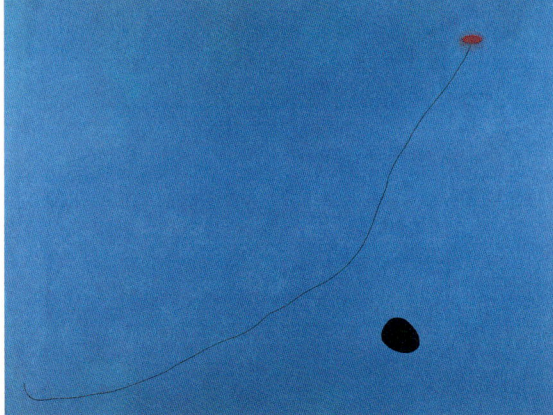

5-7

Figs. 5-7   Joan Miró
Bleu I, Bleu II, Bleu III
[*Blue I, Blue II, Blue III*],
4 March 1961, oils on canvas,
270 × 355 cm (*Blue I* and *Blue II*),
268 × 349 cm (*Blue III*)
Centre Pompidou – Musée
National d'Art Moderne – Centre
de Création Industrielle, Paris
Purchased in memory of Dominique
Bozo, with the support of the
Heritage Fund, and the help
of Sylvie and Eric Boissonnas,
Jacques Boissonnas, Hélène and
Michel David-Weill, the Friends of
the Museum Society, Pierre Bergé,
Yves Saint Laurent, the Maison
Yves Saint Laurent, and with
the participation of numerous
subscribers, 1993
AM 1993-119 (*Blue I*)
Gift of the Menil Foundation
in memory of Jean de Menil, 1984
AM 1984-357 (*Blue II*)
Purchase, 1988
AM 1988-569 (*Blue III*)

Fig. 8   James Turrell
Skyspace I, 1974, overhead
portal cut to outside sky,
interior filled with natural light;
site specific dimensions;
room: 599.4 × 360.7 × 360.7 cm;
cut: 254 × 254 cm
Solomon R. Guggenheim Museum,
New York. Panza Collection,
gift, 1992, on permanent loan
to Fondo per l'Ambiente Italiano

of that year, numerous small figures are dispersed on an almost monochrome background – *almost*: a cloudlike halo can be seen around the edge, helping to lighten the tone.

Conversely, after early Fauvist exultations,[13] blue became predominant in Matisse's work, from *La Conversation* (1911) to gouache cutouts, such as *La Vague* [*The Wave*] (1952), and was often associated with the nude, as in the *Nu assis* [*Seated Nude*], 1906, where it follows the contours of the female figure, *Poissons rouges et sculpture* [*Goldfish and Sculpture*] (1912) and, of course, in different versions of *La Danse* (1909–10). Finally, it dominates and restrains white at the Chapelle du Rosaire in Vence, from the walls and stained-glass windows to the roof. The exploration of myth was gradually replaced by the conviction that all art, if it goes beyond the anecdotal and the documentary, is of necessity religious in essence.[14] Matisse reinterpreted the sacred blue of French painting, that of the Virgin's cloak (Simon Hantaï also remembered this in the 1960s), very often saturating it, giving it a new rigour through his flat tints. Malevich's aviator was destined for the far reaches of the universe; that of Matisse, a new Icarus,[15] breaks through the clouds to rediscover the blue sky and contemplative tranquillity.[16]

"There is always a measure of truth",[17] said Matisse, at the time of *Jazz*, before dismissing the distinction between figurative and non-figurative art. The rest, he added, is up to the imagination – or to dreaming, in the case of Joan Miró's work. In *Photo : ceci est la couleur de mes rêves* [*Photo: This is the Colour of My Dreams*] (1925), a blue mark is placed on a greyish beige, reminiscent of a black and white Lambda print. It is like the Catalan *inmenso azul* of *House with Palm Tree* (1918), *The Farm* (1921–22) and *Catalan Peasant with a Guitar*, among many others, prefiguring the 1961 triptych *Bleu I, Bleu II, Bleu III* [*Blue I, Blue II, Blue III*] (figs. 5–7), in which the blue is amplified and magnified, invading the vast expanse in each of the three canvases. We remain in the colour of dreams, if by that we understand that the blue, from which red lines and black marks emanate like meteors, is less a background than it is the redefining of the surface-less intensity of the sky, which has neither beginning nor end, an evanescent and evasive substance, yet so consistent, so insistent, forever established in the recesses of the unconscious. Doubtless nothing could be as inappropriate as to evoke Stéphane Mallarmé's "eternal Blue" to comment on this triptych,[18] unless we force ourselves to forget that the 1864 poem attributes to it a "tranquil irony", damning "the powerless poet, who curses his genius/Across a sterile desert of Despair". The Catalan painter admitted that a certain cheerfulness concealed his sense of the tragic.[19] If on more than one occasion

(notably in the polychrome sculptures) he used irony, it is a playful and light-hearted irony, which makes it possible to signify two things at once.

After having called for the fogs and seen the dead sky, the poet sinks into dread, and, four times over, the Azure – the sky – continues its corrupting work. Gaston Bachelard almost totally supplants Mallarmé in Yves Klein's references:[20] quotations from *L'Air et les Songes* (1943) are recurrent in his texts, and one – "First there is nothing, then there is a deep nothing, then there is a blue depth" – became a sort of mantra. Seeking above all to warn against the instinct for decorative polychrome that he imputed to his viewers, Klein finally accorded blue an exclusive place in his work. But the essential reason for this is that "All colors bring forth associations of concrete, material, and tangible ideas, while blue evokes all the more the sea and the sky, which are what is most abstract in tangible and visible nature".[21] "All the more" here is an understatement, if it is true that "blue has no dimensions" and that it is synonymous with the infinite in which Klein claims to float, unlike Malevich, who, according to him, was content to contemplate it from afar. The disintegration of the pictorial space (*Ci-gît l'espace* [*Here Lies Space*], 1960) is, in reality, the prerequisite to "the specialisation of sensibility": monochrome as such is not an end in itself, but the means to access awareness unattached to matter.

Catholic and Rosicrucian, Yves Klein exaggerated a strange form of mysticism ("Like Christ, the painter says Mass by painting and gives the body of his soul as nourishment to others"[22]) but that was nevertheless essential to the agency of his narrative. There is no ambiguity, on the other hand, in James Turrell's assertion that God is the source and the goal of his work: the principle of "inner light" taught by the Religious Society of Friends, otherwise known as the Quakers, founded by George Fox in the 17th century, is inseparable from the experience conveyed by his 'Skyspaces' (fig. 8). They are, in Turrell's own words, viewing chambers, in which, notably at Roden Crater, in Arizona, the viewer is somehow sucked up into the infinite sky. Strictly framed and diffused, endowed with the power to make the scales drop from our eyes, sky-blue is, for Turrell, the vehicle of spiritual elevation, imparting a renewed understanding of a cosmic universe in which Winslow Homer's devil certainly has no part.

Which takes us a long way from the desymbolisation of colour in general, and blue in particular, that Modernism desired and championed in its most volontarist manifestations, and that may have given rise to scruples on the part of artists who had, moreover, freed themselves from its dogmas. I have discussed elsewhere Edward Ruscha's disconcerting denials concerning the backdrops

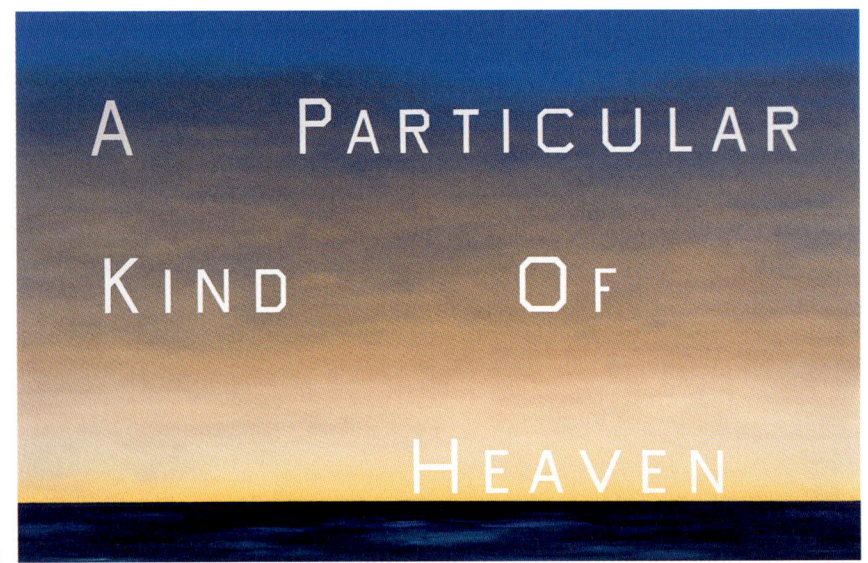

9

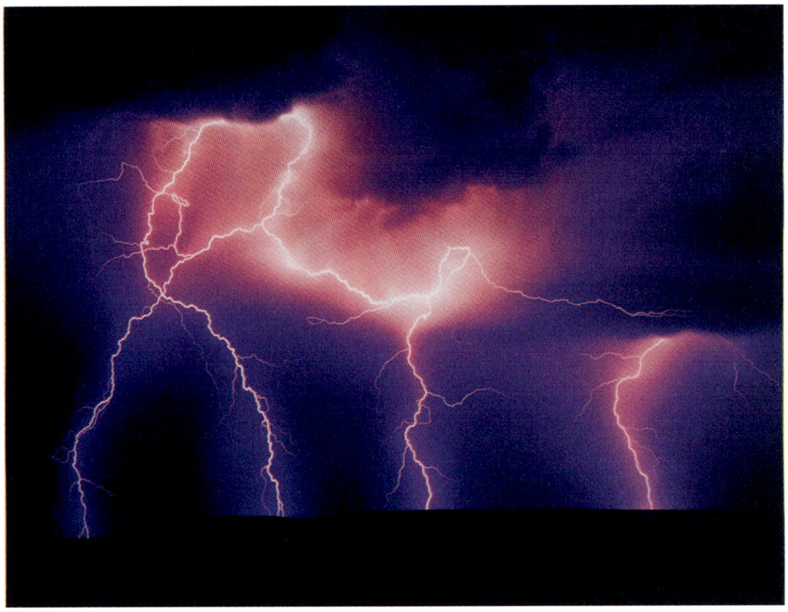

10

Fig. 9 Edward Ruscha
*A Particular Kind of
Heaven*, 1983, oil on canvas,
228.6 × 346.7 cm
Fine Arts Museums of San
Francisco, San Francisco
Museum purchase, Mrs. Paul
L. Wattis Fund. 2001.85
© Ed Ruscha. Courtesy
of the artist and Gagosian

Fig. 10 Jack Goldstein
Untitled, 1983, acrylic
on canvas, 213.4 × 273.7 cm
Lindemann Collection,
Miami Beach

of many of his paintings, backdrops that are, however, closely linked with notions of paradise (*A Particular Kind of Heaven*, 1983, fig. 9) and the sacred (*Miracle*, 1975).[23] In his work, it is less the blue that determines the sky than the very quality of his pictorial substrate, neither opaque nor transparent, from which rise words rich in thoughts, to paraphrase the quotation from Shakespeare used in *Words Over Miami* (1987). Which is more or less the opposite of what happens in Jack Goldstein's spray paintings of the 1980s (no signs or traces, the colour unaltered), where blue spreads to the clouds (*Untitled*, 1989) or is pierced by lightning and meteors (*Untitled*, 1983, fig. 10). Both reticent and fatalist, Goldstein admitted towards the end of his life: "Yes … where blue actually becomes a sky rather than a simple blue …".[24] Beyond the horizon, the space curves and takes on its rightful colours.

1
Ann Temkin, "Color Shift", in *Color Chart: Reinventing Color 1950 to Today*, exh. cat., 2 March–12 May 2008 (New York: Museum of Modern Art, 2008), p. 19.
2
Leon Battista Alberti, *On Painting*, trans. John R. Spencer (New Haven: Yale University Press, 1970 [1435]), p. 49.
3
Michel Pastoureau, *Bleu. Histoire d'une couleur* (Paris: Seuil, 2022), p. 26.
4
Goethe's Color Theory (New York: Van Nostrand Reinhold, 1971 [1820]), trans. Charles Eastlake, p. 270.
5
For Michel Pastoureau, with his own socio-cultural perspective, the opposite is true: for him, it is its symbolic vacuity that explains its popularity.

6
Pierre Daix, "Picasso et l'art nègre", in *Art nègre et civilisation de l'universel*, symposium proceedings (Dakar: Nouvelles Éditions africaines, 1975).
7
From interviews in 1903, John W. Beatty, "Recollections of an Intimate Friendship" (1923), quoted in John W. McCoubrey, *American Art, 1700–1960* (Englewood Cliffs, NJ: Prentice-Hall, 1965), p. 160. See also my essay *Ciels d'Amérique, 1801-2001* (Paris: Les Belles Lettres, 2023), pp. 122–23.
8
Goethe's Color Theory, op. cit., p. 170.
9
Kazimir Malevich, "Suprematism" (in the catalogue of the 10th State exhibition 'Non-Objective Creation and Suprematism', held in Moscow in 1919), in John Bowlt (ed. & trans.), *Russian Art of the Avant-Garde, Theory and Criticism, 1902–1934* (New York: Viking Press, 1976), p. 145.
10
Ibid.

11
Wassily Kandinsky, *On the Spiritual in Art* (New York: Guggenheim Foundation, 1946), p. 65.
12
Ibid., p. 64.
13
Fauvism "is when there is red", said Henri Matisse to Georges Duthuit; quoted by Pierre Schneider in *Matisse* (New York: Rizzoli, 1984), p. 210.
14
Georges Charbonnier, *Le Monologue du peintre*, vol. 2 (Paris: Julliard, 1960), pp. 11–12.
15
Icarus is the title of the preliminary sketch (1943) and a plate in *Jazz* (1947).
16
See Henri Matisse, *Écrits et propos sur l'art*, presented by Dominique Fourcade (Paris: Hermann, 1972), pp. 201, 236.
17
Ibid., p. 252.
18
Margit Rowell, "Bleu II, 1961 de Joan Miró", *Les Cahiers du Musée National d'Art Moderne*, no. 15 (1985).

19
Joan Miró and Yvon Taillandier, "Je travaille comme un jardinier", *xxe siècle* (1959).
20
See, however, his "Speech to the Gelsenkirchen Theater Commission" in *Overcoming the Problematics of Art: The Writings of Yves Klein* (Putnam, CT: Spring Publications, 2007), p. 40.
21
Ibid., p. 159.
22
Ibid., p. 131.
23
Alain Cueff, *Ciels d'Amérique, 1801-2001*, op. cit.
24
Meg Cranston, 'Over Here: Interview with Jack Goldstein', 2001, quoted in Philipp Kaiser, *Jack Goldstein × 10,000*, exh. cat., Newport Beach, Orange County Museum of Art, 24 June – 9 September 2012 (Munich, London, New York: Del Monico and Prestel Verlag, 2012), p. 209.

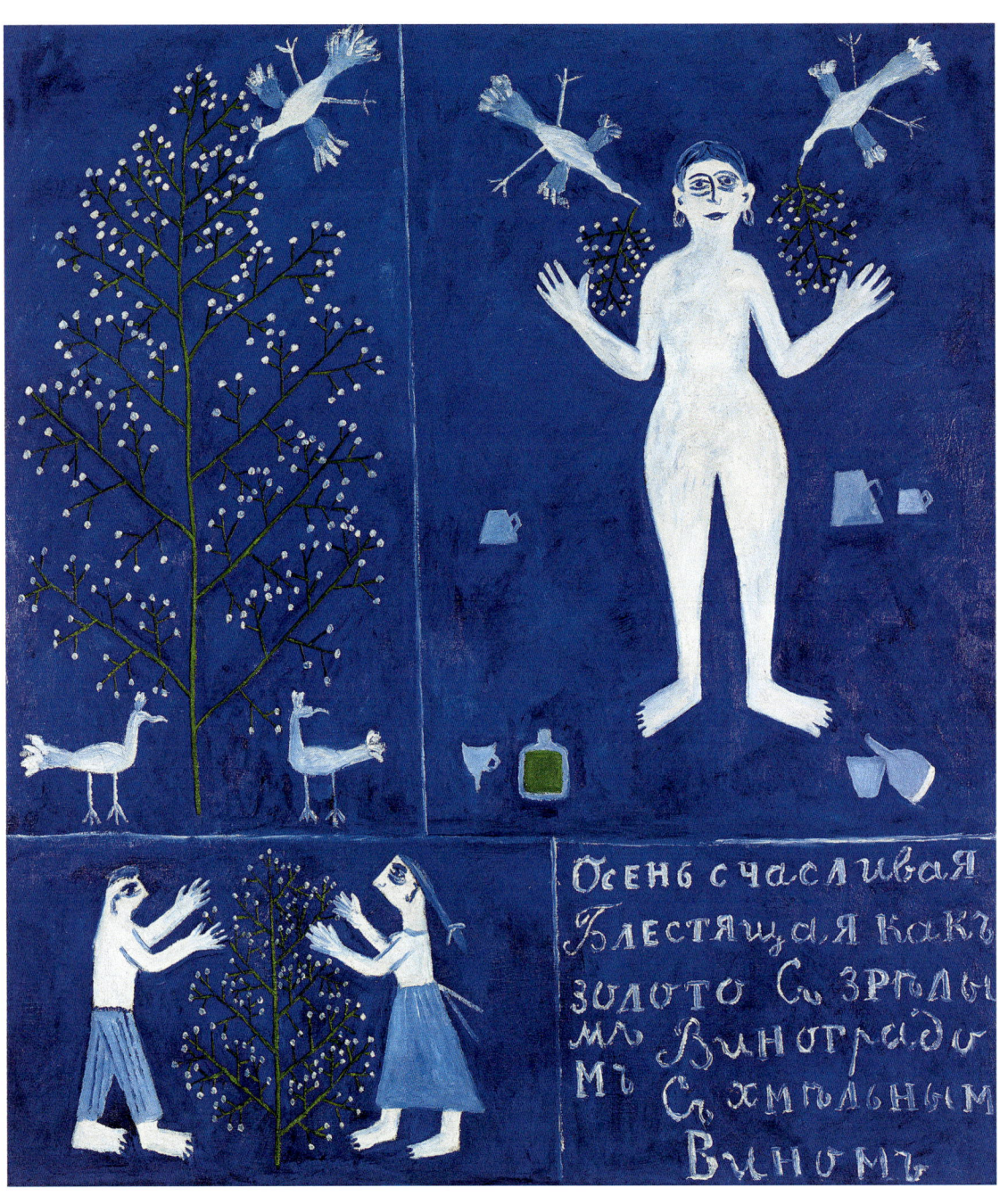

Mikhail F. Larionov   *L'Automne* [*Autumn*]   [1912]

oil on canvas   136 × 115 cm   purchase, 1970, AM 4513 P

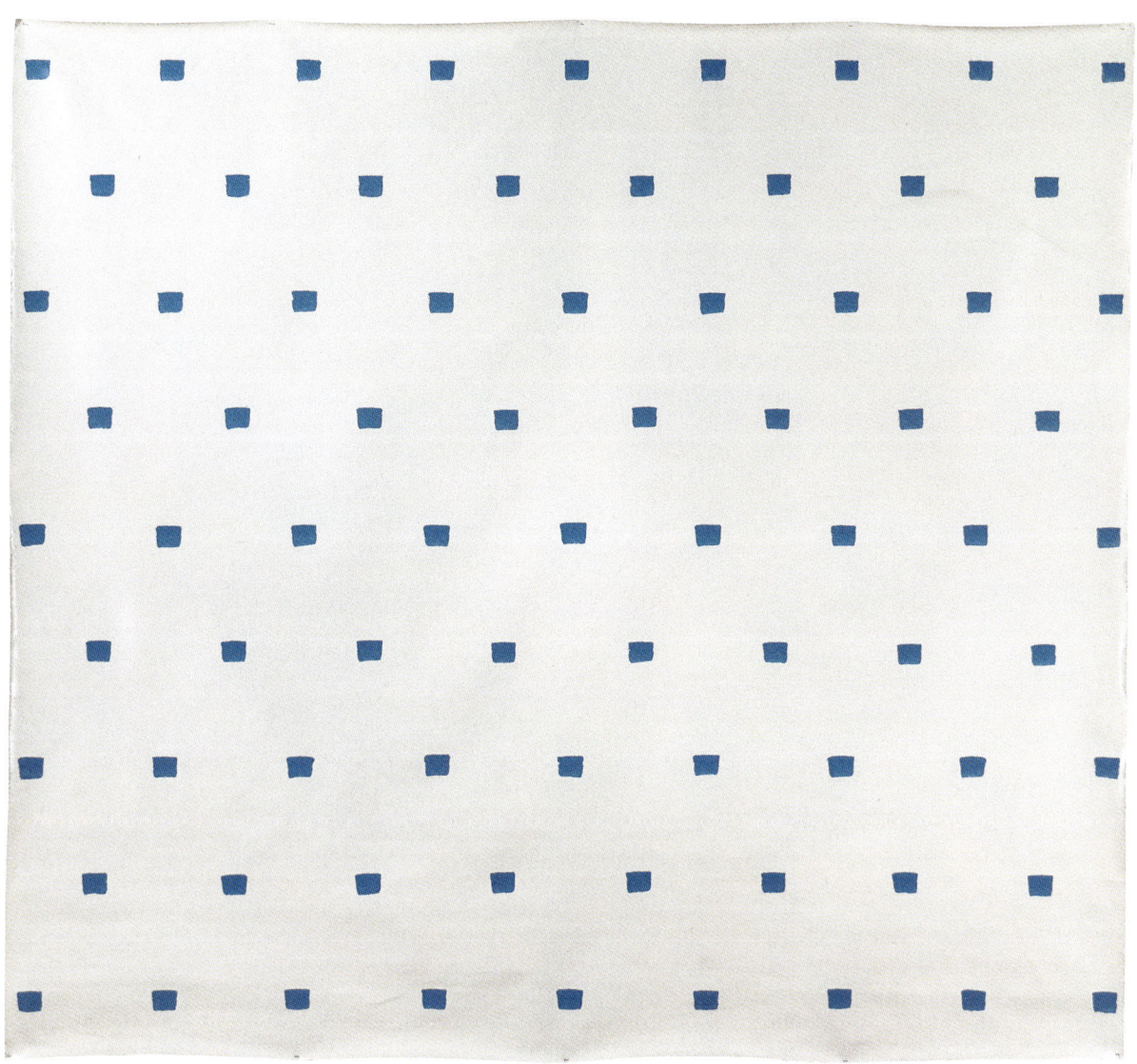

Niele Toroni   *Empreintes de pinceau nº 50 répétées à intervalles réguliers de 30 cm*
[*Imprints of a no. 50 Paintbrush Repeated at Regular Intervals of 30 cm*]   1967

acrylic on loose canvas   233 × 249 cm   purchase, 1988, AM 1988-3

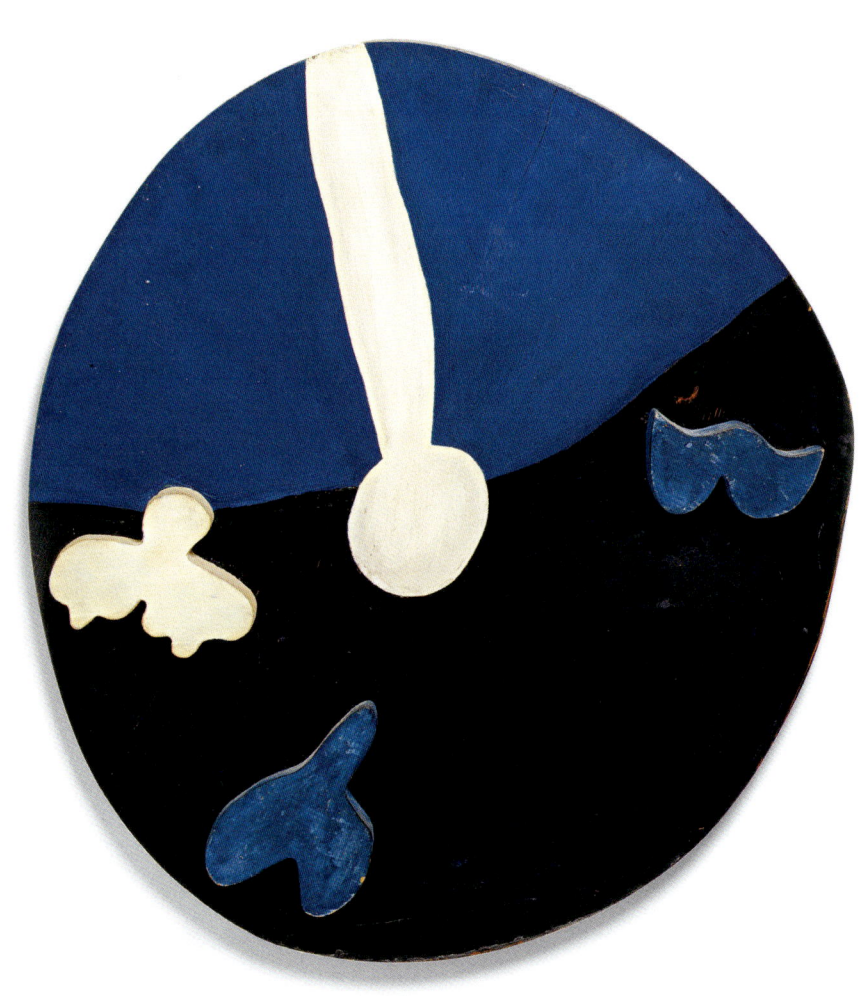

Jean Arp   *Horloge (Turmuhr)* [*Clock*]   [1924]

painted wood   65.3 × 56.8 × 5 cm   gift of Mr. Claude Gubler, 2004, AM 2004-156

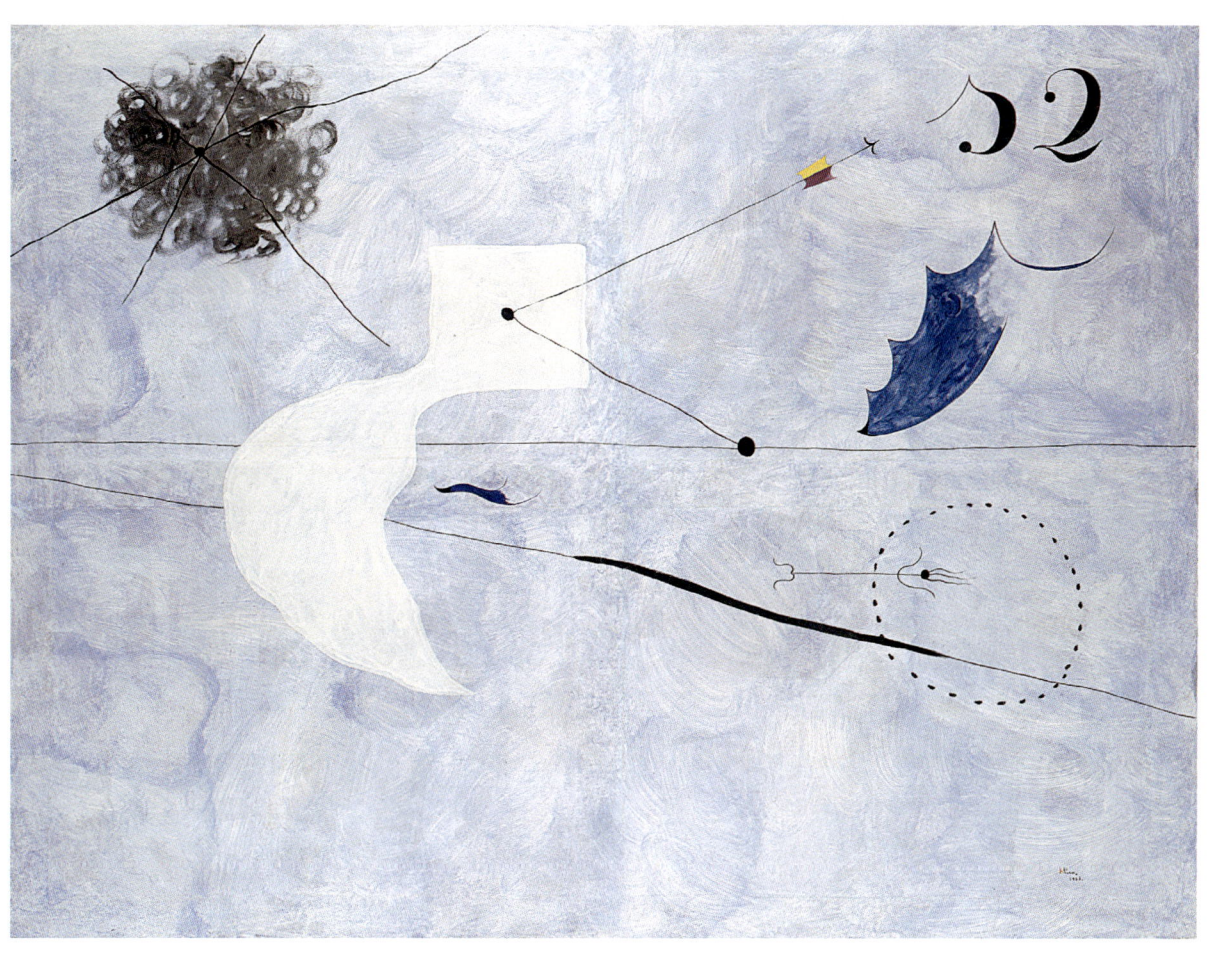

Joan Miró   *La Sieste* [*The Siesta*]   July 1925–September 1925

oil on canvas   113 × 146 cm   purchase, 1977, AM 1977-203

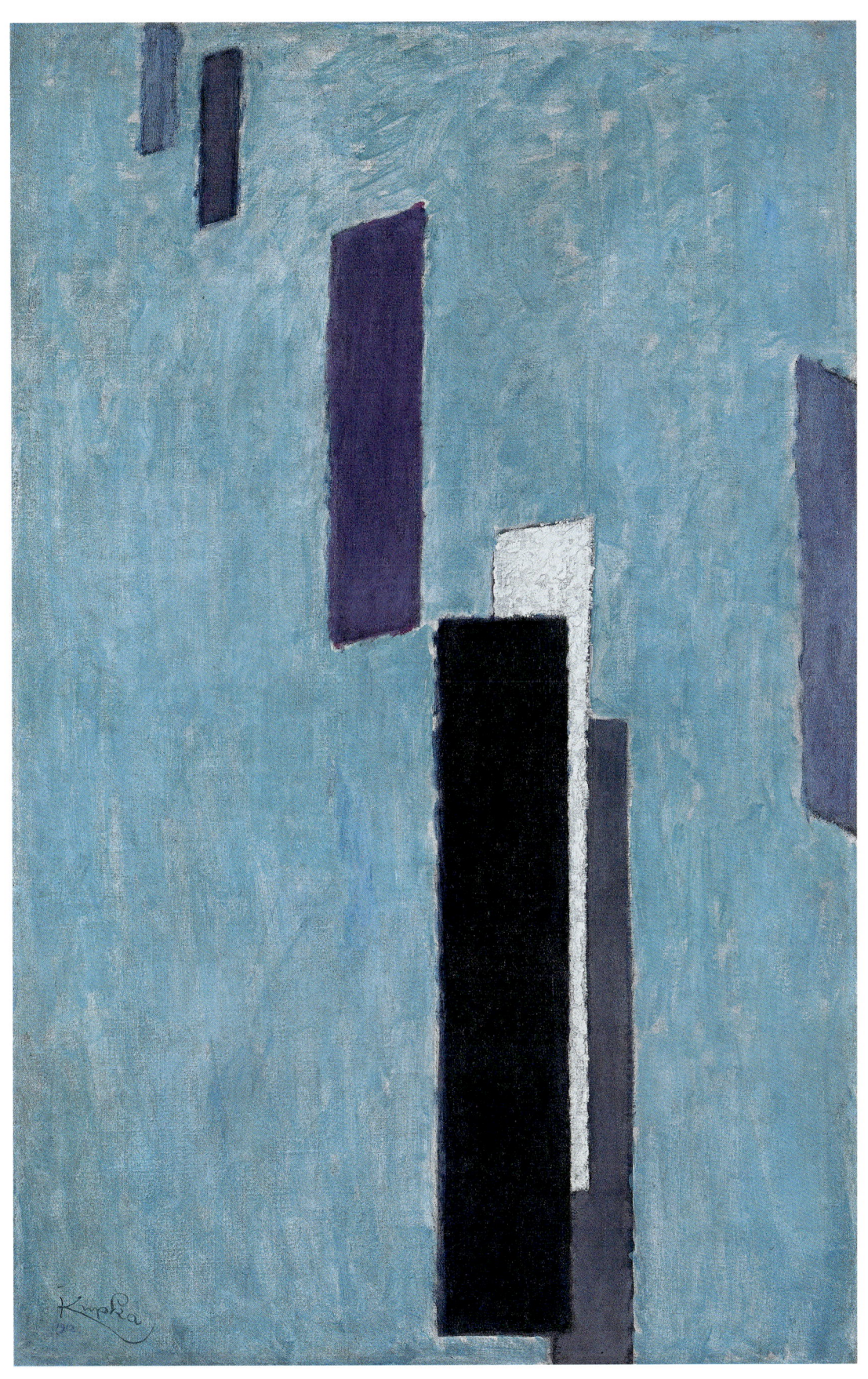

František Kupka   *Plans verticaux I* [*Vertical Planes I*]   1912

oil on canvas   150 × 94 cm   purchase of the French State, 1936, attribution, 1945, JP 807 P

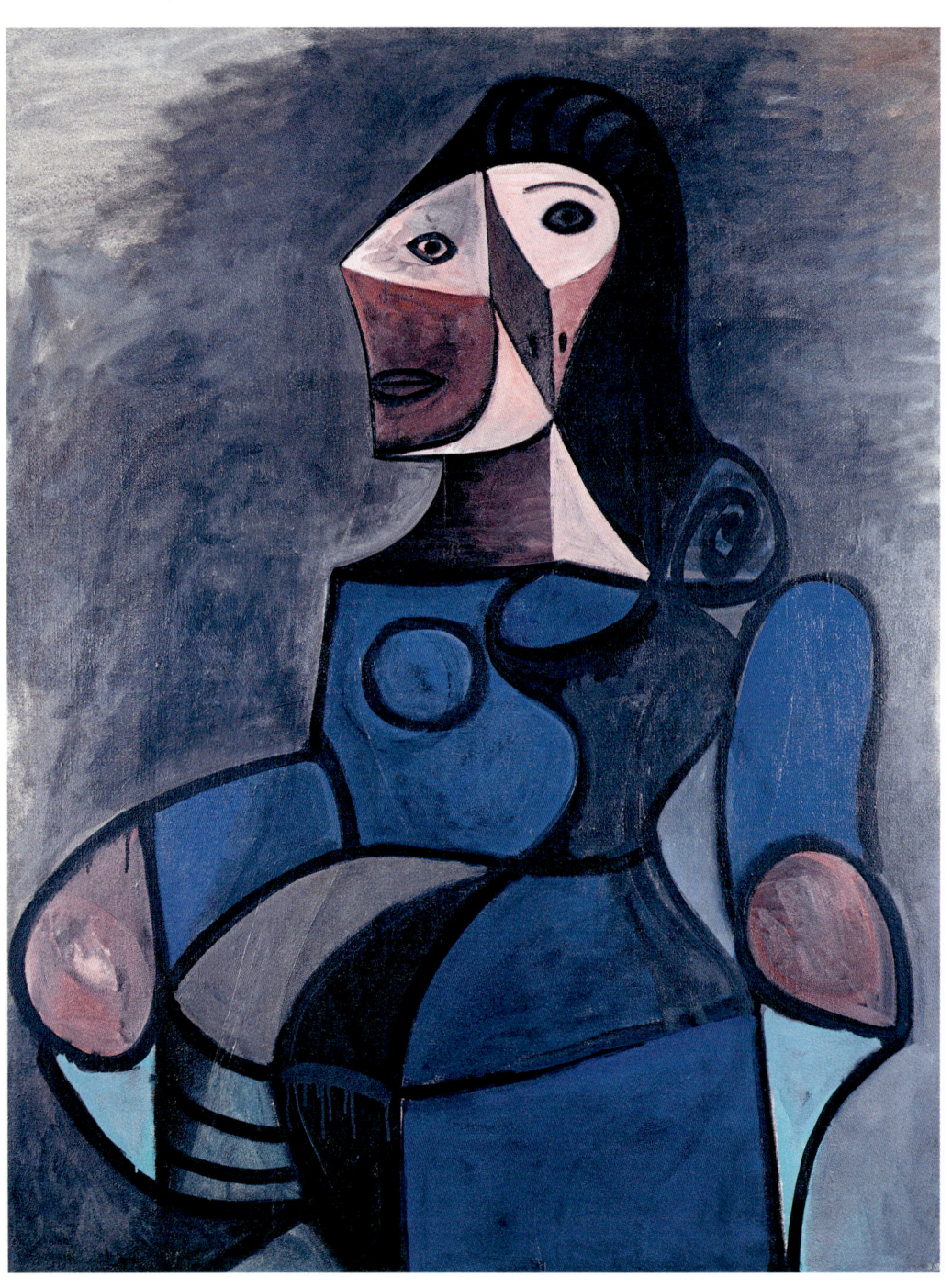

Pablo Picasso   *Femme en bleu* [*Woman in Blue*]   25 April 1944

oil on canvas   130 × 97 cm   gift of the artist, 1947, AM 2733 P

Yves Klein   *IKB 3, Monochrome bleu* [*Monochrome Blue*]   1960
pure pigment and synthetic resin on canvas mounted on wood   199 × 153 cm   purchase, 1974,
attributed to the Musée National d'Art Moderne – Centre de Création Industrielle, 1975, AM 1975-6

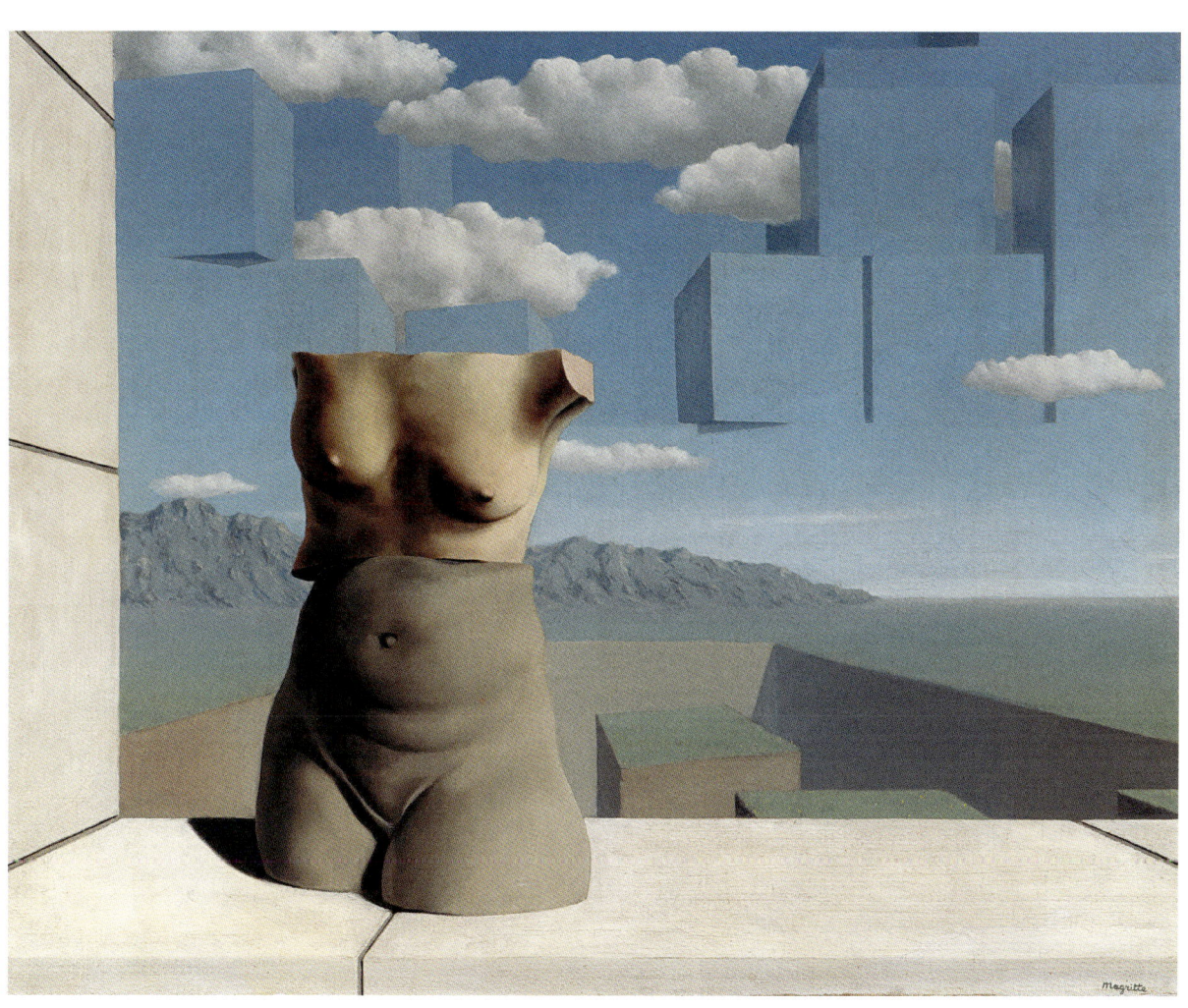

René Magritte   *Les Marches de l'été* [*The Marches of Summer*]   [1938]

oil on canvas   60 × 73 cm   purchase, 1991, AM 1991-138

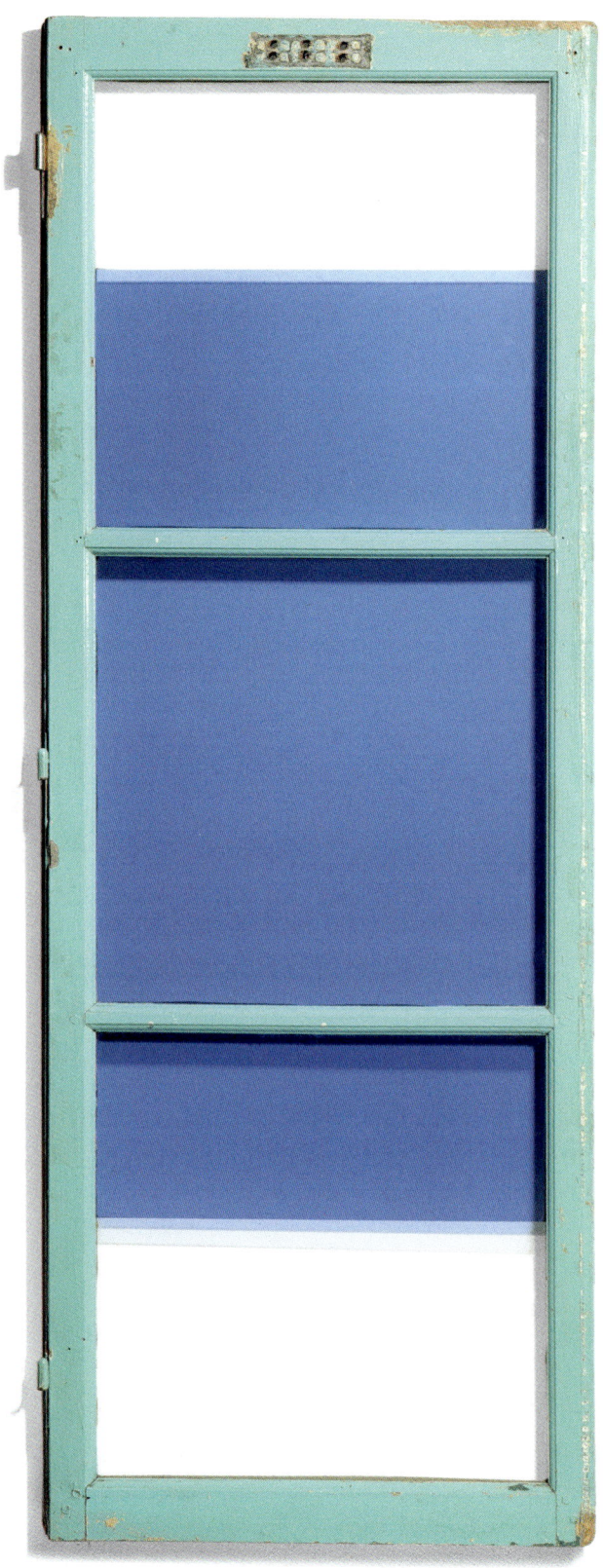

Pierre Buraglio   *Fenêtre* [*Window*]   1977
wooden leaf, clear and blue glass   178.7 × 65.1 × 3.5 cm   purchase, 1982, AM 1982-21 (1)

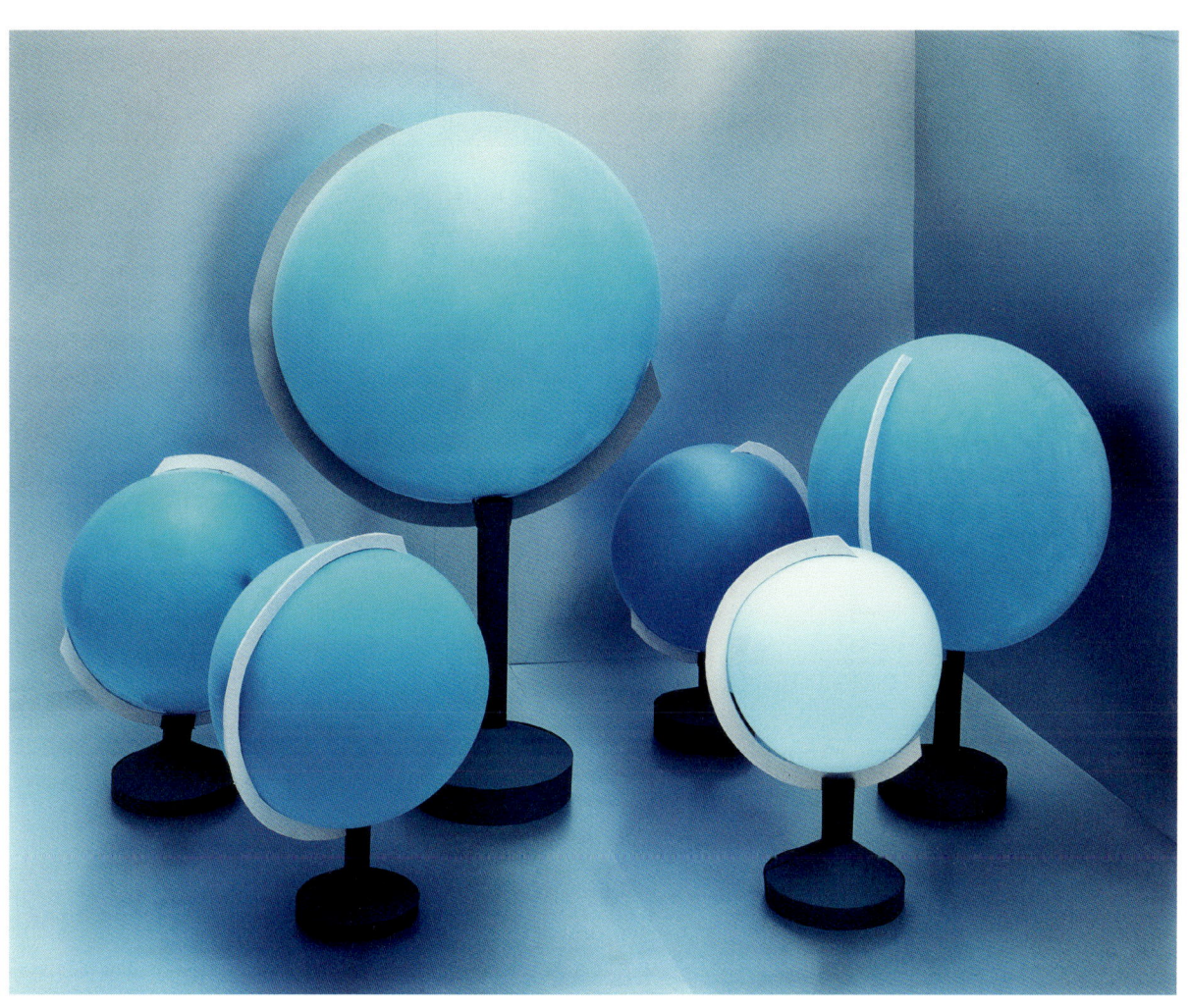

Thomas Demand   *Six Globes*   1992

Diasec chromogenic print   124 × 146 × 3.4 cm   donation by the Caisse des dépôts et consignations, 2006, AM 2006-275

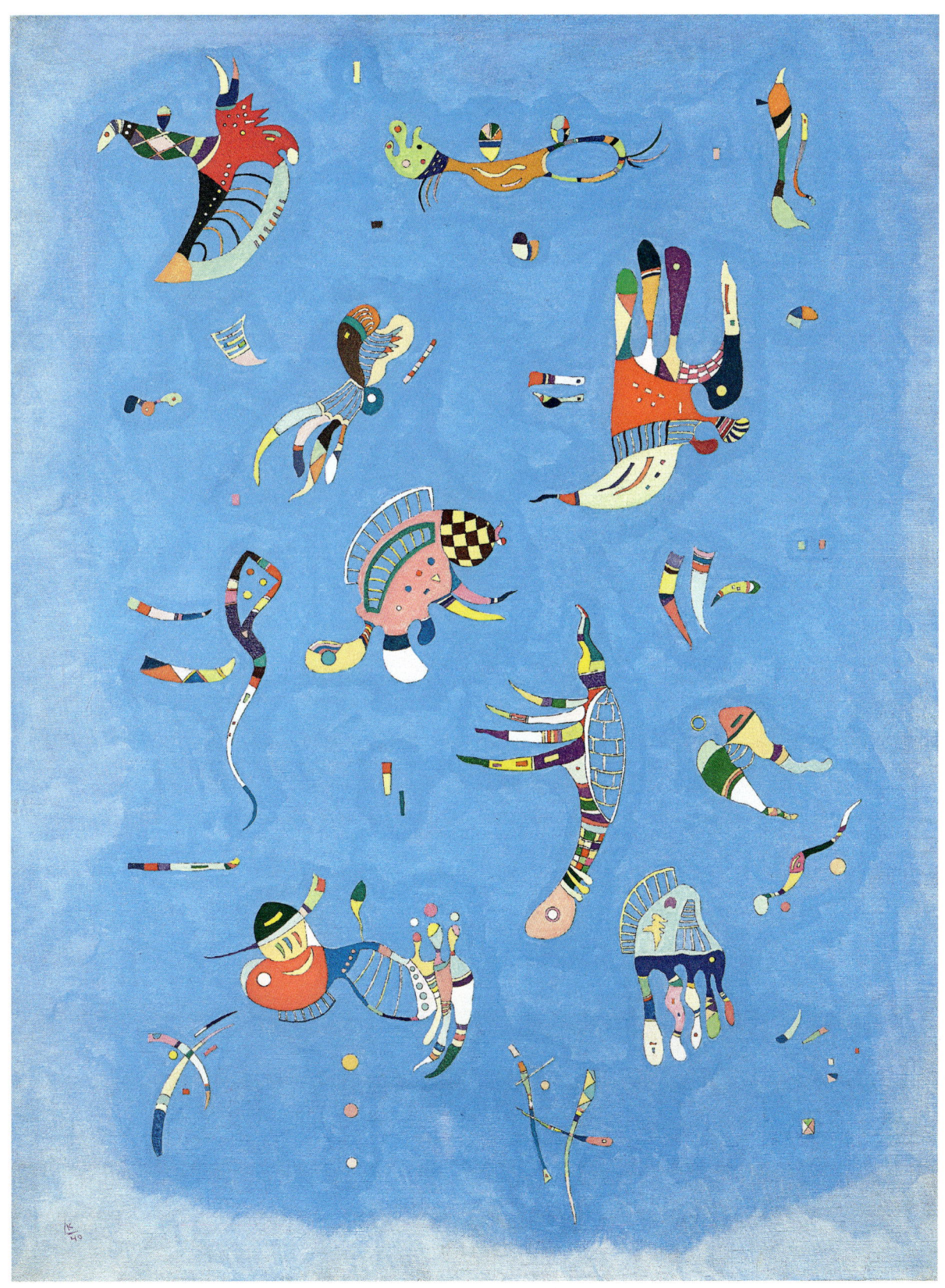

Wassily Kandinsky   *Bleu de ciel* [*Sky Blue*]   1940

oil on canvas   100 × 73 cm   donation by Nina Kandinsky, 1976, AM 1976-862

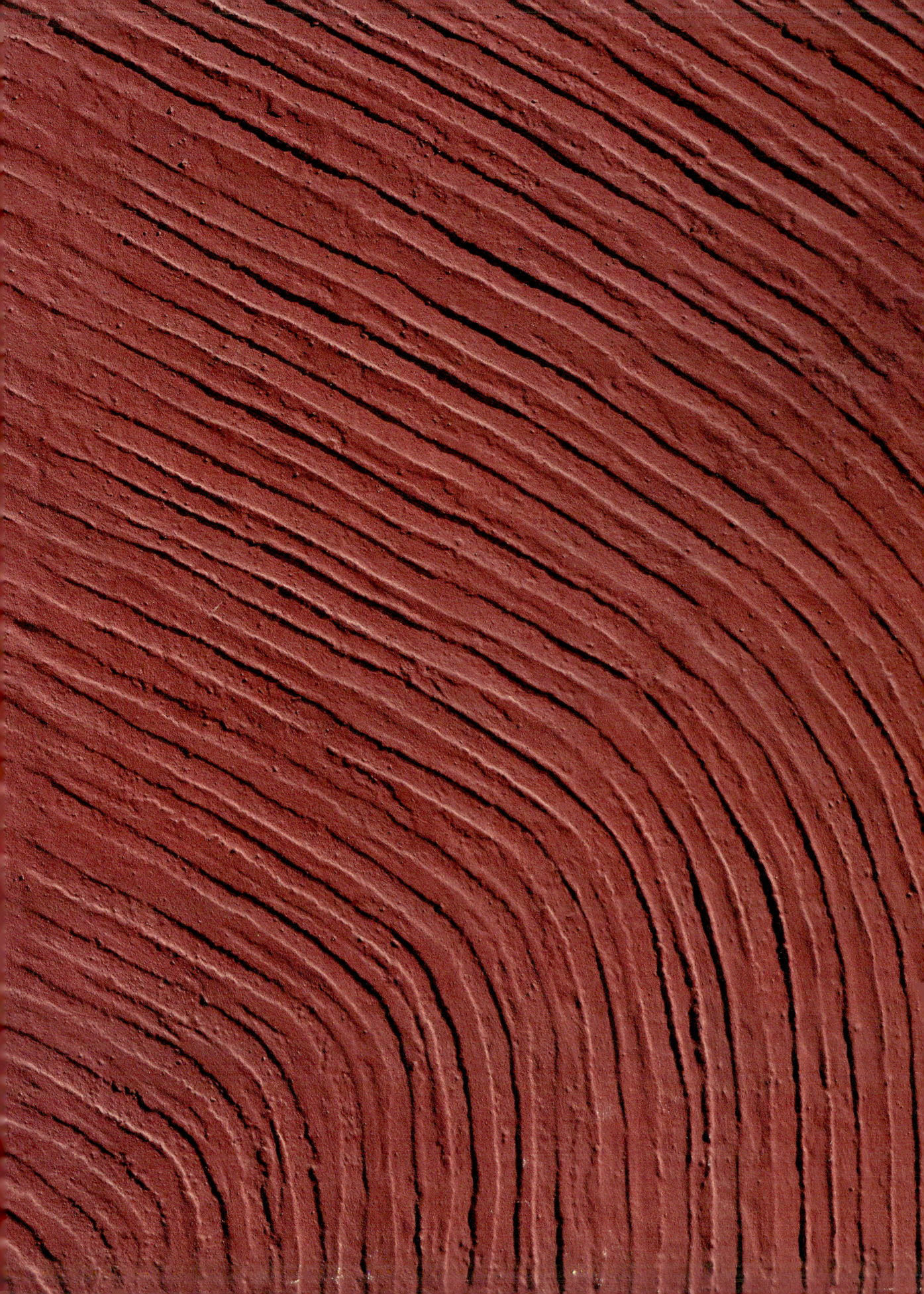

RED

AN ELEMENTARY RED

Hayley Edwards-Dujardin

IN THE BEGINNING, RED

One day in February 1997, John Christie questioned his friend John Berger about what their next project might be. The art critic gave him a nebulous reply: what if he were to send him a colour? The filmmaker complied and posted John Berger a piece of paper showing a square painted cadmium red. This scarlet pigment was the beginning of a prolific correspondence about colour, art, their memories and their emotions,[1] in which personal subjects merged with the polychrome symbolism of pictorial representations.

So everything begins with red? Red certainly expresses the human condition in a singularly complete way. Our understanding of red has to do with both the creation story of Judeo-Christian tradition – if we think of the first man in the Bible, Adam, whose name evokes red, blood and earth – and the primitive testimony of our civilisation, the same red earth embellishing prehistoric cave walls. Spirit and matter, like two substances that embody the human experience, formed in the ruddy maternal womb. Red, then, has become established as an archetypal colour that expresses both life and death, its extensive symbolic grammar facilitated by the wide availability of pigments such as red ochre, cinnabar, hematite, madder, kermes and purple used in Antiquity. It is a colour of both the intangible and the structural, which sometimes merge according to what we see and feel. Sometimes we are even led to believe that there is a symbolic purpose, when in fact the artist is not suggesting one, as Annie Ernaux alludes to when she talks about a "picture [that] consists of a cracked-up ocher surface" that the director of the gallery she is in describes to a client as "such a sensual painting":

> I try to draw a parallel between my own conception of sensuality and what appears to be a barren landscape. But I do not possess the mental agility or sensitivity this requires. I realize that I have yet to be initiated into this area of knowledge. But then it is not a question of knowledge. After all, instead of saying "sensual," they might as well have used the word "refreshing" or "violent": the non-connection between the painting and its description would still be the same. It's all a matter of learning the right code.[2]

There are too many reds to limit our impressions. While Fauvism exalted red[3] as, in the words of Kandinsky, "an endless typically warm colour [that] has an inner, highly vivid, lively, restless appeal",[4] and as is evident in Kees van Dongen's Fauvist *Self-Portrait* (1909) and its almost entirely monochrome crimson expression, modern art persisted in reflecting its primitive, violent and sensual identity.

THE BODY...

"For a long time, I had before my window a cabaret brightly painted half green, half red, which caused delicious suffering to my eyes".[5] Following Charles Baudelaire, the artists of the Belle Époque fed their imagination on the night and its women. Was it because, from the 14th to 17th centuries, prostitutes had to wear a brightly coloured, usually red, item of clothing to distinguish themselves from respectable women,[6] that this colour has become so fervently associated in iconography with sexuality, or at least with raw sensuality? Perhaps it also has something to do with the colour, pink and red, of our genitalia, as the provocative Egon Schiele suggested when he depicted himself masturbating, his penis tumescent (*Eros*, 1911). And when he drew his *Embrace* (1913, fig. 1), he so intertwined the lovers' angular bodies that if we reduced them to a line, they would become a shapeless beast. But Schiele added touches of colour that enliven the embrace and display it in all its harshness. Red tells its story in the thick wavy hair and stockings of his partner, Edith Harms, which are like pools of blood, but also in patches here and there – on knock-knees, an ear, a protruding elbow, full lips and even the curve of a buttock. Kandinsky's words come to mind: "Warm red may prove exciting, or painful, even disgusting, through possible association with blood...".[7] When such intimacy is captured so brutally, it underlines our vulnerabilities, for the unadorned and unsentimental display of our sexuality inevitably evokes a sense of unease. It is this shameless red that Louise Bourgeois uses in *La Destruction du père* [*The Destruction of the Father*] (1974, fig. 2), a cathartic, cruel and strangely familiar installation that shows a banquet of carcasses surrounded by protuberances reminiscent of phalluses and breasts. And when, in 1994, she dared to cross the threshold of the parental bedroom in *Red Room (Parents)*, it was again red that embodied intimacy, reduced to a bed in a space that is too tidy, disquieting and uncomfortable. We find the same red – "a sort of unwholesome-coloured vertigo"[8] that is both a spatial argument and a sexual metaphor of these places of prostitution – in Kees van Dongen's *Intérieur/Mlle Miroir, Mlle Collier et Mlle Sopha* [*Interior/Miss Mirror, Miss Necklace and Miss Sofa*] (1914), where, in an almost schematic composition inspired by an Egyptian living room, three women seem to be engulfed by a poisonous, possibly even venal, red. They exist now solely for the temptation of the flesh. Auguste Chabaud, too, used this "strident red"[9] of the brothel, a favourite subject for the artist, as seen in his *Nu sur fond rouge* [*Nude on a Red Background*] (1907), which shows a seductive grey body outlined in black – contradictory in that it is both voluptuous and morbid. Reminiscent of his portrait of consumptive Yvette (*Yvette ou la Robe à carreaux* [*Yvette, or The Checked Dress*], 1907–08), it can be seen as a warning of the degeneration that pleasure may lead to. It is this degeneration that so terrifies Yayoi Kusama, who, in 1965, covered the floor of the Castellane Gallery in New York with phallic shapes dotted with hallucinatory red spots. The installation is like a warning from the artist, who, through her signature spots, both conveys and exorcises her fear of sexually transmitted diseases.

… AND THE SPACE

There is a fine line between passion and violence. It is here that we see the primary contradictions of red: the pulsating blood, source of life and pleasure, but also of death, when spilt. It is these stark discordances that Otto Dix, haunted by the atrocities of the First World War, explored in his work. In the 1920s, a troubled and ambiguous decade that drowned itself in excesses as if to forget, he painted a slouched, grotesque, ugly *Sylvia von Harden* (1926, fig. 3). Otto Dix does not flatter his model, but rather makes her the archetype of an era that had an air of phoniness and was vaguely alarming, much like her unattractive red and black checked dress and the shades of "rather dull, rather faded red"[10] decorating the walls in the background: the party is over, he seems to be telling us. Red, signalling danger, is disturbing. And when the human figure leaves the painting, the sensation of unease is exacerbated. Auguste Chabaud unsettles us with his *Couloir d'hôtel* [*Hotel Corridor*] (1907–08), which we cannot help but compare to the geometric flat tints, between abstraction and reality, of Matisse's *Porte-Fenêtre à Collioure* [*French Window at Collioure*] (1914). Andy Warhol chose to juxtapose blue and a strident red in his *Big Electric Chair* (1967–68).[11] The saturated and repeated series seems to annihilate emotion, reflecting our passive consumption of the voyeuristic and sensationalist violence that we are daily presented with by the media. Nevertheless, if we isolate the work, we are struck by the ghostly and savage appearance of the unoccupied chair and the emptiness of the space surrounding it, brutally coloured red. This is the dramatic perception that Francis Bacon enshrines in *Blood on the Floor – Painting* (1986). On an orangey red monochrome background, a lightbulb illuminates a large plank of wood on which a patch of blood is visible. We do not know, in the end, which disturbs us more, this bloody splash, the cause of which remains a mystery, or the background, which is flat, infinite and lacking perspective, confusing our understanding of the space and its meaning. Should the use of spatial red, then,

be limited to fear? Of course, this would be to ignore the vital force of the colour, which the Fauves were able to make use of as an initiation into modern art, an "ordeal by fire".[12] It is this legacy, that, like a manifesto of his pictorial development, is revealed in Matisse's *L'Atelier rouge* [*The Red Studio*] (1911, fig. 4) The sprawling flat tint of Venetian red submerges the studio, dissolving the planes yet without swamping the emerging motifs and fragments, prefigurations of his gouache cutouts. The artist refused to choose between the decorative nature of the colour and its narrative power. Red evokes the studio as he describes it; it becomes the template of Matisse's gestural technique. In 1913, he explained to Ernst Goldschmidt: "Where did I find this red? I don't know. But in a while, we will go for a walk in my garden, and perhaps everything will seem simpler to you. I find that all these objects – the flowers, the pieces of furniture, the chest of drawers – become what they are for me only when I see them with this red".[13] As a single artistic motif, colour freed modern art from the figure.

"RED ON RED, THAT IS THE EXERCISE"[14]

František Kupka composed his paintings, like a musical language, under the powerful influence of colours, which dictate the form and movement and express sensations and emotions. *La Forme du vermillon* [*The Shape of Vermillion*] (1923, fig. 5), dominated by red, takes us into chromatic infinity, conveyed there by a jubilant and deafening melody. It is this absolute that we encounter in Mark Rothko's work and its elusive – both full and empty – atmospheres. The unfinished *Untitled* (1970, fig. 6) creates a tension through the falsely effortless and deceptively monochrome use of two rectangular blocks of colour that create and move away from a dialogue, that are as intense as they are muted, are brought to life by "that coarse brush that strips away the red",[15] and are confined and freed in an unframed space. Like an ironic gesture or a testament of the artist who claimed to be "the most violent of all the American painters",[16] Rothko's endless red also speaks of intimate human drama: this painting was found on the artist's easel the day he committed suicide. Donald Judd reflects on the limitation of space rather than on eternity. *Untitled (DSS #33)* (1962) was the first of his three-dimensional works, for "color, to continue, had to occur in space."[17] By painting two wooden panels, joined by a black bar, in cadmium red – the only pigment, in the artist's view, capable of defining the contours and angles of an object – Judd succeeded in delimiting the space while opening it out. In doing so, he also opened up the possibilities of red. This diversity enriches Anish Kapoor's monumental

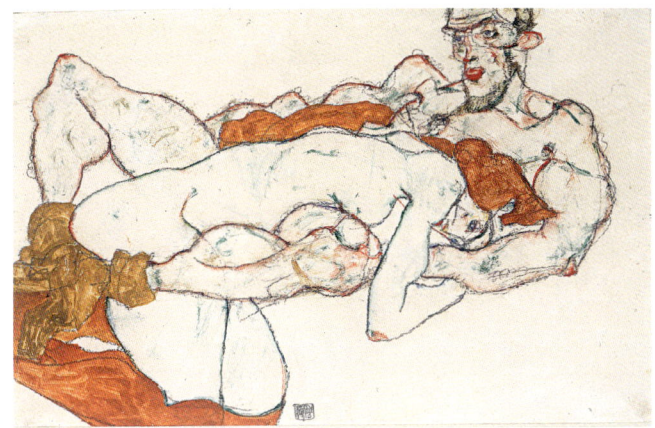

1

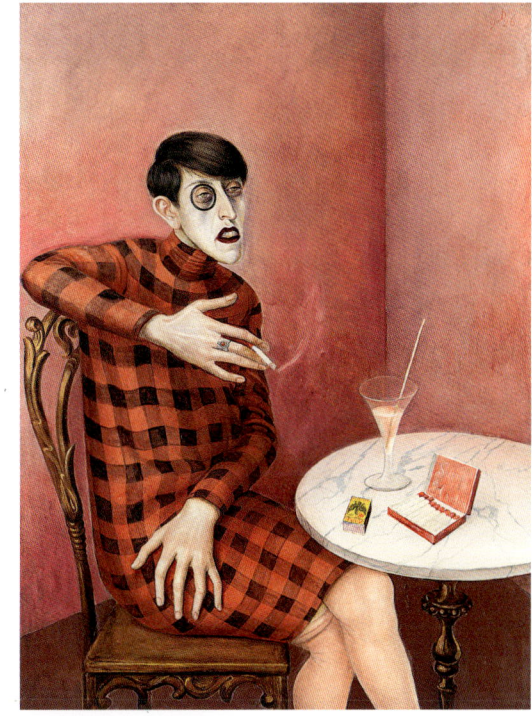

3

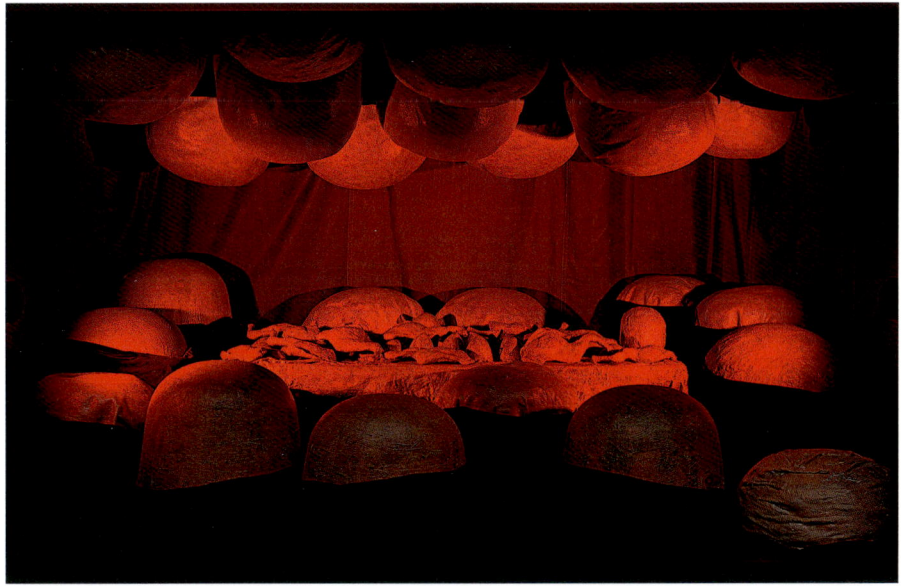

2

Fig.1 Egon Schiele
Embrace, 1913, pencil,
watercolour and opaque
paint on paper, 32 × 48 cm
Art trade London, Sotheby's,
27 November 1995, lot 24,
27/11/1995
Private collection

Fig.2 Louise Bourgeois
La Destruction du père
[*The Destruction of the
Father*], 1974, latex, plaster,
wood, textile and red light,
238 × 362 × 249 cm
Glenstone Museum, Potomac,
Maryland

Fig.3 Otto Dix
*Portrait of the Journalist
Sylvia von Harden*, 1926,
oil and tempera on wood,
121 × 89 cm
Centre Pompidou – Musée
National d'Art Moderne –
Centre de Création Industrielle,
Paris
Purchase, 1961
AM 3899 P

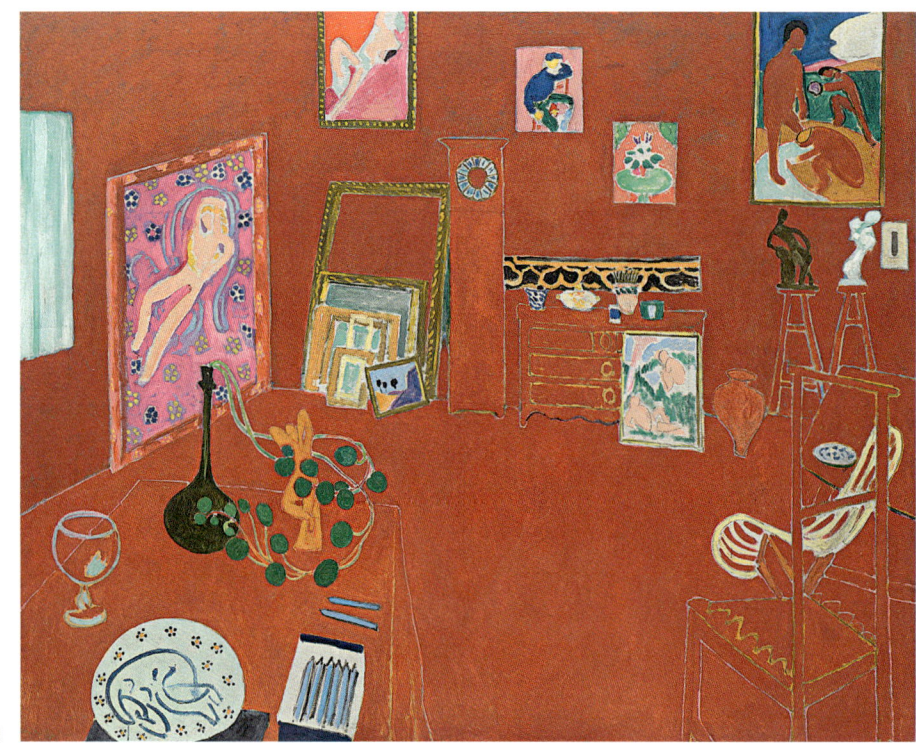

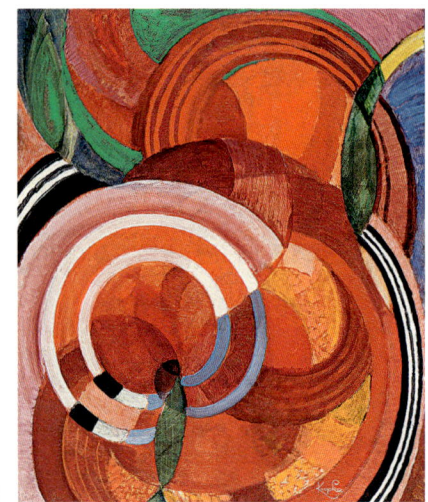

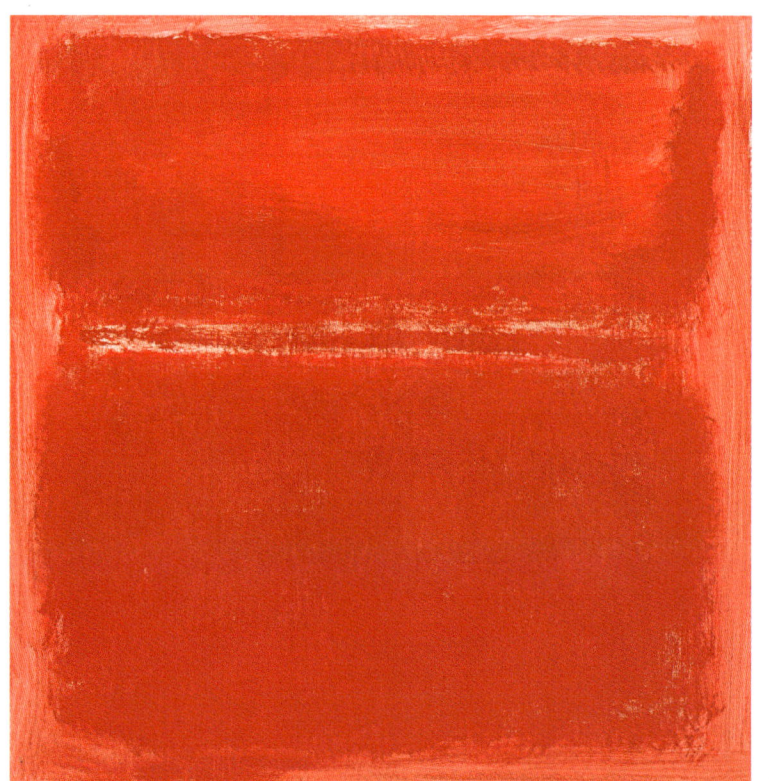

Fig. 4   Henri Matisse
L'Atelier rouge
[*The Red Studio*], 1911,
oil on canvas, 181 × 219.1 cm
Museum of Modern Art (MoMA),
New York. Mrs. Simon
Guggenheim Fund. 8.1949

Fig. 5   František Kupka
La Forme du vermillon
[*The Shape of Vermillion*],
1923, oil on canvas, 72 × 59 cm
Centre Pompidou – Musée
National d'Art Moderne – Centre
de Création Industrielle, Paris
Purchase, 1957. AM 3553 P

Fig. 6   Mark Rothko
Untitled, 1970, acrylic on
canvas, 152.4 × 145.1 cm
National Gallery of Art,
Washington, D.C.
Gift of the Mark Rothko
Foundation, Inc. 1986.43.173

installation *Svayambhu*, presented for the first time in Nantes in 2007. Composed of a massive block of red wax transported on rails that passes slowly and tightly under an arch, the work, whose Sanskrit title translates as 'modelled by its own energy', is constrained by the architecture of the places it occupies. As it moves beneath the arch, it leaves behind shreds of wax, which coat the structural elements like clots of blood. *Svayambhu* seems to convey the modern memory of humanity, that of the Industrial Revolution and slavery, of capitalism and colonialism. This bright red form, penetrating slowly but surely, also evokes a patriarchal and phallocentric masculinity. Finally, without falling for the convenient essentialist perspective, we might like to detect in it the pure pigment of Hindu culture. And so, we return to the premises of this essay: red, like a "charge of dynamite",[18] is disturbing because it is universal in what it says about the most basic aspects of our private lives and our societies. We would like to conclude as we began, with the words of John Christie: "Red is not usually innocent [...]. But the red that you sent me is. It's the red of childhood. A pretend red. Or the red of young eyelids shut tight – the red you saw when you did that. As I look at it, I wonder what will happen when it grows older. Maybe it won't be red anymore. My guess is that maybe it will become black".[19]

1
Their correspondence gave rise to a book: John Berger and John Christie, *I Send You This Cadmium Red: A Correspondence Between John Berger and John Christie* (London: Actar, 2000), n.p.
2
Annie Ernaux, *Exteriors*, trans. Tanya Leslie (New York: Seven Stories Press, 1996), pp. 19–20.
3
Henri Matisse said to Georges Duthuit that Fauvism "is when there is red"; quoted by Pierre Schneider in *Matisse* (New York: Rizzoli, 1984), p. 210.
4
Wassily Kandinsky, *On the Spiritual in Art* (New York: Guggenheim Foundation, 1946), p. 69.
5
Charles Baudelaire, *Salon de 1846*, preceded by *Baudelaire peintre* by Jean-Christophe Bailly (Paris: La Fabrique Éditions, 2021), p. 78.
6
Michel Pastoureau, *Rouge, histoire d'une couleur* (Paris: Seuil, 2016), p. 108.
7
Wassily Kandinsky, *On the Spiritual in Art*, op. cit., p. 40.

8
Jacques Rivière quoted in Anita Hopmans, *Van Dongen, fauve, anarchiste et mondain*, exh. cat., Rotterdam, Museum Boijmans Van Beuningen, 18 September 2010 – 23 January 2011; Paris, Musée d'Art Moderne de la Ville de Paris, 25 March – 17 July 2011 (Paris: Paris Musées, 2011), p. 36.
9
Serge Fauchereau, *Auguste Chabaud. Époque fauve* (Marseille: André Dimanche Éditeur, 2002), p. 89.
10
Marie Gispert, *La Femme à la cigarette* (Paris: Nouvelles Éditions Scala, 2011), p. 67.
11
The artist used the motif of the electric chair from 1964, as part of his 'Death and Disasters' series, begun in 1962.
12
André Derain quoted by Georges Duthuit, *The Fauvist Painters* (New York: Wittenborn, Schultz, 1950), p. 29.
13
Interview with Ernst Goldschmidt, *Politiken*, Copenhagen, 5 January 1913, in Ann Temkin, *Matisse. l'Atelier rouge*, exh. cat., Paris, Fondation Louis Vuitton, 4 May – 9 September 2024 (Paris: Fondation Louis Vuitton and Hazan, 2024), p. 186.

14
Joris-Karl Huysmans, *L'Art moderne* (Paris: Stock, 1903 [1883]), p. 159.
15
Yannick Mercoyrol, *Parler avec du rouge dans la bouche (face à Rothko)* (Paris: Chatelain-Julien, 2002), p. 5.
16
Mark Rothko to Brian Corney, 1959, in Chris Stephens, *Mark Rothko in Comwall*, exh. pamphlet, Tate St. Ives, 1996, p. 10.
17
Donald Judd, 'Some Aspects of Color in General and Red and Black in Particular', in Nicholas Serota, *Donald Judd*, exh. cat., London, Tate Modern, 5 February – 25 April 2004; Düsseldorf, K20 Kunstsammlung Nordrhein-Westfalen, 19 June – 5 September 2004; Basel, Kunstmuseum, 2 October 2004 – 9 January 2005 (London: Tate Publishing, 2004), p. 157.
18
André Derain quoted in Georges Duthuit, *The Fauvist Painters*, op. cit., p. 29.
19
John Berger, John Christie, *I Send You This Cadmium Red...*, op. cit.

ADDITIONAL BIBLIOGRAPHY

ERNAUX, 1993: Annie Ernaux. *Journal du dehors*. Paris: Gallimard, 1993.

PASTOUREAU, 2017: Michel Pastoureau, *Red: The History of a Color* (Princeton NJ: Princeton University Press, 2017).

VENTURI, 2023: Riccardo Venturi, "À fleur de peau. Figurer le drame humain", in *Mark Rothko*, exh. cat., Paris, Fondation Louis Vuitton, 18 October 2023 – 2 April 2024. Paris: Fondation Louis Vuitton and Citadelles & Mazenod, 2023.

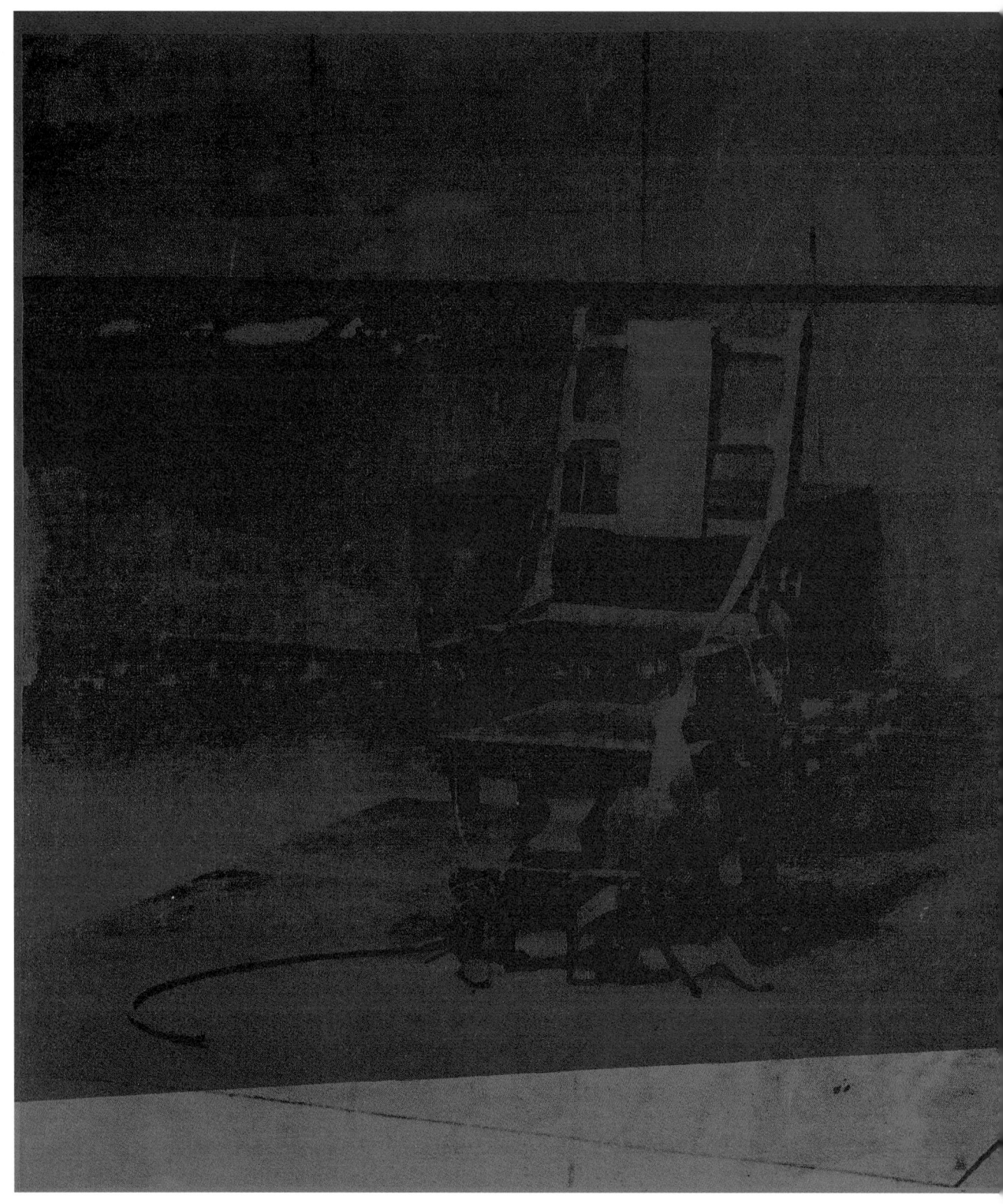

Andy Warhol   *Big Electric Chair*   December 1967–January 1968

silkscreen ink and acrylic on canvas   137.2 × 185.3 cm   gift of The Menil Foundation in memory of Jean de Menil, 1976, AM 1976-1232

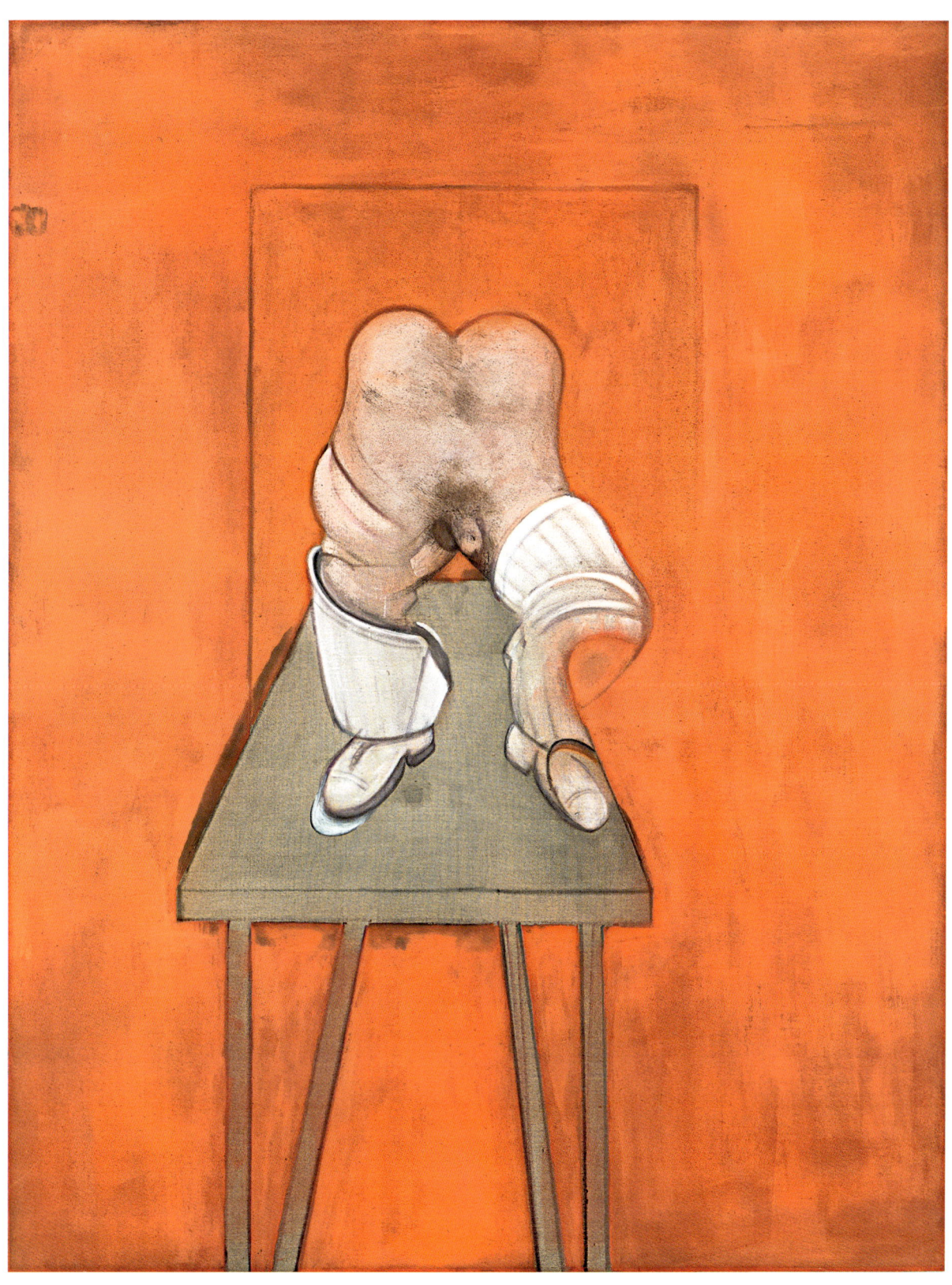

Francis Bacon *Study of the Human Body* [1981–82]

oil and pastel on canvas   198 × 147.5 cm   purchase, 1983, AM 1982-433

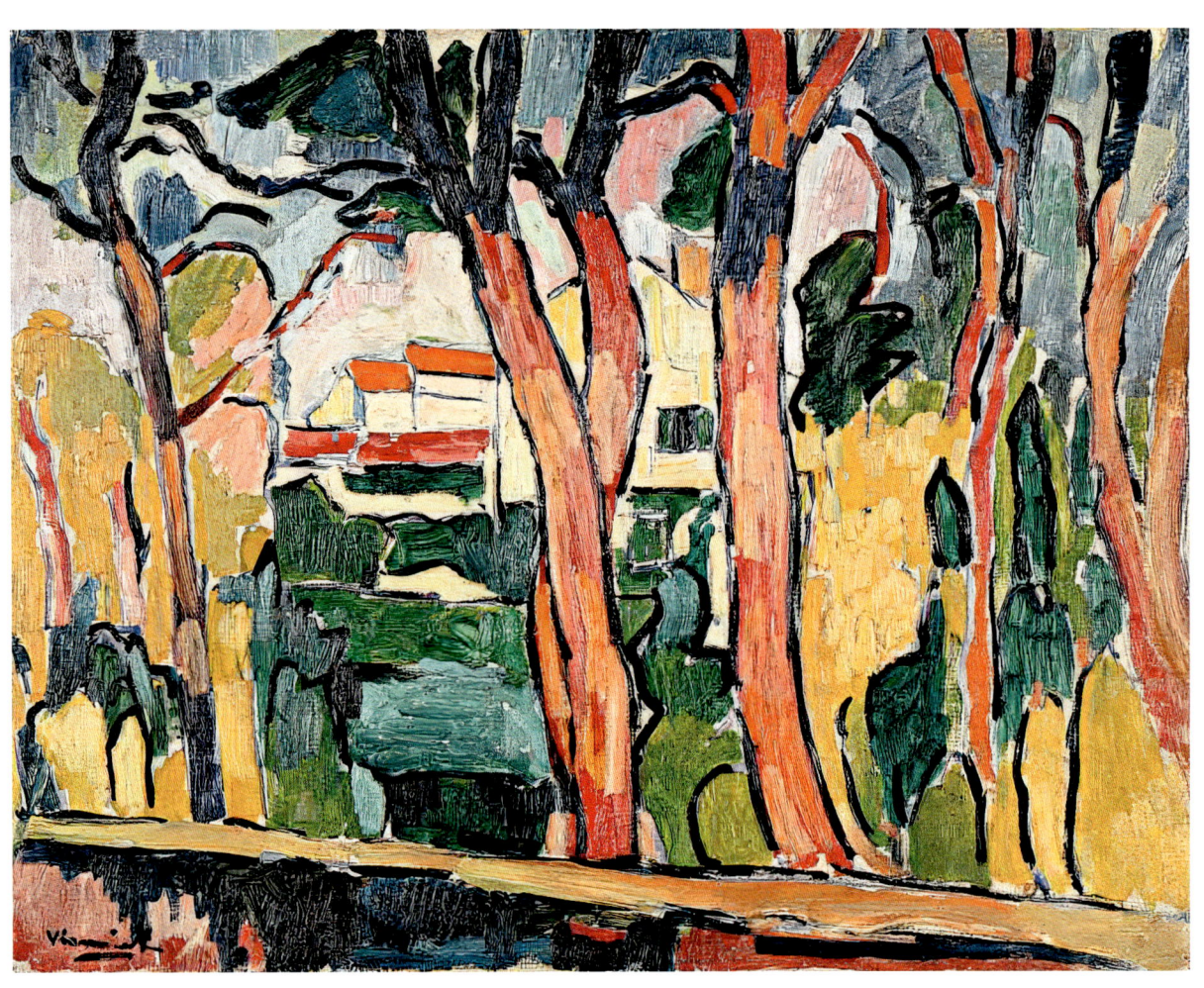

Maurice de Vlaminck   *Les Arbres rouges* [*The Red Trees*]   [1906]

oil on canvas   65 × 81 cm   purchase, 1947, AM 2673 P

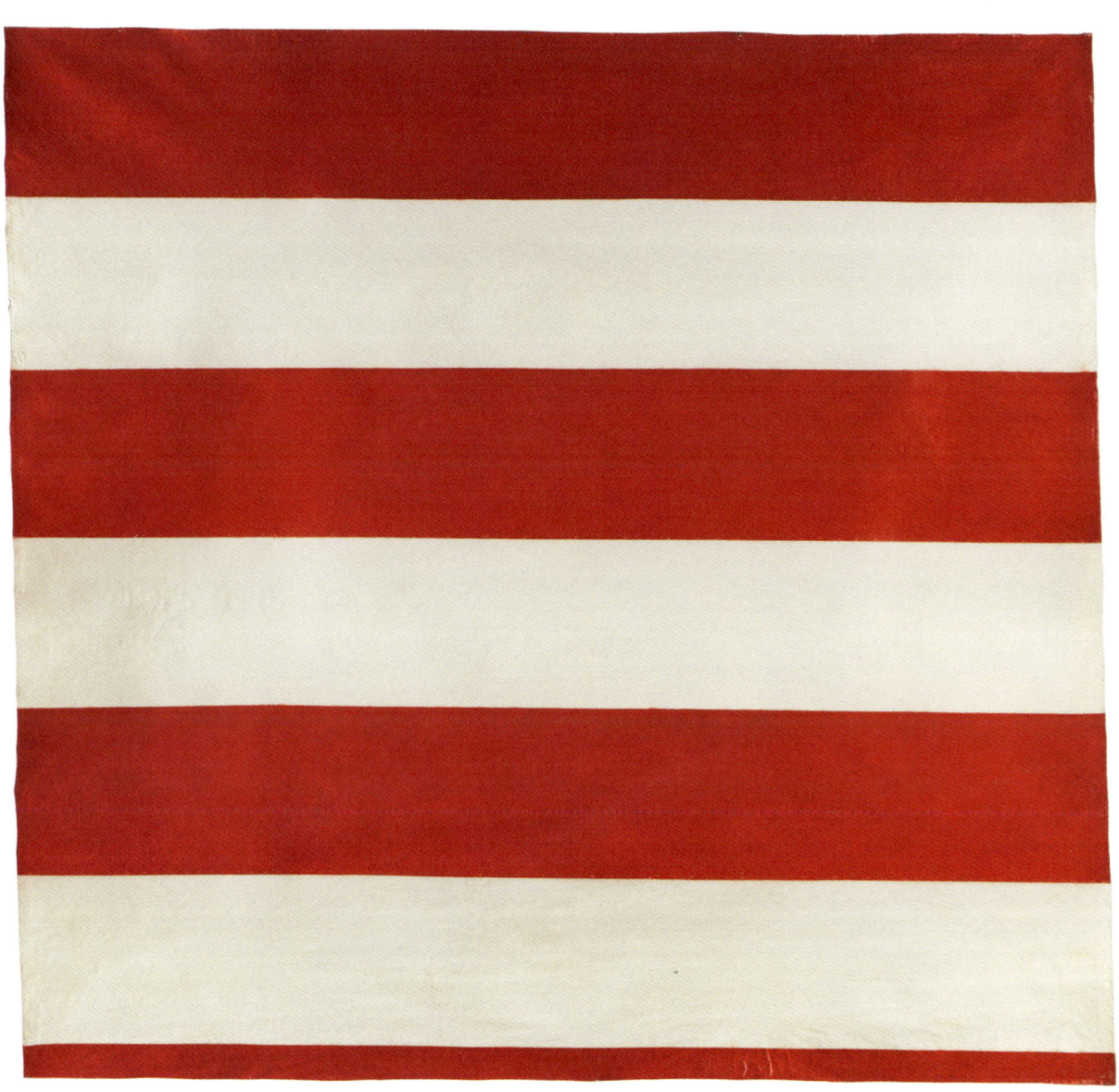

Michel Parmentier   *Rouge* [*Red*]   1968
oil on waxed canvas   233.5 × 240 cm   purchase, 1986, AM 1986-158

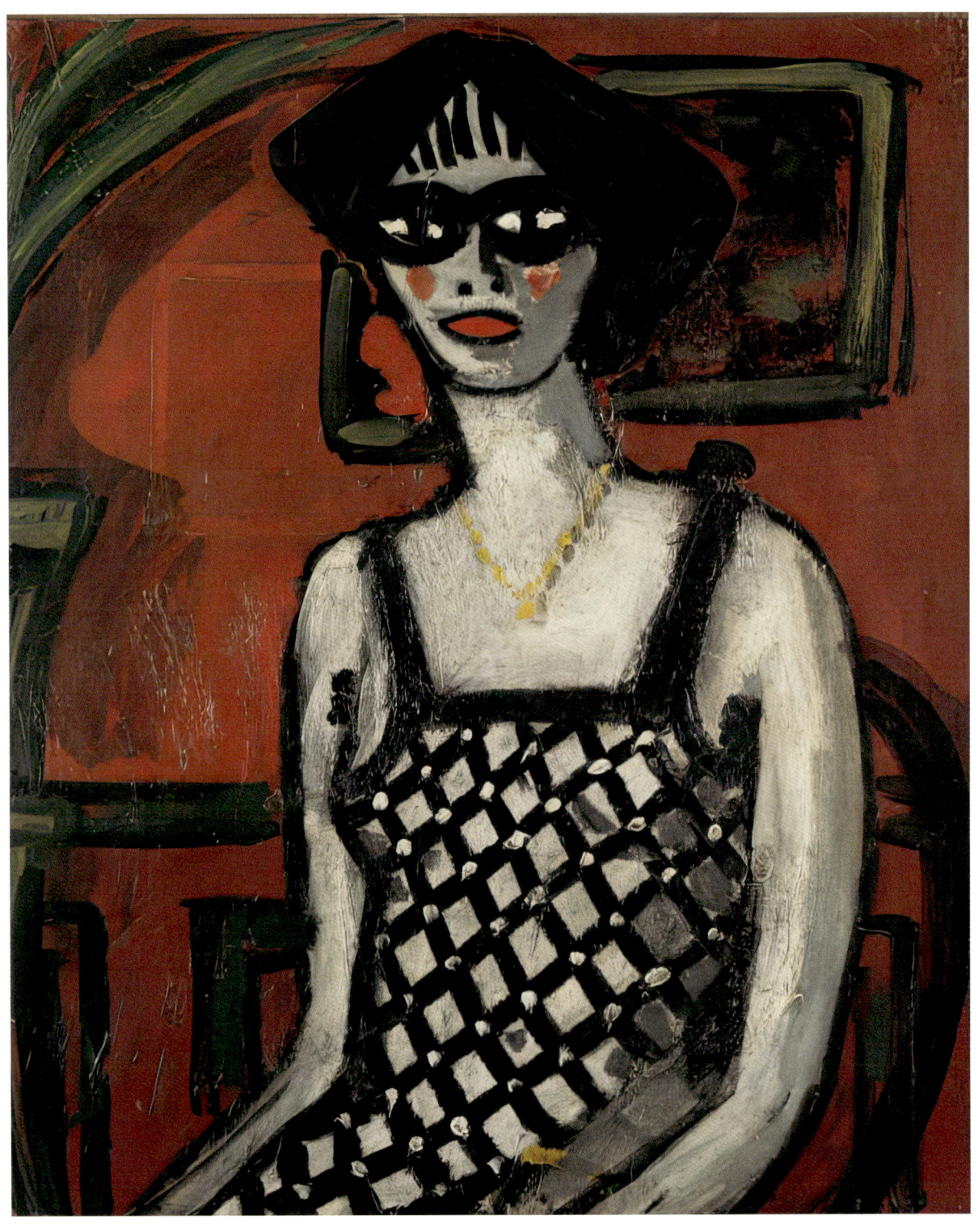

Auguste Élysée Chabaud *Yvette ou la Robe à carreaux* [*Yvette, or The Checked Dress*] [1907–08]

oil on canvas 81 × 65 cm gift of Claude Chabaud, 1995, AM 1995-299

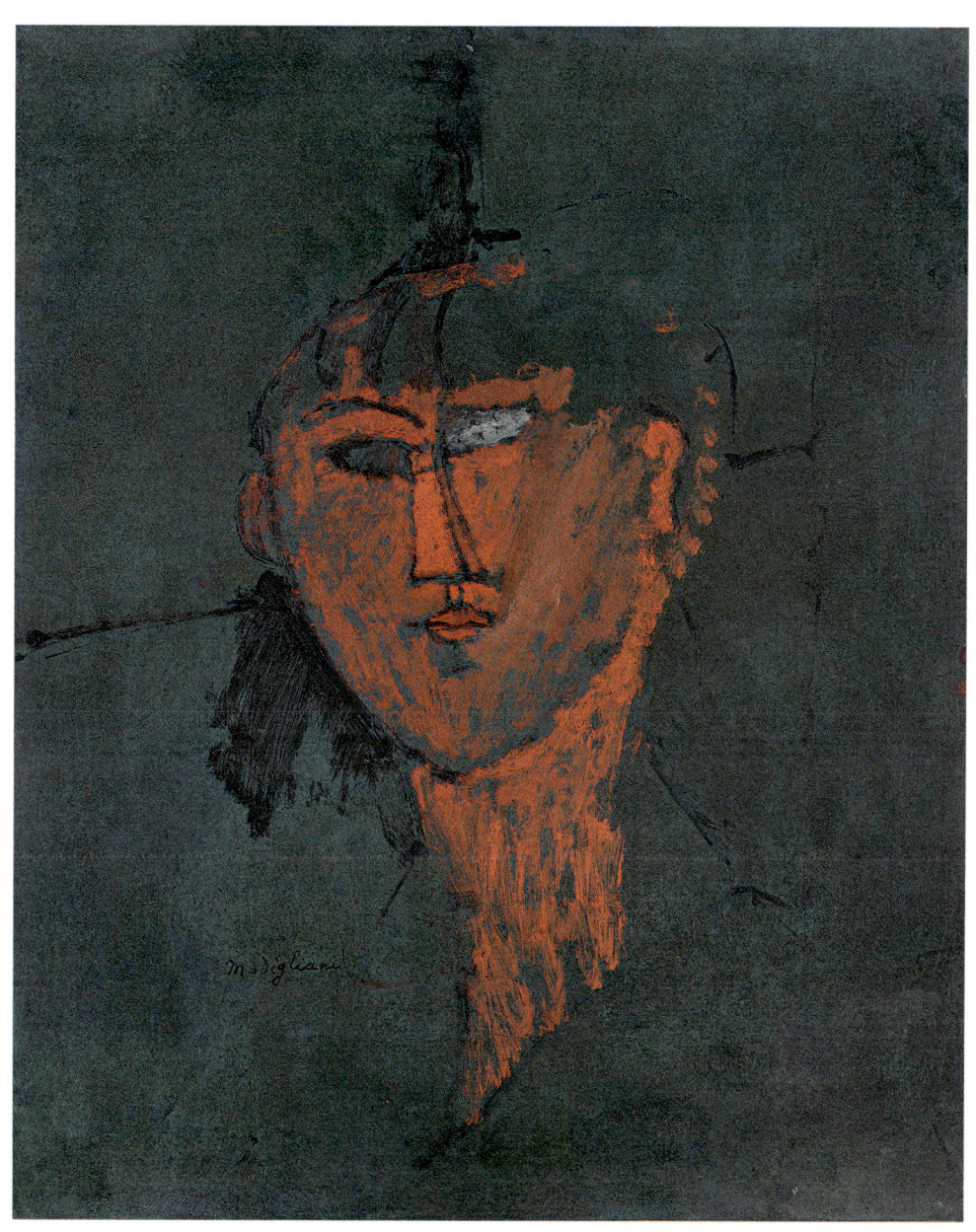

Amedeo Modigliani   *Tête rouge* [*The Red Head*]   [1915]

oil on cardboard   54 × 42.5 cm   purchase, 1964, AM 4286 P

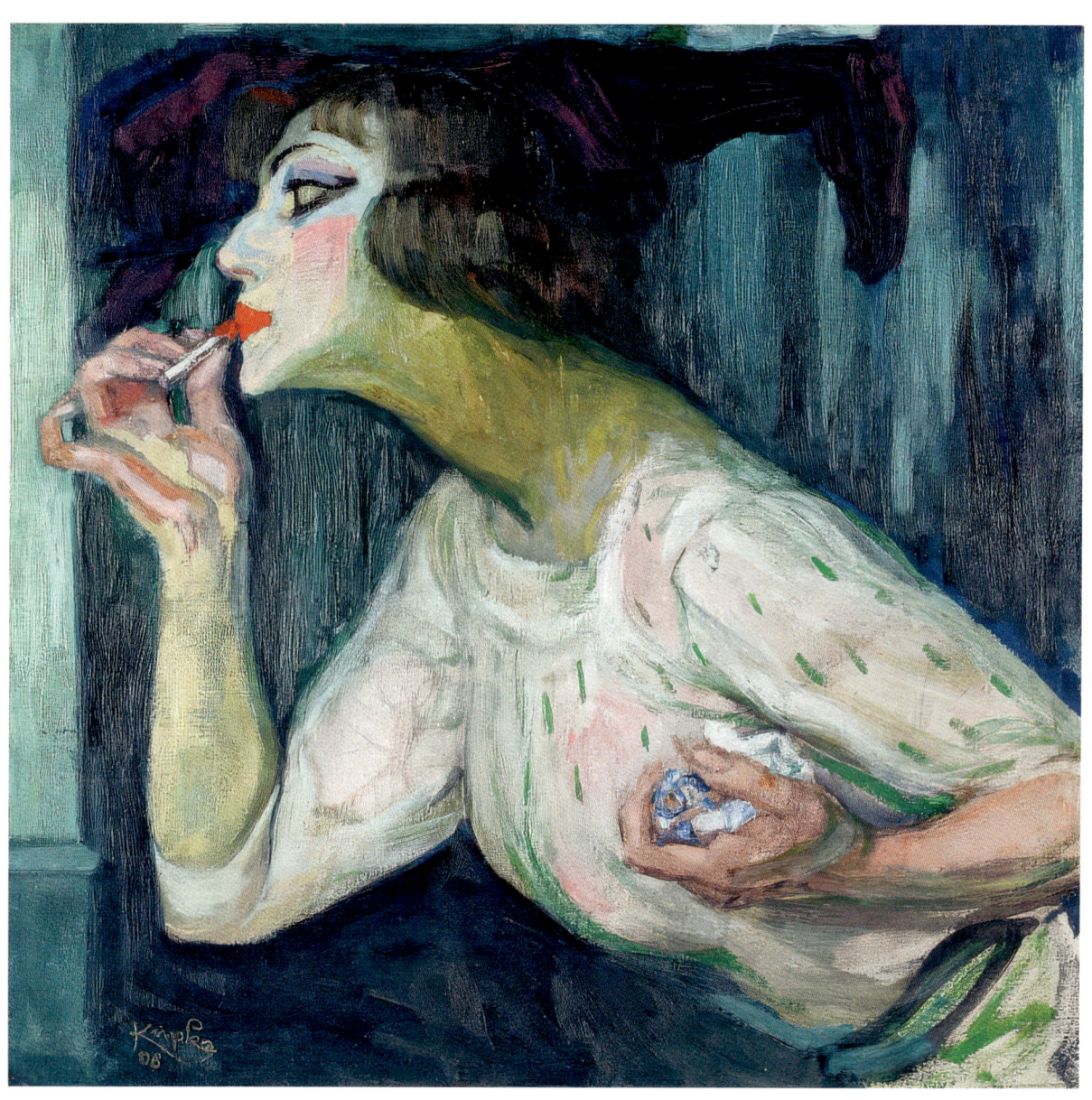

František Kupka *Le Rouge à lèvres* [*Lipstick*] 1908

oil on canvas 63.5 × 63.5 cm gift of Eugénie Kupka, 1963, AM 4167 P

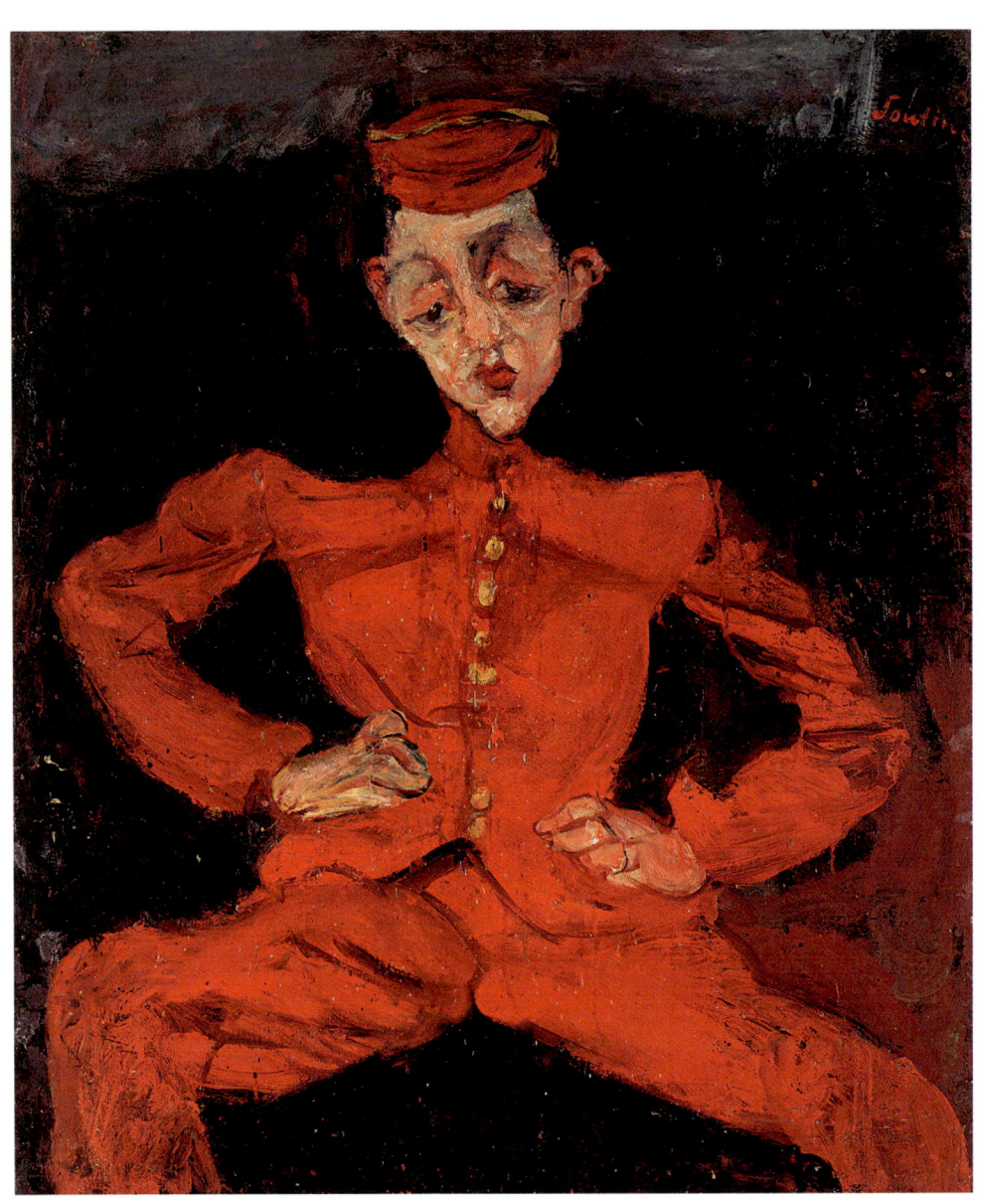

Chaïm Soutine *Le Groom* [*The Bellboy*] [1925]

oil on canvas   98 × 80.5 cm   former collection of Baron Kojiro Matsukata transferred in 1959
to the Musée National d'Art Moderne in application of the 1952 peace treaty with Japan, AM 3611 P

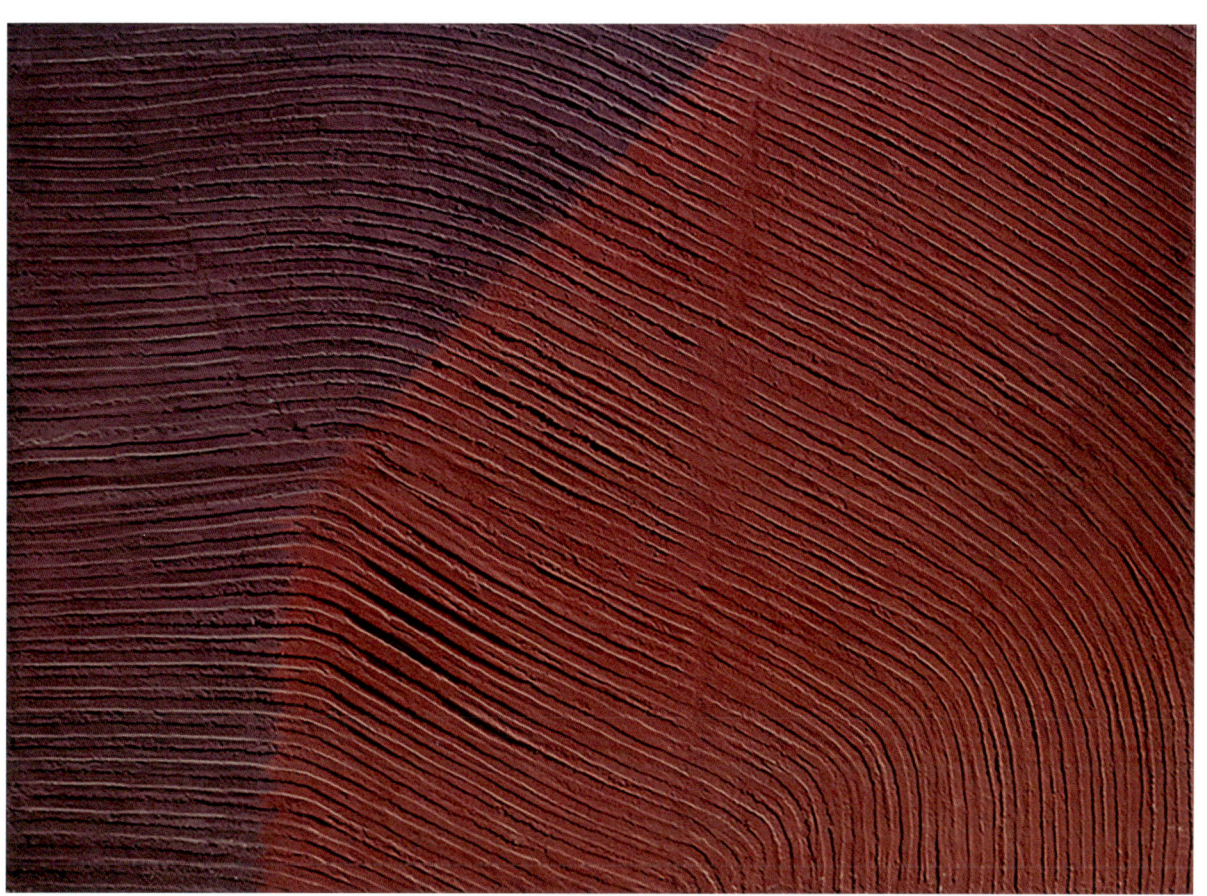

Raoul Ubac   *Grande Terre rouge* [*Large Red Earth*]   1971

amalgamated resins on Isorel   155 × 210.5 cm   dation, 1989, AM 1989-541

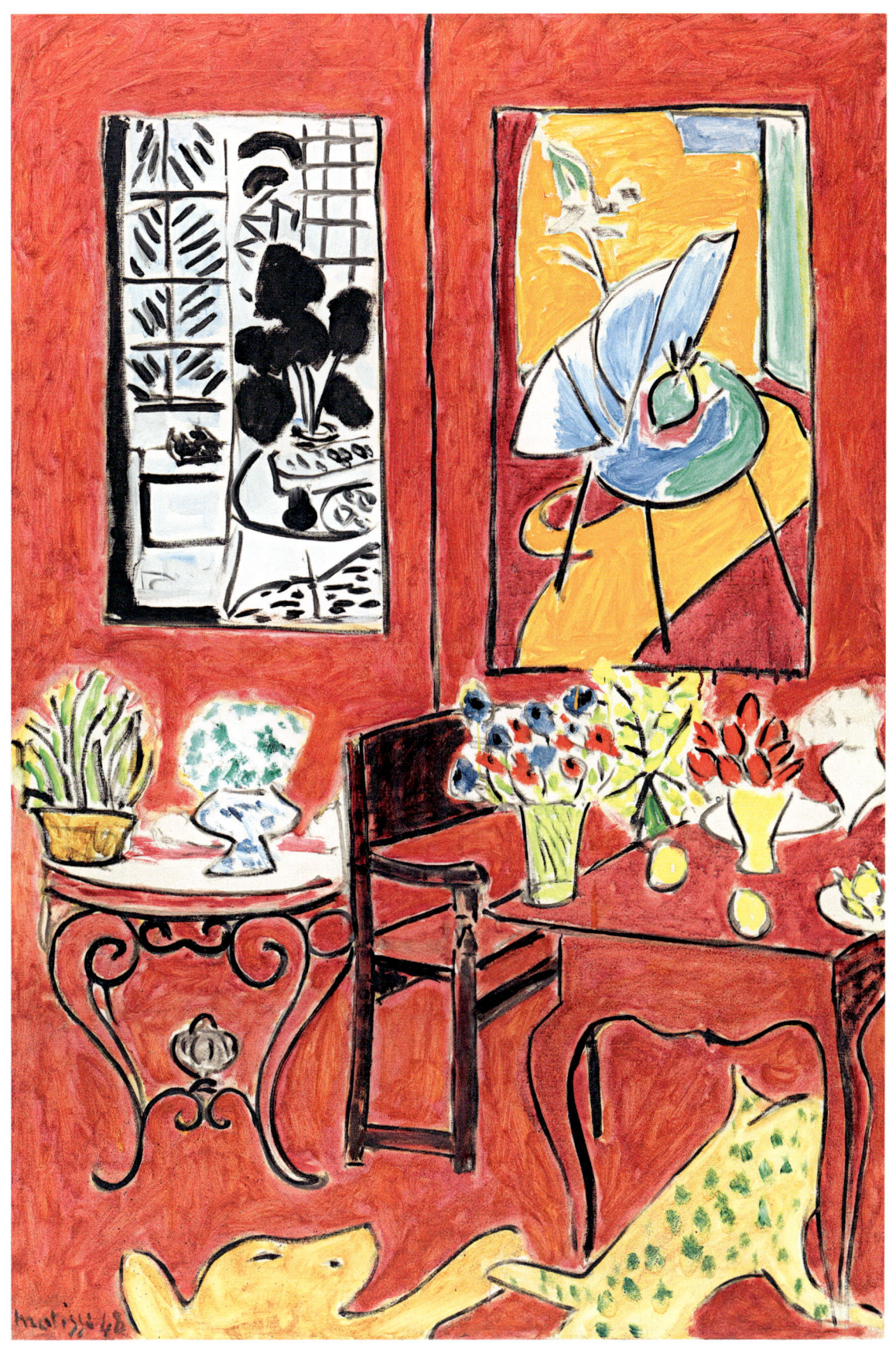

Henri Matisse   *Grand Intérieur rouge* [*Large Red Interior*]   Spring 1948

oil on canvas   146 × 97 cm   purchase by the French State, 1950, attribution, 1950, AM 2964 P

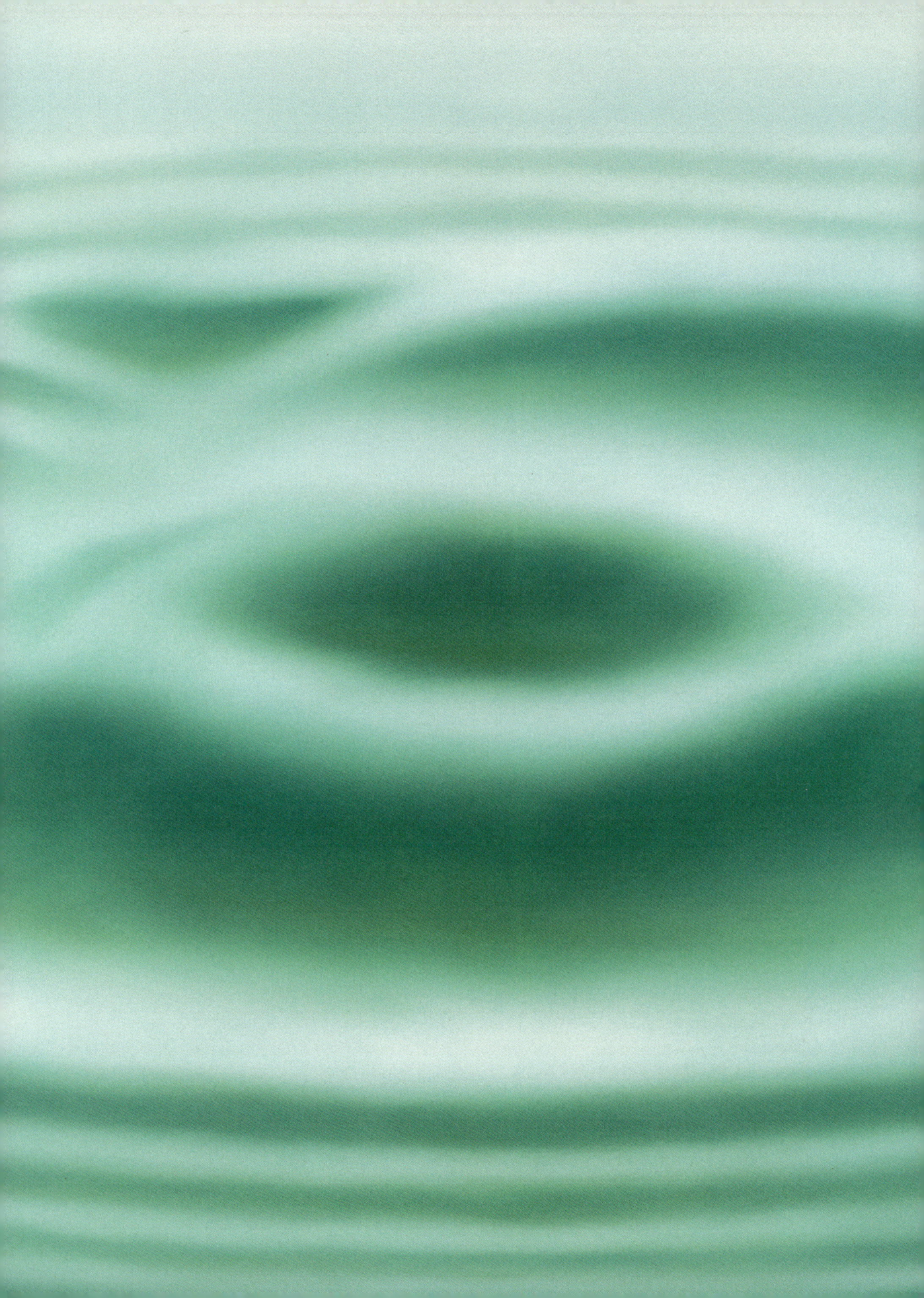

GREEN

GREEN AND MODERNITY

Marie Gispert

"GREEN HAS A WEARISOME EFFECT"

Does green have a place in artistic modernity? Although the question may seem a simple, even provocative, one, it remains relevant – or at least has been so for many artists.

Green was, of course, part of the Fauvists' palette: it was, after all, the "apple-coloured"[1] forehead in the portrait of Henri Matisse's wife[2] that drew the attention of critics at the Salon d'Automne in 1905. The green stripe across her face even gave another of his portraits its title.[3] André Derain, meanwhile, depicted the Thames in a green that is almost fluorescent in his London paintings (fig.1).[4] Here, the choice of green appears to be a rejection of the river's actual colour, a departure from reality in favour of a colour-based composition. But if we start from the idea that art finds its modernity by finding itself, by demonstrating its autonomy as art, by extricating itself from nature to achieve universality or pictorial realism, then the use of green has often been problematic. In works that have become abstract, it obviously tends to evoke nature – plants, foliage or meadows. Indeed, in its analytical phase, Cubism abandoned the greens inherited from Cézanne and that were still being used by Georges Braque. In *On the Spiritual in Art*, Wassily Kandinsky maintains that "green has a wearisome effect (passive effect)", and even that it resembles "a fat, healthy, immovably resting cow, capable only of eternal rumination, while dull, bovine eyes gaze forth vacantly into the world".[5] Piet Mondrian, too, seems to have been a sworn enemy of green, preferring the three primary colours. According to stories related by Michel Seuphor, Mondrian refused to stand in front of the window so as to avoid seeing the trees outside and painted the leaf of the artificial tulip in his studio white in order "to banish entirely from his studio any recollection of the green he found so intolerable".[6] Although the quotation often attributed to the Dutch painter, "green is a useless colour",[7] is probably apocryphal, he did write: "I had come to feel that the colors of nature cannot be reproduced on canvas".[8]

However, we should emphasise the difference between theory and practice. Kandinsky saw green not only as a "tiresome" colour, but also as "the most restful [*ruhigste*] colour in existence",[9] cancelling out the contradictory movements of yellow and blue of which it is composed, "forces which can be reactivated", so that green "has a possibility of movement which is completely lacking in gray".[10] Importantly, green is, in fact, often present in his works, in particularly those of the 1930s. Sometimes, he even made it the focus of a painting: in *Green Emptiness* (1930, fig.2), Kandinsky contrasts a wide expanse of bright sea green with a complementary long rectangle of pink, dividing the

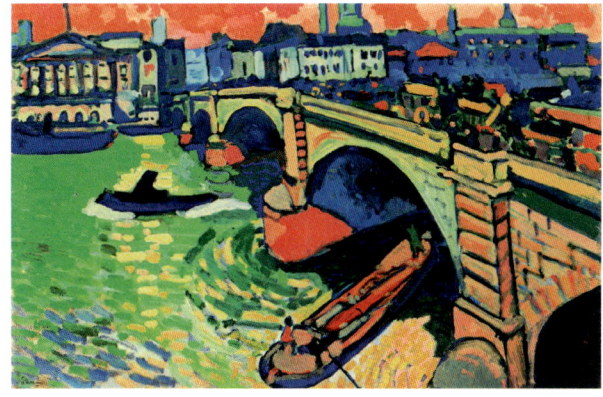

Fig.1 André Derain, *Pont de Londres* [*London Bridge*], 1906, oil on canvas, 66 × 99.1 cm
Museum of Modern Art (MoMA), New York. Gift of Mr. and Mrs. Charles Zadok. 195.1952

canvas into two unequal parts. The green is brought to life both by the shape of a door, or a lighthouse, outlined in red and with sections painted in golden yellow, and by the graphic red and blue symbols that appear in the upper left corner of the composition, the yellow and blue recalling the forces that make up green. During his Parisian period, he employed a detail to construct the rest of the composition – the *deux points verts* that gave their name to a painting in 1935[11] represent only a small part of the whole – or combined mint-green and emerald-green contours to form figures that had become biomorphic.[12] The same was true of some Cubists: while Braque and Picasso opted for shades of brown, ochre and grey to unify form and background, Juan Gris offered still lifes with objects that, though fragmented, have clear contours, and sought to accentuate contrasts between flat areas and reliefs and between unity and fragmentation. In this perspective, green plays a unique role: sometimes in the form of monochrome stripes alternating with and distorting objects,[13] sometimes as an element that disturbs the image by its incongruous use as a surface for the outline of a cafetière, an object in relief or the unexpected colour of a newspaper (*Le Petit Déjeuner* [*The Breakfast*], 1915, fig.3).

In fact, green does exist in artistic modernity. But, if it seems to have received a bad press, few works have been devoted to it,[14] doubtless because it exists *with* other colours rather than having been *chosen*, *preferred* or *isolated* as other colours have been. Josef Albers, it is true, composed many of his 'Homages to the Square' around the colour green (fig.4), but he produced as many in red, orange or yellow; Lucio Fontana certainly slit green canvases,[15] but his 'Spatial Concepts' also include works in white, pink and blue. Yves Klein's book *Yves Peintures* (1954) – a collection of ten rectangles of colour, cut out, mounted on paper and given titles relating them to various cities in which he had lived – includes two green monochromes: a pale green *Yves à Madrid* and a stronger green *Yves à Paris*.[16] He also produced monochrome paintings in different colours between 1954 and 1957, including green ones in various shades and formats.[17] But ultimately, it was a pure and saturated ultramarine – IKB (International Klein Blue) – that was Klein's first choice and to which he added pink and gold to compose his colour trinity.

In fact, considering green as a choice, rather than as simply one of many possibilities, involves a rethinking of our relationship to artistic modernity. Firstly, because the rather secondary role of green in modernity is a West-centric view. We would doubtless be writing a very different history of green if we addressed, for example, the works of Tarsila do Amaral (fig. 5), whose use of green is, rightly, one of the ways of affirming the existence of Brazilian modernism. She wrote: "I have found in Minas the colours I loved when I was a child. I had been taught that they were ugly and crude. Thereafter, I took revenge for this oppression by using them in my paintings: the purest blue, pink-violet, bright yellow, strident green …".[18] A few years later, she maintained: "Our green is primitive".[19] Green is also predominant in Chéri Samba's work, where it has an eminently political significance in the pagne, printed with the outline of Africa, worn by the reclining woman in *Un vieil enfant* [*An Old Child*], which explores the reality of African independence,[20] or in the uniforms of the immigrant street sweepers in *Paris est propre* [*Paris is Clean*] (fig. 6).[21] And although the colour of his last self-portrait, created during the Covid-19 pandemic, relates primarily to the lifting of lockdown[22], the swirling shapes in different shades of green enhanced with glitter, the almost psychedelic-effect background on which the figure of the artist seems to float, could also constitute a sort of signature.

Modernity, then, needs to be reconsidered, precisely because green has often been used as a means to reread history. The most obvious example is probably that of Martial Raysse, whose series 'Made in Japan' began a practice of reimagining the masterpieces of classical painting. Whether reproducing works by Lucas Cranach, Piero del Pollaiuolo or Jean-Auguste-Dominique Ingres, Raysse focused on artists celebrated for their precise design and linear style. He flattened the figures by applying *martialcolor*, which covers the bodies of Apollo,[23] a young Renaissance woman and an odalisque,[24] in a fluorescent green. He also glued onto the canvas elements that both develop and distort the original picture. Although his reason for choosing these particular works remains unclear,

they are united in the use of green, which elicits a smile but also explores a society of image consumption. Although Raysse addressed classical painting, modernity itself and its rejection of green have been revisited by contemporary artists. In the environment he created in 1966 for the exhibition "Kunst Licht Kunst" [Art Light Art] at the Stedelijk Van Abbemuseum in Eindhoven, Dan Flavin crossed two series of green neon lights, creating a barrier that prevented rather than facilitated access to the gallery (fig. 7). The choice of green here was deliberate, as the artist explains: "Green is used throughout because it is a pleasant color at this extent, brilliant as fluorescent light and soft in the total barrier (*sic*)".[25] But the most interesting thing is without doubt the title, which, as is often the case in Flavin's works, includes a dedication: *greens crossing greens (to Piet Mondrian who lacked green)*. While this aligns with the viewer's perception – a green light bathes the room, but the neon tubes appear white – it is also a way of playing on De Stijl's dogma of primary colours. Likewise, Vera Molnár, in *Car je n'aime pas la couleur verte* [*Because I Don't Like the Colour Green*],[26] a collage in the form of a graduated scale of some 40 shades of green, carried out this experiment precisely "because she had learnt in Mondrian's credo that the colour green was horror".[27] The incongruity of green in the Neoplastic artist's work has also been exploited by other contemporary artists. The Canadian collective General Idea created a series of works entitled 'Infe©ted Mondrian' (1994, fig. 8), in which one of the geometric forms in Mondrian's grid has been changed from yellow to green. The associated title suggests that a virus has contaminated the work and drew the attention of contemporary viewers to the rampant AIDS epidemic of the 1990s.

Finally, the choice of green allows us to rethink the relationship between modernity and nature and landscape, and thus to question the supposed autarky of the canvas. Several artists have worked with green in abstract compositions that reject any form of mimetism or direct allusion to nature, while playing on the evocative power of this colour. Helen Frankenthaler accords a special place to green, which she applies using her original soak-stain technique: diluted paint spread like a dye over the blank canvas laid out on the ground. Influenced by the landscapes of 19th-century painters and a natural world that is sometimes beautiful, sometimes sublime and terrifying, she often opted for the horizontal format typical of landscape paintings. However, her greens are never a direct quote from nature, but rather an evocation of it and coloured forms in dialogue with other coloured forms – "landscapes distilled into a chromatic essence", as Hilton Kramer described them.[28] So *Lush Spring*

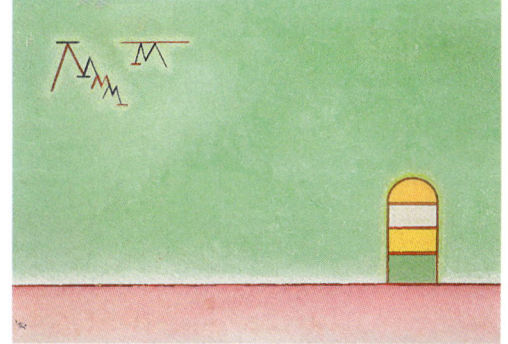

2

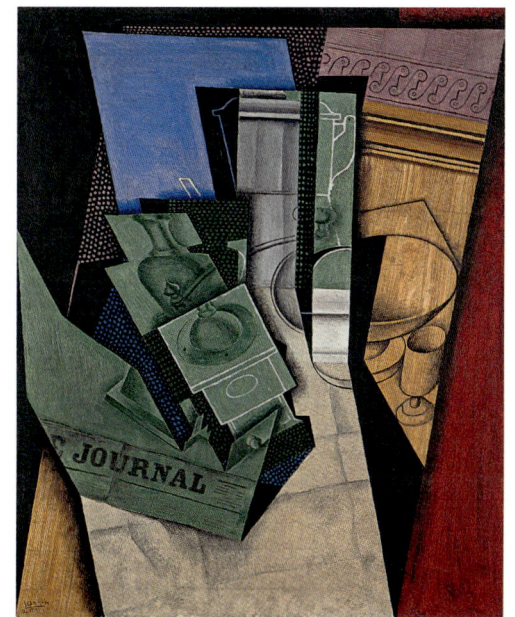

3

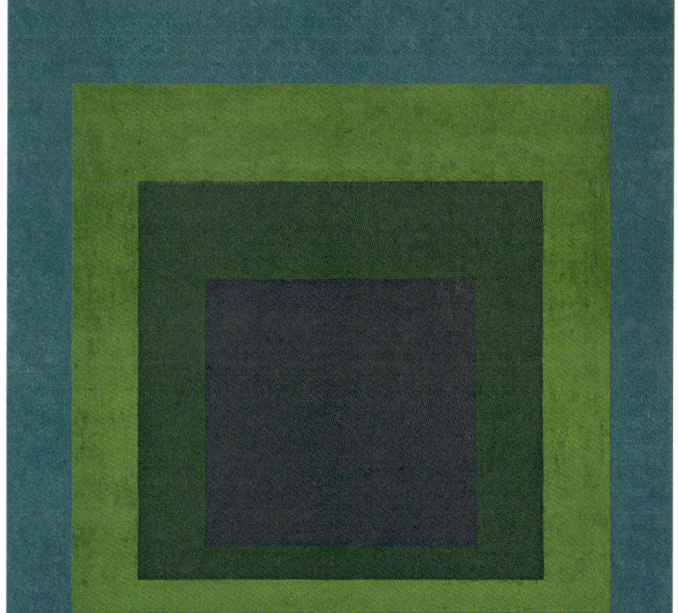

4

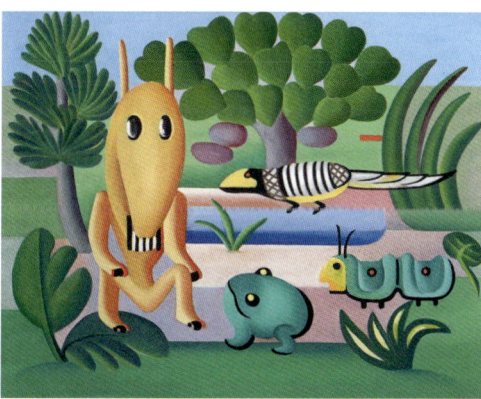

5

Fig. 2 Wassily Kandinsky
Green Emptiness, 1930,
oil on cardboard, 35 × 40 cm
Centre Pompidou – Musée
National d'Art Moderne – Centre
de Création Industrielle, Paris
Bequest of Nina Kandinsky, 1981
AM 81-65-61

Fig. 3 Juan Gris
Le Petit Déjeuner [*The Breakfast*],
October 1915, oil and charcoal
on canvas, 92 × 73 cm
Centre Pompidou – Musée
National d'Art Moderne – Centre
de Création Industrielle, Paris
Purchase, 1974. AM 2678 P

Fig. 4 Josef Albers
*Homage to the Square: Soft
Spoken*, 1969, oil on Masonite,
121.9 × 121.9 cm
The Metropolitan Museum of Art,
New York. Gift of the artist, 1972
1972.40.7

Fig. 5 Tarsila do Amaral
A Cuca, c. February 1924,
oil on canvas, 60.5 × 72.5 cm
Centre national des arts plastiques,
on long-term loan to the Musée
de Grenoble since 1928
Donated by the artist to the
French State, 1926. FNAC 9459

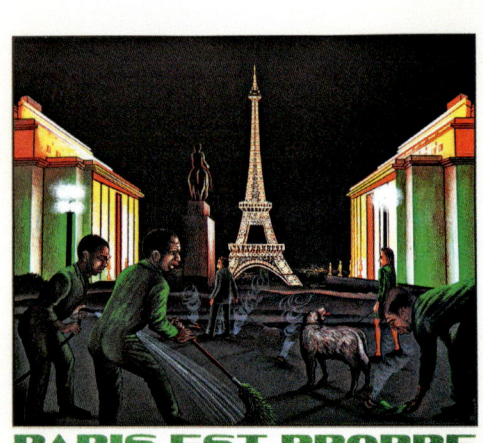

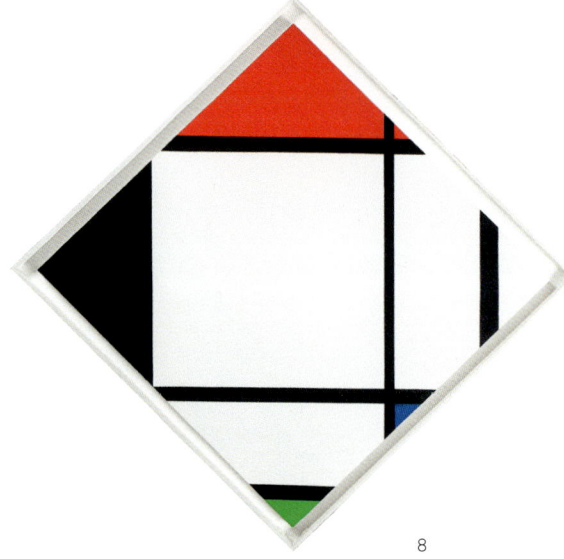

6

8

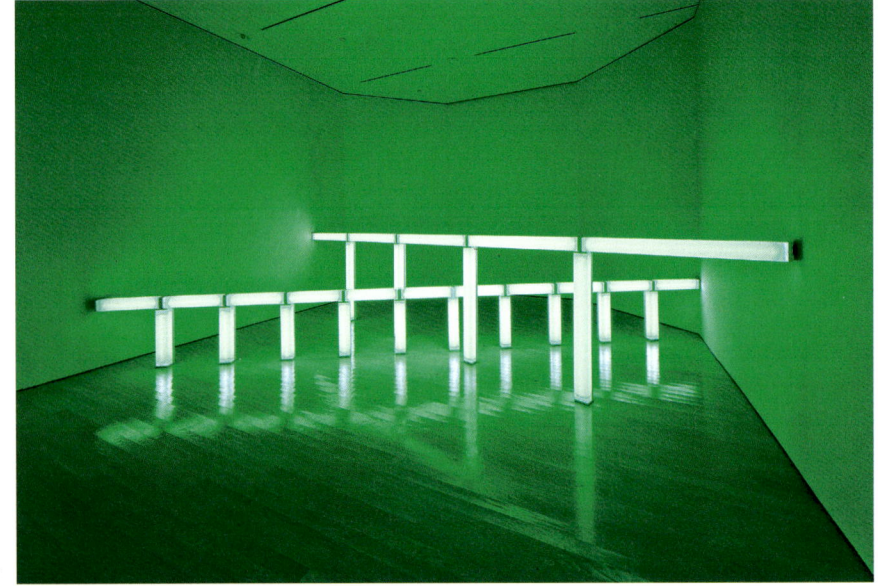

7

Fig. 6 Chéri Samba
Paris est propre [*Paris
Is Clean*], 1989, colour
lithograph, 75 × 55.5 cm
Musée National de l'Histoire
de l'Immigration, Paris. 2006.3.1

Fig. 7 Dan Flavin
*greens crossing greens
(to Piet Mondrian who
lacked green)*, 1966, green
fluorescent lights; first
section 122 × 609.6 cm;
second section: 61 × 670 cm
David Zwirner Gallery
Courtesy of David Zwirner Gallery,
© ADAGP, Paris, 2025

Fig. 8 General Idea
Infe©ted Mondrian #2,
1994, acrylic on cardboard,
119 × 119 × 6.3 cm
Stedelijk Museum, Amsterdam
Acquired with the generous
support of the Mondrian Fund and
the International Collector Circle
and Curator Circle of the Stedelijk
Museum Fund. 2019.1.0033

(1975, fig. 9) portrays nothing of the vernal vegetation of its title but rather presents areas of vibrant shades of green in varying tones on a background that is also tinged with green. A central blue line and an oblong pinkish shape at the top of the painting add contrast. Monochrome itself can also be reinterpreted in green. The paintings created by Brice Marden between 1972 and 1976 and assembled under the title 'Grove Group' are a striking example of this. All were inspired by an olive grove on the Greek island of Hydra, where Marden had stayed. None, however, is a reproduction of a landscape. Rather, these works are the restoration, through memory and colour, of the sensations gathered in this place: surfaces of monochrome colours, sometimes isolated,[29] sometimes placed next to each other in vertical[30] or horizontal[31] bands, in greyish, silvery or bluish greens – the shades that the artist had recorded in his sketchbook. In Marden's own words: "I begin work with some vague color idea; a memory of a space, a color presence, a color I think I have seen".[32] While the choice of monochrome would seem to draw a parallel with Minimalism, his quest for

a certain lyricism and the use of a blend of paint with oil and wax distinguishes it from the latter. The result is a matt surface, dense and opaque, but never flat, that is luminous, capturing the shimmer of the silver leaves of the olive trees. It was also using green that, forty years later, the artist continued his research into colour, surface and media. In his 'Terre verte' [Green Earth] series, he uses terra verde, a pigment derived from glauconite or celadonite, widely used as an undercoat in late medieval Italy, and whose diversity of extractions results in a variety of shades, from a pale yellow-green to a deep olive green. By adding fine layers of terre verte to different works, he brings to the surface what was previously hidden, while gradually darkening each shade. The margin at the bottom of each painting, in the form of a predella, and on which drops and splatters remain visible, is painted in a single layer of each pigment, as evidence of the gradual covering of the canvas, which becomes the very motif of the work. "A color should turn back into itself. It should reveal itself to you while, at the same time, it evades you", wrote Marden.[33] Even green.

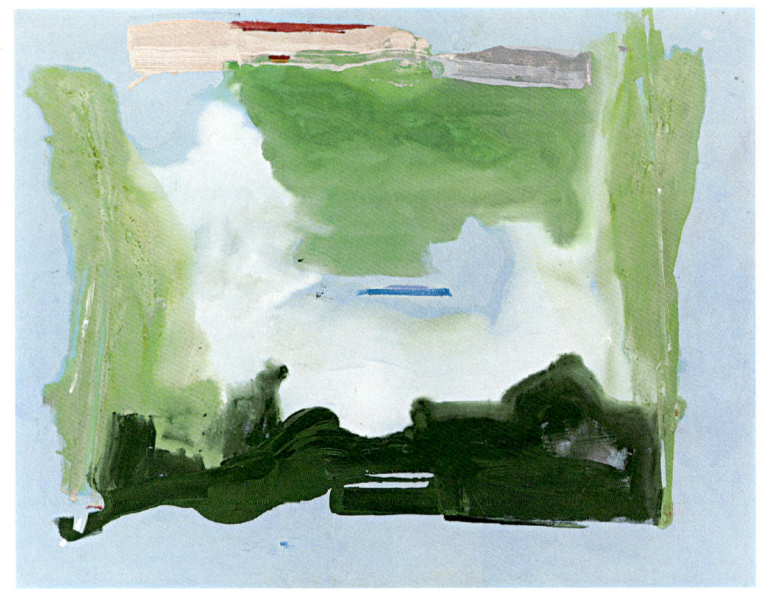

9

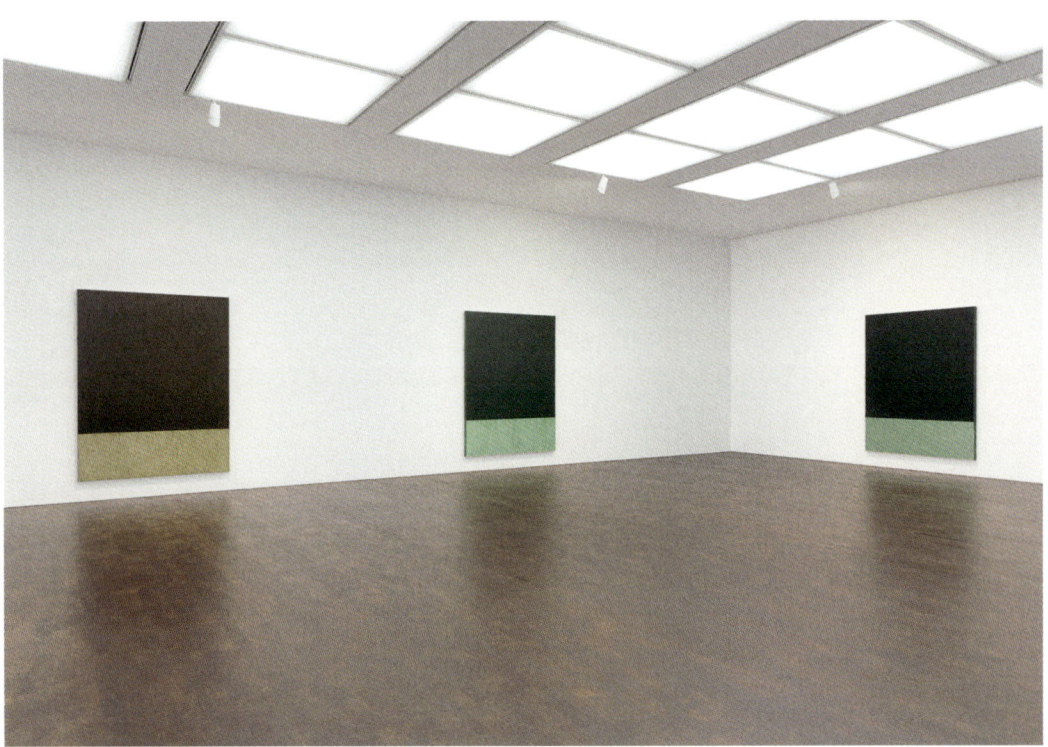

10

Fig. 9 Helen Frankenthaler
Lush Spring, 1975, acrylic
on canvas, 236.2 × 299.7 cm
Phoenix Art Museum, Phoenix
Museum purchase with funds
provided by the National Endowment
for the Arts. 1975.52

Fig. 10 Installation view,
"Brice Marden" 4 October –
22 December 2017
Gagosian Gallery,
Grosvenor Hill, London
© ADAGP, Paris, 2025. Photo:
Mike Bruce, Courtesy Gagosian

1
André Gide, "Promenade au Salon d'Automne", *La Gazette des beaux-arts* (1 December 1905), p.483.

2
Henri Matisse, *La Femme au chapeau* [*Woman with a Hat*], 1905, oil on canvas, 80.6 × 59.7 cm, Museum of Modern Art, San Francisco.

3
Henri Matisse, *La Raie verte* [*The Green Stripe*], 1905, oil on canvas, 40.5 × 32.5 cm, Statens Museum for Kunst (National Gallery of Denmark), Copenhagen.

4
See also André Derain, *La Tamise et le Tower Bridge* [*The Thames and Tower Bridge*], 1907, oil on canvas, 66 × 99 cm, private collection.

5
Wassily Kandinsky, *On the Spiritual in Art* (New York: Guggenheim Foundation, 1946 [1911]), pp.65–66.

6
Michel Seuphor, *Piet Mondrian: Life and Work* (New York: H.N. Abrams, 1955), p.160.

7
The quotation is cited in Michel Pastoureau, *Green: The History of a Color* (Princeton, NJ: Princeton University Press, 2014), p.200, and in Stella Paul, *Chromaphilia: The Story of Colour in Art* (London: Phaidon, 2017), but I was unable to find the exact reference in Mondrian's writings.

8
Piet Mondrian, "Toward the True Vision of Reality", 1941 NANL, autograph copy; printed copies by Valentine Gallery, New York (1941).

9
Wassily Kandinsky, *On the Spiritual in Art*, op.cit., p.65.

10
Ibid., p.63.

11
Wassily Kandinsky, *Deux points verts* [*Two Green Points*], 1935, oil and sand on canvas, 115 × 169.2 cm, Centre Pompidou, Musée National d'Art Moderne, Paris.

12
Wassily Kandinsky, *Figure verte* [*Green Figure*], 1936, oil on canvas, 117.5 × 89.3 cm, Musée d'Art Moderne et Contemporain, Strasbourg, on loan from the Centre Pompidou, Musée National d'Art Moderne, Paris.

13
Juan Gris, *The Guitar*, 1913, oil and collage on canvas, 61 × 50 cm, Centre Pompidou, Musée National d'Art Moderne, Paris.

14
Only one exhibition seems to have been dedicated solely to green: "Green on Green", which was held at Sperone Westwater, New York, from 1 November to 15 December 2001, and featured works by Alighiero Boetti, Nicola De Maria, Dan Flavin, Lucio Fontana, Peter Halley, Howard Hodgkin, Jasper Johns, Ellsworth Kelly, Jonathan Lasker, Frank Moore, Nabil Nahas, Bruce Nauman, Gerhard Richter, Susan Rothenberg, Julian Schnabel, Richard Tuttle, Cy Twombly and Andy Warhol. A catalogue introduced by an essay by Robert Rosenblum was published for the occasion.

15
Lucio Fontana, *Spatial Concept: Expectations*, 1964–65, vinylic paint on canvas, slits, 61.2 × 50.4 cm, Sotheby's, Contemporary Art/Milan, 24 November 2021.

16
Yves Klein, *Yves peintures* (Madrid: Fernando Franco de Sarabia, 1954).

17
See, for example, *Yves Klein, M 77, monochrome vert*, 1957, pure pigment, synthetic resin, primer on canvas glued and nailed onto plywood, 105.3 × 26.8 × 4.7 cm, Centre Pompidou, Musée National d'Art Moderne, Paris. See also *M 124, M 5, M 75* and *M 35*.

18
Tarsila do Amaral, 'Pintura Pau-Brasil e Antropofagia', *RASM – Revista Anual do Salão de Maio*, no.1, São Paulo, quoted in Geaninne Gutiérrez-Guimarães, "Un retour à la tradition. Les œuvres sur papier de Tarsila do Amaral", in *Tarsila do Amaral. Peindre le Brésil moderne*, exh. cat., Paris, Musée du Luxembourg, 9 October 2024 – 2 February 2025; Bilbao, Musée Guggenheim, 21 February – 1 June 2025 (Paris: GrandPalaisRmnÉditions, 2024), p.57. See also Aracy Amaral, *Tarsila. Sua obra e seu tempo* (São Paulo: Editora 34/Edusp, 2003 [1975]), p.149.

19
Ibid., p.297.

20
Chéri Samba, *Un vieil enfant* [*An Old Child*], 2010, acrylic and glitter on canvas, 135 × 200 cm, Henri Seydoux collection.

21
The lithograph features the following text: "Paris est propre/ Grâce à nous les immigrés qui n'aimons pas voir les urines et les crottes des chiens/Sans nous, cette ville serait peut-être la scorie de crottes" ["Paris is clean/Thanks to us immigrants, who don't like to see dog urine and turds/Without us, this city would perhaps just be a dumping ground of turds"].

22
Chéri Samba, *Merci, merci je suis dans la zone verte* [*Thank You, Yes, I'm in the Green Zone*], 2020, acrylic and glitter on canvas, 135 × 200 cm, Jean Pigozzi collection.

23
Martial Raysse, *Conversation printanière* [*Spring Conversation*], 1964, oil, collage and mixed media on canvas and wood panel, 229.5 × 131 × 26.5 cm, Pinault Collection.

24
Martial Raysse, *Made in Japan – La Grande Odalisque*, 1964, acrylic paint, glass, appliqué, synthetic-fibre trim, on photograph mounted on canvas, 130 × 97 cm, Centre Pompidou, Musée National d'Art Moderne, Paris.

25
Dan Flavin, "About 'Greens Crossing Greens' of May 17 1966", signed handwritten statement, 22 September 1966, Kröller-Müller Museum, Otterlo.

26
Vera Molnár, *Because I Don't Like the Colour Green*, 1983, gouache on paper, 38 elements of 57.9 × 48 cm, 1983, Musée des Beaux-Arts de Rouen.

27
"Les variations constructivistes de Vera Molnár. Entretien avec Renaud Faroux", *Art absolument*, no.42 (21 June 2011). On Vera Molnár and green, *see* Isabelle Ewig, "Portrait des artistes concrets en botanistes. Florilège en guise d'introduction", in Isabelle Ewig (ed.), *Art concret + nature = homme vu par une fleur* (Paris: Fage, 2024), pp.9–33.

28
Hilton Kramer, "Art: Lyric Vein in Frankenthaler Paintings", *The New York Times* (15 November 1975), p.21.

29
Brice Marden, *Grove Group I, 1972–73*, oil and wax on canvas, 184.2 × 274.6 cm, Museum of Modern Art, New York.

30
Brice Marden, *Grove Group IV*, 1976, oil and wax on canvas, two panels, 182.9 × 274.3 cm, Solomon R. Guggenheim Museum, New York.

31
Brice Marden, *Grove Group V, 1973–76*, oil and wax on canvas, three panels, 182.9 × 274.6 cm, The Museum of Contemporary Art, Chicago.

32
Brice Marden in Carl Andre, "New in New York: Line Work", *Arts Magazine*, vol.41, no.7 (May 1967), p.50.

33
Brice Marden, "Notes: A Mediterranean Painting", in Marcia Tucker (ed.), *The Structure of Color*, exh. cat., 25 February – 18 April 1971 (New York: Whitney Museum of American Art, 1971), p.20.

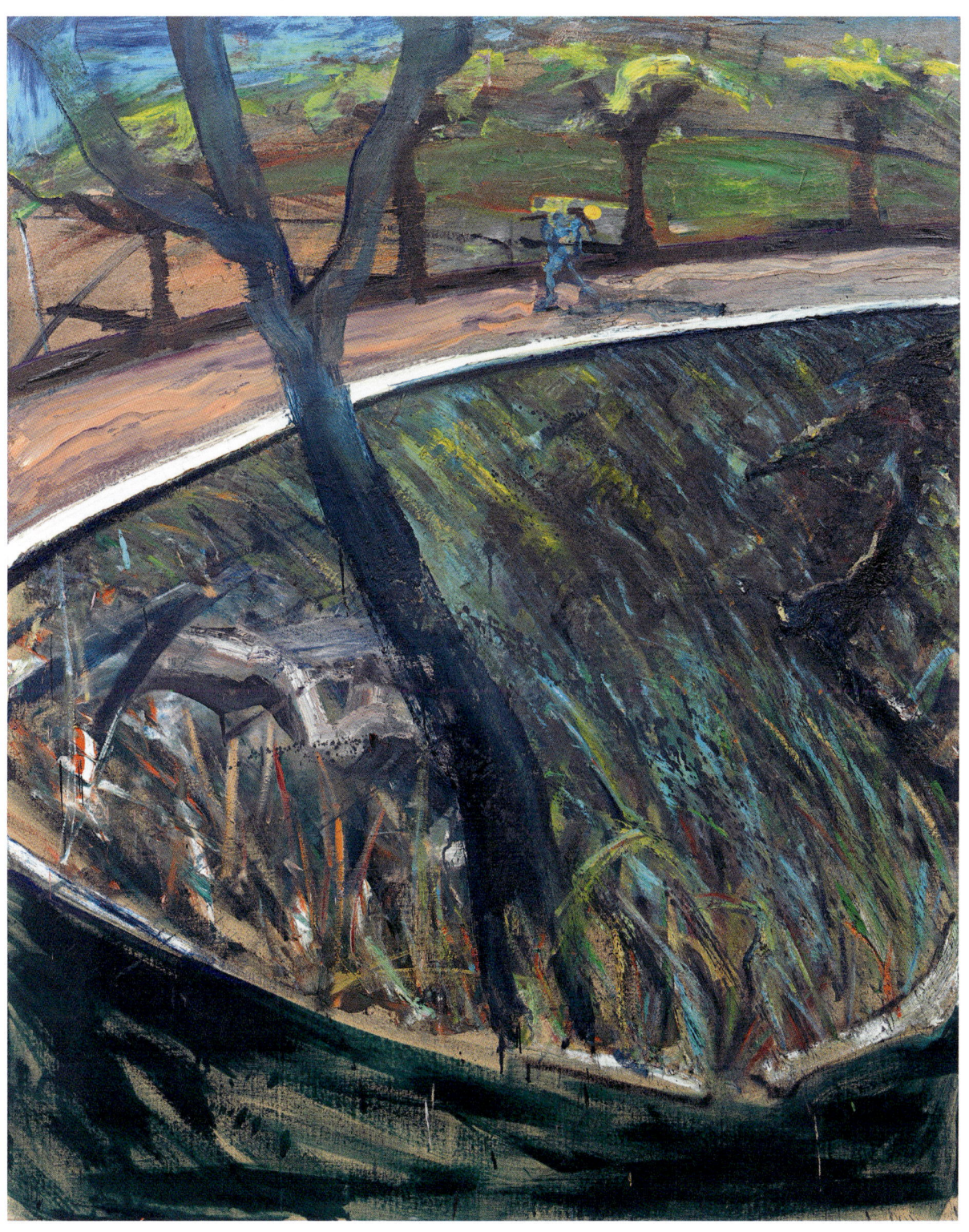

Francis Bacon   *Van Gogh in a Landscape*   [1957]

oil on canvas   153 × 120 cm   purchase, 1982, AM 1982-2

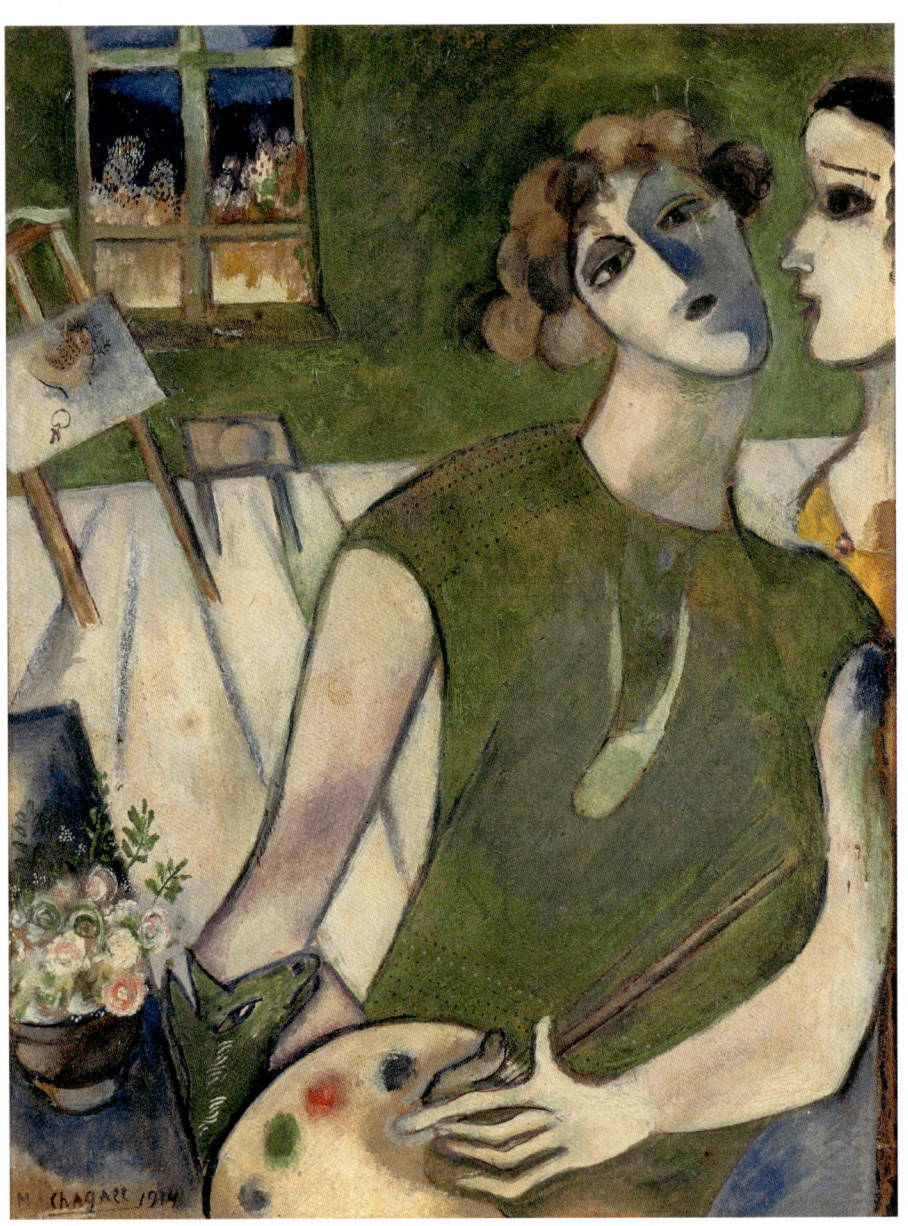

Marc Chagall   *Autoportrait en vert* [*Self-Portrait in Green*]   1914

oil on cardboard mounted on canvas   50.7 × 38 cm   dation, 1988, AM 1988-59

Yves Klein   *M77, Monochrome vert* [*Monochrome Green*]   [1957]

pure pigment, synthetic resin, coating on canvas glued and nailed to plywood   105.3 × 26.8 × 4.7 cm   purchase, 1985, AM 1985-14

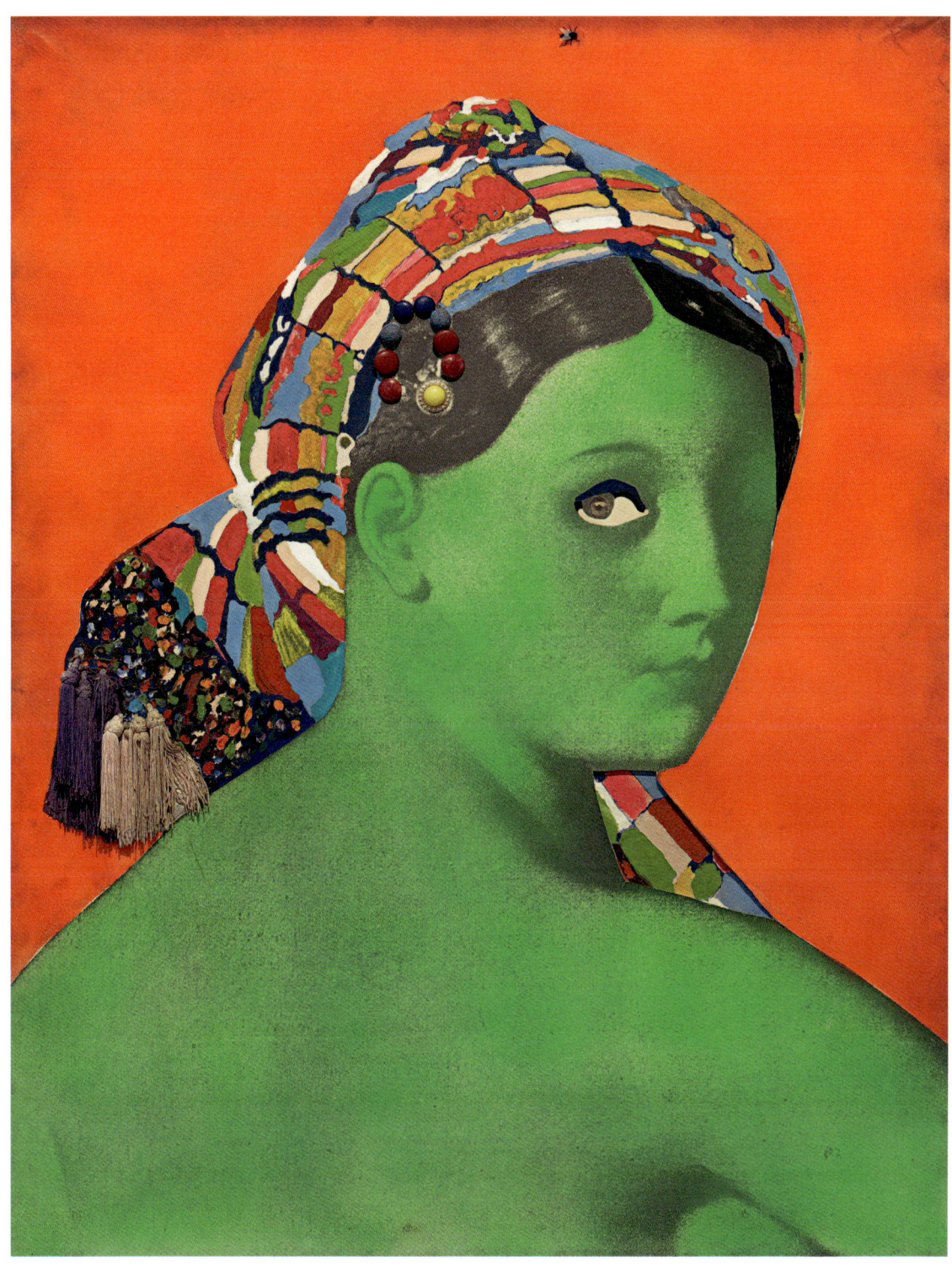

Martial Raysse   *Made in Japan – La Grande Odalisque*   1964

acrylic paint, glass, appliqué (a fly), synthetic-fibre trim, on photograph mounted on canvas   130 × 97 cm   gift of the Scaler Foundation, 1995, AM 1995-213

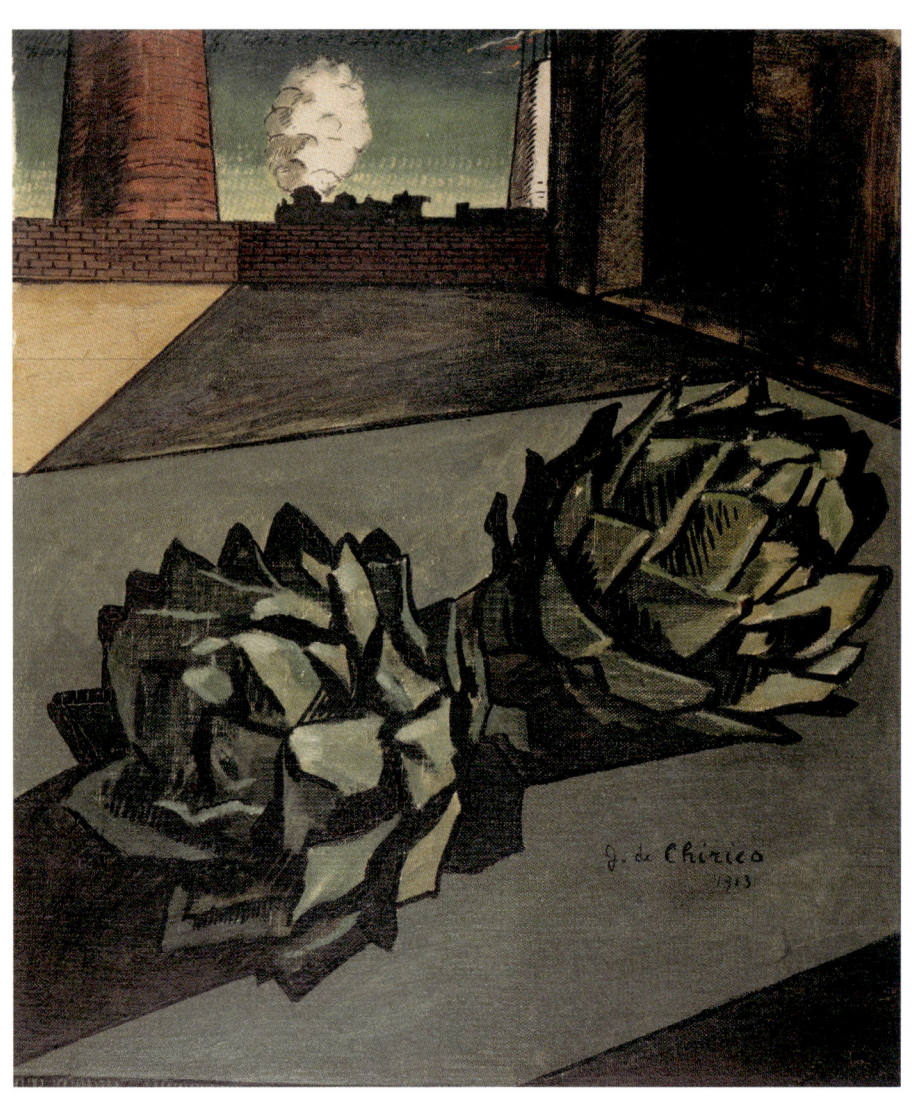

Giorgio De Chirico   *Mélancolie d'un après-midi* [*The Melancholy of an Afternoon*]   1913

oil on canvas   56.7 × 47.5 cm   dation, 1999, AM 1999-24

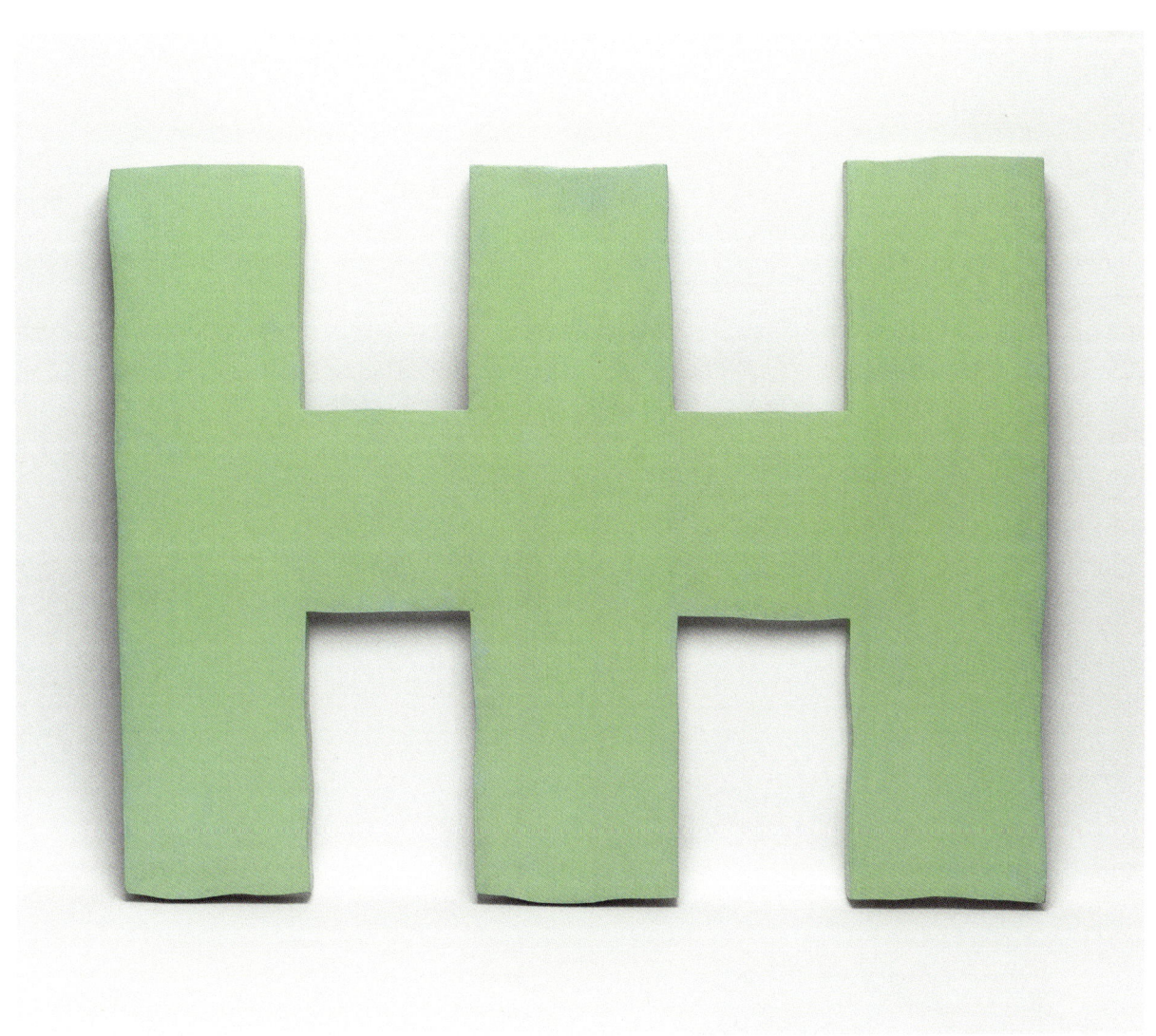

Richard Tuttle *House* 1965

acrylic on wood   68 × 84.5 × 3.5 cm   purchase, 1983, AM 1983-2

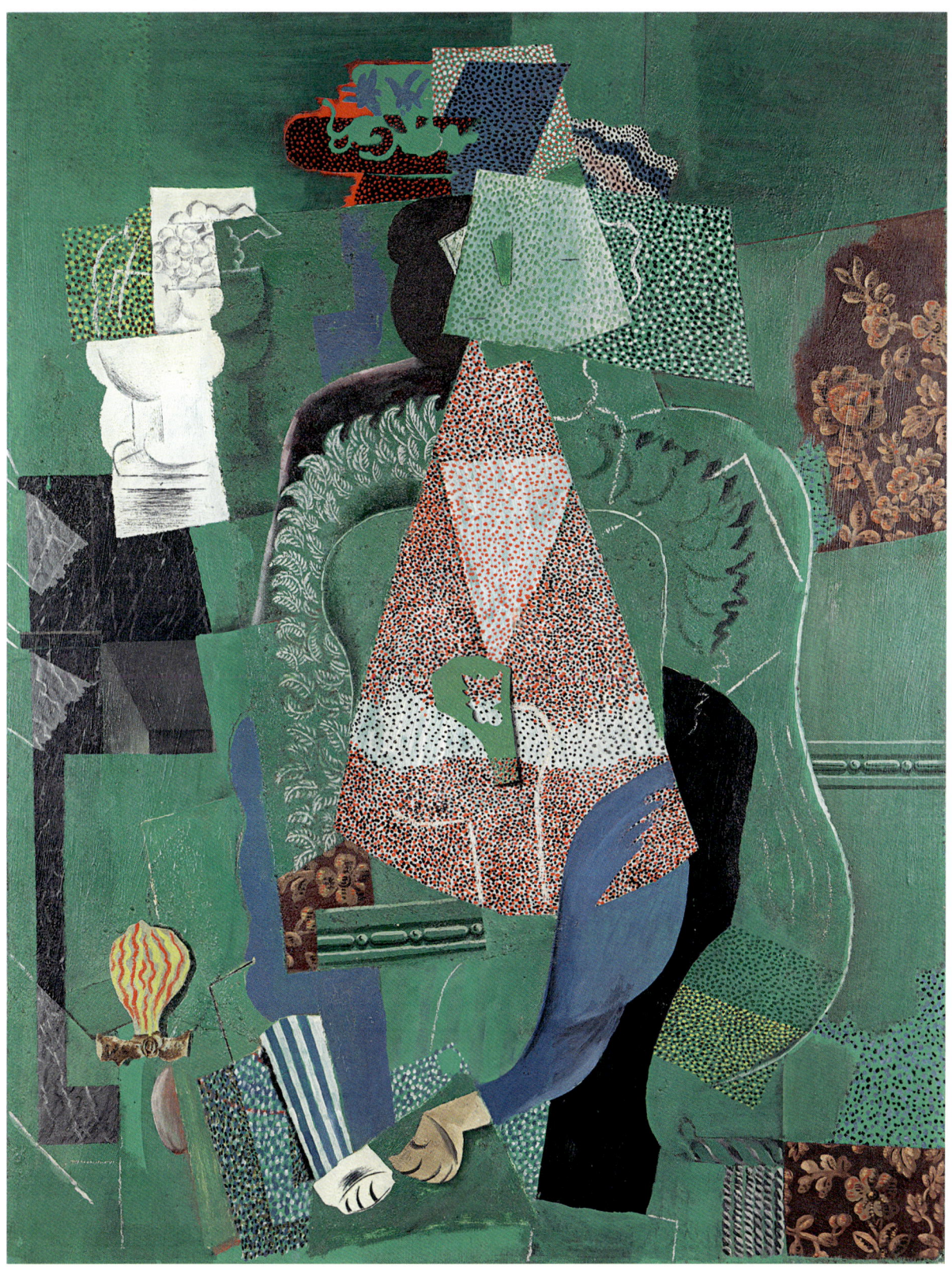

Pablo Picasso   *Portrait de jeune fille* [*Portrait of a Young Girl*]   [July 1914–August 1914]

oil on canvas   130 × 96.5 cm   bequest of Mr. Georges Salles, 1967, AM 4390 P

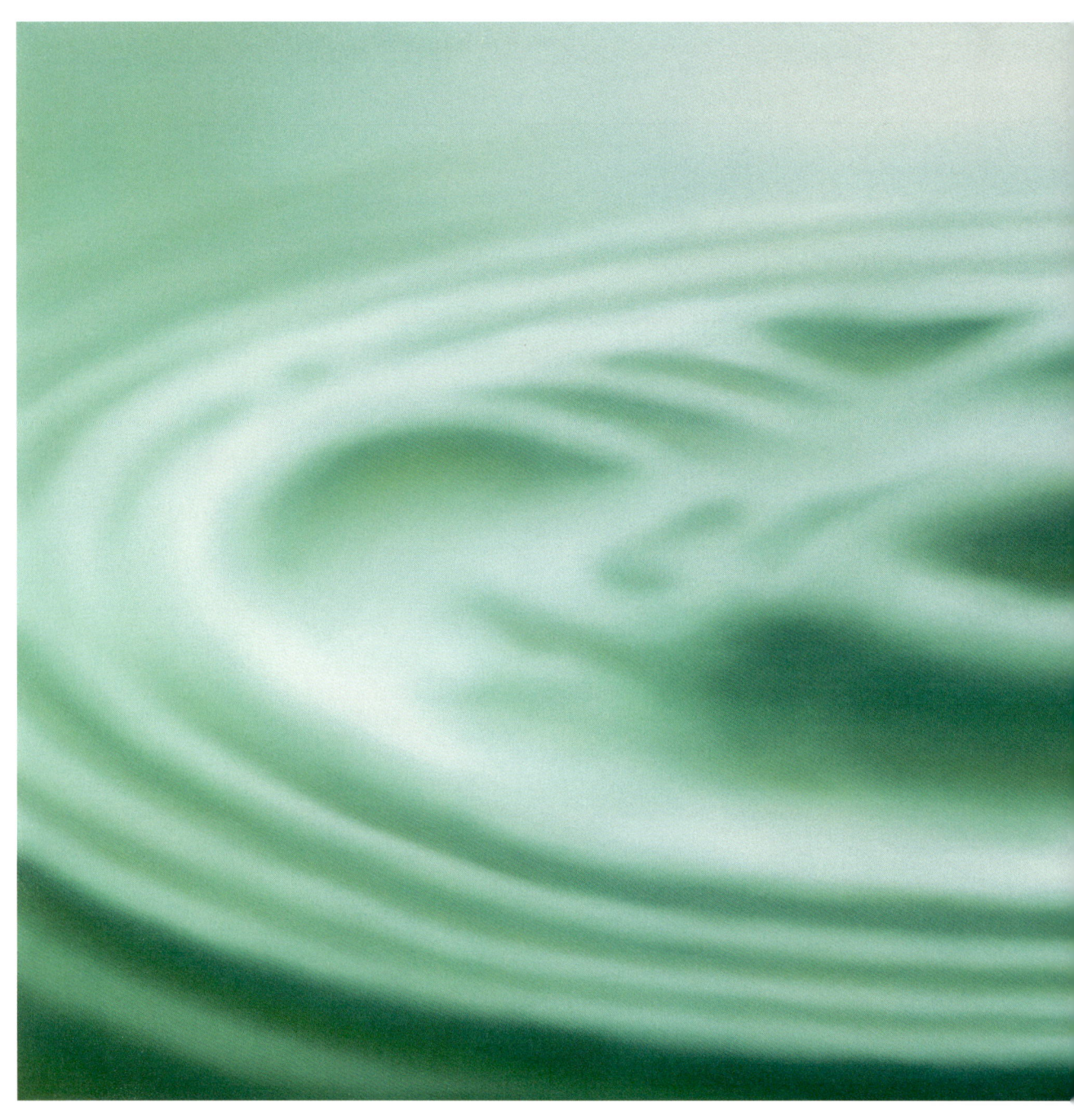

Christophe Vigouroux *Brassé nature (Je sais ce que je mange)* [*Plain Brew (I Know What I Eat)*] 1995

oil on canvas   100.5 × 200.5 × 2.6 cm   purchase, 1996, AM 1996-404

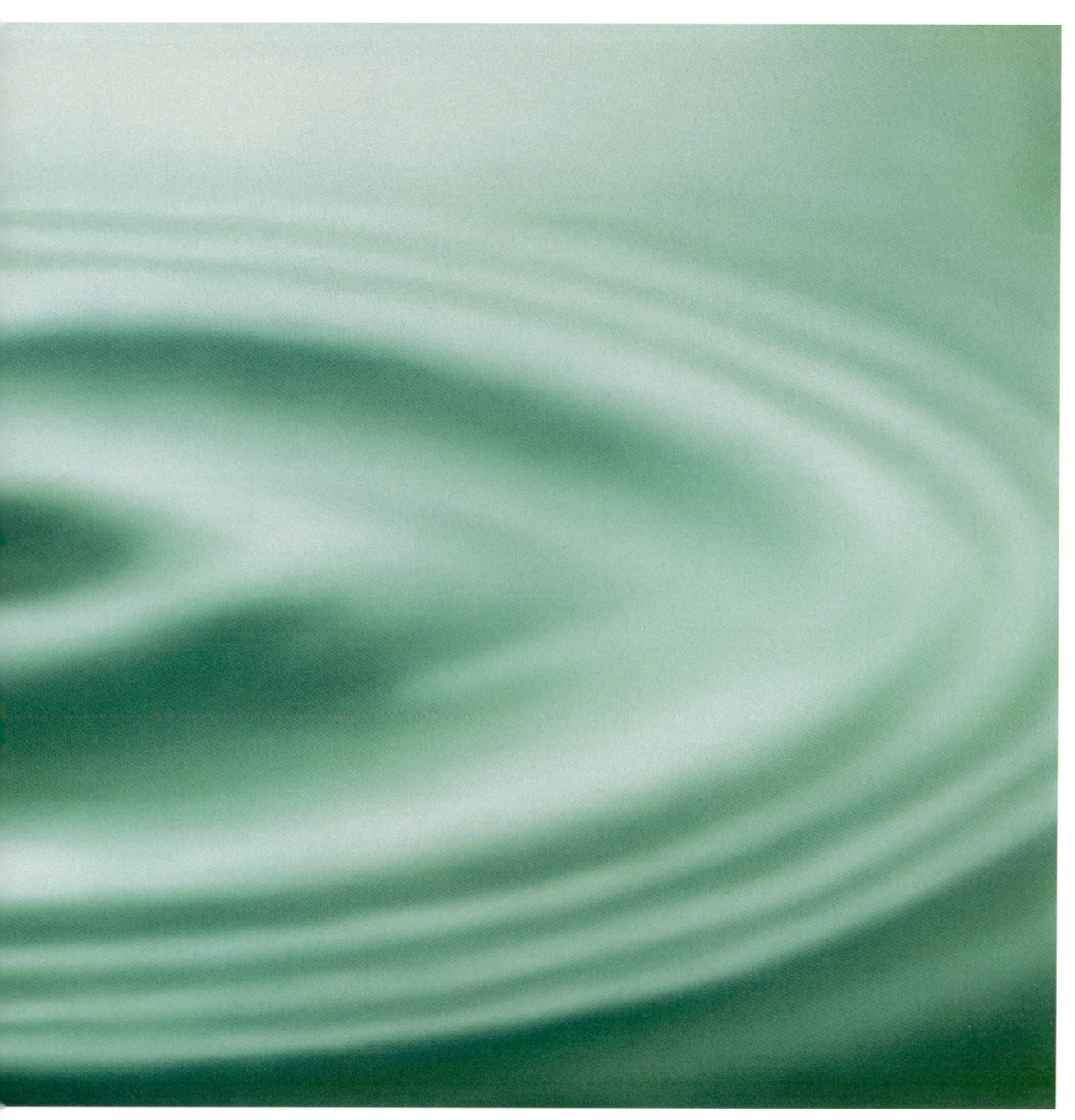

Jean-Michel Sanejouand   *Charge-Objet*   1964

vinyl paint, plastic, ping-pong net   162 × 130 cm   purchase, 1988, AM 1988-582

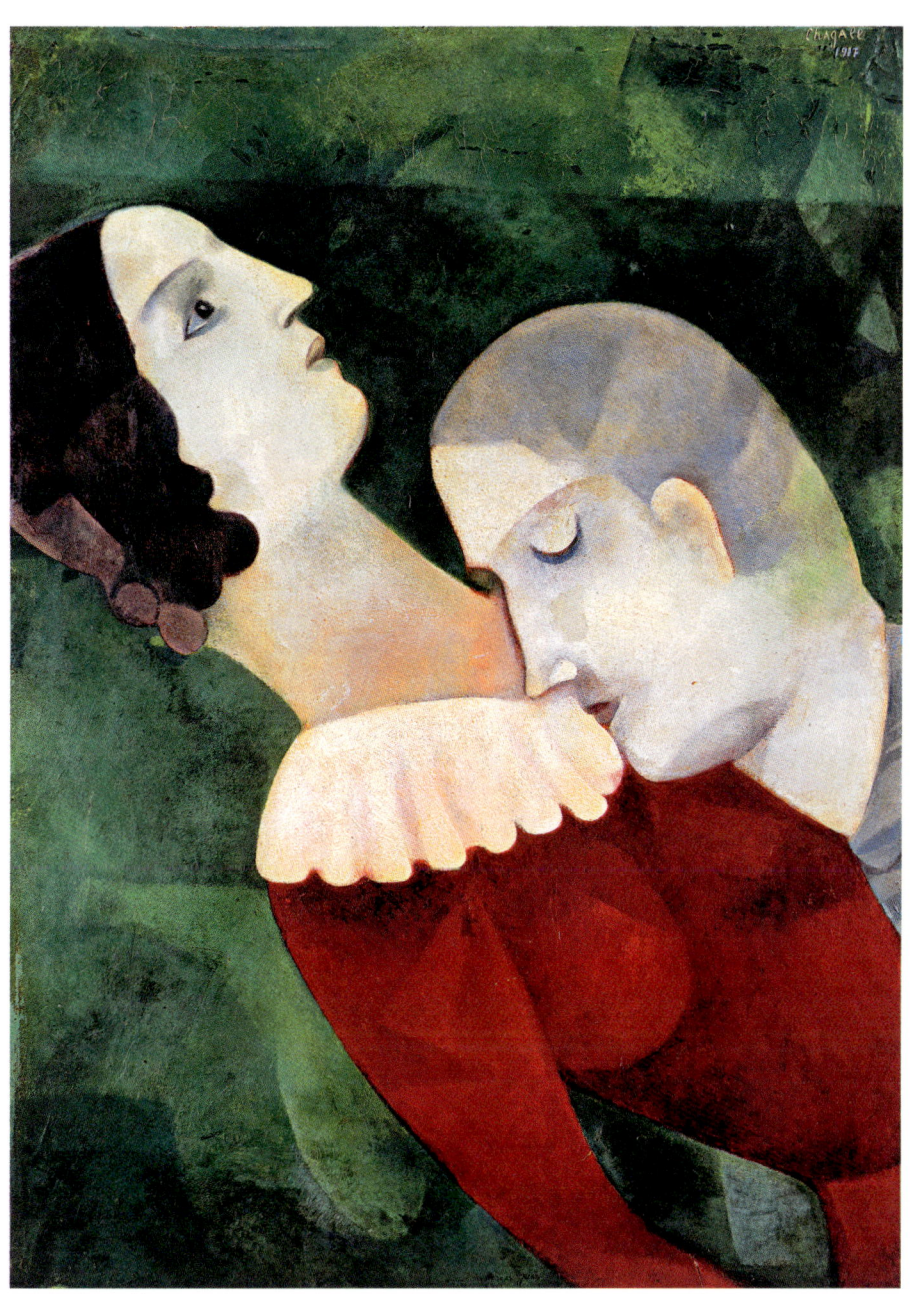

Marc Chagall *Les Amoureux en vert* [*Lovers in Green*] 1916–17

oil on cardboard mounted on canvas   69.7 × 49.5 cm   dation, 1988, AM 1988-60

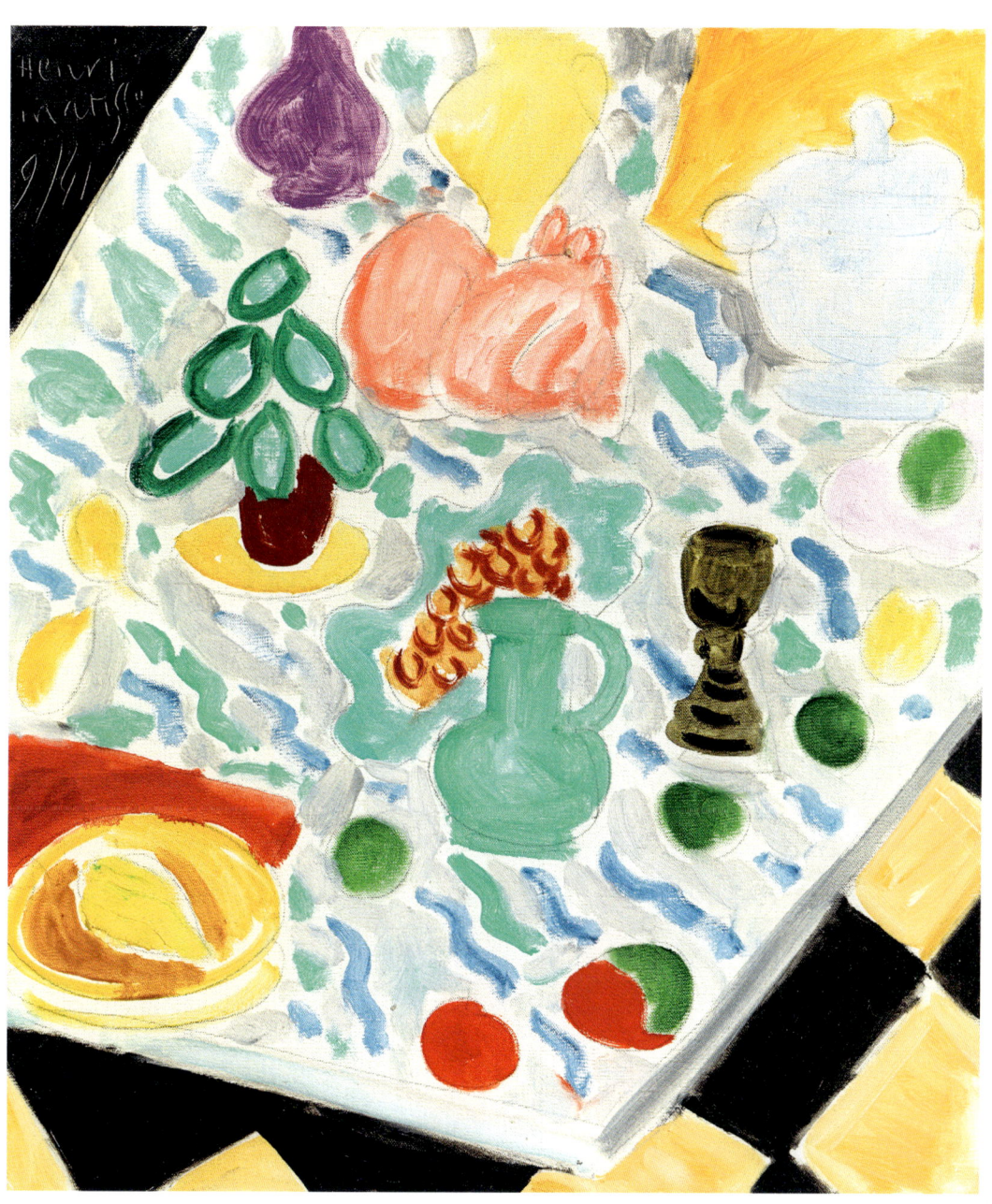

Henri Matisse   *Nature morte à la table de marbre vert*
[*Still Life with a Green Marble Table*]   September 1941

oil on canvas   46 × 38.5 cm   purchase, 1945, AM 2591 P

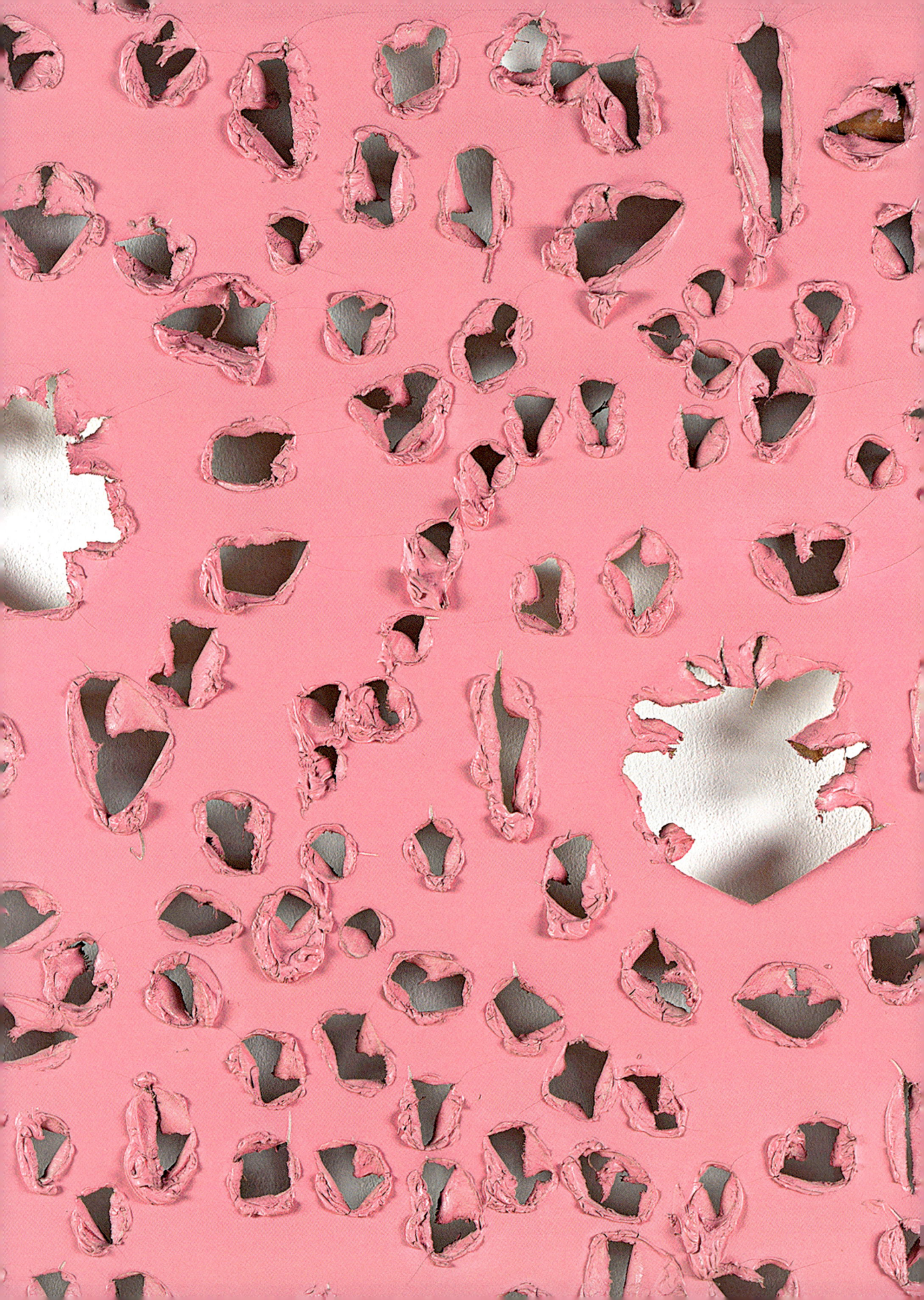

PINK

THE PHYSICALITY OF PINK

Hayley Edwards-Dujardin

THE GENDER OF PINK

"Pink is feminine. It represents love and self-acceptance".[1] We could almost resent Louise Bourgeois for describing pink in this way and so perpetuating the gendered and stereotypical appraisal that accompanies this colour. It was when Rococo painting was flourishing that pink – used extensively by artists to depict clothing, flesh and emotions – was finally given a name. In the lead up to the French Revolution, however, the Rococo style was disapproved of, derided by its detractors, including Denis Diderot, who criticised it harshly as a "frivolous, ridiculous and feminine genre",[2] in contrast to Neoclassicism. From then on, "the rococo [was] associated with an innately feminine smallness of mind and love of adornment and artificiality and also with a feminized, arriviste aristocracy, both of which are markers of inferiority and the decline of French culture".[3] A mix of red and white, considered as a "half colour",[4] pink is consequently subject to the same pejorative labels that limit it to the 'feminine', a phenomenon exacerbated by the clothing chromophobia that accompanied the evolution of menswear in the 19th century, when colour became "the property of some 'foreign' body – usually the feminine, the oriental, the primitive, the infantile, the vulgar, the queer or the pathological".[5] Polychromy became the domain solely of women, who, according to Charles Blanc, "governed by their emotions, attach more importance to colour than we [men] do".[6] In the late 19th century, Claude Monet's skies streaked with pink clouds (*Soleil couchant sur la Seine à Lavacourt, effet d'hiver* [*Sunset on the Seine at Lavacourt, Winter Effect*], 1880) was similarly condemned, when Camille Mauclair described Impressionism as "very feminine art".[7] In his Futurist manifesto, Carlo Carrà was no more accommodating: "The concept of the harmony of colours, a typically French concept, which inevitably limits them to the lightsome, to the style of Watteau, and in consequence to an excess of sky blue, light green, pale mauve and pink. We have already stated several times how much we deplore this tendency towards the feminine, the gentle, the tender".[8] Some women artists made an asset of these gendered affectations of art. One such was Marie Laurencin, whose paintings favour idealised feminine figures, treated in light pastel tones, that convey an alternative reality from which men are excluded. Long ignored by a feminist art theory, which dismissed her gender-essentialist aesthetic, Marie Laurencin nevertheless created an assertive female gaze, affirming lesbian desire. Artist Gerda Wegener views her transgender partner, Lili Elbe (*Lily*, 1922, fig. 1) with a similar eye, in a portrait that clothes her in pink, from her painted nails to her rouged cheeks, via her flapper dress

and bracelets. By having her pose in front of a table that seems to borrow its shapes from Cubism, she portrays Lili Elbe as a modern woman, a woman of her time, dismissing the backward clichés associated with the pink that inundates her painting. While pink is specifically feminine, it has served the visual language of certain feminist activists, who have clearly and subversively reappropriated the colour; artists like Guerrilla Girls, who, in 1986, sent written notes to various art collectors (*Dearest Art Collector*, fig. 2). Writing on candy-pink paper in a deliberately naive cursive script, the members of the collective challenged their recipients on the absence of women artists in their collections. Using the immediate and familiar style of advertising, the Guerrilla Girls created a paradoxical work whose sarcastic rhetoric contrasts with its sugary-sweet iconography. The use of pink and its attributions supports contemporary artists' reflections on gender identity and the re-evaluation of heteronormative features of self-representation. It is this pink that Urs Lüthi convokes in his video installation *Shame* (2020). Like a culmination of the work he began in the 1970s, in which he questions his identity through self-portraiture and cross-dressing, the video depicts him as an old man, bald and with a doleful expression, while a pink veil settles over his face, as though it were reddening in distress – a very feminine blushing intensified by Rococo artists, who would apply it to their female figures like "a substitute for the genital organs that could not be represented".[9] What is this confusion the artist is feeling? That of ageing? Of arousal? Or, possibly, of daring to betray an emotion contrary to masculine symbolism. In revealing himself in this way, Urs is entering a world long forbidden to men, for "the association of painting, of the woman, of flesh, of emotion and of sexuality forms a significant chain".[10]

OF FLESH AND BLOOD

While female nudes populate the history of Western art, pink is closely linked to the colour of flesh, and "he who has acquired the feeling of flesh, has taken a great step; the rest is nothing in comparison".[11] Pink not having been named as such until the 18th century, the word '*incarnato*' was used from the end of the Quattrocento to designate flesh tones, or, more precisely, the blood that flows under the skin, giving it a pinkish appearance: "How I love you in that dress that reveals you so well".[12] Whereas Peter Paul Rubens created voluptuous, sublimely imperfect flesh and Auguste Renoir painted radiant nudes that acknowledge their classical heritage, contemporary art seeks the truth of raw flesh. Such is the case with Jenny Saville's monumental nudes (*Strategy*, 1994), which subvert the prescribed canons of feminine beauty and challenge the tyranny of masculine desire. It is difficult not to grasp Francis Bacon's pictorial vocabulary in the violence of his images. *Study of the Human Body* (1981–82) carves up the human form, reducing it to a grotesque fragment of a man (identifiable by his phallus) in movement. Francis Bacon captures flesh at its most erotic and crude, admitting: "It's true, I love reds, blues, yellows, the fat of the meat. We're meat, aren't we? When I go to the butcher's, I'm always surprised not to be there, where the pieces of meat are".[13] Is it this skinned and soft flesh that Louise Bourgeois alludes to in her double-jointed, pink-fabric doll (*Arched Figure*, 1999), which is reminiscent of Hans Bellmer's work? This use of pink as a skin tone poses the problem of a monolithic perspective of skin colour that relates only to white people, however. It is this visual and linguistic conflict that Carrie Mae Weems explores in her series 'Untitled (Colored People Grid)' and more specifically, with her *Magenta Colored Girl* (1987), which is part of this series (fig. 3). By colouring the photograph of an African American teenager in pink, she plays on the absurd vocabulary designating African Americans and challenges the very signification of colour.

Reduced to pink, flesh is now no more than a plastic motif, yet its symbolic significance remains undiminished, as is evidenced by Henri Matisse's *Nu rose assis* [*Seated Pink Nude*] (1935–36), and his concise female body outlined in black, emerging in a rapidly brushed pink background. In their conquest of the spatial environment, the monochromes of abstract art dialogue timidly with pink, like "Yves Klein's 'Monopinks' (1956–62), the 'momentary state' of the flesh",[14] or Lucio Fontana's gashed canvas (*Spatial Concept, Expectations*, 1958). Despite Fontana's claim that he wanted to "use the colour pink, that bright pink of fashion, or else black, but [that] the colour was not important",[15] it is difficult to resist the desire to see a metaphor of the vulva in this slit painting, for pink flesh is a clear reference to eroticism at its most performative. Is this not what Marcel Duchamp was revealing in cross-dressing as Rrose Sélavy? Robert Morris, who had exhibited his own naked body in 1962, stretched physical investigation and material with his spontaneous and malleable felt sculptures: epidermal shreds that are paradoxically more carnal than a figurative nude (*Untitled [Pink Felt]*, 1970). In Alina Szapocznikow's work, sensuality is mixed with unease. Her resin sculpture-lamps dismember the human body, retaining from it only sexual signs, as with her lampstand shaped like a veined pink phallus, topped by a fragile shell enclosing a scarlet mouth (*Sculpture-Lamp XIII*, c. 1970). Monster-objects at the service of catharsis. Marlene Dumas, too, invokes the mouth (*Lips*, 2018): close-up lips, bitten, moist and coloured bright pink. Borrowing from the Pop Art repertoire, she trades objectification for sexual bliss. While make-up helps dramatise femininity, it also creates shifts towards masculinity through the transvestism evoked by Andy Warhol's 'Marilyns' (1967, fig. 4), excessively made-up paragons of a stereotypical hyperfemininity reappropriated by drag-queens in a camp style, the essence of which "is its love of the unnatural: of artifice and exaggeration"[16] and reconciles the masculine and the feminine by demolishing their narrow-minded boundaries. Cindy Sherman uses her own body to explore the polymorphic nature of femininity. Her use of cross-dressing reveals the masquerade of our social norms.

AN ARTIFICIAL PINK

The 19th century produced magenta – a shockingly artificial, even gaudy, bright pink – which is reflected in the *Madame de Pompadour née Poisson (1721-1764)* soup tureen (1990, fig. 5), part of Cindy Sherman's 'History Portraits/Old Masters' series. The work relegates the affected and grotesque marchioness to the status of an object, a brightly coloured porcelain piece offering "a self-critique of the responsibility women bear for their own fetishisation".[17] The pink of the porcelain is enough to suggest womanhood, or at least decorative femininity – an analysis that Portia Munson developed with her *Pink Project* (1994–2016), a scientific archiving of pink objects (toys, sex toys, accessories, etc.), the accumulation of which lays out a cosmetic lexicon of femininity reduced to the status of merchandise. *Her Coffin* (2016), with its Plexiglas coffin packed with pink objects, invites fresh questions: what is the health and environmental impact of this pink plastic? Christo and Jeanne-Claude had already used a chemical pink in *Surrounded Islands* (1980–83), eleven islands encircled with polypropylene in Biscayne Bay, Miami. Involving brazen human intervention, the installation exploits the artificiality of pink as a warning. Along the same lines, Judy Chicago created *Atmospheres* (1968–74), a spatial performance in the form of pyrotechnical clouds, created in response to a California arts scene she considered to be chauvinistic and destructive. Judy Chicago's vaporous land art is ephemeral and volatile. Respectful of nature, it places feminism back at the heart of ecological issues and concerns. Pablo Picasso, for his part, invites nostalgia and melancholy into his pink- and ochre-tinted paintings with reticence, as if to convey the anxieties of human experience. We want to see the light-hearted life of a street performer here, but it is the harshness of a precarious and nomadic existence that we discern in the angular, sharp bodies, the gloomy expressions

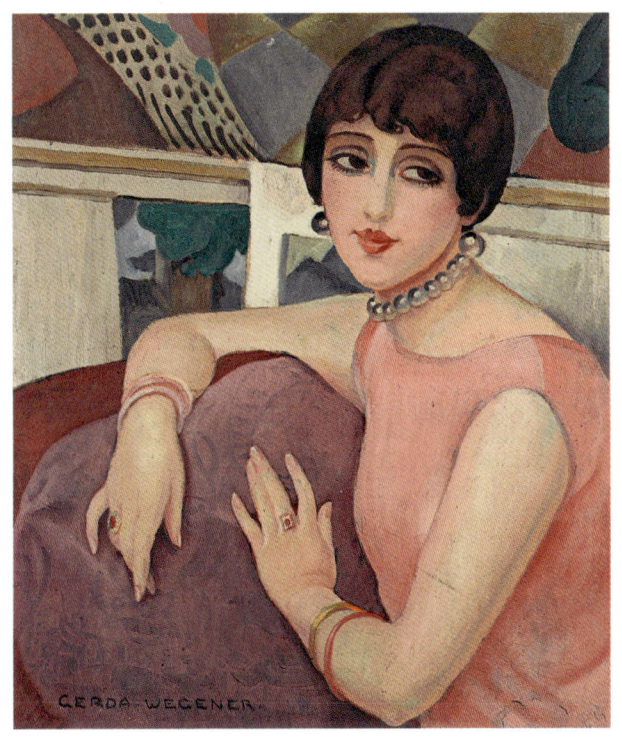

1

Fig. 1 Gerda Wegener
Lily, 1922, oil on canvas,
73.2 × 60 cm
Centre Pompidou – Musée
National d'Art Moderne – Centre
de Création Industrielle. Purchase
of the French State, 1927. JP 445 P

Fig. 2 Guerrilla Girls
Dearest Art Collector, 1986,
from *Guerrilla Girls Talk Back*,
Screenprint on paper, 56 × 43 cm
Tate Modern, London
Purchase, 2003. P78802

Fig. 3 Carrie Mae Weems
Magenta Colored Girl, 1987,
Gelatin silver prints with
vinyl lettering on acrylic 2/3,
43.2 × 124.5 cm
George Eastman Museum,
Rochester, NY. Purchase with funds
from the Charina Foundation
1995.0161.0001a-c

Dearest Art Collector,
It has come to our
attention that your
collection, like most,
does not contain
enough art by women.
We know that you
feel terrible about this
and will rectify the
situation immediately

All our love,
Guerrilla Girls

CONSCIENCE OF THE ART WORLD

2

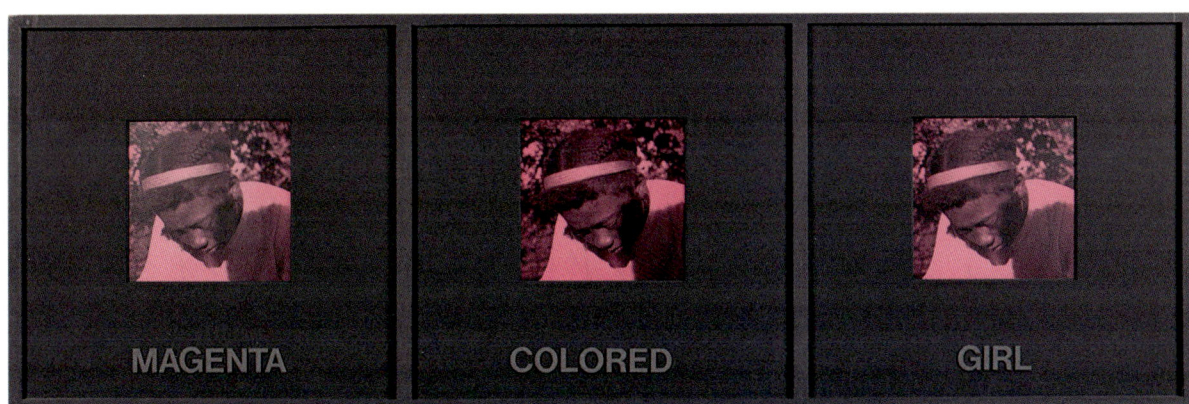

3

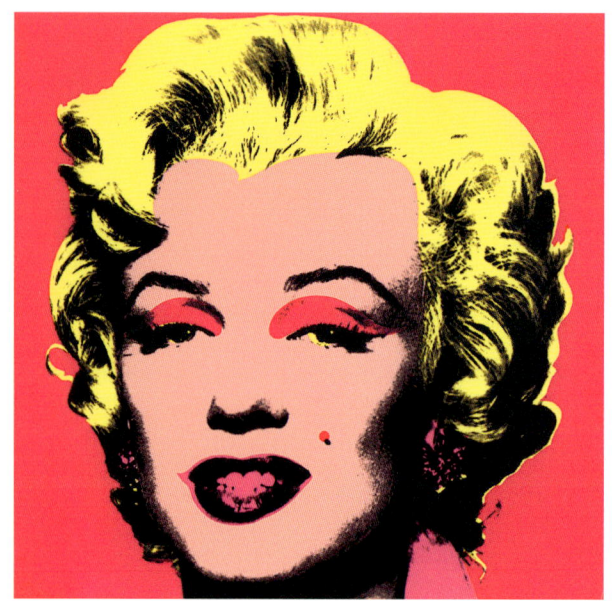

4

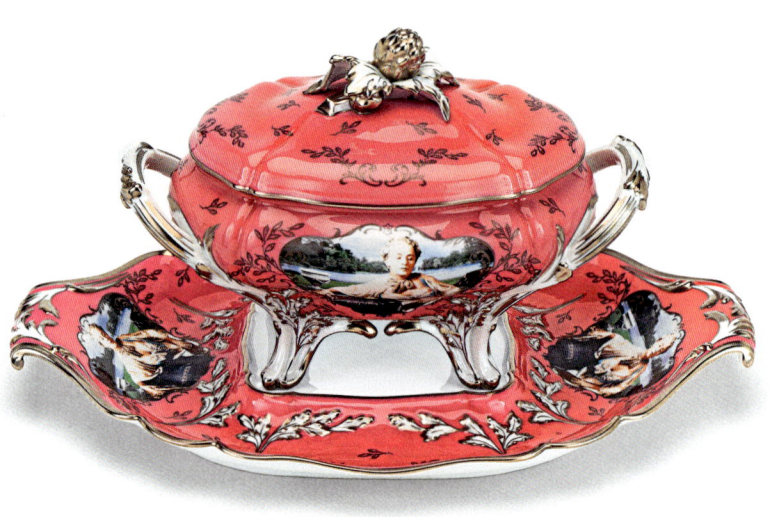

5

Fig. 4 Andy Warhol
Untitled from 'Marilyn Monroe',
1967, one from a portfolio of ten
screenprints, 91.5 × 91.5 cm
Publisher: Factory Additions, New York.
Printer: Aetna Silkscreen Products, Inc.,
New York. Edition: 250. Museum
of Modern Art (MoMA), New York
Gift of Mr. David Whitney 70.1968.1

Fig. 5 Cindy Sherman
Soup tureen *Madame
de Pompadour née Poisson
(1721–1764)*, 1990, porcelain,
screen-printed photograph and
hand-painted fish design on pink
background, 37 × 56 × 30 cm
Centre National des Arts Plastiques,
on long-term loan to the Musée
des Beaux-Arts d'Agen since 2019
Purchase at Artes Magnus, 2000
FNAC 2000-389 (1 to 3)

and the dull tones of *Acrobate et jeune arlequin* [*Acrobat and Young Harlequin*] (1905). Pablo Picasso does not want us to be fooled by appearances. Pink also wards off inner anxieties for Philip Guston, who abandons the expressive vocabulary of abstract colour in favour of figurative paintings – his alter egos – in a distinctly cartoon-like style. They record

an exploration of his inner turmoil using crude, familiar characters who evolve in the pink-coloured paintings, provoking an absurd and troubling visual dissonance. When these characters don the white tunics of the Klu Klux Klan, the tension rises further (*In Bed*, 1971). Here, pink reveals its duplicity. It is disturbing, evasive and unyielding.

1
Louise Bourgeois, *Destruction du père, Reconstruction du père. Écrits et entretiens 1923-2000*, texts selected, compiled and presented by Marie-Laure Bernadac and Hans Ulrich Obrist (Paris: Daniel Lelong Éditeur, 2000), p. 230.
2
Hayley Edwards-Dujardin, "Apparences, apparat et féminité: le goût et la postérité de la mode rococo", in Hélène Jagot, Jessica Degain and Guillaume Kazerouni (ed.), *L'Amour en scène! François Boucher, du théâtre à l'opéra*, exh. cat., Tours: Musée des Beaux-Arts, 4 November 2022 – 30 January 2023 (Paris: Snoeck and Musée des Beaux-arts de Tours, 2022), p. 217.
3
Melissa Hyde, *Making Up the Rococo: François Boucher and His Critics* (Los Angeles: Getty Publishing, 2006), p. 46.

4
Michel Pastoureau and Dominique Simonnet, *Le Petit Livre des couleurs* (Paris: Panama, 2005), p. 112.
5
David Batchelor, *Chromophobia* (London: Reaktion, 2000) p. 23.
6
Charles Blanc, *L'Art dans la parure et le vêtement* (Paris: Henri Laurens, 1887), p. 18.
7
Camille Mauclair, "Les Salons de 1896", *La Nouvelle Revue* (May–June 1896), p. 342.
8
Carlo Carrà, "La peinture des bruits, des sons et des odeurs" (Milan: Direzione del Movimento Futurista, 11 August 1913).
9
Kévin Bideaux, *Rose. Une couleur aux prises avec le genre* (Paris: Éditions Amsterdam, 2023), p. 87.

10
Anne Larue, *Histoire de l'art d'un nouveau genre* (Paris: Max Milo, 2014), p. 115.
11
Denis Diderot, *Essais sur la peinture*, chap. II, 'Mes petites idées sur la couleur', 1766, included in *Denis Diderot, Œuvres esthétiques*, Paul Vernière (Paris: Garnier, Classiques Garnier, 1994), p. 677.
12
Théophile Gautier, 'À une robe rose', *Émaux et camées* (Paris: Crès et Cie, 1913), p. 92.
13
Franck Maubert, *L'odeur du sang ne me quitte pas des yeux. Conversations avec Francis Bacon* (Paris: Mille et une nuits, 2009), p. 38.

14
Camille Morineau, "De l'imprégnation à l'empreinte, de l'artiste au modèle, de la couleur à son incarnation", in *Yves Klein, corps, couleur, immatériel*, exh. cat., Paris, Musée National d'Art Moderne, 5 October 2006 – 5 February 2007 (Paris: Éditions du Centre Pompidou, 2006), p. 121.
15
Lucio Fontana, quoted in Valérie Da Costa (ed.). *Écrits de Lucio Fontana. Manifestes, textes, entretiens* (Dijon: Les presses du réel, 2013), p. 334.
16
Susan Sontag, essay 'Notes on "Camp"', *Partisan Review* no. 31 (4) (1964), pp. 515–30.
17
Hélène Jagot, notice, in Hélène Jagot, Jessica Degain and Guillaume Kazerouni (eds.), *L'Amour en scène! François Boucher, du théâtre à l'opéra*, op. cit., p. 214.

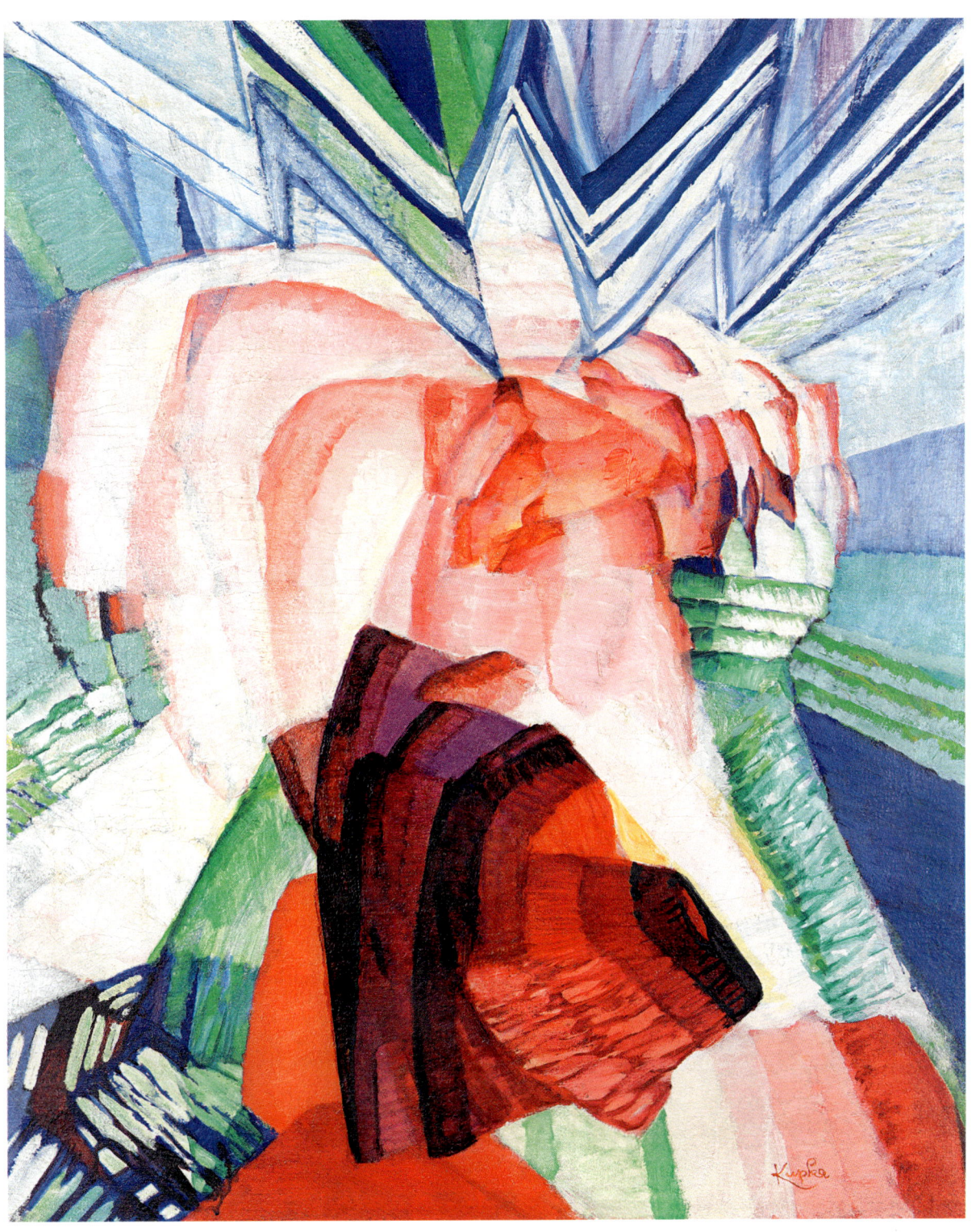

František Kupka   *Le Roman du rose no. 1*   [1923]

oil on canvas   92 × 73 cm   gift of Mrs. Eugénie Kupka, 1963, AM 4208 P

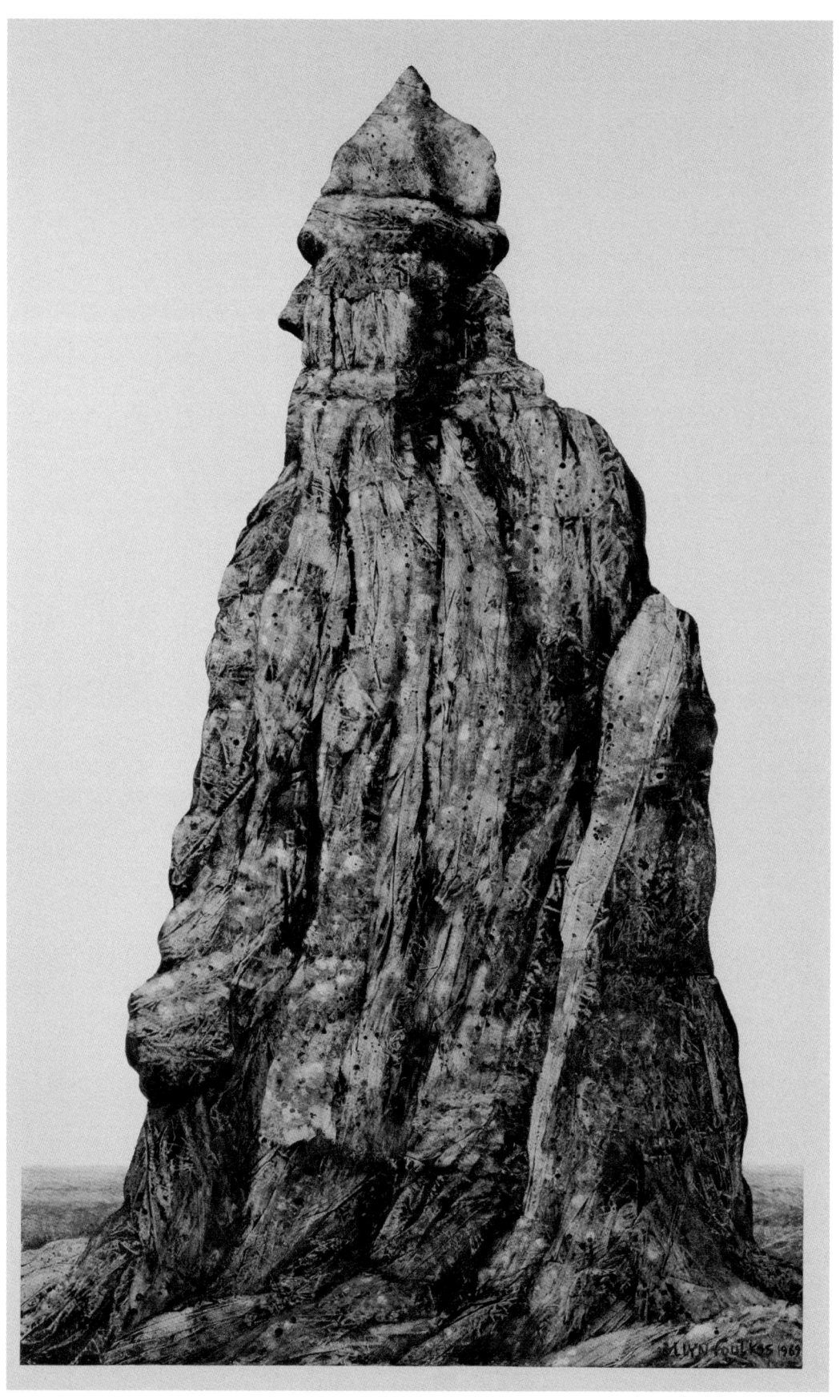

Llyn Foulkes *Cardinal Rock* 1969

acrylic on canvas   274.5 × 165.5 cm   gift of Mrs. Alexander C. Speyer, 1978, AM 1978-577

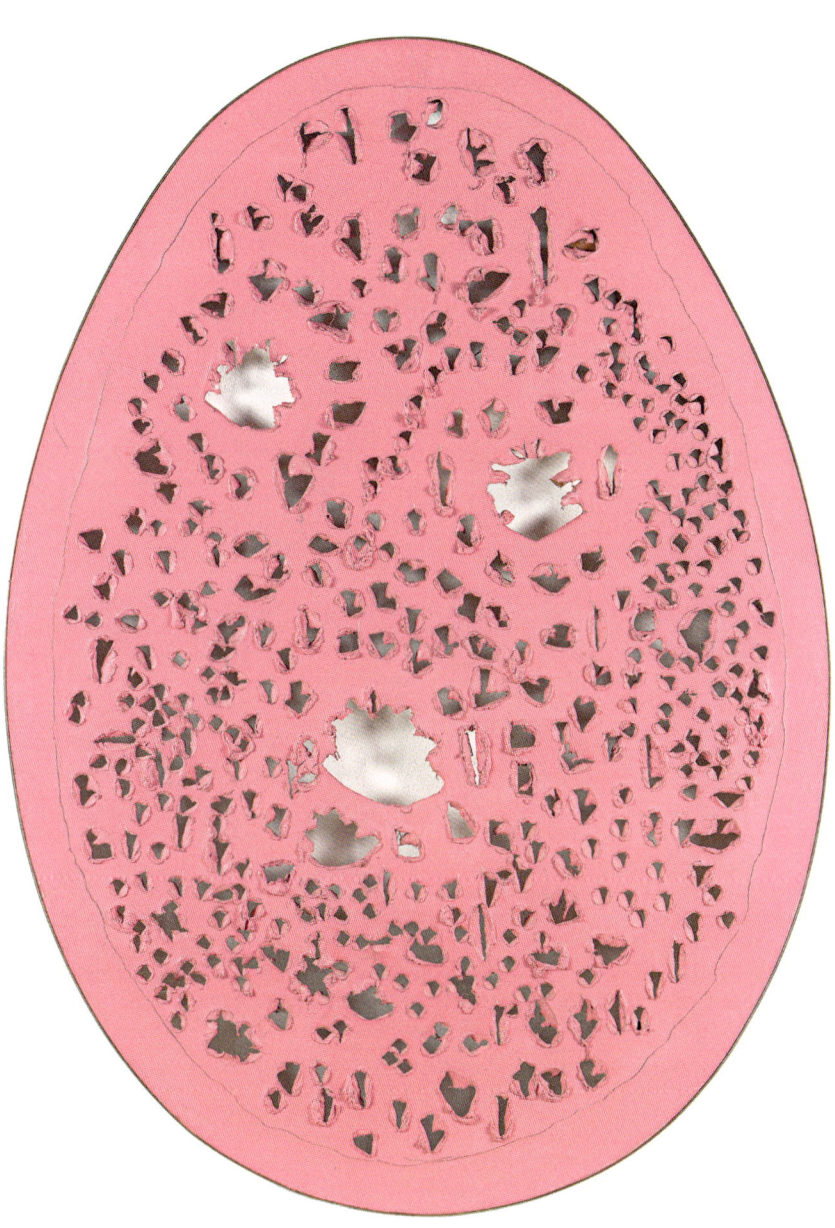

Lucio Fontana   *Spatial Concept, The End of God (67-FD.17)*   [1963]

oil on canvas, perforations   178 × 123 cm   dation, 1997, AM 1997-94

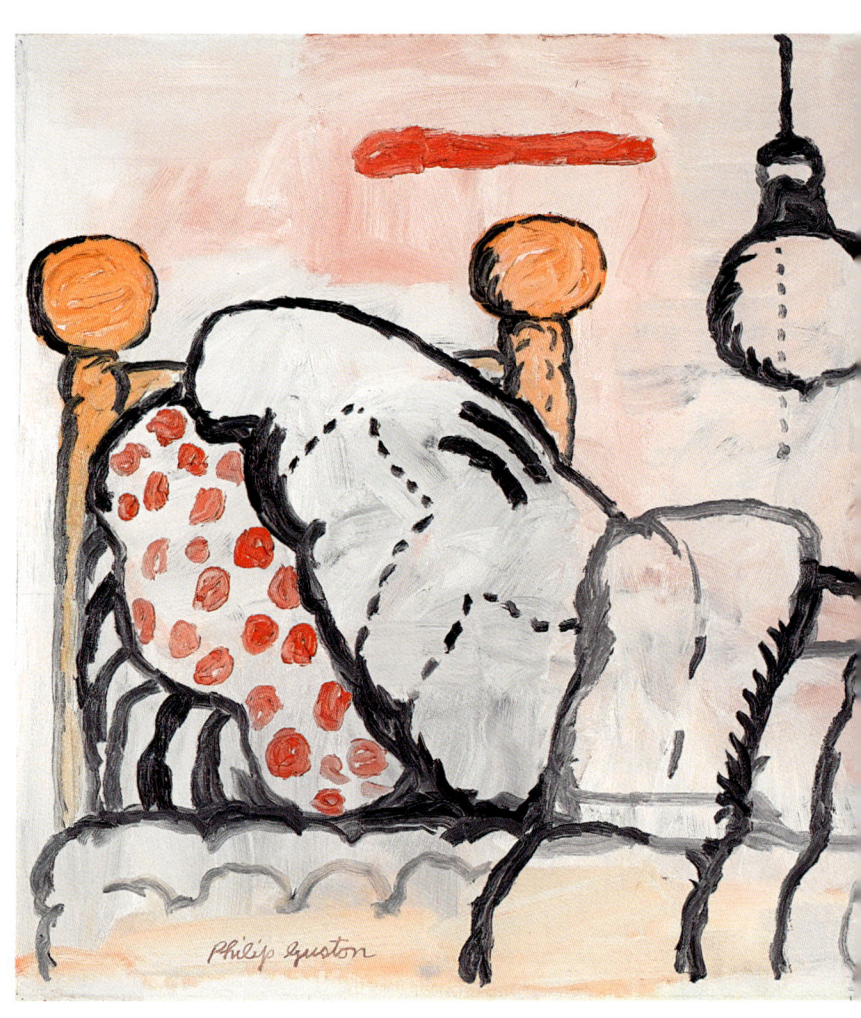

Philip Guston   *In Bed*   1971

oil on canvas   128.5 × 295.7 × 3 cm   gift of the Centre Pompidou Foundation, 2016, AM 2016-942

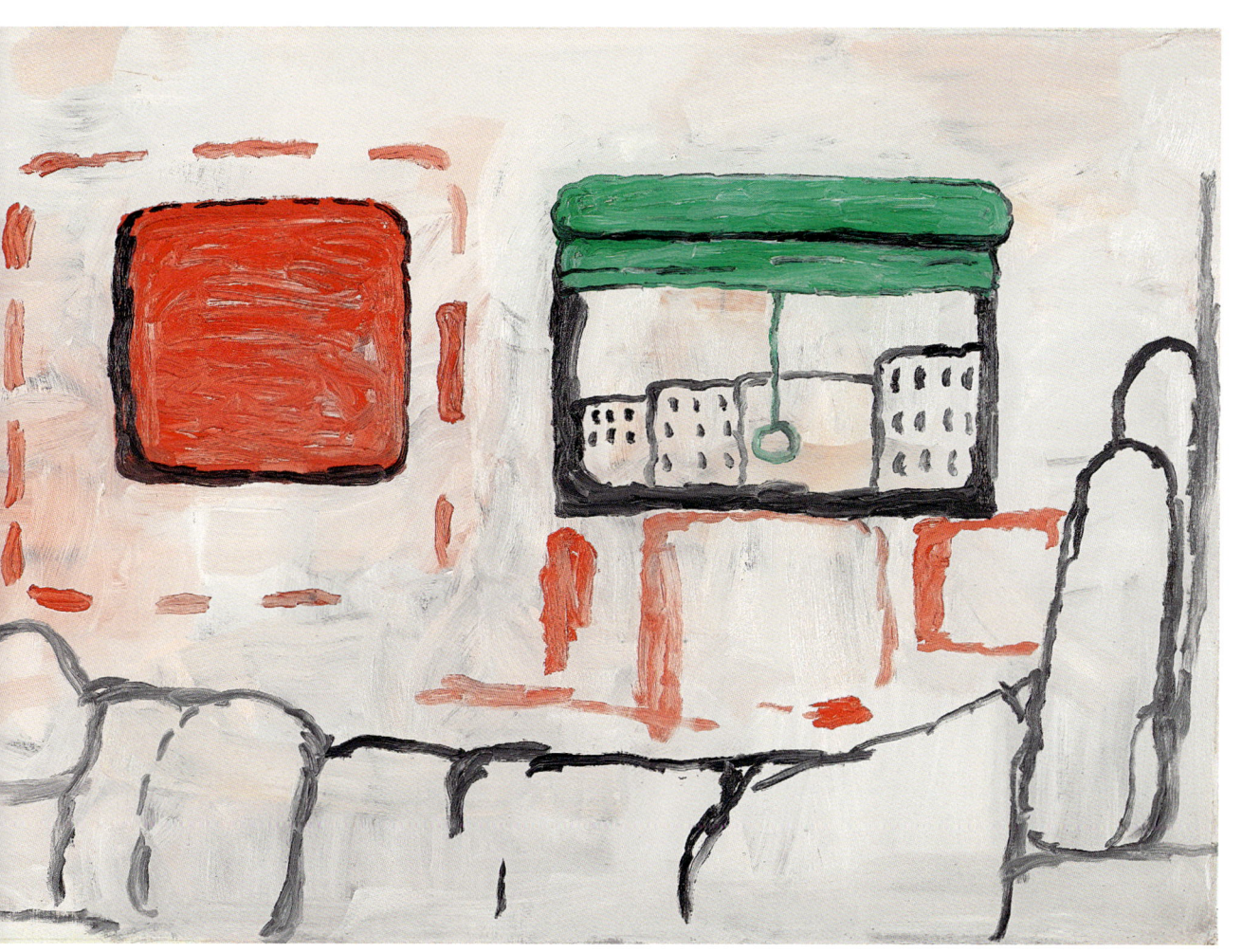

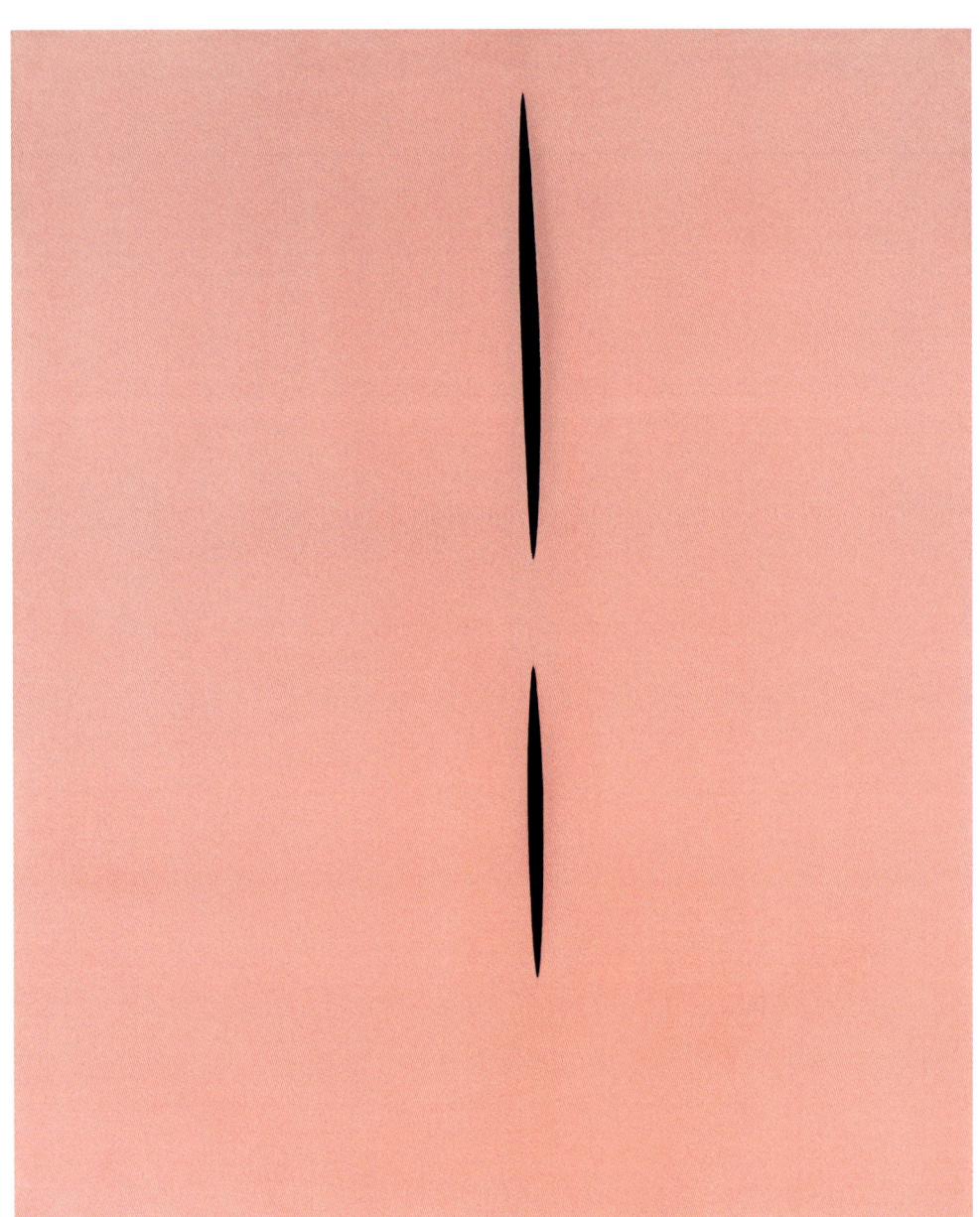

Lucio Fontana   *Spatial Concept, Expectations (T.104)*   1958
vinyl paint on canvas, cuts   125 × 100.5 cm   gift of Mrs. Teresita Fontana, 1979, AM 1979-30

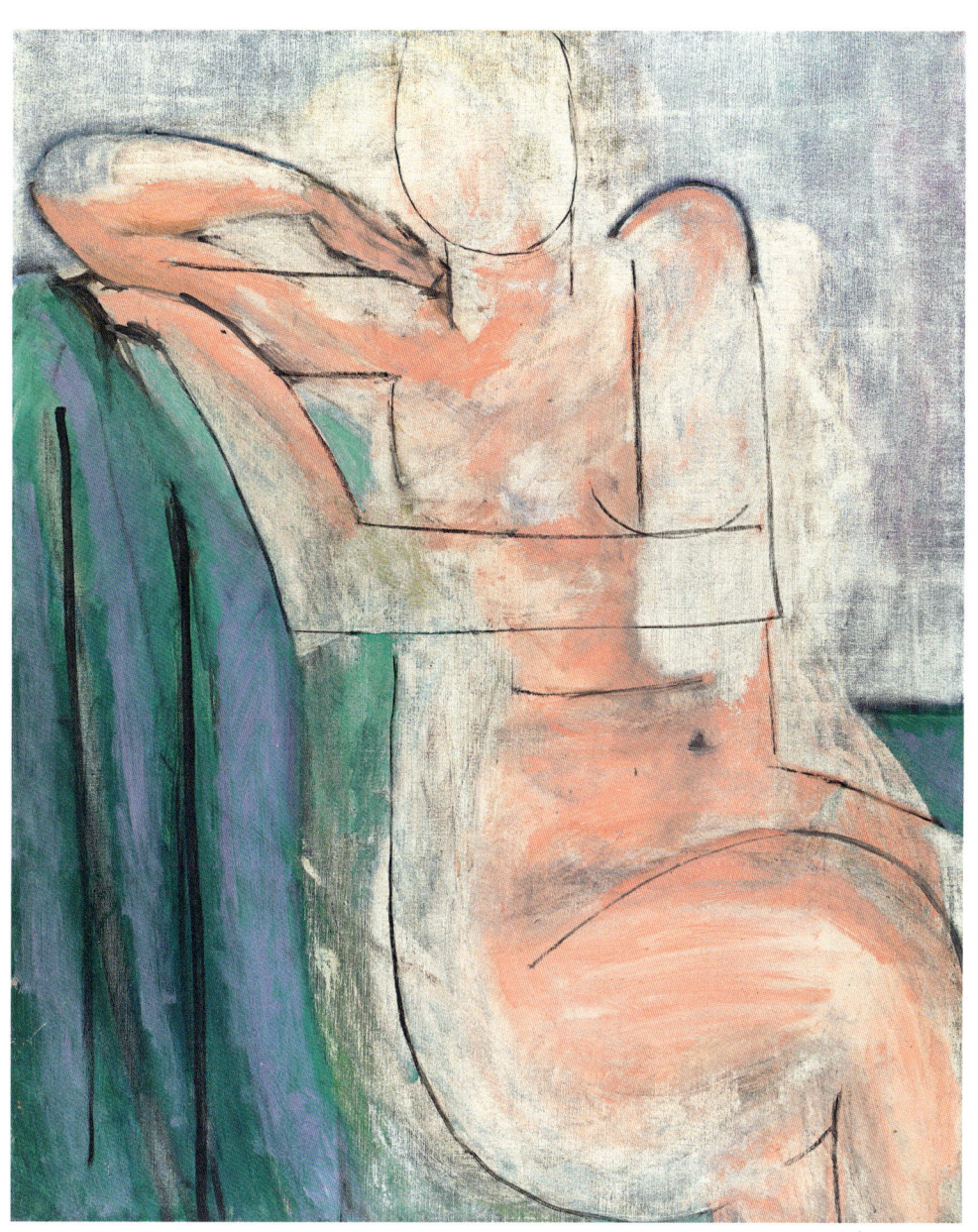

Henri Matisse   *Nu rose assis* [*Seated Pink Nude*]   [April 1935–36]

oil on canvas   92 × 73 × 2.7 cm   dation, 2001, AM 2001-215

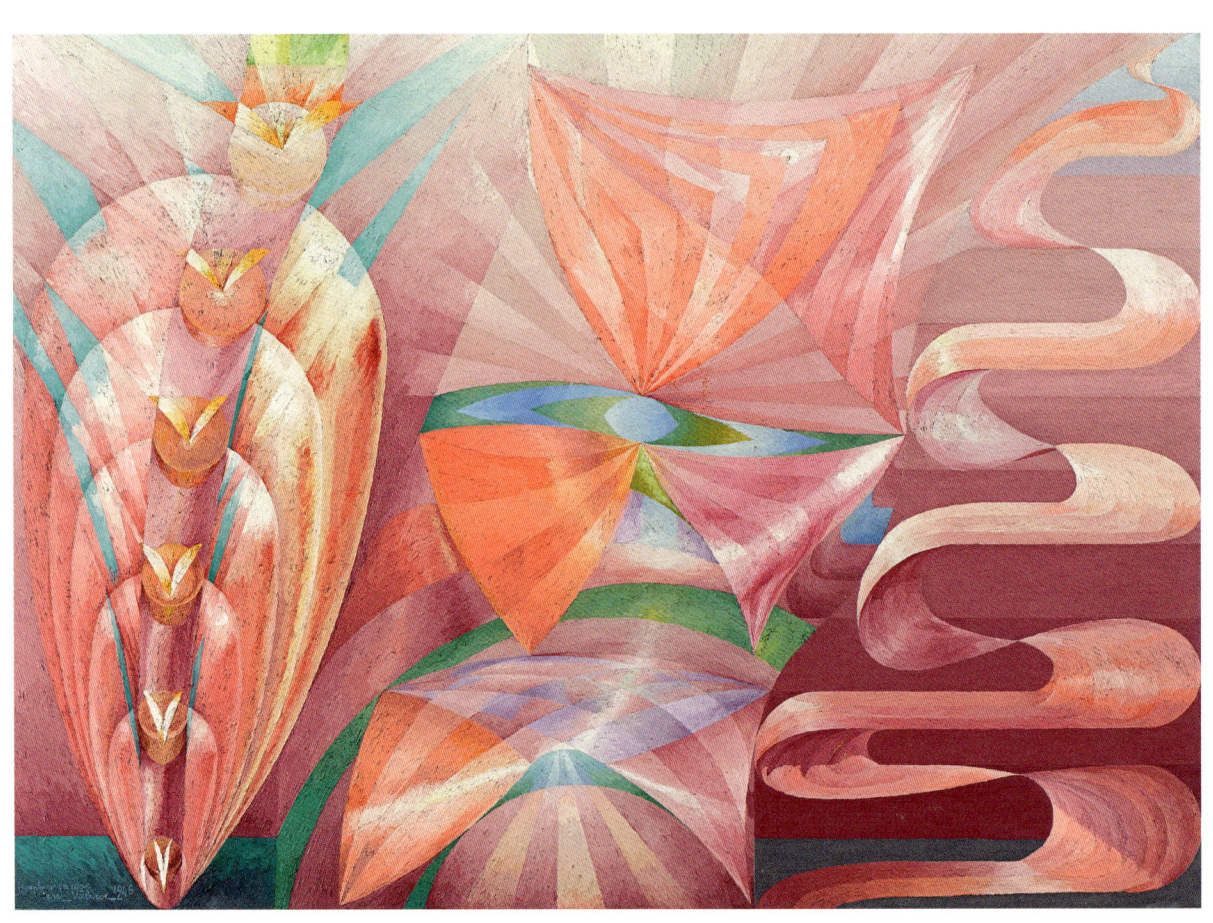

Henry Valensi   *Symphonie en rose* [*Symphony in Pink*]   1946

oil on canvas   97 × 130.5 cm   bequest of the artist, 1960, AM 3870 P

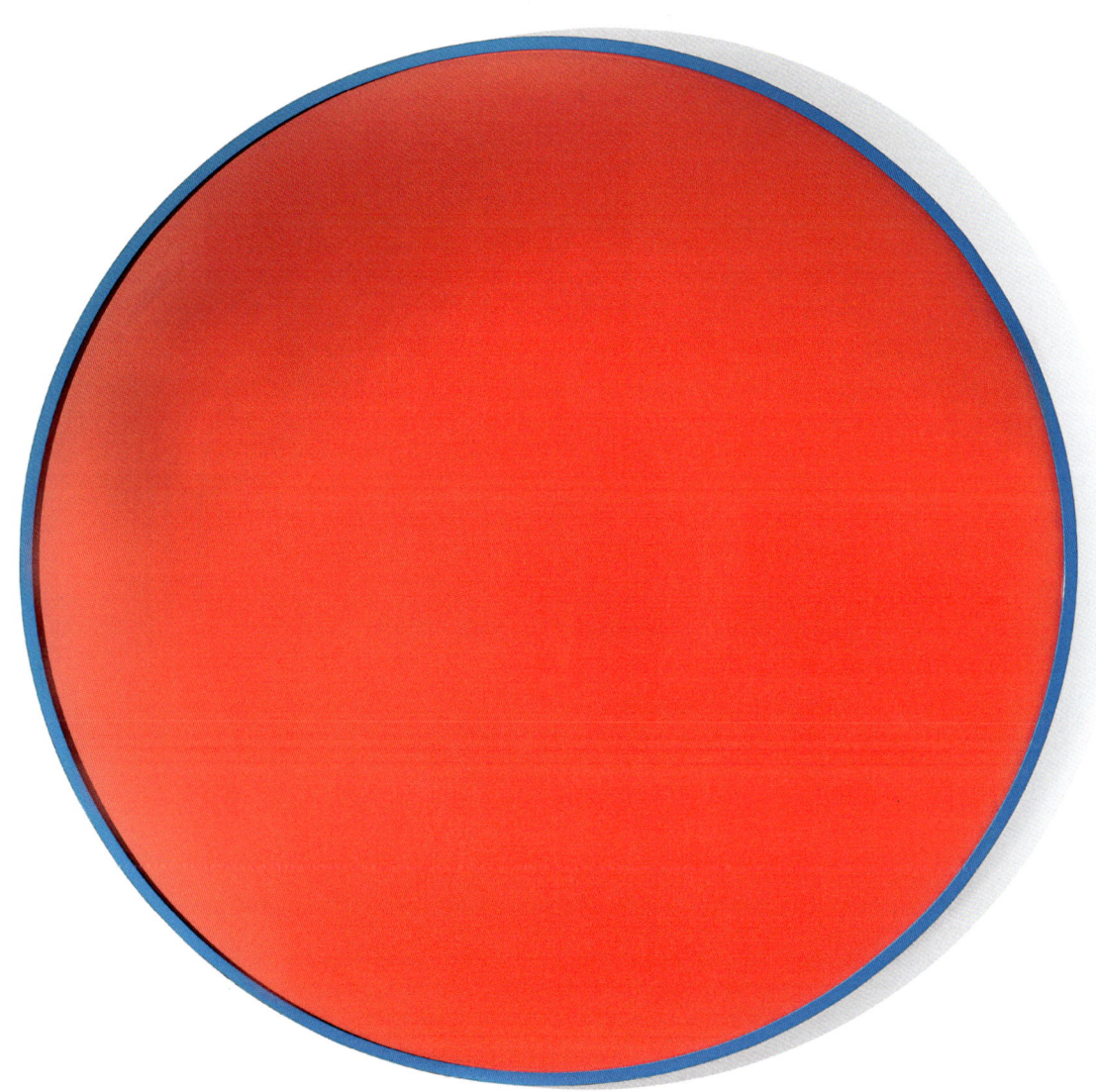

Olivier Mosset   *Sans Titre* [*Untitled*]   1999–2000

acrylic on stretched canvas on aluminium chassis, lacquered metal frame and glass   diameter 203 cm
purchase in 2002, long-term loan from the Centre National des Arts Plastiques, 2002, FNAC 02-234, AM 2003-DEP 33

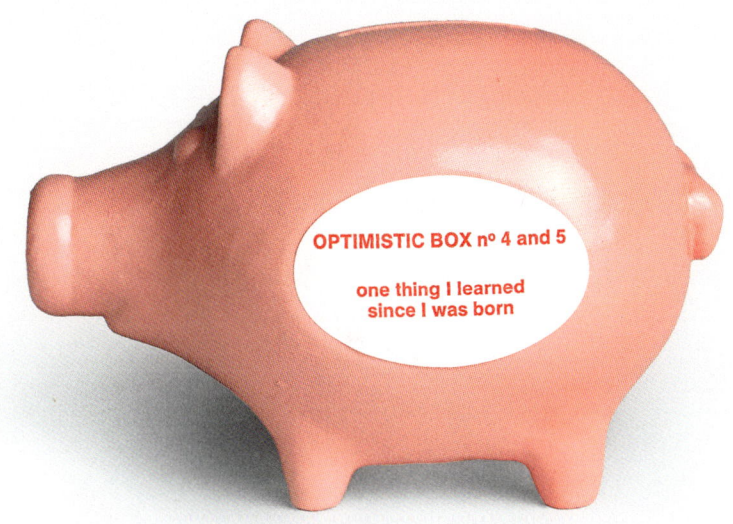

Robert Filliou *Optimistic Box nos. 4 and 5* 1981

painted ceramic 9.5 × 12.5 × 11 cm purchase, 2003, AM 2003-116

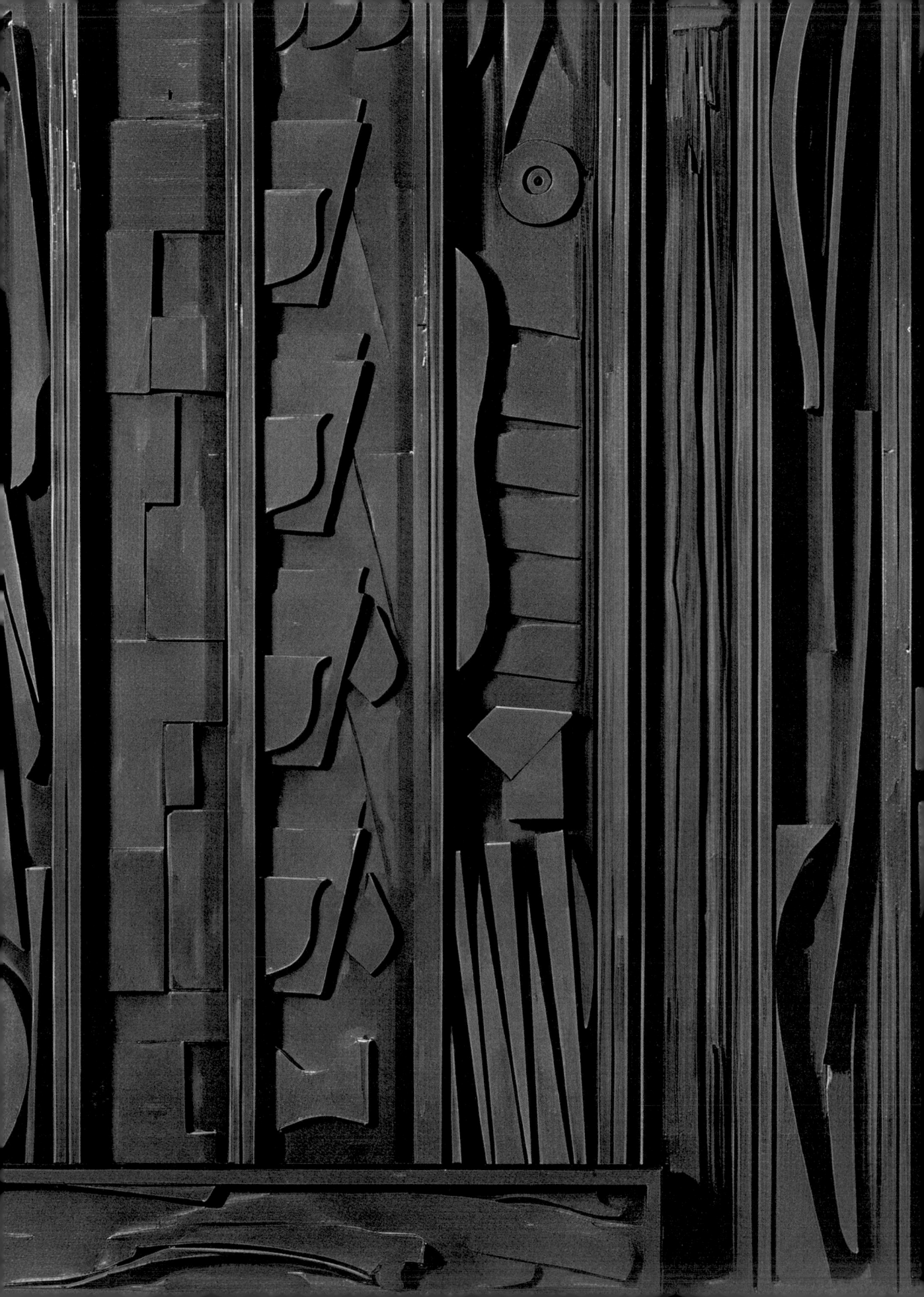

BLACK

Miguel Egaña

NON-COLOUR AND MODERNITY: A 'ROMAN NOIR'

LUMINOCENTRISM AND MELANOPHOBIA

We can understand the modern status of black only in the context of the rupture brought about by Isaac Newton and his followers:[1] in definitively derealising colour, which became merely an element of a superior, non-substantial entity – light – they condemned the material world of painters – pigments, blending on the palette, etc. – to be nothing more than its negative counterpart. Indeed, as a way of thinking about their beloved colours, the new science could conceive only of that strange oxymoron, 'subtractive colour mixing', with black now reappraised as the culmination of this; a negative theology defined it as a privative addition, the sum of erasures: each coloured wave was systematically removed from the spectrum, and, in the end, nothing remained but the death of light. Henceforth, black gave its name to this colourless void.

We can see that this duality, characteristic of Enlightenment rationality, reaffirms the field of the visible as structured by a light/dark polarity. Paradoxically, in providing an irrefutable scientific basis, it also confirmed traditional prejudices concerning black, night and darkness. Modern scientific 'luminocentrism'[2] ontologically assigned black to negativity.

LUMINISM VERSUS TENEBRISM

A new Manichaeism was forming. On the one hand, there were the 'Luminists', who categorically refused this negativity. They were the first avant-garde: colourist, optimist and progressive, excluding black (Impressionists, Divisionists), whose fundamental work, significantly, was sunny. Claude Monet, *Impression, soleil levant* [*Impression, Sunrise*] (1872, fig. 1).

Summarising this process at the turn of the century, Paul Signac illustrated this radical melanophobia, which was less artistic than moral: "[…] adding black is not adding a halftone … it is tainting the tone […]".[3] For this mix, this accursed 'subtractive colour', which leads fatally to black, is evil, 'contamination': "They will always respect the purity of these pure colours, refraining from tainting them, by mixing them on the palette".[4] What he was trying to preserve here, through the definitive exclusion of evil and death, assimilated with black, was the fantasy of a colourful utopia, a luminous paradise, as exemplified perfectly in *Au temps d'harmonie* [*In the Time of Harmony*], (1893–95, fig. 2), the immense (3 × 4 m) 'anarchist' manifesto,[5] painted at Saint-Tropez, future 'paradise' of modern consumerist neo-Edenism.

Opposing them were the 'Tenebrists', followers of the "black sun of Melancholy",[6] who marked the reaction to the triumph of the Enlightenment and the masochistic plunge into the hell of negativity. Preceded by philosopher Edmund Burke, who had reactivated the ancient notion of the 'sublime', associating it this time with terror and night,[7] and his Gothic compatriots, who were filling contemporary imaginations with Gothic fiction,[8] Francisco de Goya summed up this invasion of dark forces in his famous etching *The Sleep of Reason Produces Monsters*, which portrays the barbaric violence of the fight to the death of obscurantist guerrillas against the modern armies of Napoleon. Like the demented writings of his contemporary, the Marquis de Sade, his 'Black Paintings' exalt cruelty, death and crime (fig. 3). Swiss painter Johann Heinrich Füssli, discovering the dark nature of the unconscious (the negative of Rationalist consciousness), painted the nightmare of the sleeper as a lair filled with hideous monsters. The Romantic Victor Hugo, a master of antithesis, torn between light (he was a 'progressive') and darkness (he made the dead speak and penned the poem *La Fin de Satan*), devoted his drawings to the expression of his 'dark side', using the blackest ink to depict the apparition of spectral burgs, the plunge into funereal oceans and the fall into unfathomably deep chasms.

ABSOLUTE BLACK: THE LAST PAINTING

Between 1863 and 1875, as far from Romantic darkness as from the colourist wave of his Impressionist friends, dandy James Whistler invented a third way, 'pure painting', with two 'variations' of (quasi-)monochromes: whites and blacks. The most radical of these, *Nocturne in Black and Gold, the Falling Rocket* (1875, fig. 4), so infuriated chromophile John Ruskin that he insulted the painter, who then famously sued him.[9] This unprecedented 'absolute black' would only truly achieve posterity with Kazimir Malevich's *Black Square* (1915).[10]

Malevich, an important figure in Futurism and Suprematism, both of which derived from Cubism, and the first avant-garde painter to break with the colour-loving utopia, was a 'Modernist'. Modernism is the synthesis of two teleologies: on the one hand, the autotelicity of the painting, meaning it is its own end; on the other, the progressive historicity of art history. Very quickly, these two 'ends' merged in the ultimate Modernist work: the 'last' painting. As Whistler had already anticipated, this would be 'unist' – of a single colour – and achromatic – made up of 'non-colours', white or black. Malevich, who produced two versions, acclaimed this 'end of art'. So his *Black Square* (fig. 5), a Suprematist work, venerated as an 'icon' in its presentation in the top corner of two walls, was, according to the artist, "beyond the zero point of creation", the "start of a new culture" and "the first step of pure creation in art".[11] This paradoxically 'positive' interpretation of absolute black can be understood only in the context of going 'beyond painting': "Painting has long since had its day, and the painter himself is a prejudice of the past",[12] declared the father of Suprematism.

In 1929, another Russian, philosopher Alexandre Kojève,[13] saw in absolute black the 'end' of all expression (artistic, philosophic); he wrote to his uncle, the avant-garde colourist Wassily Kandinsky:

> To express not only the different aspects of the world itself – which would be the entirety of its aspects (everything) – [...] [reduced] to (mystical) silence and, in painting, to black canvases. It would no longer mean dialectically mastering any form of painting but painting itself as such. In absolute understanding, there is no longer any differentiation: philosophy, art and so on. There, there is only 'total', 'black' and 'unintelligible' silence.[14]

It was precisely this 'nihilist' manifesto that the American painter Ad Reinhardt, repeating the avant-gardism of the early 20th century, strived to implement in his 'Ultimate Paintings' (1960–67, fig. 6), developing a unique, definitive and self-centred formula: "[...] a work that merges everything into a single dissolution and inseparability, each painting subject to unique uniformity and unique non-irregularity".[15] His black paintings – "knowledge of nothingness and emptiness (abyss, night, desert)"[16] – are thus the expression, both unique and reiterated, of negativity, that of the 'last painting' as the very fulfilment of art history: "I'd like to stick with permanent negativity", declared Reinhard. "If you read and reread art history [...], you can see that there is a negative progression".[17]

Reinhard's legacy is two-fold. On the one hand, it is plastic: in his famous striped 'Black Paintings' (1959, fig. 7), Frank Stella revisited Ad Reinhardt's 'absolute black' in another way, eliminating any metaphysical dimension to it. His desacralised, 'profane' 'absolute' is likewise purely tautological, self-referential. He stated it thus: "My painting is based on the fact that only what can be seen there is there. It is really an object".[18] Revealing "an almost stupid obstinacy",[19] his intentionally deceptive black revisits the semantic nullity of Whistler's earliest monochromes; a deliberate refusal of meaning, described as 'nihilistic' by contemporary critics.[20]

On the other hand, Reinhardt's legacy is conceptual. Joseph Kosuth, pushing the philosophic development of art to its limits, transformed the 'unism' of his compatriot into a tautologism that would become the definitive trope of his verbal aesthetic. Refusing all plasticity, he nevertheless made a concession, if not to painting then at least to the 'black surface': his first 'statements' were 'white on black', the 'negative' inversion of the pages of the dictionary.[21] As if the completion of the 'verbal painting' could literally only be realised on the last painting, the status of which had changed from transcendent concept to simple support.

DIALECTIC BLACK: THE EXPRESSIONIST DRAMA

Radical Modernists, driven by a fascination with black, were therefore either new mystics or atheist tautologists, who shared the same obsession with 'One', and the same indifference to the world. Other artists, conversely, devoted themselves to the desperate quest for the truth of reality. Yet, they thought of this truth, whether subjective or social, as dual: Manichaean and agnostic. Likewise rejecting the appeal of colour, they settled into a dualistic aesthetic, expressing their 'tragic view of life' through a fight to the death of black and white, the artistic battle between darkness and light. Vehemently opposed to all forms of historicism, they were, on the contrary, 'presentists', favouring actuality and the immediacy of the moment, and 'primitivists', exalting the energy of beginnings.

Félix Vallotton, revisiting Caravaggio's tenebrism, adapted the latter's theatrical tragedy to the mediocrity of his bourgeois and proletarian century. His woodcuts (fig. 8) – characterised by a deep, engulfing blackness, in which white fragments of dismembered bodies seem to float – reveal, through a pessimistic and misanthropic lens, the dark negative of modern society and its intimate underbelly: the battle between the sexes (*The Confession*, *Triumph*, *The Lie*) and its social antithesis, the class struggle (*The Demonstration*, *The Anarchist*, *The Charge*). His immediate successors, the German Expressionists (Ernst Ludwig Kirchner, Erich Heckel, Max Pechstein), revisited this plastic binarism in multiple woodcuts, refocusing it subjectively on the mental and physical suffering of the artist, whose body and face became the scene of existential drama. Eliminating any aestheticising element in favour of a deliberately rudimentary, maladroit, 'primitive' technique, they produced a pathetic, tragic, dispirited black, charged with expressing the eternal dereliction of the human condition.

THE BLACK GESTURE

In their turn, American Abstract Expressionists reactivated this tragic dualism, moving it into the 'reality' of the studio: the positive pole remained

Fig.1 Claude Monet
Impression, soleil levant
[*Impression, Sunrise*], 1872,
oil on canvas, 50 × 65 cm
Musée Marmottan Monet, Paris
Bequest of Eugène and Victoire
Donop de Monchy. 4014

Fig.2 Paul Signac
Au temps d'harmonie [*In the
Time of Harmony*], 1893–95,
oil on canvas, 300 × 400 cm
Hôtel de Ville de Montreuil

Fig.3 Francisco de Goya
A Way of Flying, 1864,
Etching, aquatint and
drypoint, 24.8 × 35.7 cm
Final state. From the
compendium *Los Proverbios*,
first edition, Madrid, unknown
publisher, 1864, no.13
Bibliothèque nationale
de France, RÉSERVE BF-4
(J,44)–BOÎTE ECU

Fig.4 James Abbott
McNeill Whistler
*Nocturne in Black and Gold,
the Falling Rocket*, 1875,
oil on panel, 60.3 × 46.7 cm
Detroit Institute of Arts, Detroit
Gift of Dexter M. Ferry, Jr.
46.309

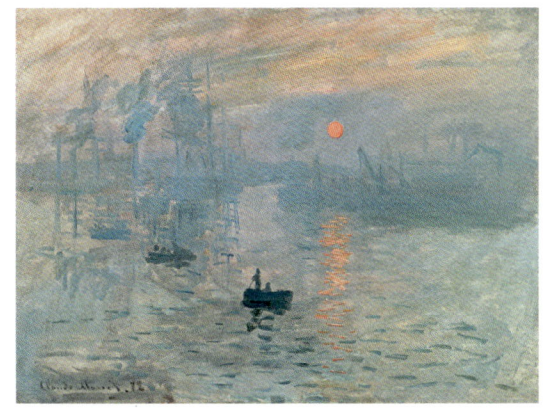

1

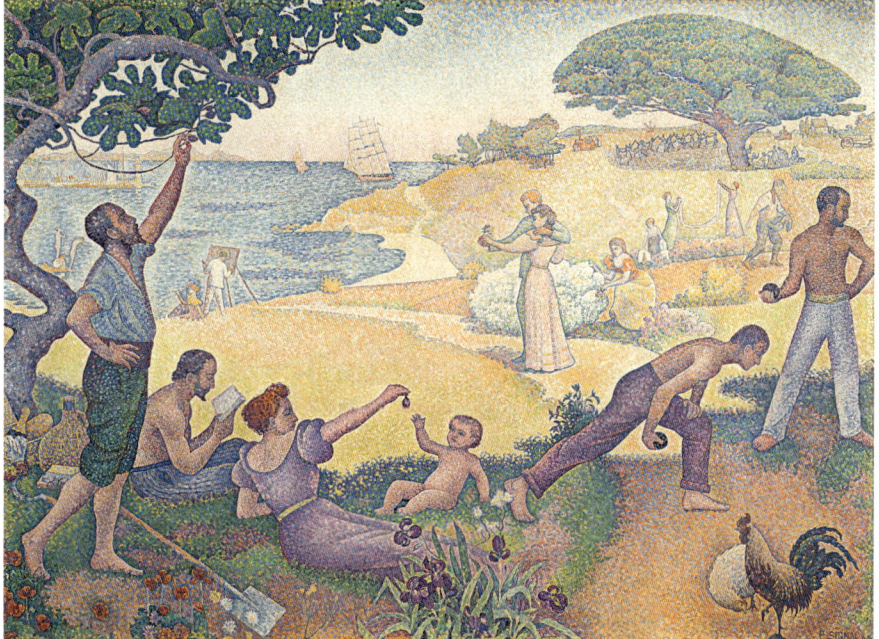

2

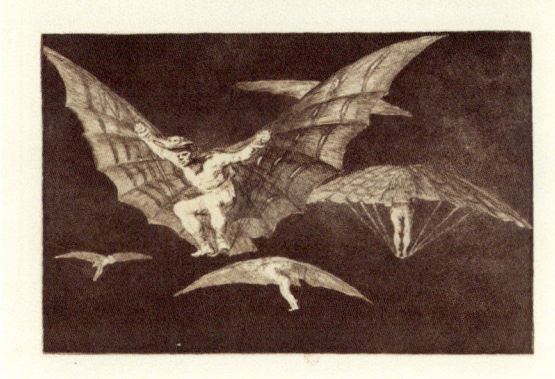

3

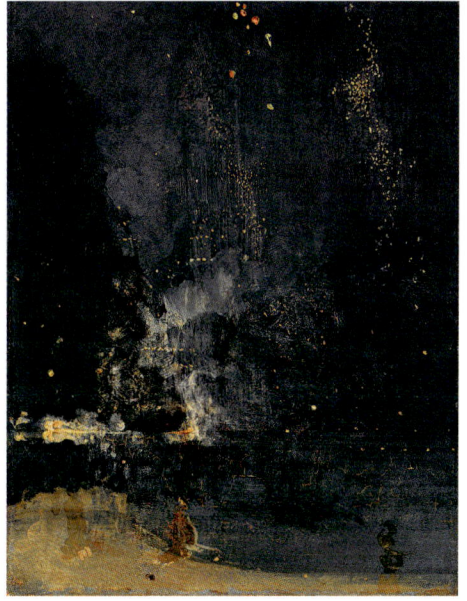

4

5

6

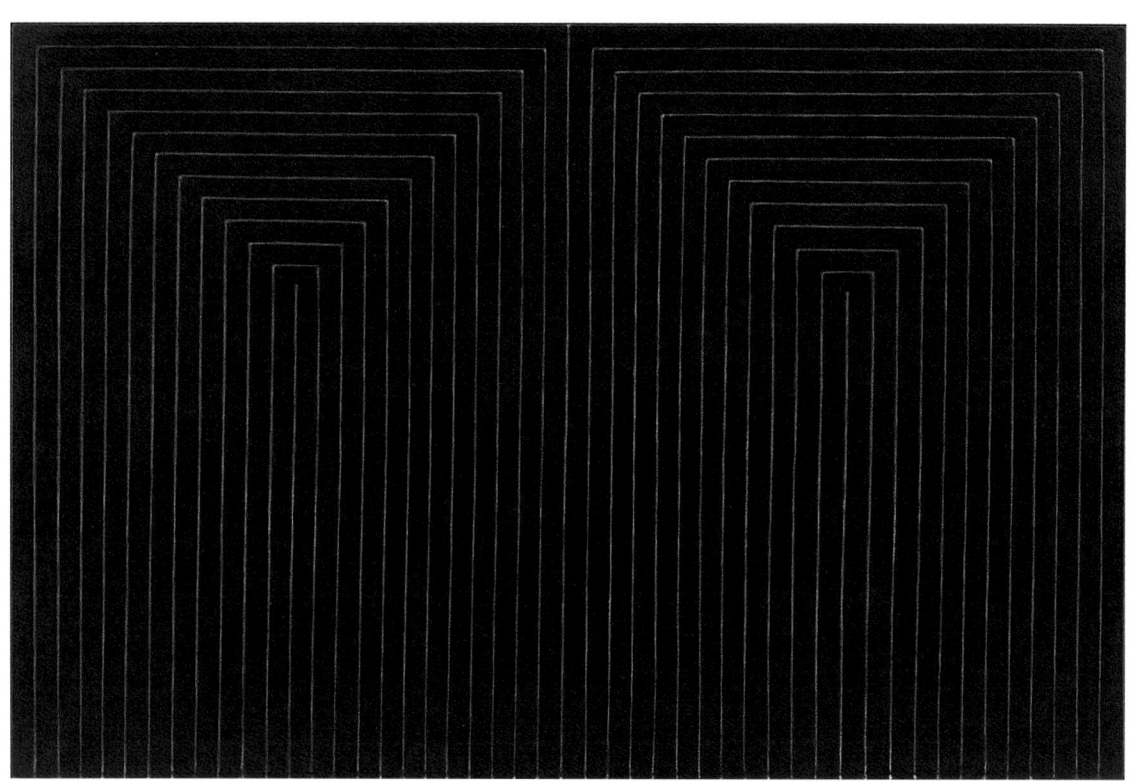

7

Fig. 5 Kazimir Malevich
Black Square, 1923–30, oil on
plaster, 36.7 × 36.7 × 9.2 cm
Centre Pompidou – Musée
National d'Art Moderne – Centre
de Création Industrielle, Paris
Anonymous gift, 1978
AM 1978-631

Fig. 6 Ad Reinhardt
Ultimate Painting, no. 6, 1960,
oil on canvas, 153 × 153 cm
Centre Pompidou – Musée
National d'Art Moderne – Centre
de Création Industrielle, Paris
Purchase of the French State, 1974
AM 1974-19

Fig. 7 Frank Stella
*The Marriage of Reason and
Squalor, II*, 1959, enamel
on canvas, 230.5 × 337.2 cm
Museum of Modern Art (MoMA),
New York. Larry Aldrich Foundation
Fund. 725.1959

the white space of the canvas or paper, but the negative pole now took the form of the artist's own body, the violent projection of the paint onto the canvas serving to express his or her antagonistic energy. It was now the duel – the dynamic struggle of the creator with the painting surface – that would convey the metaphysical tragedy. As famous American art critic Harold Rosenberg enthused: "At a certain moment the canvas began to appear to one American painter after another as an arena in which to act".[22] This famous bullfighting metaphor once again takes us back to Hegelian negativity: the hero who risks his life in the area is the matador, the 'killer';[23] yet, according to Hegel, a 'death in action' is the very definition of the 'active' human subject: "[…] if Man is Action, and if Action is Negativity 'appearing' as Death, [then] Man is, in his human or speaking existence, only a death […]".[24]

In this vision, the material used to embody this subject that asserts itself only in negation, the oxymoronic living – "a death that lives a human life"[25] – can only be black; black are Franz Kline's sweeping brushstrokes, black is the paint thrown by Jackson Pollock, whose first drip paintings (1947) are predominantly black and covered with a chaos of colours. And, above all, when Hans Namuth filmed the painter in action[26] (fig. 9), the dramatised gestural painting that would be exhibited was black. The gesticulations of the paint on glass, black flows filmed from below, from the viewpoint of the support, are the quintessence of Pollock's art and of the very concept of 'action painting': before any immersion in the 'One' future of the canvas, in the all-over painting hailed by the monist critic (Clement Greenberg), Namuth demonstrated that there is first, in all its radicality, a primary, original gesture and that it is a 'black gesture'.

BLACK LIKE POST-PAINTING

What remains after the last painting? After the history of art? Two survivors, Arnulf Rainer and Pierre Soulages, gave us their response. Arnulf Rainer, a direct descendant of German Expressionism,[27] was torn between the quest for a 'before' – that of the primitive gesture, the infantile doodle, or even something below it: monkey painting – and

a contemporary 'after', which, for want of a better term, we call 'post'. But the contemporary painter is neither a child nor a primate; to believe in the dawn of painting required the innocence of the pioneer, like that of the 'Yankee' Pollock, seizing hold of the New World like a blank slate. Rainer, who came after Pollock, despite his primitivist dreams, could no longer rely on the virginity of a canvas that would never again be white. Rainer the Austrian was too European, too marked by history. His black gesture, like a veritable impulse, became a tainted gesture, an act of covering up that fell into the negativity of defilement: scribbling, smearing the works of others, Rainer tarnished not only the history of art but History itself; in a striking leap, he used black to move from the beginnings to the end, destroying not only the first gesture but also, and especially, the last image: death masks ('Totenmasken' series, 1978, fig. 10), photos of Hiroshima ('Hiroshima' series, 1982). These 'ultimate paintings', like discarded black shrouds, joined Reinhard's glorious nihilist assertions. He stated it thus: "The fullness of this void represents the Absolute, and the artist must always be this heroic negator, because he is the believer".[28] His black is a palimpsest black: under the layer of black, the entire memory of painting, all the images of humanity, are buried. No longer the end of History but its very impossibility. Neither beginning nor end but its suspension, its cessation. An immobile time. That of catastrophe.

Soulages, although he was a contemporary of Kline and Pollock, never made a 'black gesture'. A tenebrist painter but also a 'constructor', adept at large formats, he moved logically from calligraphy to overpainting and found his post-pictorial solution in going beyond the plane, by sculpting his 'non-colour' – black – in the layers of a thick medium, which, thanks to the non-colour's transformation into a bas-relief, is reinvested almost subliminally with the light that had been excluded from it. Paradoxically, then, it is Soulages, with his 'outrenoir' shining in the darkness, who completes the Newtonian chromatic narrative: denial or redemption, his gleaming shadows mark the improbable return of the 'accursed' tone to light-filled Paradise: "Outrenoir means 'beyond black', light reflected, transmuted by black. Outrenoir: black that, ceasing to be such, becomes the emitter of clarity, secret light".[29]

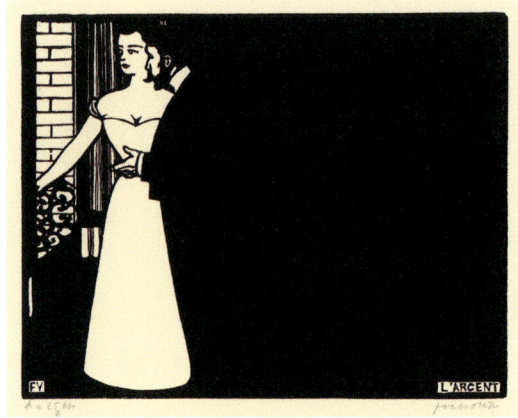

8

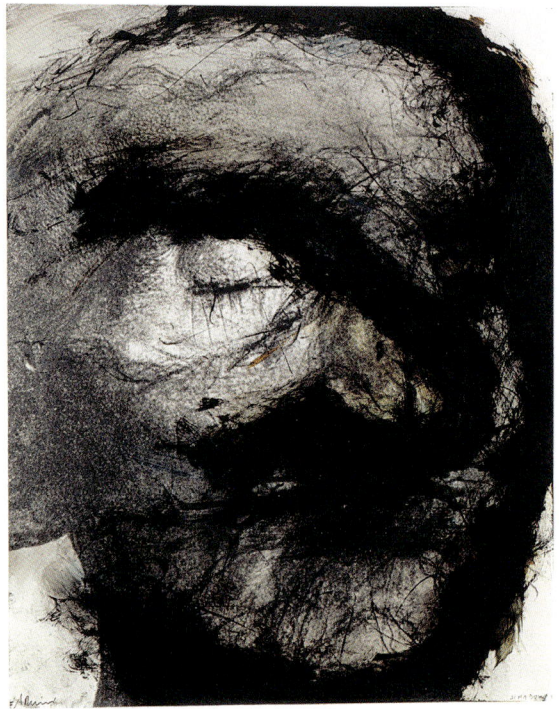

10

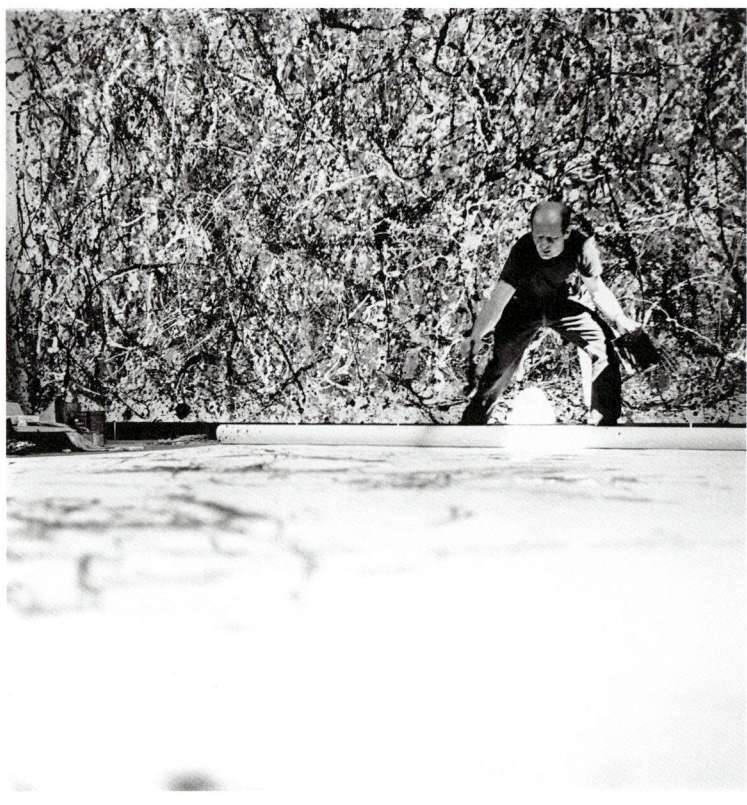

9

Fig. 8 Félix Vallotton
L'Argent [*Money*], from the
series 'Intimités', 1897–98,
woodcut in black on wove
paper, 24.9 × 32.2 cm
Van Gogh Museum (purchased
with support from the
VriendenLoterij and the members
of the Yellow House Circle),
Amsterdam. p2747-006S2014

Fig. 9 *Jackson Pollock*,
1950, photograph by
Hans Namuth, gelatin silver
print, 60.5 × 60.5 cm
Centre Pompidou – Musée
National d'Art Moderne – Centre
de Création Industrielle, Paris
Purchase, 1983. AM 1983-87

Fig. 10 Arnulf Rainer
*Death Mask (Gottfried von
Schadow)*, 1978, oil and India
ink on gelatin silver print,
60.2 × 45.8 cm
Centre Pompidou – Musée
National d'Art Moderne – Centre
de Création Industrielle, Paris
Purchase, 1984. AM 1984-394

1
Isaac Newton, *Opticks: or, A Treatise of the Reflections, Refractions, Inflexions and Colours of Light* (London: S. Smith and B. Walford, 1704).

2
See Paul Virilio: "Le centre de l'univers […] c'est le point lumineux d'un 'héliocentrisme' ou plutôt d'un 'luminocentrisme'", in Paul Virilio, *L'Espace critique* (Paris: Galilée, 1984), p. 52.

3
Paul Signac, *D'Eugène Delacroix au néo-impressionnisme* (Paris: Hermann, 1987 [1899]), p. 42.

4
Ibid., p. 37.

5
The original title of the work was *Au temps d'anarchie* [*In the Time of Anarchy*].

6
Gérard de Nerval, "El Desdichado" sonnet, in *Les Chimères*, 1854.

7
Edmund Burke, *A Philosophical Enquiry into the Origin of Our Ideas of the Sublime and Beautiful* (London: Penguin Books, 1998 [1757]).

8
For example, the writings of Horace Walpole (1717–1797), Matthew Gregory Lewis (frequently referred to as 'Monk' Lewis, 1775–1818) and Ann Radcliffe (1764–1823).

9
John Ruskin (1819–1900) thought of colours as 'heavenly' and was close to Paul Signac. James Abbott McNeill Whistler was ruined by the lawsuit against the British writer and art critic, despite winning it.

10
If we exclude the satirical *Combat de nègres dans la nuit* (1882), by Paul Bilhaud, exhibited in 1882 at the Exhibition des Arts Incohérents.

11
Kazimir Malevich, quoted in Jacqueline Lichtenstein (ed.), *La Peinture* (Paris: Larousse, 1995), pp. 890–91.

12
Ibid., p. 895.

13
Born in Moscow in 1902, Aleksandr Kozhevnikov obtained French nationality in 1937 and gallicised his name to Alexandre Kojève.

14
Letter from Alexandre Kojève to Wassily Kandinsky, quoted by Dominique Auffret in *Alexandre Kojève* (Paris: Le Livre de poche, 1990), p. 286.

15
Ad Reinhardt, quoted by Heribert Heere in "La théorie de l'art pour l'art d'Ad Reinhardt", *Artistes*, trans. Martine Keyser and Max Reithmann, special edition no. 1 (13 June 1984), p. 6.

16
Ibid., p. 9.

17
Ibid.

18
Bruce Glaser, *Questions to Stella and Judd*, in Battcock, Gregory (ed.), *Minimal Art: A Critical Anthology* (Berkeley, CA: University of California Press, 1995), p. 158.

19
Robert Rosenblum, quoted by Irving Standler, *Le Triomphe de l'art américain. L'École de New York*, vol. 3 (Paris: Carré, 1990), p. 260.

20
Brian O'Doherty, quoted by Irving Standler, ibid., p. 76.

21
Ben, a visual artist from Nice, did the same in parodic style: his neo-incoherent verbal fantasy, as tautological as that of Kosuth and Reinhardt, was repeated over decades on the same absolutely black background.

22
Harold Rosenberg, "The American Action Painters" (1952), quoted in Joan M. Marter, *The Grove Encyclopaedia of American Art*, vol. 1 (New York: Oxford University Press, 2011), p. 27.

23
In Spanish, the word *matar* is the verb 'to kill'.

24
Alexandre Kojève in Dennis King Keenan (ed.), *Hegel and Contemporary Continental Philosophy* (New York: State University of New York Press, 2004), p. 44.

25
Ibid., p. 46.

26
In 1950, the German-born American photographer Hans Namuth (1915–1990) immortalised Jackson Pollock at work in a series of black-and-white photographs. He also made a documentary, also in black and white, entitled *Jackson Pollock 51* (1951) showing the artist in action.

27
He is close to the Viennese Actionists, who, in order to go beyond painting, chose to use body fluids: blood, urine, etc.

28
Arnulf Rainer, in *Arnulf Rainer*, exh. cat., Paris, Musée National d'Art Moderne, 2 February – 26 March 1984 (Paris: Éditions du Centre Pompidou, 1984), p. 64.

29
Pierre Soulages, quoted by Camille Morando, *Soulages* (Paris: Éditions du Centre Pompidou, 2015), p. 54.

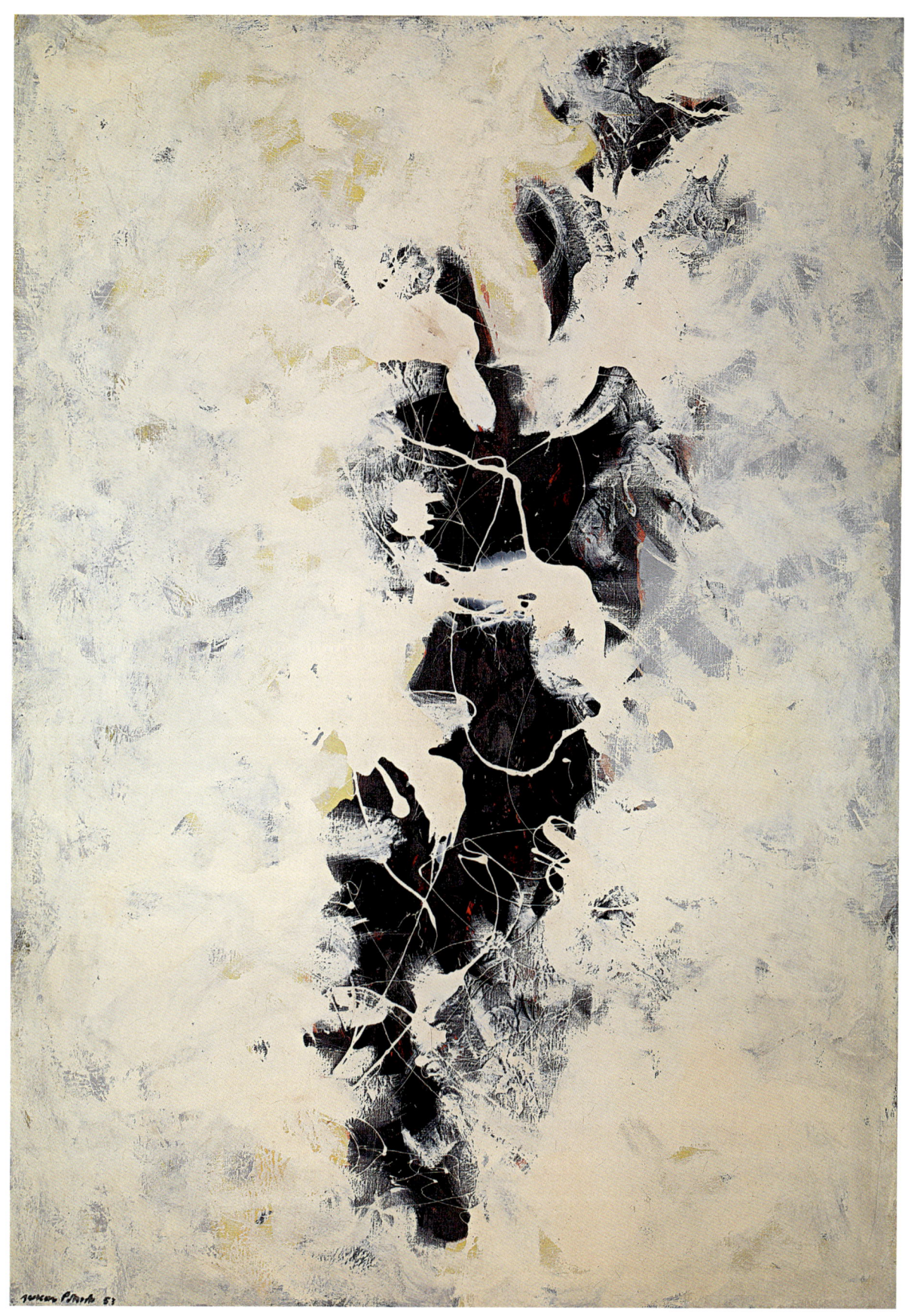

Jackson Pollock   *The Deep*   1953

paint on canvas   220,4 × 150,2 cm   donation in memory of Jean de Menil by his children and the Menil Foundation, 1976, AM 1976-1230

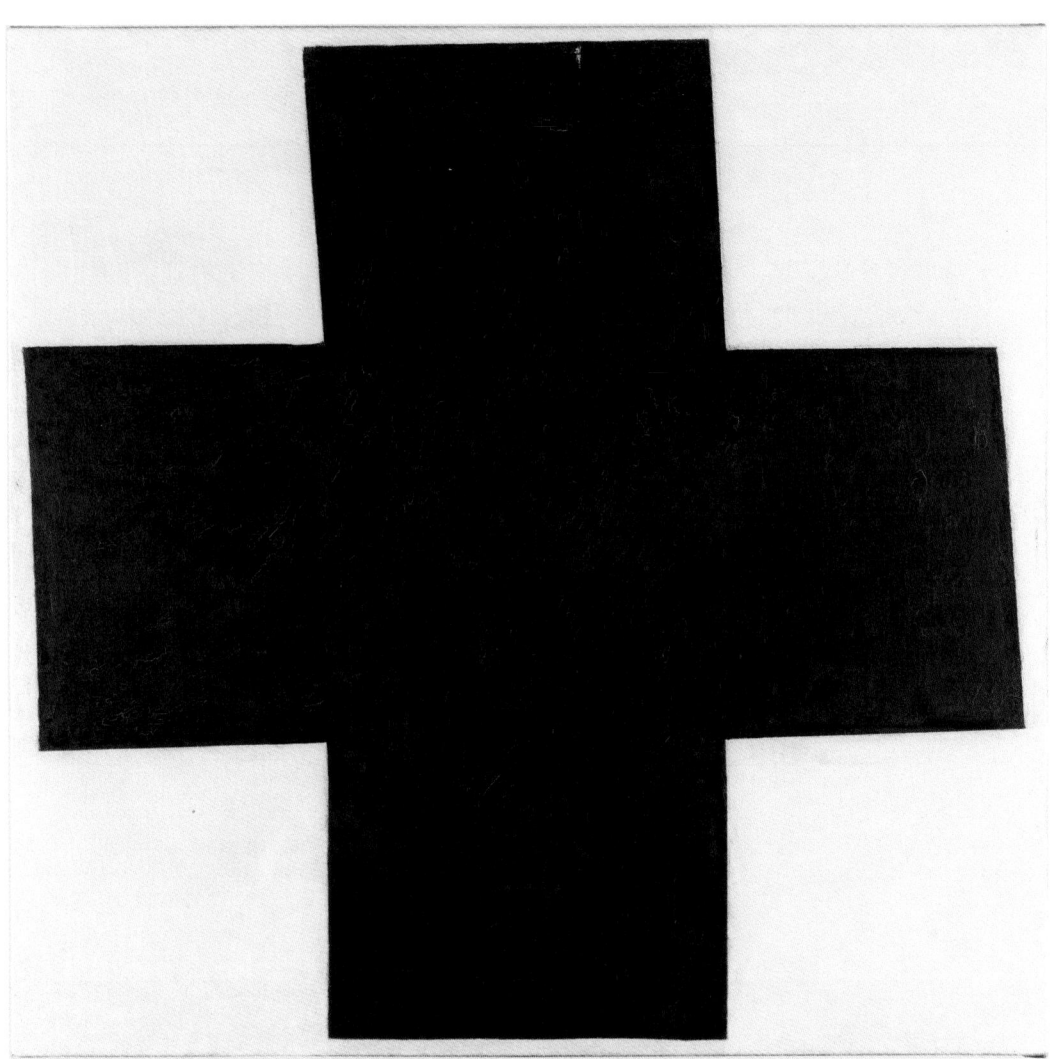

Kazimir Malevich   *Black Cross*   [1915]

oil on canvas   80 × 80 cm   gift of the Scaler Foundation, 1980, AM 1980-1

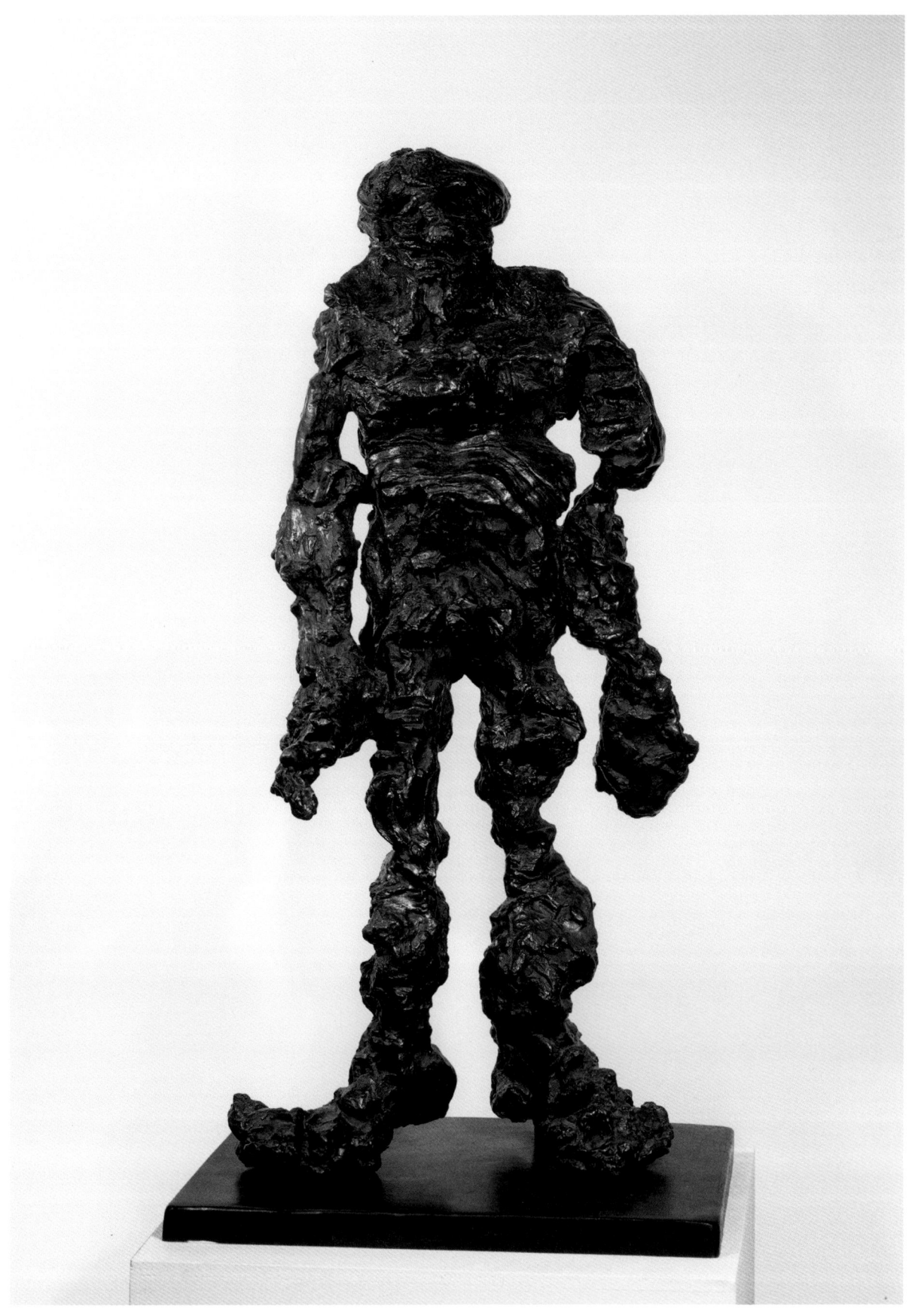

Willem de Kooning   *Clam Digger*   [1972]

bronze   151 × 63 × 54 cm   purchase, 1979, AM 1P978-735

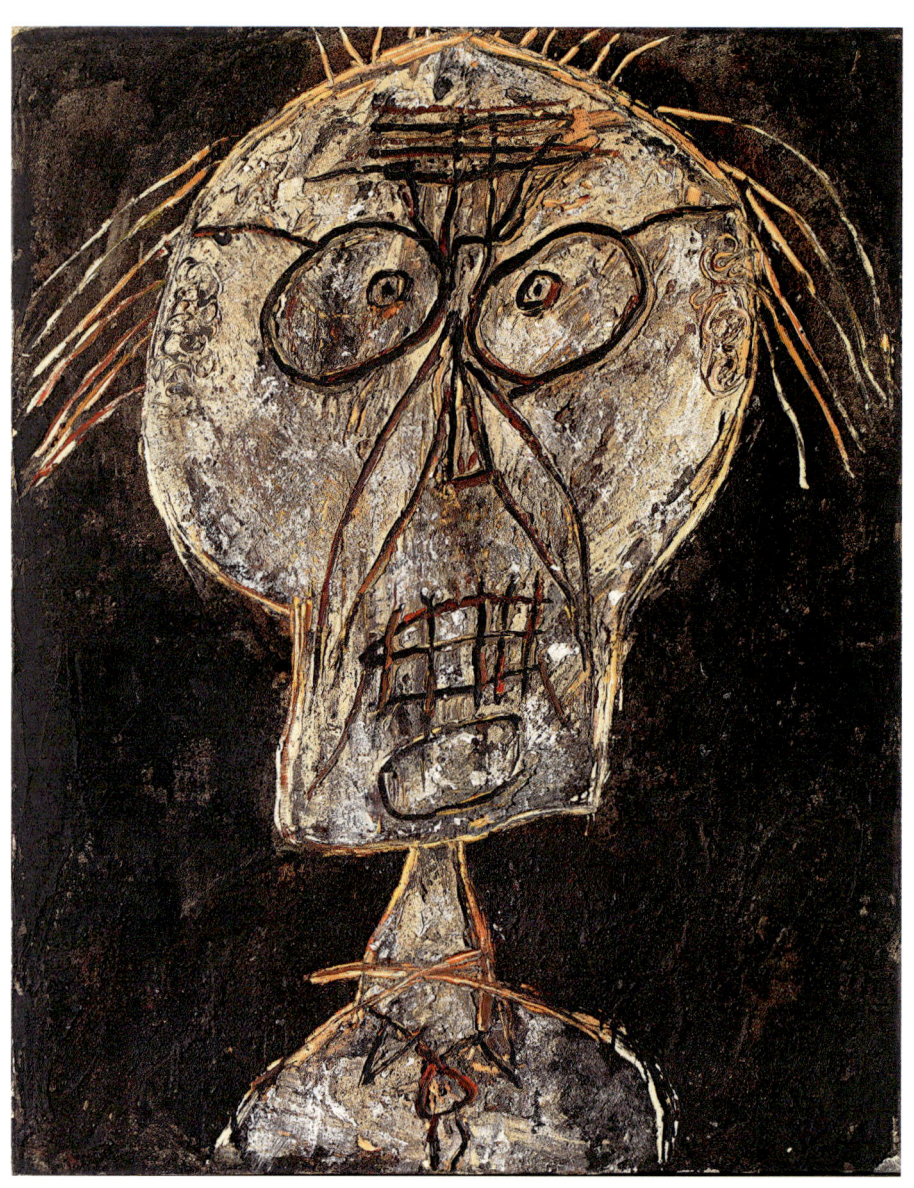

Jean Dubuffet   *Dhôtel nuancé d'abricot* [*Dhôtel Tinged with Apricot*]   July 1947–August 1947

oil on canvas   116 × 89 cm   purchased with the participation of the Scaler Foundation, 1981, AM 1981-501

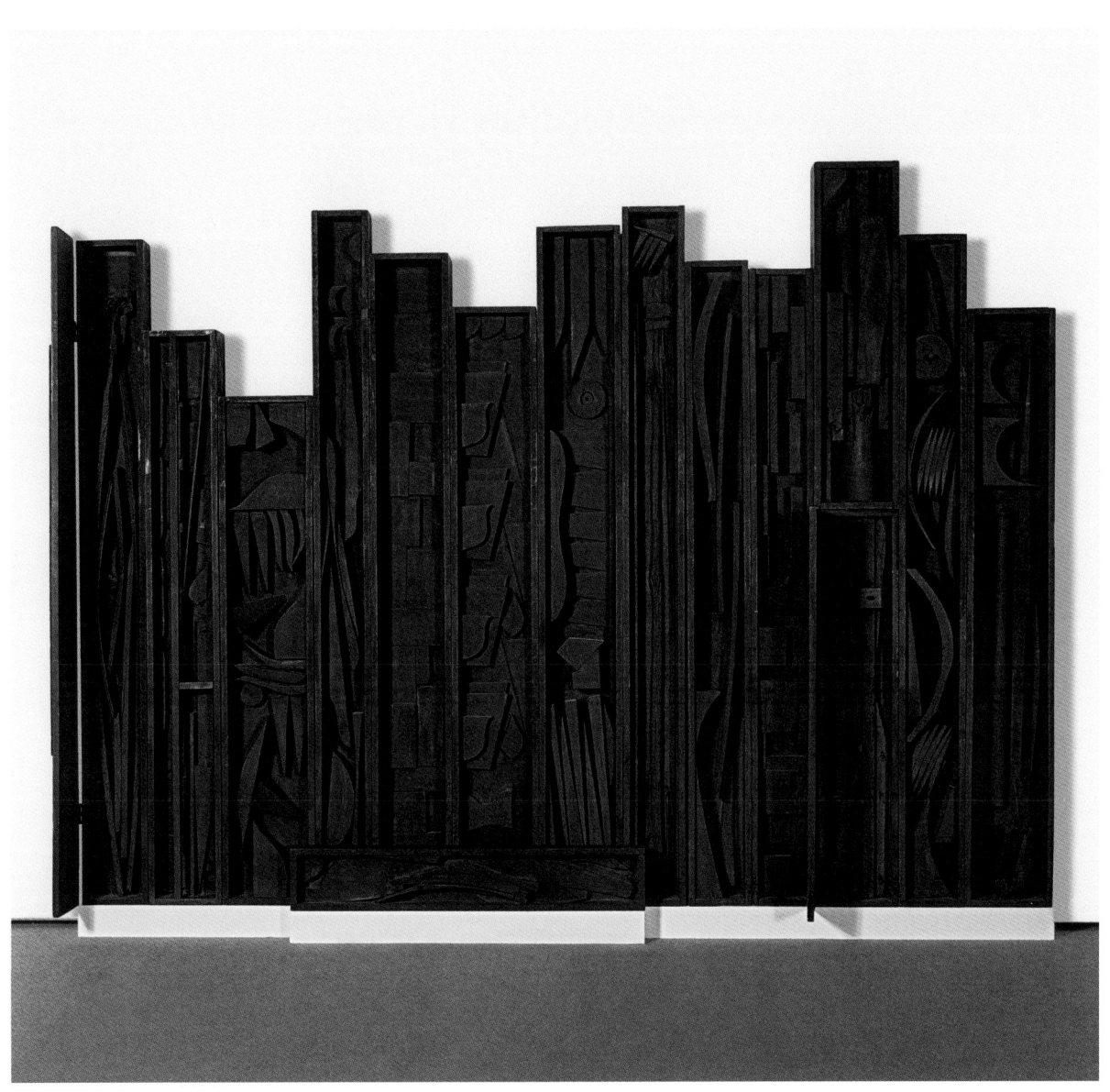

Louise Nevelson   *Tropical Garden II*   1957

carved painted wood   229 × 291 × 31 cm   purchase by the French State, 1968, attribution, 1976, AM 1976-1002

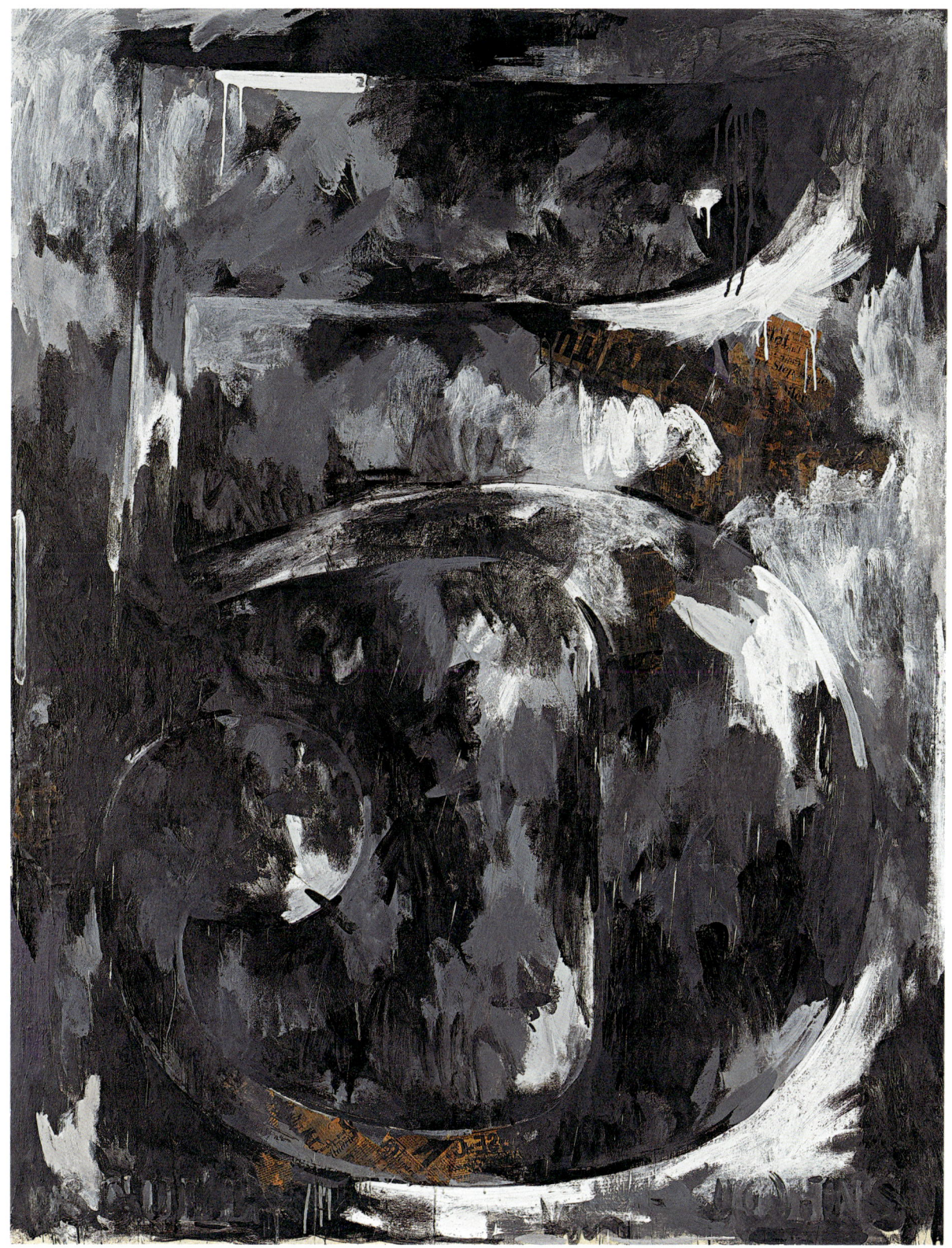

Jasper Johns *Figure 5* 1960

encaustic paint and glued newspaper on canvas 183 × 137.5 cm gift of the Scaler Foundation, 1976, AM 1976-2

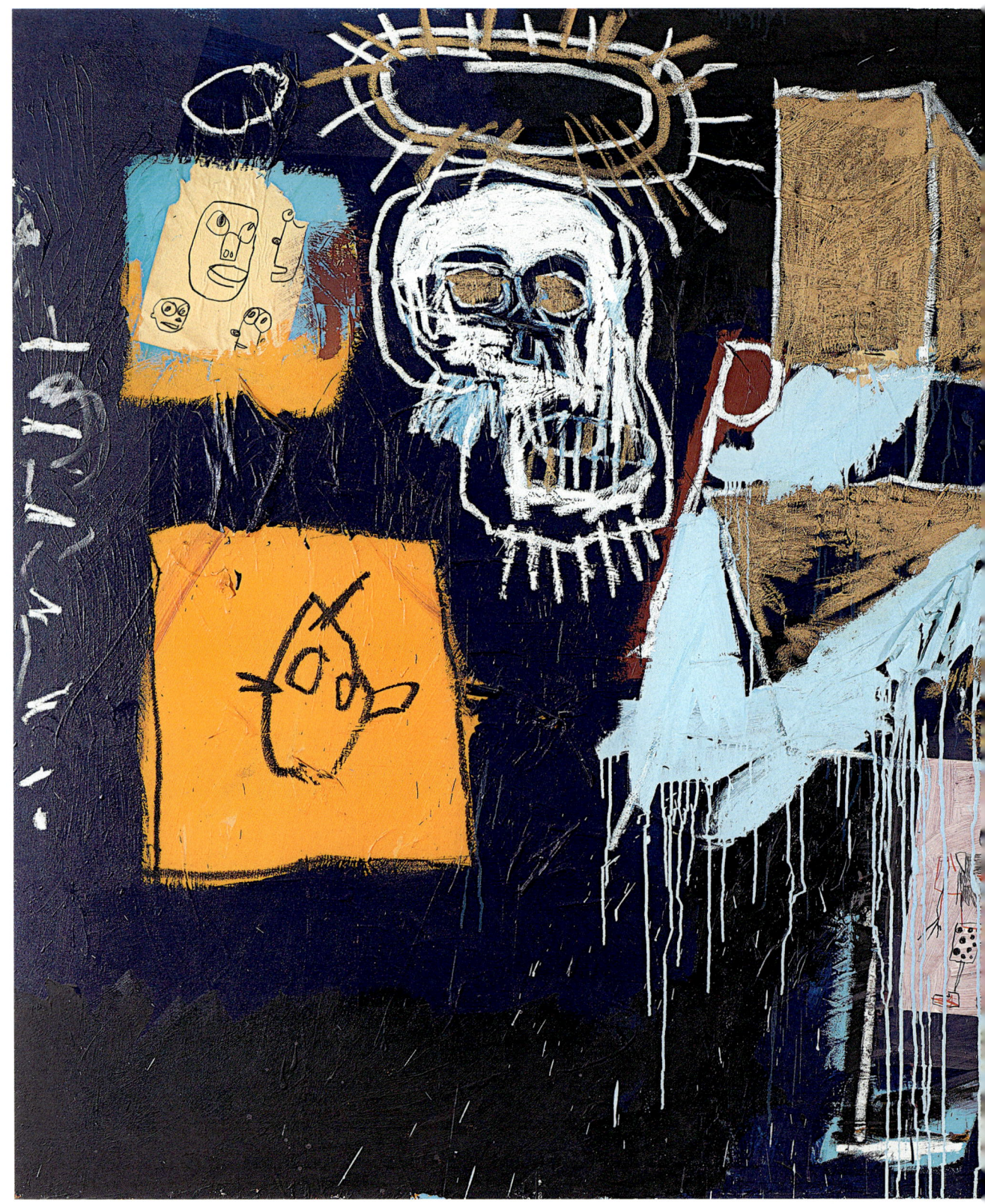

Jean-Michel Basquiat *Slave Auction* 1982

collage of crumpled paper, oil pastel and acrylic on canvas   183 × 305.5 cm   gift of the Société des Amis du Musée National d'Art Moderne, 1993, AM 1993-99

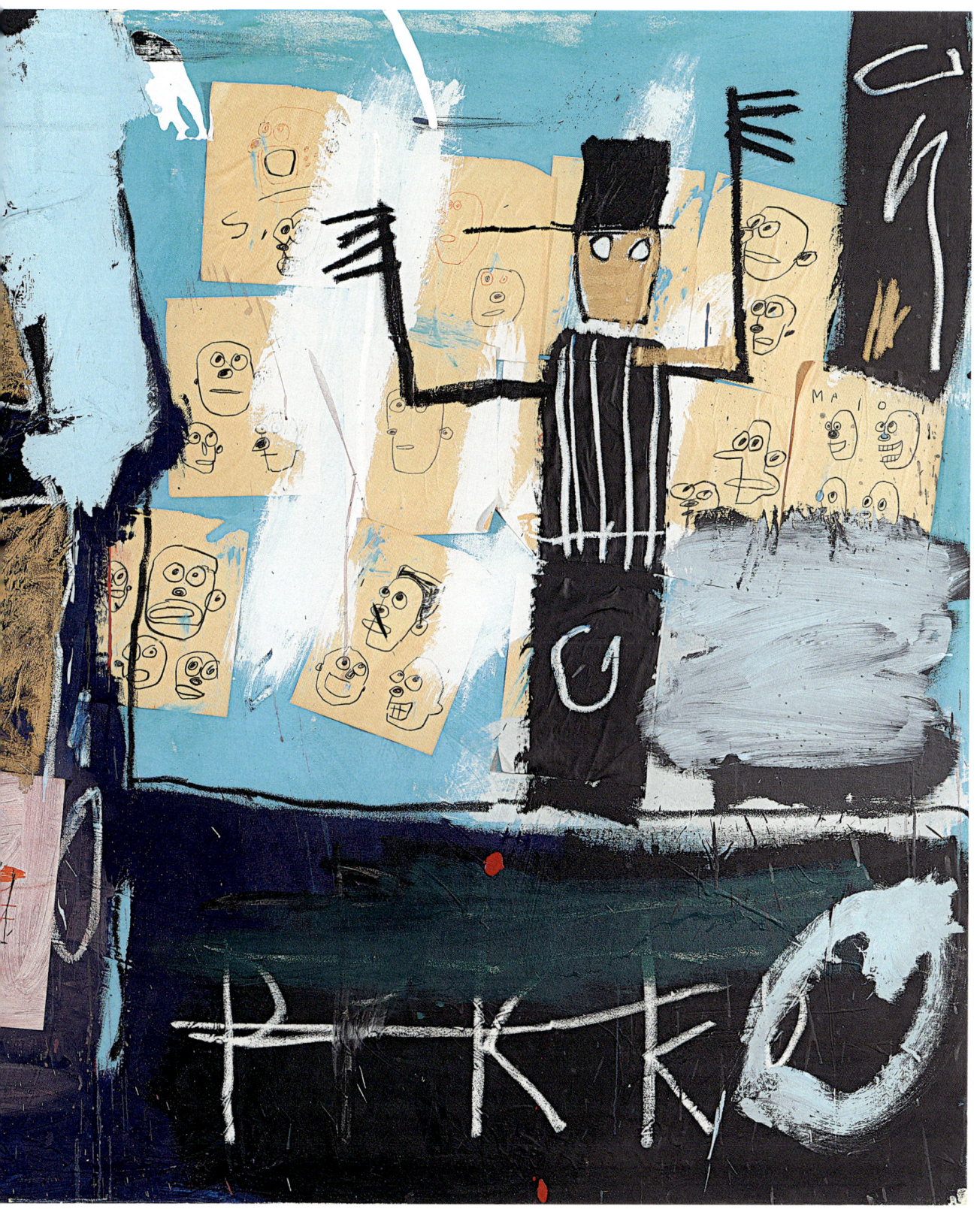

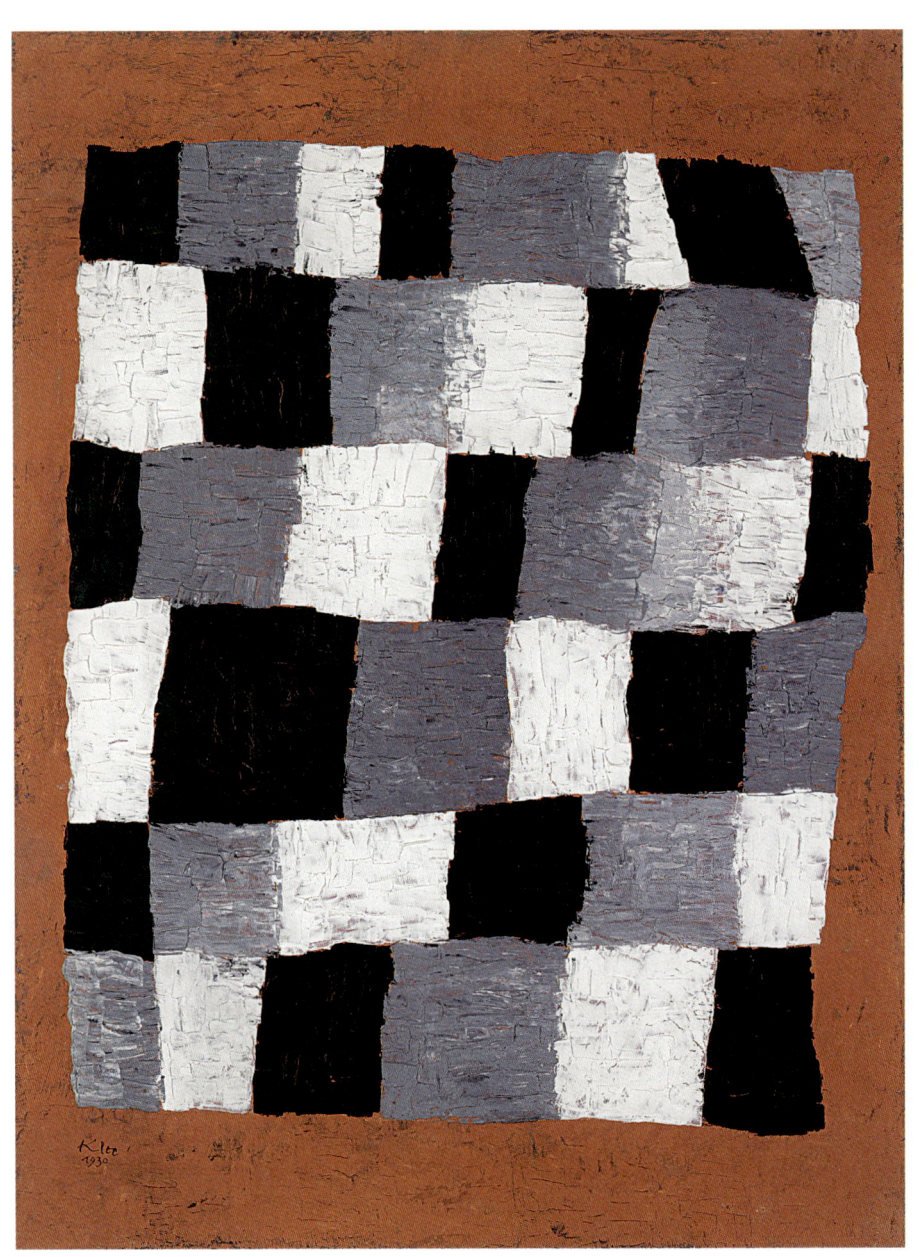

Paul Klee *Rhythmical* 1930

oil on burlap cloth   69.6 × 50.5 cm   purchase, 1984, AM 1984-356

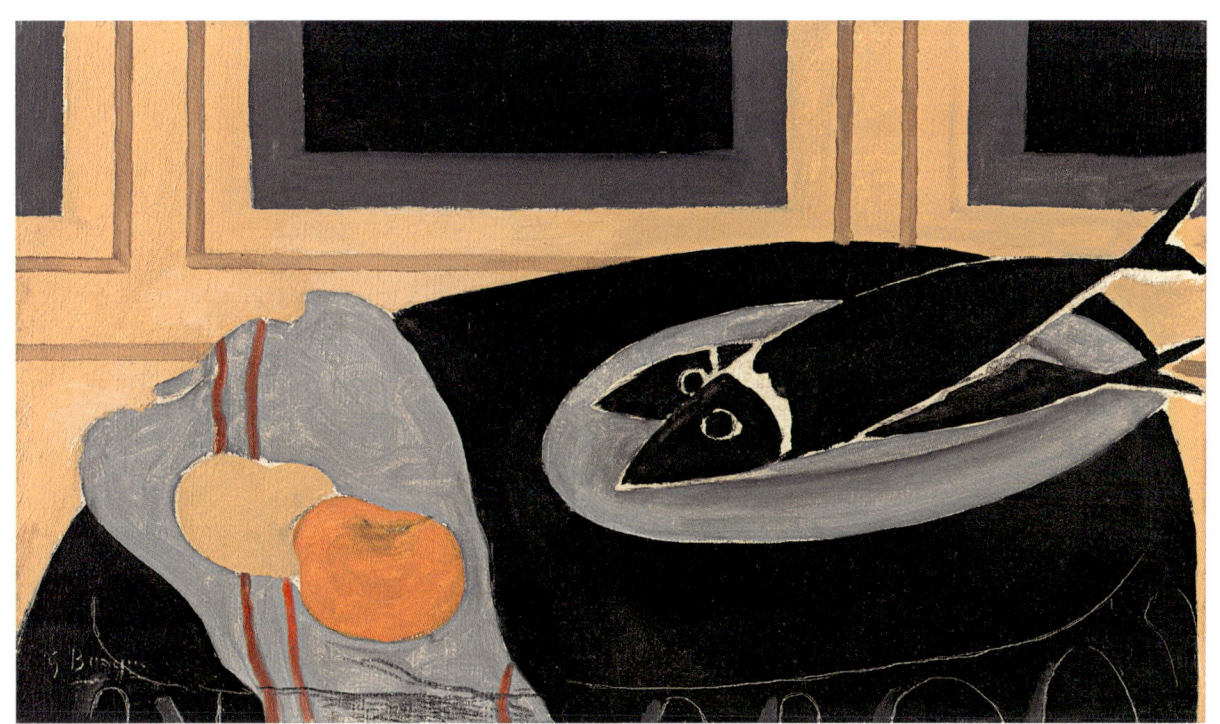

Georges Braque   *Les Poissons noirs* [*Black Fish*]   [1942]

oil on canvas   33 × 55 cm   gift of the artist, 1947, AM 2762 P

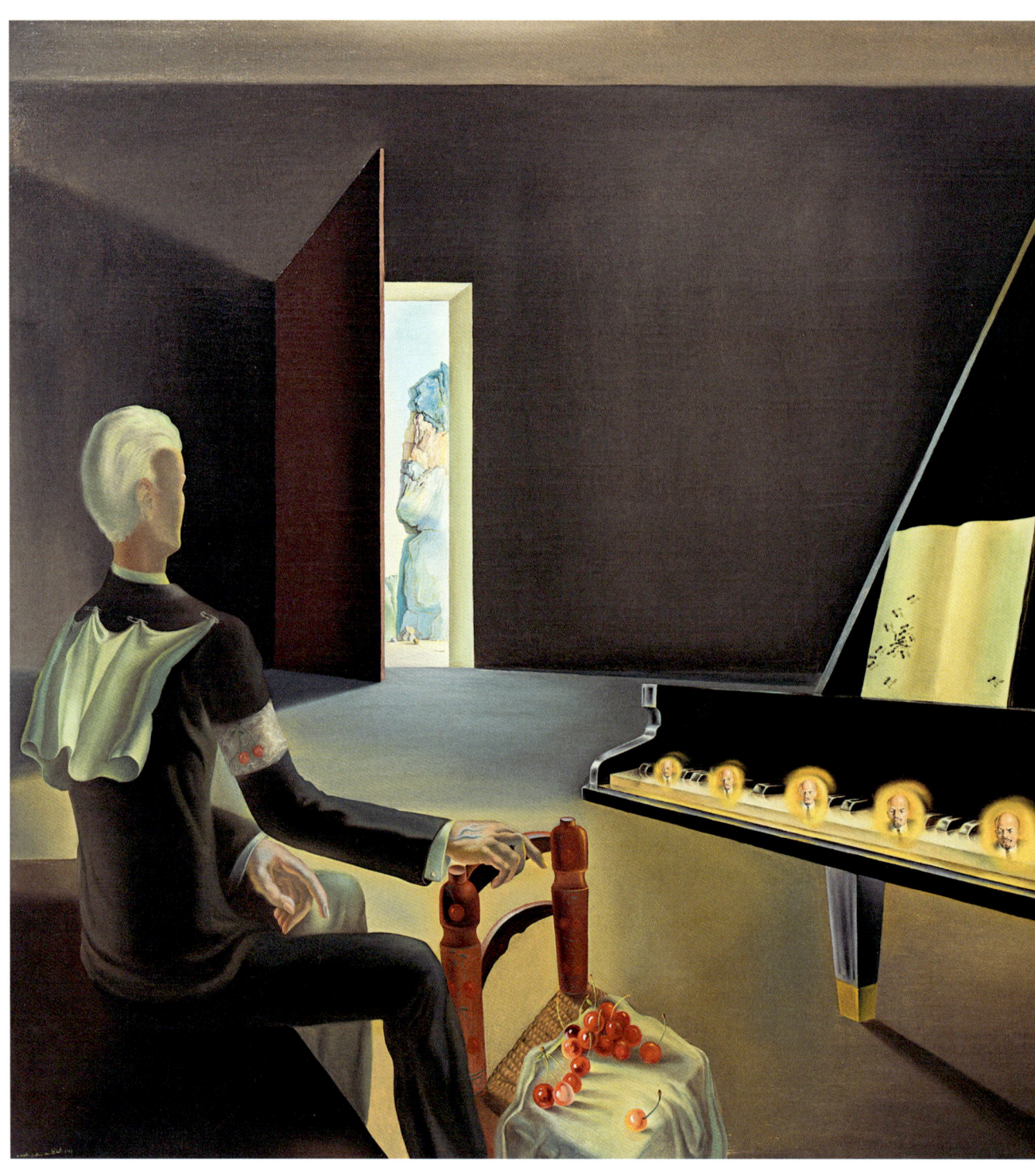

Salvador Dalí   *Hallucination partielle*. *Six images de Lénine sur un piano*
[*Partial Hallucination, Six Apparitions of Lenin on a Piano*]   1931

oil and varnish on canvas   114 × 146 cm   purchase by the French State, 1938, attribution, 1938, AM 2909 P

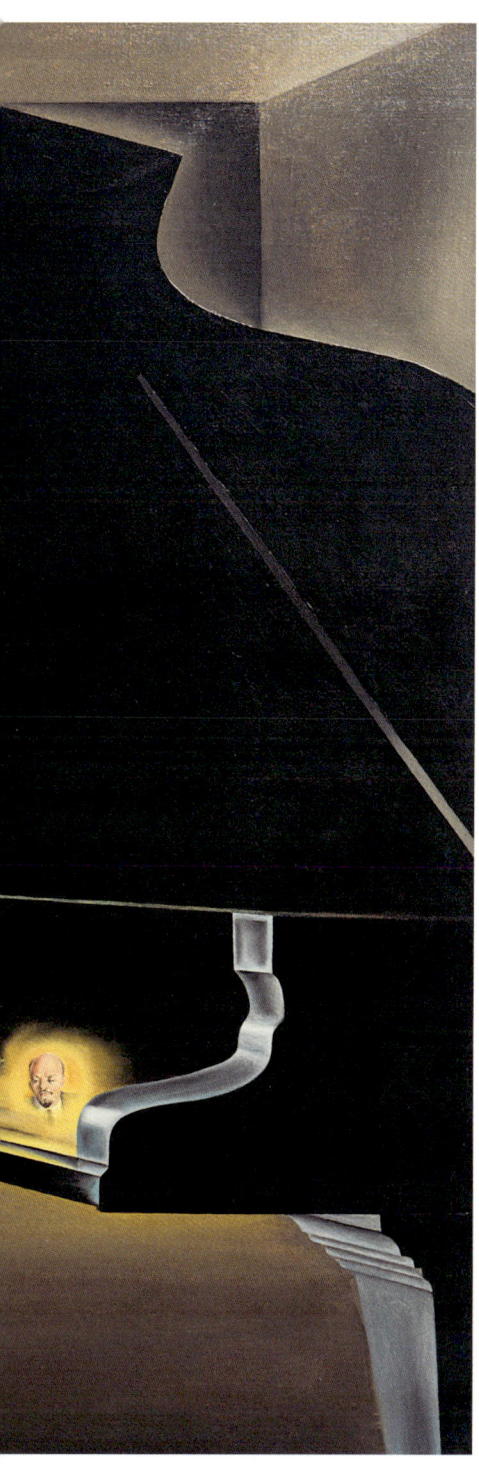

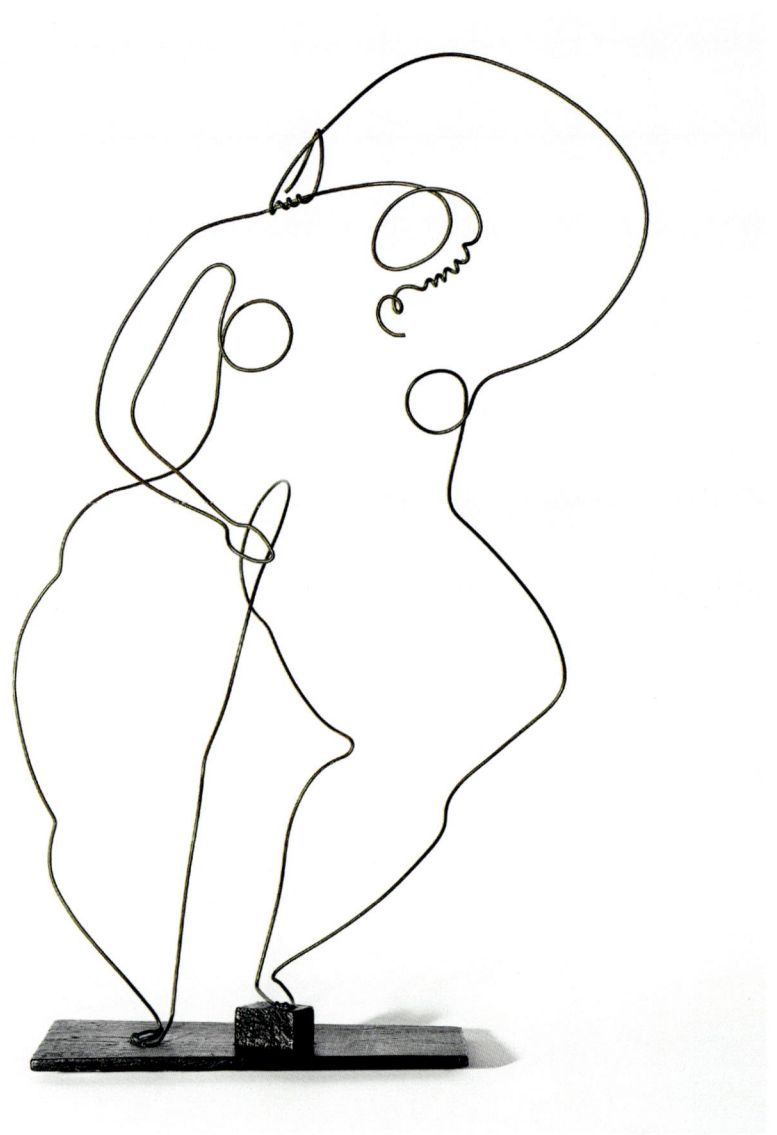

Alexander Calder   *Femme nue* [*Female Nude*]   [c. 1929]

wire on a base   72 × 38 × 31.5 cm   gift of the artist, 1966, AM 1516 S

Bernar Venet *Relief carton* 1965
industrial painting on cardboard mounted on a frame   158 × 128 × 7 cm   gift of ArcelorMittal, France, 2006, AM 2006-85

SEEING THE SPECTRE

Jacques Soulillou

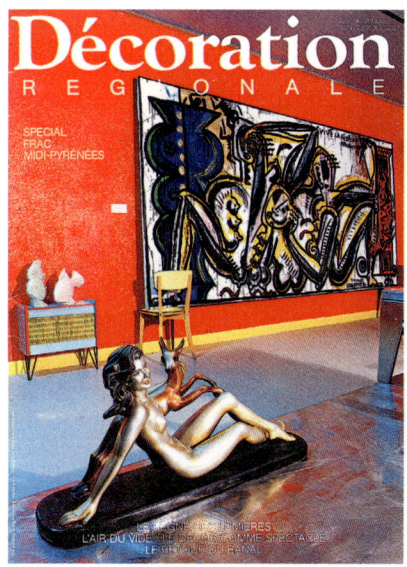

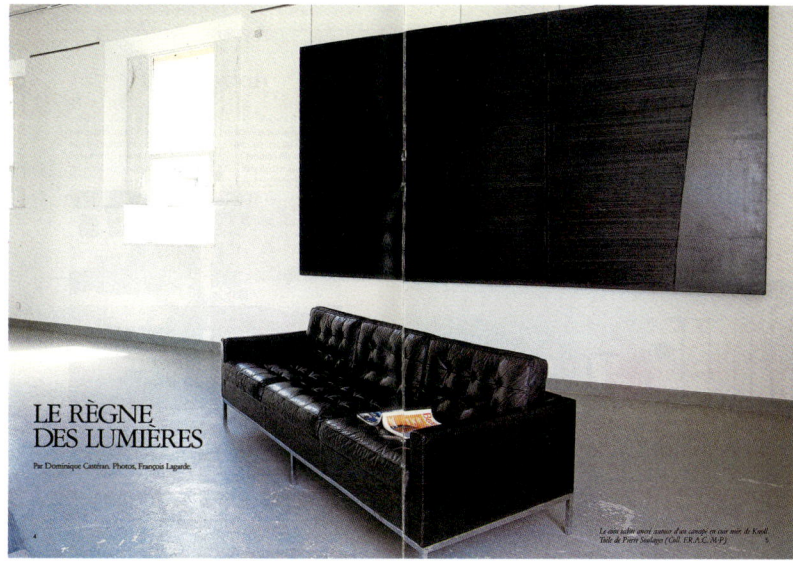

Fig.1 *Décoration régionale. Coquet, lumineux, meublé*
cover, 1986, photograph, catalogue presenting the furnished staging
of a selection of works from the Fonds Régional d'Art Contemporain
Midi-Pyrénées orchestrated by the artist collective Présence Panchounette
Published by Fonds Régional d'Art Contemporain (FRAC) Midi-Pyrénées, 1986

Fig.2 View of the decorative staging
Coquet, lumineux, meublé, by the artist collective
Présence Panchounette, 1986, photograph, published
in *Beaux Arts Magazine*, special issue, October 1998
Fonds Régional d'Art Contemporain (FRAC) Midi-Pyrénées

On 7 June 1943, Adolph Gottlieb and Mark Rothko, two eminent representatives of Abstract Expressionism, renamed 'colour field' painting by Clement Greenberg, addressed a letter to the art editor of the *New York Times*, Edward Alden Jewell, expressing their indignation at a review that had been published in the daily paper about their exhibition. Enumerating five aesthetic convictions (the first, expressed in bullish tones: "to us, art is an adventure into an unknown world [...]"), they concluded: "Consequently, if our work embodies these beliefs, it must insult anyone who is attuned to interior decoration; pictures for the home; pictures for over the mantle [...]."[1] A way of reminding the art editor not of the privileges of "the institutionalisation of anomie" (Pierre Bourdieu), but of the existence of hierarchies whose origins go back much further, and that are imposed on everyone (including the sociologist), without anyone even being aware of them.

On reading this 'quasi-manifesto', one might naturally be led to believe that what these three musketeers (Barnett Newman contributed to the writing of the letter) were calling for was nothing less than respect for the sacrosanct hierarchy between major and minor arts (always denounced, never overthrown) – interior decoration (a field so generously accorded by men to women) being part

of the latter. However, things were more complicated than that. More complicated, because the threat that Gottlieb, Rothko and Newman had in mind was less that of interior decoration, in the strict sense of the word, than it was a vague, almost spectral foreboding, to which Rothko had developed a particular sensitivity, as two episodes in his career illustrate.

The first, and no doubt the most famous, concerned the massive commission he received in 1954, in New York, when the Seagram Building and its luxury restaurant were being built. Believing that his paintings would serve merely as a decorative backdrop for millionaires, Rothko refused this commission – having naively hoped that his paintings would put them off their food.[2] The second episode, also in 1954, occurred at his exhibition at the Art Institute of Chicago. We know, from a letter he wrote to the curator Katharine Kuh, that the presentation caused him genuine distress: "Since my pictures are large, colorful, and unframed, and since museum walls are usually immense and formidable, there is the danger that the pictures relate themselves as decorative areas to the walls. This would be a distortion of their meaning, since the pictures are intimate and intense, and are *the opposite of what is decorative*".[3] What Rothko had caught sight of in these two events, and more clearly in the second,

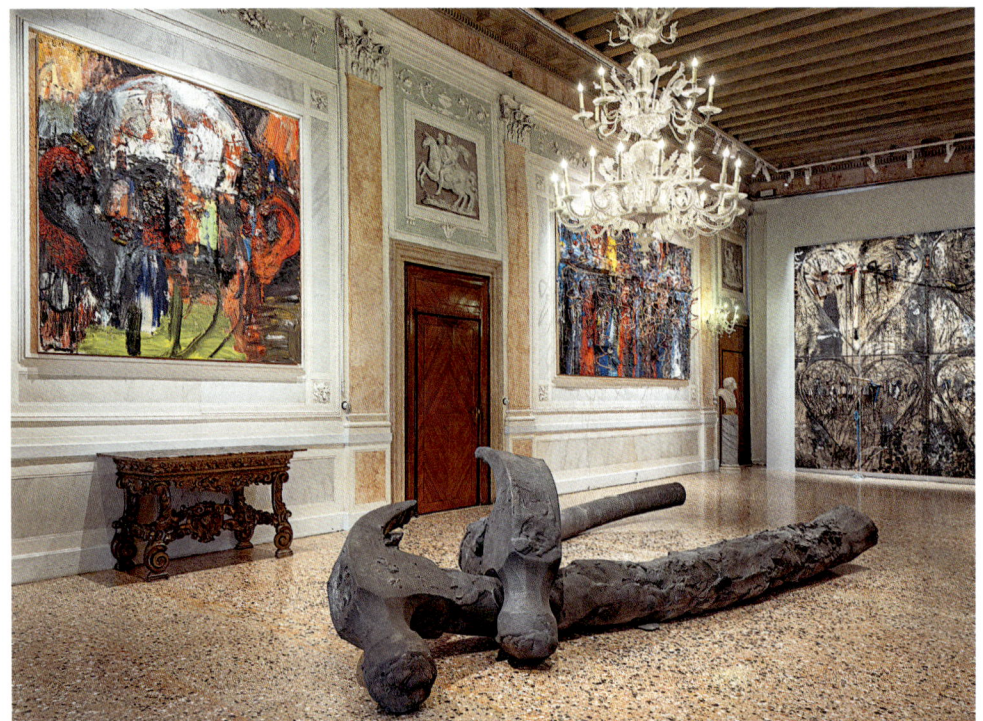

3

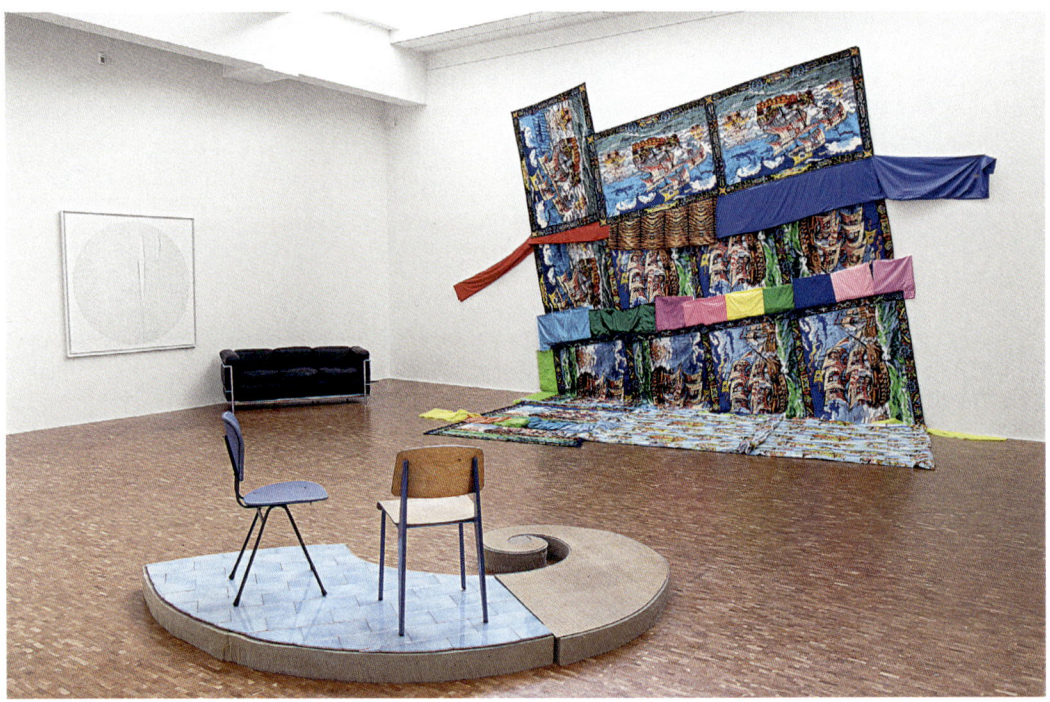

4

Fig. 3   View of the exhibition
"Dog on the Forge" by Jim Dine, 2024,
60th Venice Biennale of Art,
Palazzo Rocca, Venice,
20 April – 24 November 2024

Fig. 4   View of the exhibition "L'Envers
du décor. Dimensions décoratives
dans l'art du xxᵉ siècle", 1999
Lille Métropole Musée d'Art Moderne, d'Art
Contemporain et d'Art Brut (LaM), Villeneuve
d'Ascq, 17 October 1998 – 21 February 1999

was a spectre: the head of a Gorgon, a skull, such as can be seen in the foreground of Hans Holbein's painting *The Ambassadors* (1533). This spectre is what I call the 'decorative spectre', which is a concept stemming not from art history, but from aesthetics.[4]

Like the god Janus, this spectre has two faces. One – of less interest to us here – is visible, colourful, we might say, attracting attention with its incongruous character and presence: Jeff Koons at Versailles, for example – provoking laughter or indignation. This face of the spectre defies the canonical rule of decoration, of submitting oneself fully to "that which is fitting". The other face is invisible, but its presence is indisputably felt. Wassily Kandinsky was no doubt one of the very first to have perceived it, when he discovered one of his paintings in his studio stored on its side rather than vertically: "The danger of decorative art was clear to me; the dead, illusory existence of stylised forms could only repel me."[5] An exclusively Western and recent syndrome. To these two restrictions, I would add a third: the decorative spectre chiefly concerns painting, sculpture and architecture; video art and photography have little to fear from its apparitions.

A short time later, on the other side of the Atlantic, another young artist found himself face to face with the head of a Gorgon: Yves Klein, whose career began practically at the same time as Rothko's exhibition at the Art Institute of Chicago. After his second solo exhibition, held at the Colette Allendy Gallery in 1956, he wrote the following on the subject – in words so candid they compel admiration:

> I displayed [at this exhibition] a selection of PROPOSITIONS of colors in various formats. […] Unfortunately, this occasion made apparent that many spectators were slaves to their manner of seeing: they were much more sensitive to the relationships of the PROPOSITIONS to each other and tended to recreate decorative and architectural elements out of the colors. This forced me to go much further in my experiments and to present in January 1957 at the Galleria Apollinaire in Milan a show devoted to what I dared to call my 'Blue Period'.[6]

The only solution he found for escaping the spectre was to sacrifice polychromy and make the choice of blue monochrome, more evocative of the sky and air.

In 1986, the collective Présence Panchounette was invited to present a new perspective on the collections of the Frac Midi-Pyrénées, which were relocated for the occasion to the premises of the Centre culturel de l'Albigeois in Albi. Entitled "Coquet, lumineux, meublé" [Stylish, Bright, Furnished], the exhibition reconfigured the collections into three parts, each of which formed a subdivision of a 'show home':

> Respectively: 1 hippy room with Parent, Ben, Dufour, etc.; 1 trendy room with Combas, Blanchard, Di Rosa and so on; 1 chic room with Viallat, Tapiès, Soulages […]. The first had wallpaper, tired Art Deco, Récamier and a café corner. The second, Minitel, motorbike, '60s furniture and Paic Citron. The last, Knoll, Knoll and green plants.[7]

Behind the Knoll sofa hung a triptych by Pierre Soulages, in front of it lay a rug by Sonia Delaunay, revisited by BazileBustamante.[8]

Note 11 in the text "L'air du vide" (Air of Emptiness, an allusion to Gilles Lipovetsky's book *L'Ère du vide*, published in 1983), in the catalogue irreverently entitled *Décoration régionale*[9] (another allusion, this time to the journal *Décoration internationale*), reads as follows: "It would be a shame if none of the 'exhibited' artists protests", on the grounds that their work had been reduced to the level of "merchandise", or rather, in this instance, to a "spot of colour". Only one artist, painter Bernard Dufour, protested in writing against this decorative staging. His letter, dated 28 August 1986, was addressed to "Madame Présence Panchounette/ artiste-ensemblier-décorateur".[10] Dufour, who explicitly made reference to *Décoration régionale*, resisted reacting with typical indignation, instead responding with ironic hauteur: "Contrary to what, provocatively, you were hoping for, I am not protesting, especially since your feeble and fashionable ideology is simply laughable." But Dufour was not the only protester[11] (there is no doubt that writing to say "I am not going to protest" is tantamount to doing precisely that) – there were also Claude Viallat and Pierre Soulages.[12] *Décoration internationale*, which clearly had not appreciated the allusion, threatened Frac Midi-Pyrénées with legal proceedings. All was well.

Underlying these protests is an interesting and potentially explosive question: can artists (or their beneficiaries) who esteem that their work has been reduced to the rank of a decorative element, consider this as constituting an infringement of their moral rights? Perhaps it was faced with the impossibility of erecting a protective sanctuary around every work of art, that, feeling blue one evening in 1970, Rothko realised the futility of seeking to reach the heights of the sublime and pierce the vaults of heaven if it was only to see his work finish up as a patch of colour brightening up a room, matching, if such was required, the colours of the sofa, the pattern on the carpet or the dress of the lady of the house. In those conditions, he might as well kill himself. Happy are those who do not see the spectre.

But not everybody does see it. Questioned by Philippe Dagen in 2024 about the presence of his works in the Palazzo Rocca Contarini Corfù, and in response to the question "What are Dine and his works doing in a place that seems so unsuitable for them?", Jim Dine replied: "Confronting it [...]. When the paintings arrived from my studio, I saw them in a completely different light: it was as though they belonged to the palazzo".[13] And Philippe Dagen continued: "On the ground floor, [...], the small paintings of heads are completely at home; the same is true of the very large paintings in the main gallery, on the first floor, which harmonise well with the decorative elements and the allegorical frescos".[14] Jim Dine, the *enfant terrible* of pop art, had blended into the background; he had not seen the spectre.

Décoration régionale had an interesting epilogue, in two stages. Firstly, in 1989. At FIAC, facing the Galerie Eric Fabre stand, a work could be seen by Présence Panchounette entitled *Black is Back*: a black triptych "in the style of Soulages", with, in front of it, a Le Corbusier–Perriand chaise longue. No rug. Soulages looked at the work, even met the person who had painted the triptych, and apparently took it all with a sense of humour. He no longer saw the spectre. The second time was in 1998. At LaM in Villeneuve-d'Ascq an exhibition was held entitled "L'Envers du décor. Dimensions décoratives dans l'art du xxᵉ siècle" [Behind the Scenes: decorative dimensions in 20th-century art]. Présence Panchounette (which, at that time, no longer existed as a collective) offered to recreate the 'decorative staging' of 1986, with the triptych and black sofa of the same year. Soulages refused:[15] he had seen the spectre again. Finally, it was a white monochrome by Geneviève Claisse that was hung behind the Knoll sofa. The label was as follows:

> The living room area, centred around
> a black leather sofa by Knoll.
> Reconstruction
> First presentation: 1986
> Installation: "Le Corbusier" sofa,
> painting: Pierre Soulages

As we know, the 'colour' white is often associated with spectres, and this 'work', which was neither by Présence Panchounette nor by either Geneviève Claisse or Pierre Soulages, was literally an 'apparition' that defied the laws of optics. No photograph of this 'reconstruction' appears in the exhibition catalogue. However, in a special edition that *Beaux Arts Magazine* devoted to it in October 1998, there is a full-page feature titled "Objects" by Xavier Douroux and Éric Troncy, which shows the Soulages painting and the Knoll sofa, with a copy of *Beaux Arts Magazine* open.

Kandinsky, Rothko, Klein and Soulages (but not Jim Dine) all felt, with varying degrees of intensity, the presence of the spectre. No artist to date has ever been able to prevent their work being used for 'decorative purposes'. But 'decorative purposes', 'decorative dimension', 'decorative feeling' and many other similar phrases do not describe the 'decorative spectre'. The essential difference between the decorative as defined by art historians and the decorative spectre is that the former is entirely subordinate to the décor – merely one of its elements, identifiable and datable by its style. It can even be touched, understood, photographed. This is totally impossible with the decorative spectre, which is an ominous shadow that the artist sees passing in front of the painting and that seems to strip it, in a fraction of a second, of all its substance.

With the chapel that bears his name in Houston, Rothko understood the extent of the repellent force that décor exerts on the spectre. He used no fewer than three architects to complete the plans of what the *Wikipedia* entry 'Rothko Chapel' neatly describes as "a meditative space filled with his paintings". Like Piet Mondrian, he knew that to create a "new plastic reality", it would be necessary to unify architecture, sculpture and painting, as a bulwark against any intrusion by the spectre.[16]

There is no trace of the spectre either in the Rothko Chapel or in Mondrian's *Salon for Madame B... in Dresden* or in Monet's 'Waterlilies', as there never was, either, in the Scrovegni Chapel decorated by Giotto or the Sistine Chapel decorated by Michelangelo – but not for the same reasons. In the last two examples, the reason that the spectre had no chance of emerging from the wall and blinding the artist, as happened to Rothko at the Art Institute exhibition, was because the whole space was a celebration of the union between man and God, leaving no room for doubt. This celebration required the creation of a magnificent setting that bears witness both to the power of the commissioner and the glory of God to whom it pays homage. The only doubts Giotto or Michelangelo may have had would have been whether they were equal to the task they had been set.

The reason that the decorative spectre is exclusively an 'affair' of Western culture is that in no other culture has the work of art achieved autonomy in this silent and gradual way, against decoration (of which the setting is just one element). In 1860, basing his research on both Western and non-Western creations, Gottfried Semper published his voluminous *Der Stil* [Style], in which he attempted to protect the fundamental unity between decoration and the work of art, which until that point had functioned as a binary relationship that no one imagined could ever

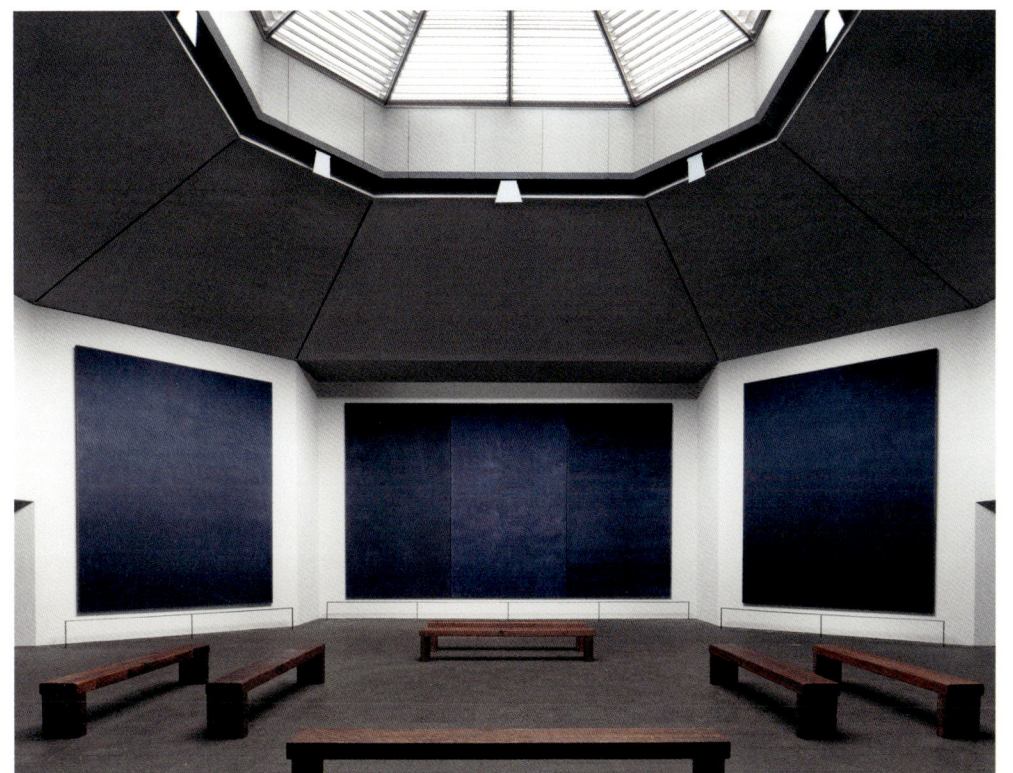

5

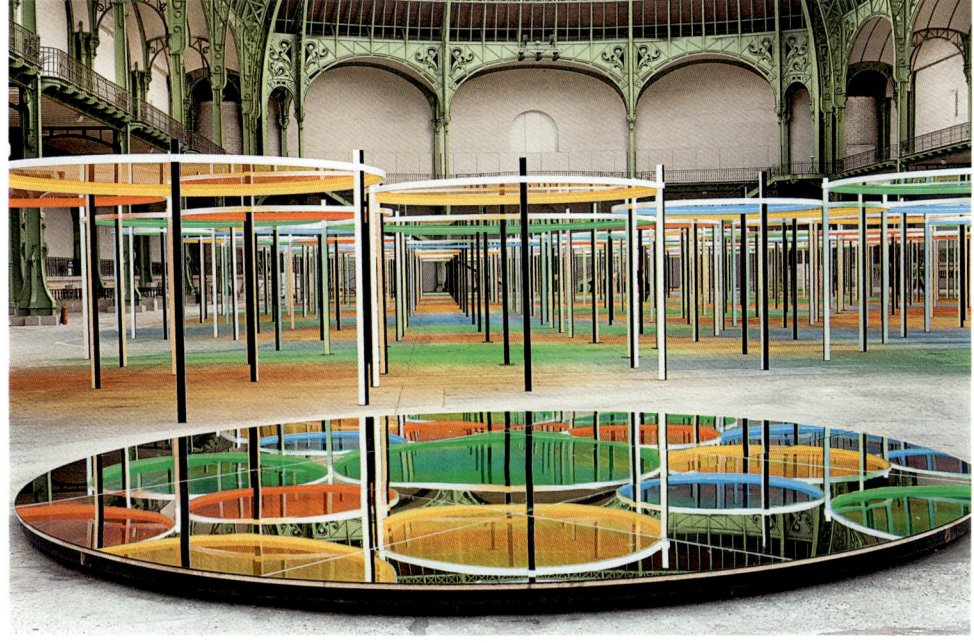

6

Fig. 5 Paul Hester
Rothko Chapel Interior, 2021,
photograph

Fig. 6 Raphaël Gaillarde
View of the exhibition "Monumenta
2012. Excentrique(s), travail in situ,
œuvre de Daniel Buren",
2012, digital print
Raphaël Gaillarde Collection, Paris
Grand Palais, Paris, 10 May – 21 June 2012

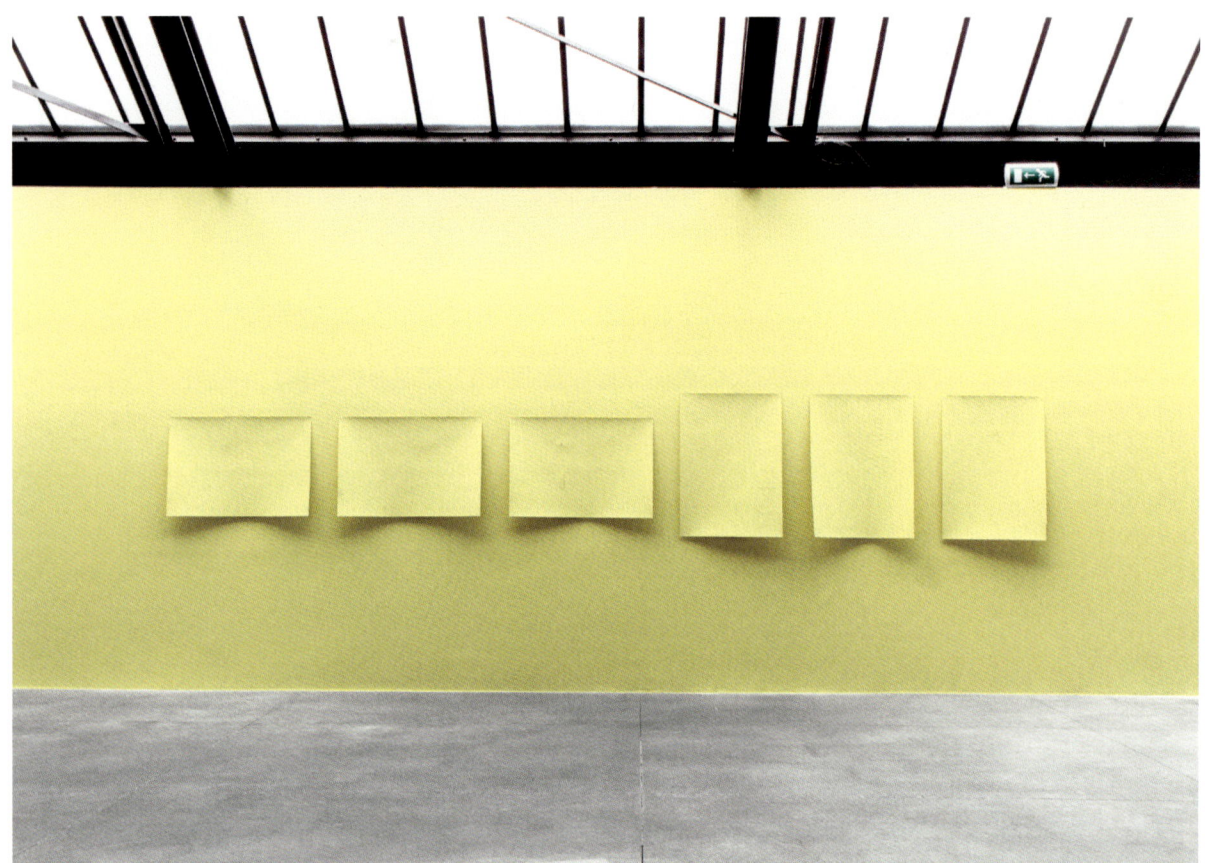

7

Fig. 7   Claude Rutault
repeint 2019, 2019, paint on paper,
variable dimensions according
to the individual staging,
view of the exhibition "Claude
Rutault – monochrome 5 sur
une grille de marelle"
Fondation CAB, Brussels,
3 September – 14 December 2019

be cast aside. But it was too late: his message had become inaudible. It is worth remembering in passing that Semper was also known as one of the first to argue that ancient buildings were originally coloured – a notion considered at the time a veritable offence to good taste by those convinced of the Parthenon's pristine whiteness and who saw only an indecent spectre in its reconstructed, colourful façade.

However, even in the most radical experiments that marked the first quarter of the 20th century, we can still identify signs of attachment to some of the fundamentals of the old world: "In its first stage", wrote Malevich, "Suprematism is a purely philosophical movement, a movement of cognition through colour; in its second stage, it is the form that can be applied, constituting *the new Suprematist style of decoration*".[17]

The modern transposition of the concept of décor is known as 'installation' or 'in situ' or 'site-specific installation'. The difference between décor – always local, linked to a place – and site-specific installation resides in the fact that the latter occurs in a world that has acknowledged the death of God. In France,

two artists with diametrically opposed approaches, Daniel Buren and Claude Rutault, have understood particularly well how site-specific décor can serve as an impenetrable bulwark against the intrusion of the decorative spectre. Daniel Buren has created site-specific installations that are rigorously classic in style, such as *Les Deux Plateaux* [*The Two Plateaux*], in the great courtyard of the Palais Royal, or, on the contrary, of a wild Baroque style bordering on Rococo, such as at the Louis Vuitton Foundation and the Grand Palais. Claude Rutault, seemingly duller but in reality unswervingly radical, transposed the problem of the white cube[18] into the apartment of the collector who agreed to have one of his walls painted the same colour as the monochrome canvas that was to adorn it. But he also exposed the ambiguity and duplicity of the white cube, which claims to set aside the external world, thereby restoring the optimal conditions that preside over the 'act of the mind' (Marcel Proust) that gives rise to the work of art, while feigning ignorance of the fact that the gallery – preferably with white, erroneously neutral walls – is merely a transitional space between the gallery and the collector's living room.

1
The letter contained a list of ten terms that served as foils for everything that the two painters detested. See *From the Archive: Adolph Gottlieb and Mark Rothko*, 23 September 2022, Adolph and Esther Gottlieb Foundation, online: https://www.gottliebfoundation.org/blog/2022/9/23/from-the-archives-adolph-gottlieb-and-mark-rothko [accessed 29 November 2024].

2
"To ruin the appetite of every son of a bitch who ever eats in that room", as he famously put it. See, in particular, James E.B. Breslin, *Mark Rothko: A Biography* (Chicago: The University of Chicago Press, 1998).

3
Quoted on https://www.nga.gov/features/mark-rothko/mark-rothko-classic-paintings.html (accessed 28 April 2024). Italics author's own.

4
This term is introduced for the first time in Jacques Soulillou, *Le Livre de l'ornement et de la guerre* (Marseille: Éditions Parenthèses, 2003).

5
Wassily Kandinsky, "Rückblicke [Regards sur le passé]", 1913, in *Regards sur le passé et autres textes, 1912-1922*, Jean-Paul Bouillon (ed.) (Paris: Hermann, 1974), p. 110.

6
Yves Klein, "My position in the battle between line and color" [1958], in *Overcoming the Problematics of Art: The Writings of Yves Klein*, trans. Klaus Ottmann (Putnam: Spring Publications, 2007), pp. 19–20.

7
Letter from Frédéric N. Roux to Jacques Soulillou, 26 June 1986.

8
François Lagarde immortalised this installation in a photograph used by the author for the cover of the reissue of the book *Le Décoratif* (Paris: Klincksieck, 2016). The Soulages, the Knoll and the Delaunay-Bustamante appear in the same image, which was not the case in *Décoration régionale* (see *infra*), where the Delaunay-Bustamante was shot separately with other pieces.

9
Jean-Marc Ferrari and Brigitte Rambaud (ed.), *Coquet, lumineux, meublé / Décoration régionale, Spécial FRAC Midi-Pyrénées*, exh. cat., Albi, Centre culturel de l'Albigeois, 11 June – 9 August 1986 (Toulouse: Frac Midi-Pyrénées, 1986).

10
This letter comes from the collection of Les Abattoirs, Musée-Frac Occitanie Toulouse. I would like to thank Les Abattoirs documentation department for passing it on to me, and in particular Joëlle Pijaudier-Cabot, who successfully undertook the research.

11
In his letter, Bernard Dufour had added: "I would also like to inform you, Madam, that I have refused both to reply to the protestations that certain painters made to me by telephone and to associate myself with them".

12
Claude Viallat, in no uncertain terms; Soulages more moderately (telephone interview by the author on 28 June 2024 with Jean-Marc Ferrari, then director of Frac Midi-Pyrénées). Note that all the artists mentioned were reacting to the catalogue and not following a visit to the exhibition. In the catalogue, the photograph of the Soulages and the Knoll (in the chapter "Le règne des lumières") was captioned as followed: "The living room area, centred around a black leather sofa by Knoll".

13
Philippe Dagen, "Les rêves de palais de Jim Dine", *Le Monde* (12 May 2024), p. 25.

14
Ibid.

15
In an email dated 19 May 2024, Joëlle Pijaudier-Cabot, who was director of LAM, co-curator, with Catherine Delvigne, of the exhibition and who, in 1986, worked at the Ministry of Culture's Delegation for the Plastic Arts, responsible for the Midi-Pyrénées region, wrote to me as follows: "I well remember Soulages's anger at the time of *Décoration régionale*, and his opposition to the PP

[Présence Panchounette] piece then." "Opposition" here refers to what Soulages conveyed to Joëlle Pijaudier-Cabot, when she called him to know whether he would allow part of the 1986 exhibition to be recreated with the triptych and sofa.

16
On this subject, see also Piet Mondrian, *Natural Reality and Abstract Reality: An Essay in Trialogue Form* (New York: George Braziller, 1995).

17
Kazimir Malevich, "Le Suprématisme", *Écrits*, trans. Andrée Robel-Chicurel (Paris: Champ Libre, 1975), p. 214. Italics author's own. The great art historian Camilla Gray-Prokofieva (1936–1971) has shown how the creation of the *Black Square* could be linked to be the design of the sets and costumes of the Suprematist opera *Victory over the Sun* (1913), which sparked a scandal as significant as Picasso's Cubist sets and costumes for *Parade* did in Paris, four years later.

18
On this subject, see Brian O'Doherty, *Inside the White Cube: The Ideology of the Gallery Space* (Berkeley: University of California Press, 2000 [1976]). Brian O'Doherty also successfully pulled off the Oulipian feat of not resorting to the word 'décor' once throughout his entire text.

Marion Mailaender

INTERIORS

"Colour is a joy that has nothing to do with architecture but is part of architecture".

Philippe Starck

Responding to Didier Ottinger's invitation to play in the colour wheel has been a delightful experience. Each colour, within its own domestic context, comes to life and encourages us to reflect on our immediate environment.

Arranged by colour, the works are mixed with no hierarchy and displayed in everyday settings – a living room, a utility room, a bedroom, a doctor's surgery – in which paintings, sculptures, videos, furniture, household appliances and light fittings all take their place. This helps demystify the objects and invites us to reflect more deeply on their emotional and sensory impact. I love the idea of taking these works out of their 'white box' and seeing them displayed in a garage or a student's studio.

"Sometimes, colour can be brought into an interior not with paint or furniture but via the most unexpected objects, such as a Bloody Mary. Colour can be subtly introduced into the atmosphere through the objects and moments of daily life", said Andrée Putman. I like the idea that we can also introduce colour into a space through a piece of clothing, a cocktail or a packet of crisps.

The role I accepted was that of a decorator – the one who selects colours, arranges furniture and places artworks; an interior designer–decorator. It is a very different role to that of the architect, who builds and rationalises. Sometimes, out of snobbery, we consider white, grey-beige and black to be the epitome of style,

modernity, radicalism and purity. We are often afraid of colour. I find myself tempted by the idea of not choosing, of opting out of colour, but I am immediately drawn back to the colourful objects and works of art that shape the spaces in which we really live.

"The colour of objects transforms the space. It is one of the most powerful ways to create an atmosphere and influence our emotions", said David Hicks.

The link between these monochromatic works could be that they belong to the collection of a fanatic who selects works and objects by colour. It is different as an idea, but on reflection, it seems as valid an approach to collecting as any other. After all, why not collect blue? The principle would be to assemble objects by their dominant colour rather than by period, creator or style. Each nuance could tell a different story or evoke a different emotion. Each colour has an infinity variety of shades, which I have joyfully jumbled together in each room. Some nuances are almost contradictory, dissonant even, yet together, they cohere into a loosely unified ensemble. Whether in a 'total look', or assembled in a more subtle way, these are the scenarios of colour that are presented to us, expanding on the equally subjective idea that colours have a sound or a smell.

Finally, the scenography of this exhibition offers as many levels of interpretation as there are shades of colour.

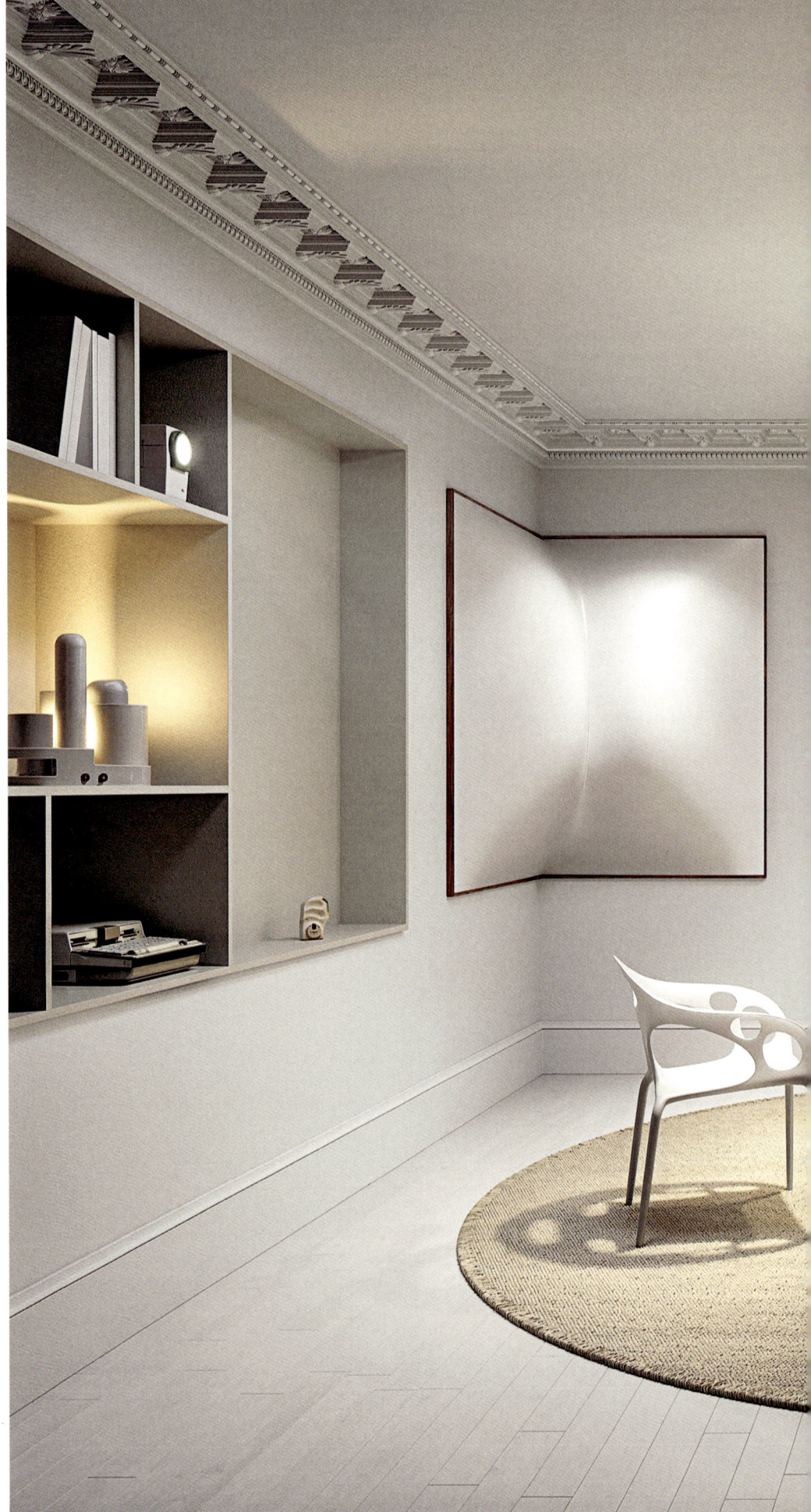

Marion Mailaender
Blanc pour
une bibliothèque
[*White for a Library*]

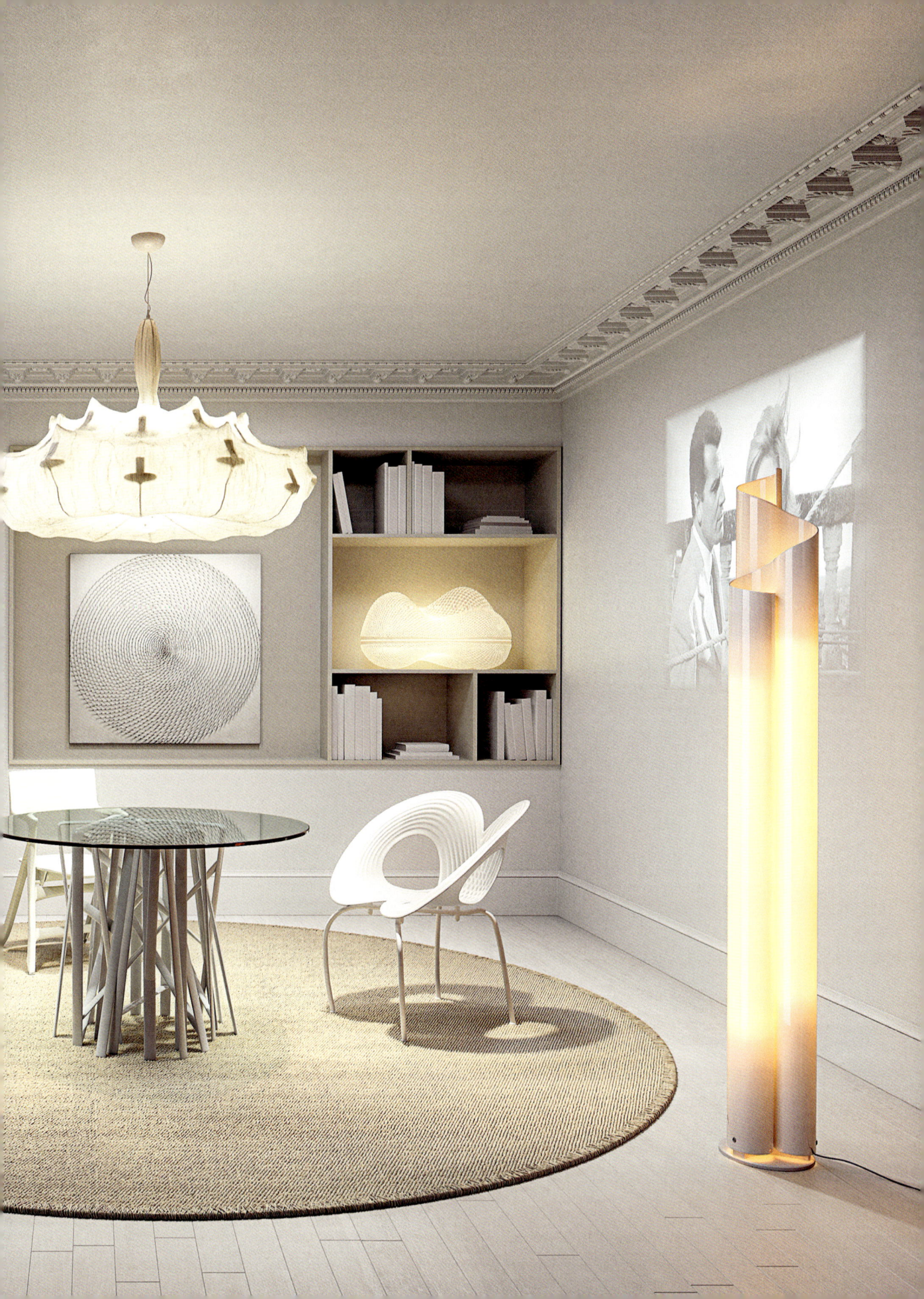

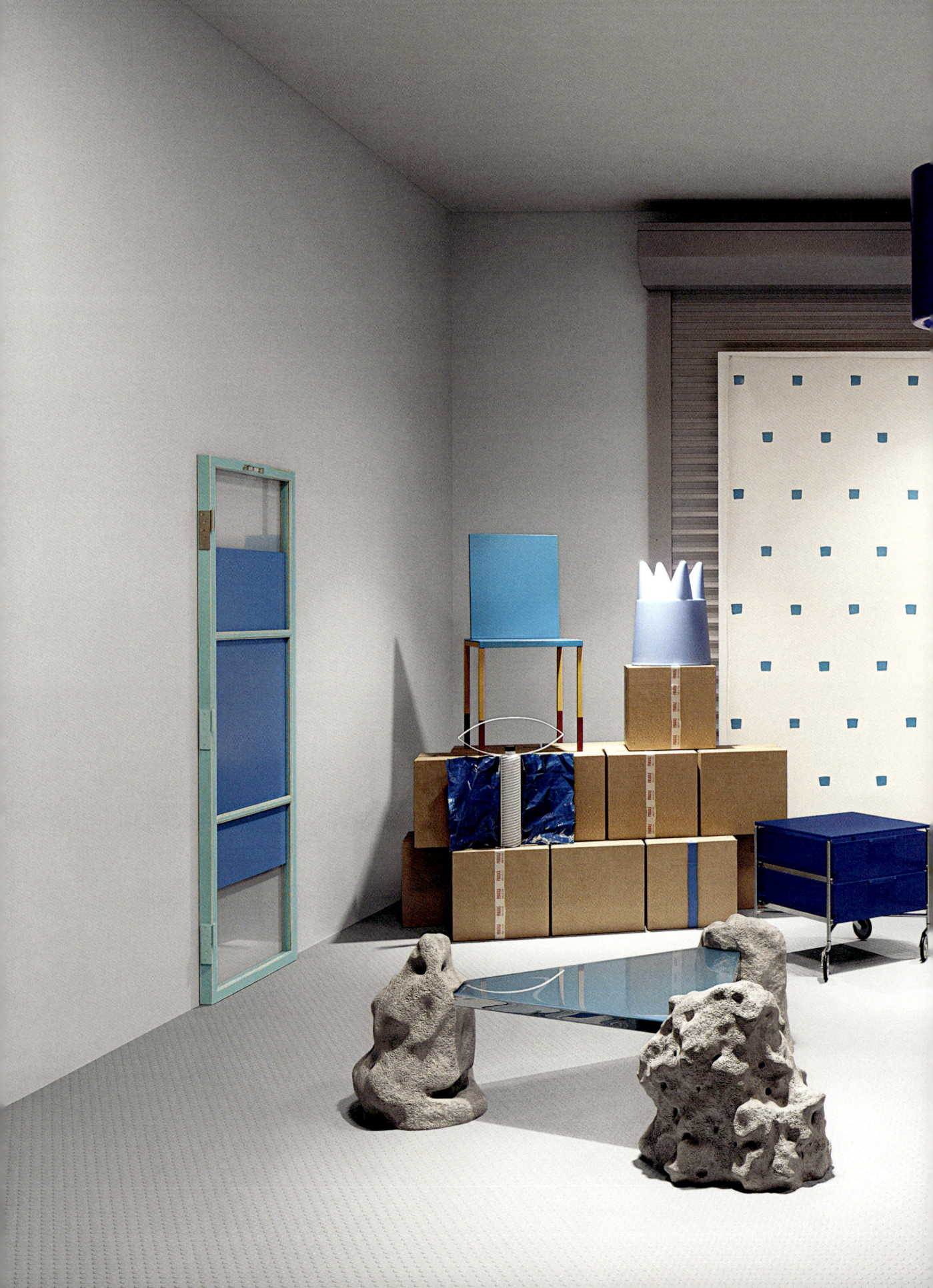

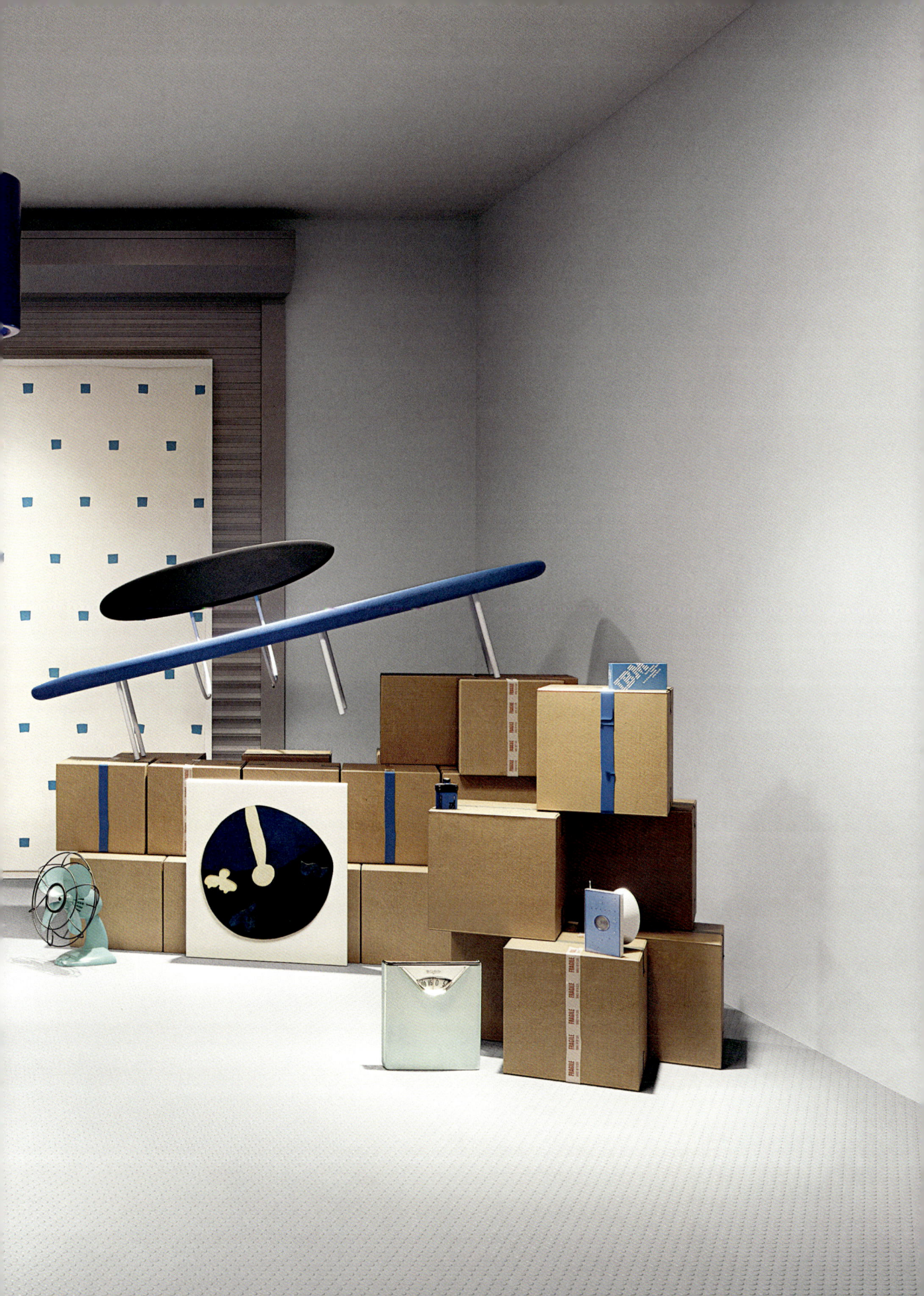

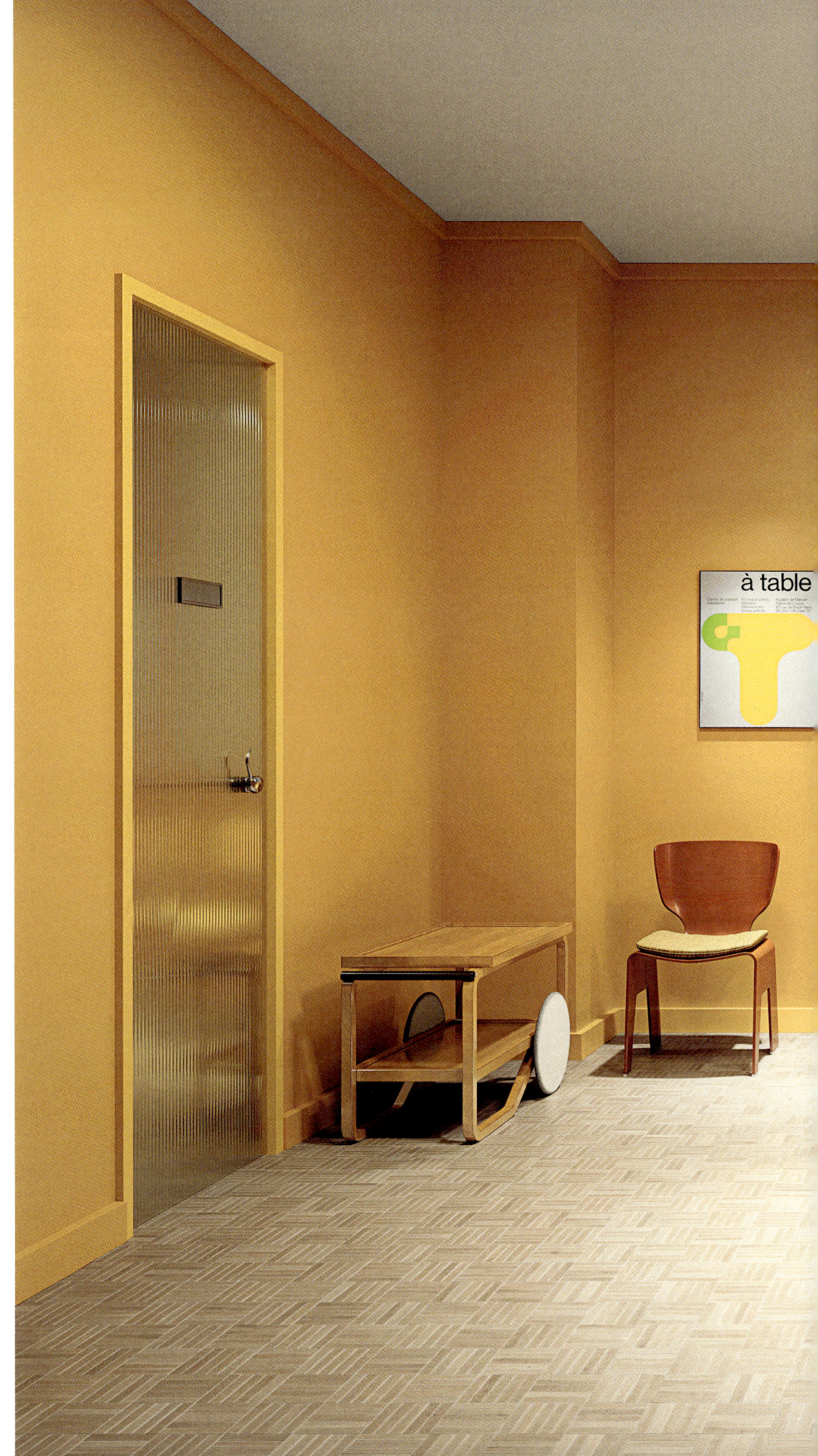

Previous pages:
Marion Mailaender
Bleu pour un garage
[*Blue for a Garage*]

Marion Mailaender
*Jaune pour
une salle d'attente*
[*Yellow for
a Waiting Room*]

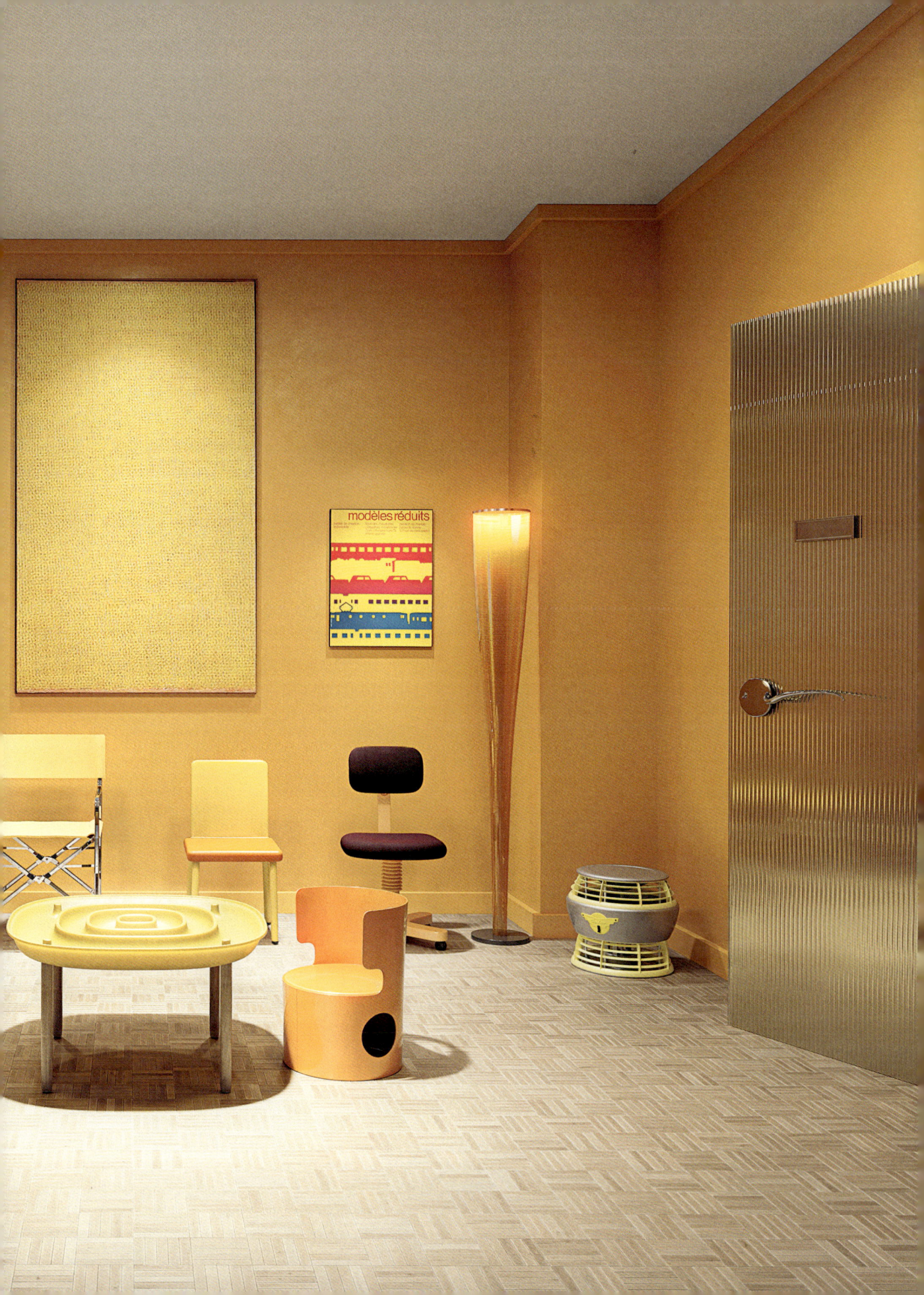

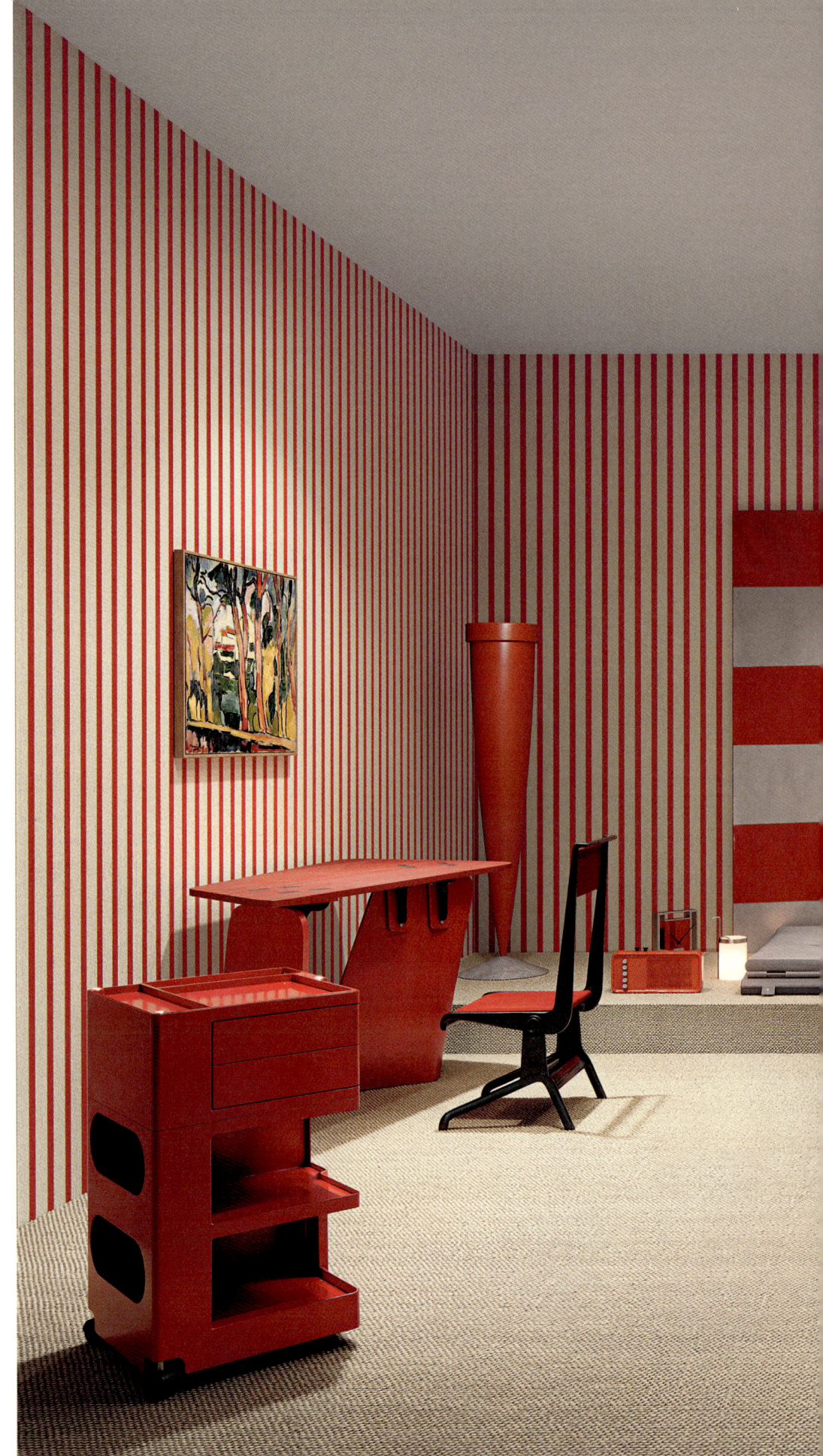

Marion Mailaender
*Rouge pour une
chambre d'étudiant*
[*Red for a
Student's Room*]

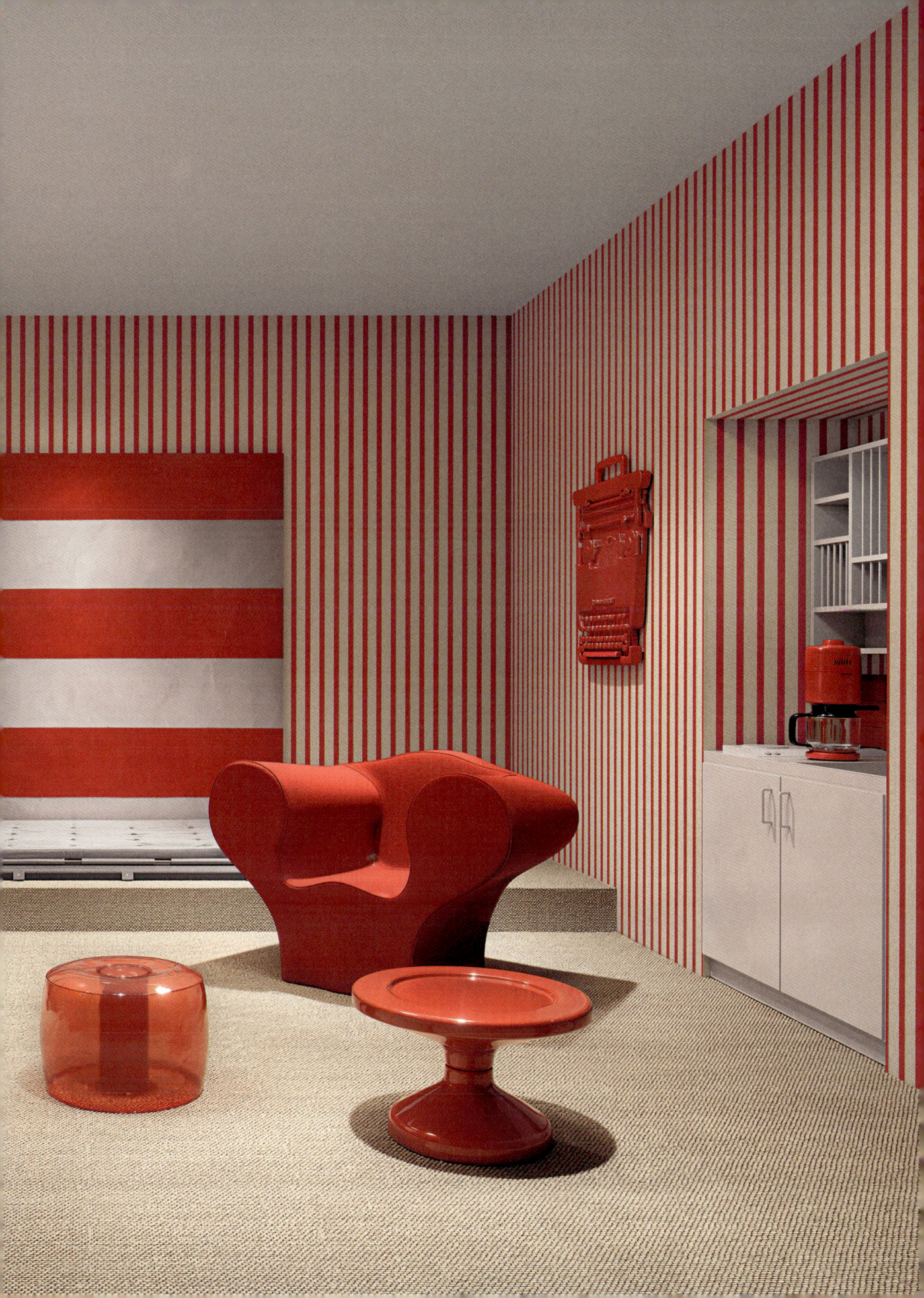

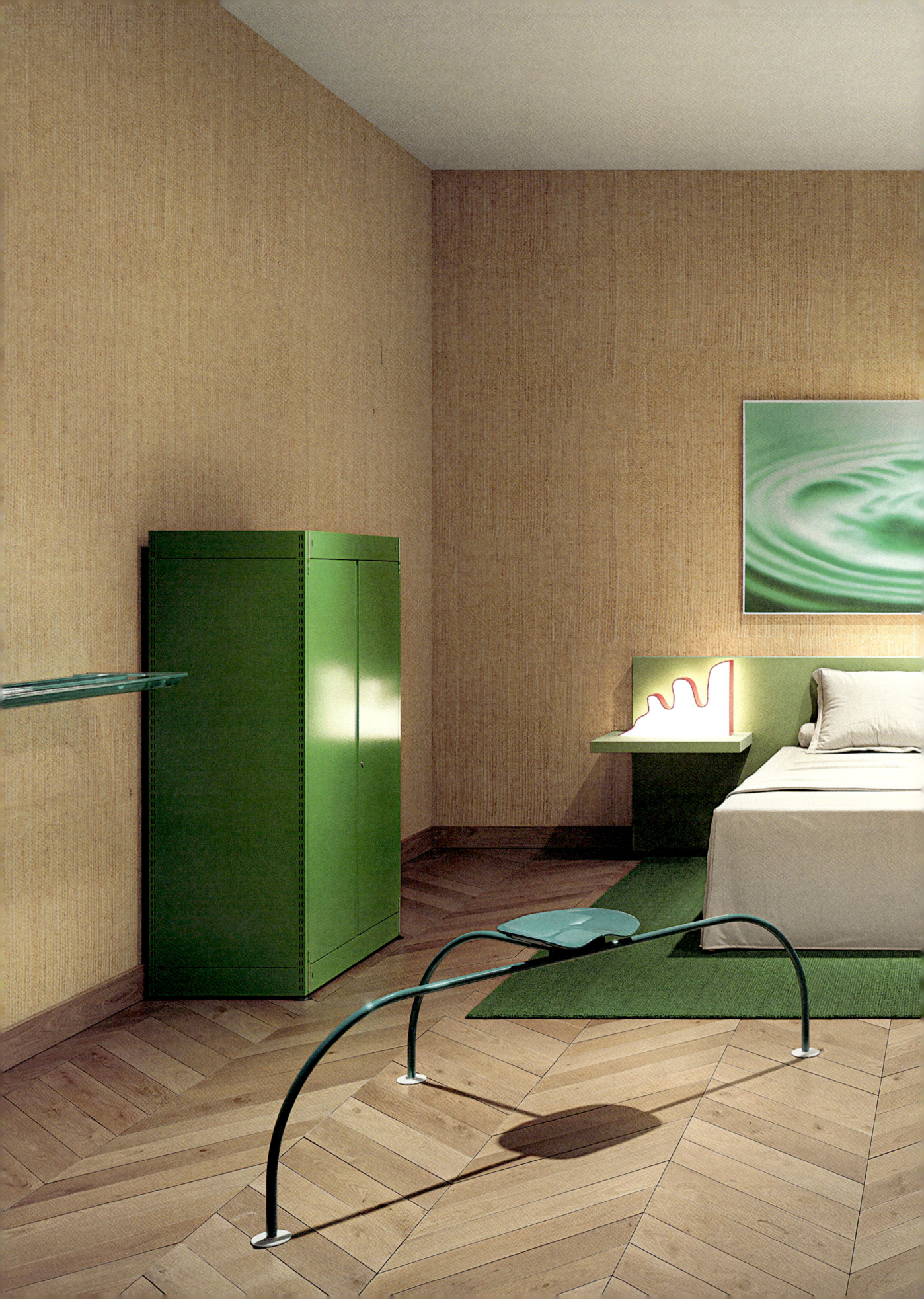

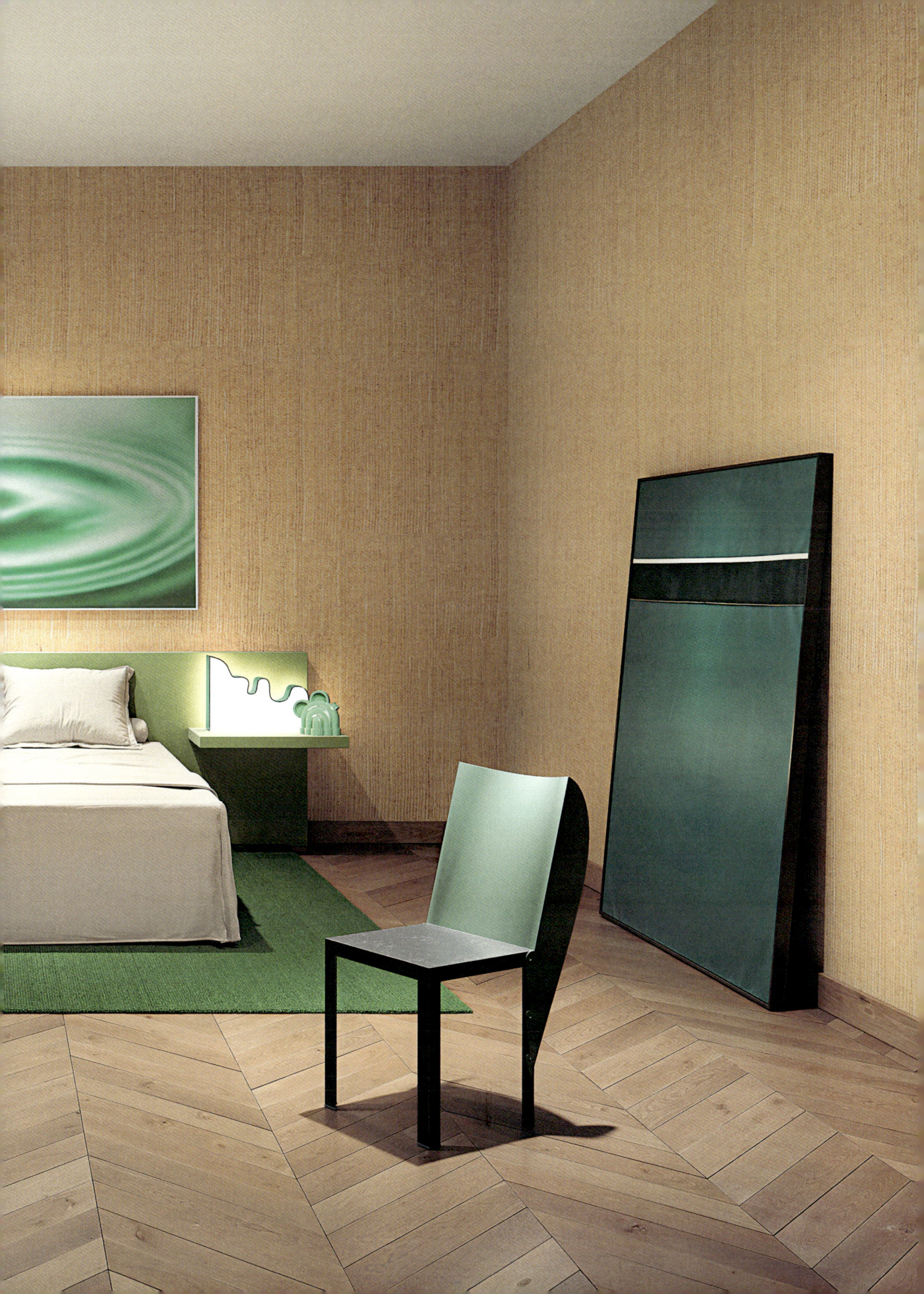

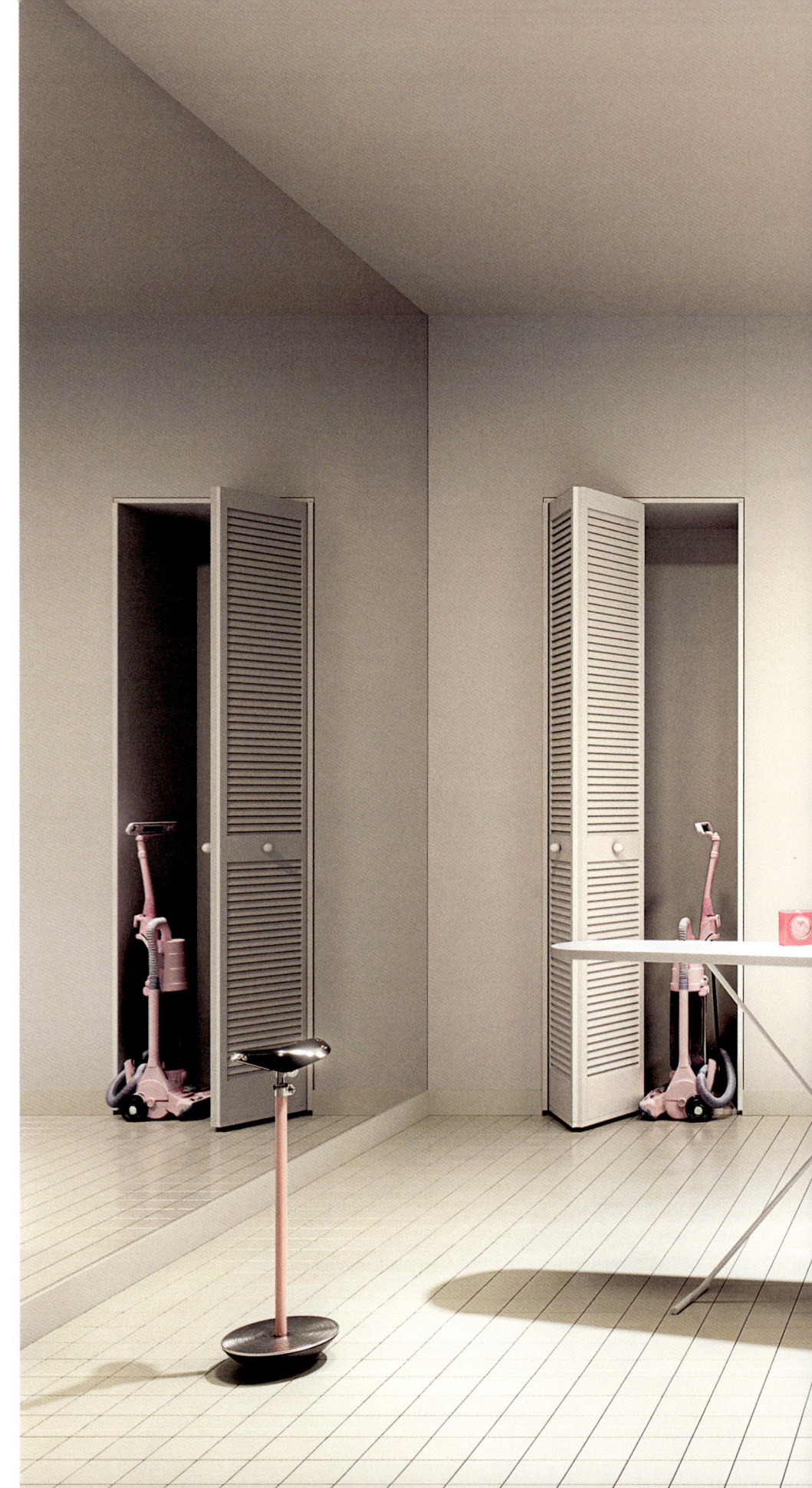

Previous pages:
Marion Mailaender
*Vert pour
une chambre
[Green for
a Bedroom]*

Marion Mailaender
*Rose pour
une buanderie
[Pink for
a Laundry Room]*

Following pages:
Marion Mailaender
*Noir pour
une garçonnière
[Black for
a Bachelor Flat]*

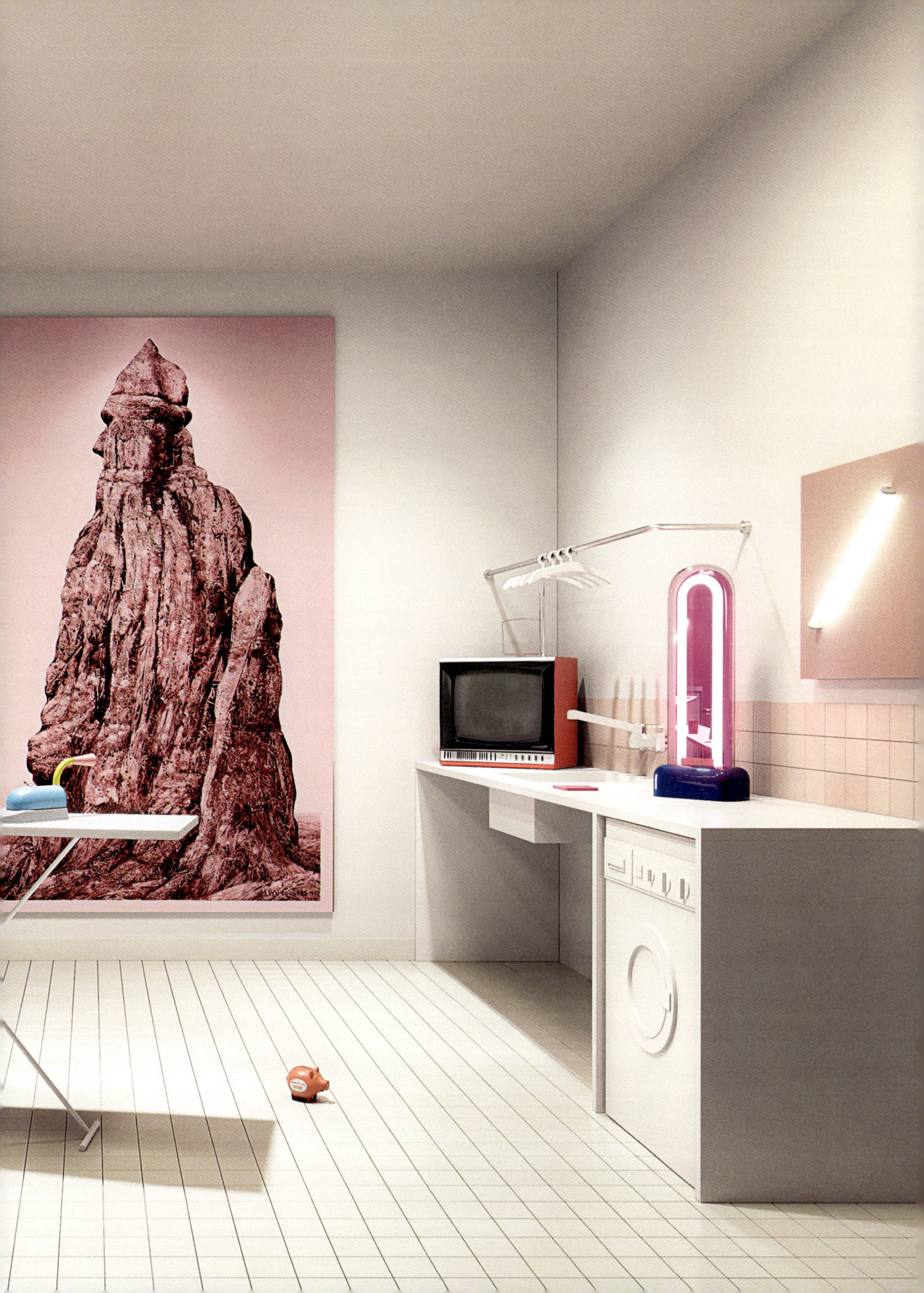

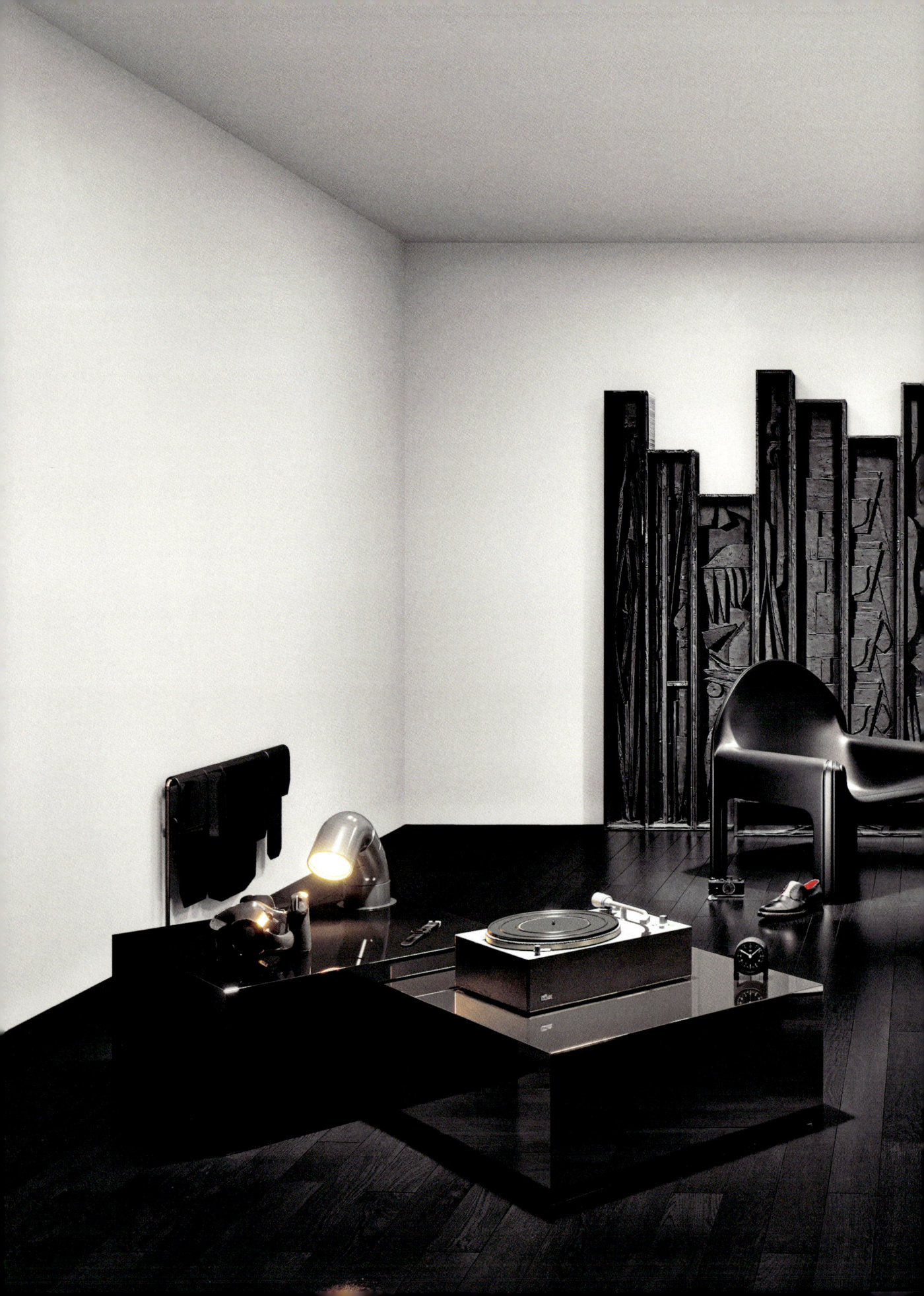

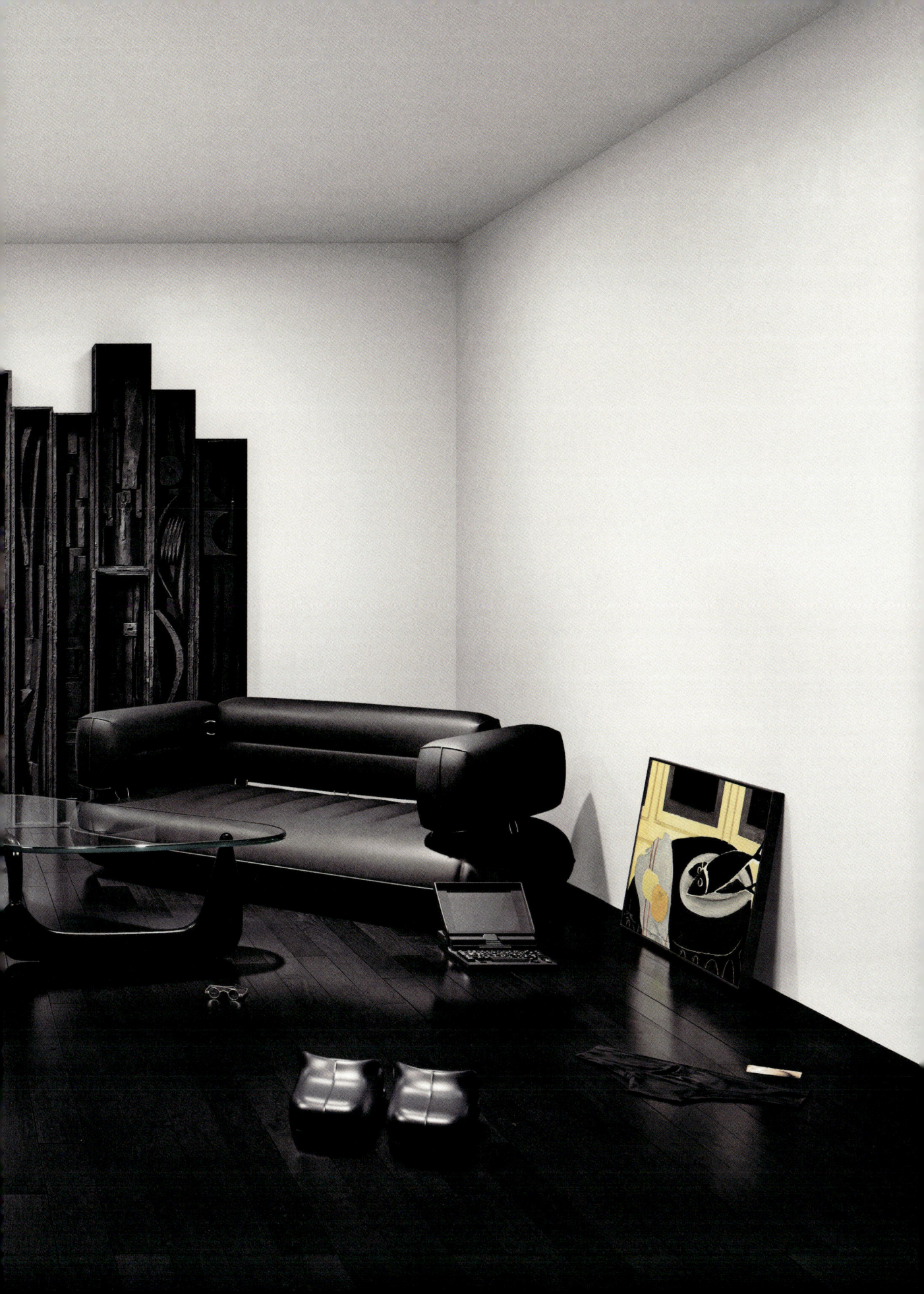

SYNAESTHESIA

Pascal Rousseau

ON THE CORRELATIONS BETWEEN SOUND, COLOUR AND SCENT IN ARTISTIC MODERNITY

In the historiography of 20th-century modernism, thinking in terms of colour alone appears to be both an ultimate goal and a limit not to be exceeded. With the monochrome painting, modern artists pushed the anti-illusionist literality of the canvas to its very limits: "a flat surface covered with colours assembled in a particular order",[1] as famously described by Maurice Denis. In this schema, which inspired the first steps towards abstraction, it is colour alone that confronts the viewer's gaze and arouses their curiosity with a self-reflective surface whose only narrative is that of the pictorial covering itself. This is a well-known stance within formalist orthodoxy, fixated on the 'opticalist' specificity of the medium – a stance that proves relatively weak when faced with other interpretations, suggesting that 'pure' or 'autonomous' colour can be understood only in relation to a broader, more encompassing field of sensibility. So, exploring the visual field of pure colour is about coming into direct contact with its pigmentary or vibratory density; it is about engaging in a tactile or proprioceptive experience. It is not a matter of isolating it within an optical expanse, but of intuitively identifying a correspondence that establishes links unifying different modes of perception. What formalist interpretation overlooks is quite simply a long history of rapprochements between the arts (the *paragone*), the central argument of which has been, over time, the idea not of the separation but of the coordination of the senses. Within this associative logic, a harmony emerged: the synchronisation between the range of sounds, colours and smells and its corollary: the organic coordination of their perception. This became known as 'synaesthesia'.[2]

At the origin of this story is a physical world that relies on an analogous logic of continuity and unification, where colours and sounds are vibrationally connected. It was Isaac Newton (1642–1727) who made one of the first scientific attempts to reconcile the scale of sounds with the range of colours. His first attempts, in Cambridge, led him to select five fundamental colours (red, yellow, green, blue and violet), which he mentions many times in his *Opticks* in 1704.[3] He added two, in order, as he said in his optical lectures, to "divide the image into parts more elegantly proportioned to one another".[4] It was this "more refined symmetry"[5] that gave him the idea of a possible link with the seven notes of the diatonic scale, although it is tempting to think it was the acoustic analogy that prompted him to make this

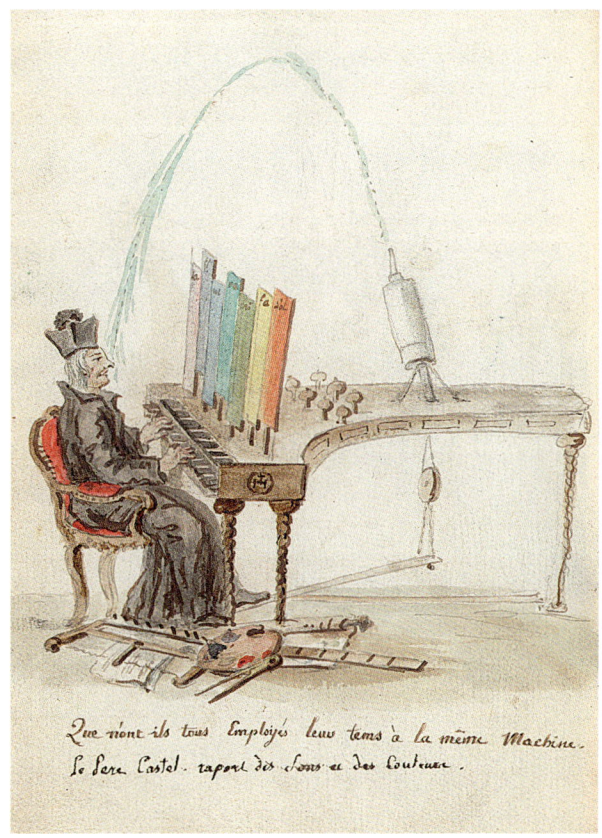

Fig. 1 Charles-Germain de Saint-Aubin, "Que n'ont ils tous Employés leurs tems à la même Machine. / Le Père Castel, raport [*sic*] des Sons et des Couleurs", 1740–57, watercolour, ink and graphite on paper, 18.7 × 13.2 cm Waddesdon image Library, bequest of James de Rothschild, 1957. Part of *Livre de Caricatures tant bonnes que mauvaises*, Paris, 1775. 675.302

choice. Newton was able to compare colours to the seven whole-tone intervals within the octave. At the same time, he created a tabular system for comparing colours and sounds as well as a way of representing the colour spectrum in the form of a wheel, producing the illusion of a circulation of colours similar to that of the system of octaves. Despite this, the corpuscular theory on which his physics of colours was based was powerless to explain the difference between the mix of colours–materials (the painter's pigments, for example) and the mix of colours–light (the beams from a magic lantern). Following on from Newton, while criticising the postulates of his physics of colours, Louis-Bertrand Castel (1688–1757)[6] had the idea of putting this analogy into practice. A professor of mathematics and physics at the Jesuit College of Paris, he developed a theory on the correspondence between sounds and colours. In his *Optique des couleurs* (treatise on the melody of colours, 1740),

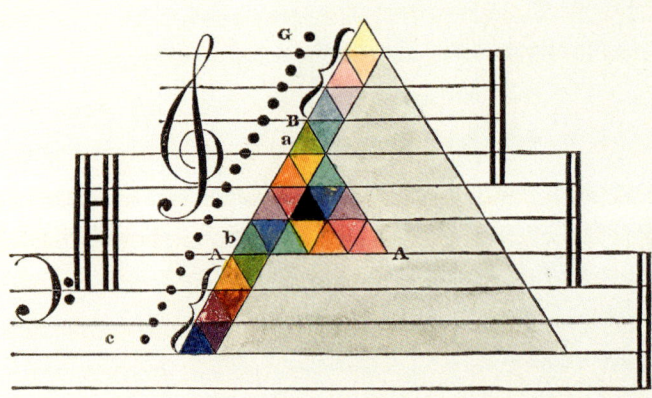

EXAMPLE XVI.

ANALOGOUS SCALE OF SOUNDS AND COLOURS.

2

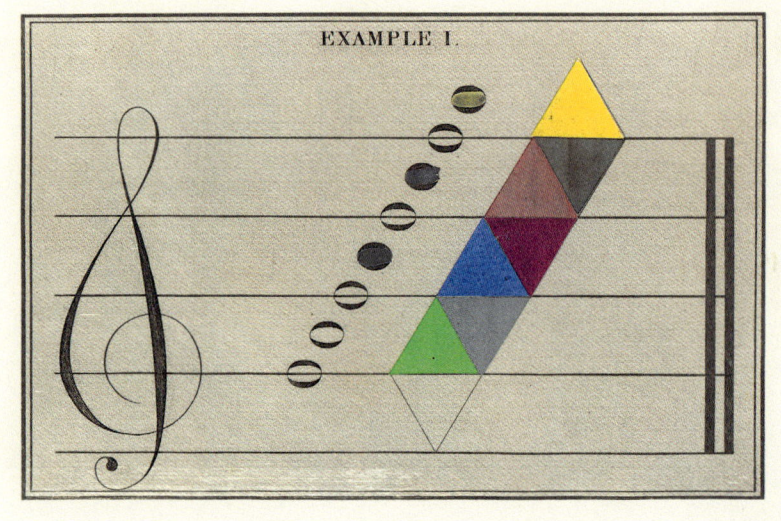

EXAMPLE I.

3

Fig. 2 George Field
"Diagram of the analogous
scale of sounds and colours",
1817, hand-coloured wood-
engraving with letterpress
caption, 7.5 × 12.4 cm
Royal Academy of Arts, London
From *Chromatics, or An Essay
on the Analogy and Harmony of
Colours*, London, 1817. 06/4495

Fig. 3 David Ramsay Hay
*The Laws of Harmonious
Colouring. Adapted to Interior
Decorations, Manufactures,
and Other Useful Purposes*,
1836, publisher: William and
Robert Chambers and
Orr & Smith (London),
printer: Edinburgh Printing
Company, illustrations:
engraving with applied colour
triangles, 23 × 14.1 × 1 cm
The Metropolitan Museum of Art,
New York. Gift of Lincoln Kirstein,
1970. 1970.565.147

he established a sequence of colours between black and white, starting from blue, the first colour to emerge from black, which he immediately associated with the note *do* (C):

> Dark blue, I have said, always contains an appearance of red. Is it not the C string that causes the dominant G to resonate? Red is clearly the dominant colour in nature. And yet the deepest red is always a shade less dark than dark blue – the colour from which it emerges as it rises toward brightness. And yellow, which is by nature a degree lighter than red, seems to correspond precisely to the mediant E [...].[7]

Castel distinguished the three primary colours – blue, red and yellow (the number three reflecting the Holy Trinity) – to which he curiously added green and '*aurore*' [dawn], to obtain five tonic colours, and two 'semitones', 'violet' and 'violant' [deep purple]. The result was a gradation of colours aligned with the diatonic scale – *do* (C) blue, *re* (D) green, *mi* (E) yellow, *fa* (F) aurore, *sol* (G) red, *la* (A) violet, *si* (B) violant – which inspired his 'ocular harpsichord', a strange instrument on which, when "moving the fingers as on an ordinary harpsichord, the motion of the keys makes colours appear, along with their combinations and harmonies"[8] (fig. 1). An initial text presenting the project was published in 1725 in the columns of the *Mercure de France*. Its title announced the possibility of "painting" with sounds: "A harpsichord for the eyes with the art of painting sounds and pieces of music of all sorts".[9] A 'description' was published by Georg Philipp Telemann in an appendix to Castel's *L'Optique des couleurs*.[10] In concrete terms, the 'ocular harpsichord' had a keyboard with keys that activated thin strips of fabric impregnated with different colours, that, when a note was played, passed in front of a flame, producing, along the principle of a magic lantern, a spectral projection of coloured light. The focus here is less on the "physical" correlations between sounds and colours than on the rules of "progression", "since harmony has never been, after all, anything other than number, measure and proportion".[11] From there, he went on to construct a 'chromatic rule', which he called the 'optico-acoustic analogue', enabling him to establish a whole system for weighting colours on the screen: "a slight movement, alternately and frequently interspersed with rest" – what Castel referred to as the '*piquant*' of "the alternation of movement".[12] Castel said himself that the idea for his harpsichord emerged from a reflection on the "static" limitations of painting: "At first glance, a thousand flowers in a flowerbed are a diversity; at second glance, it's the same diversity, and thereafter, without waiting for the third, it is monotony, boredom, aversion. The same is true of the colours in a painting".[13] Castel reproached painting for the static nature of its "inanimate bodies", an *incarnato* devoid of *anima*. He contrasted it with "moving and mobile pictures"; in other words, a variation on colour that is in itself a variety, a "variety of varieties" that addresses a modern awareness seeking to (re)produce a feeling of infinitude in these perpetually moving forms: "Only infinite diversity, the infinite number, only infinity, can give us true, solid and perfect pleasure without aversion".[14]

To increase this "piquant" effect, Castel multiplied the interplay of associations, with perfume adding to and perfecting this organological variation: "Set out forty or so cassolettes filled with various perfumes and open the valves – there you have the sense of smell. On a board, lay out in an orderly fashion a variety of objects capable of producing different sensations on the hand – there you have touch. Likewise, arrange items pleasing to the palate, mixing in a few bitters – and there you have taste [...]".[15] In the wake of a "music for the eyes", Polycarpe Poncelet (1720–1780) imagined a "music for the tongue" or "flavoursome music", along with the realisation of its instrumentation in a "keyboard of flavours":

> There may therefore be a music for the tongue and the palate, just as there is for the ears; it is quite possible that flavours, in order to awaken different sensations in the soul, have, like sounds, their generative tones, their dominant, major, minor, low and high notes, even their commas, and all that derives from them: consonances and dissonances alike. Seven full tones form the foundation of sound music; the same number of original flavours form the basis of flavour music, and their harmonic combination follows a similar logic. It is possible to make a harmonious instrument from flavours, much more easily than a colour harpsichord; it would be, if you like, a sort of new organ, on which one could play all sorts of flavoursome airs, provided the new organist masters his keyboard with discernment.[16]

Castel and Poncelet were not alone in seeking the sensation of the infinite through this Pythagorean exploration of series and numbers, capable of 'deciphering' the code of sensory correlations. One of the very first hypotheses about a direct comparison between sounds and colours was advanced by mathematician Leonhard Euler (1707–1783), who, at the same time as Castel was developing his harpsichord, was formulating the principle in his famous *Letters to a German Princess*: "What the various sounds in music are to hearing, the various colours are to sight".[17] Euler concluded from this that the difference between colours depends on the number of their vibrations, even though he recognised that he was unable to assign a specific number to each colour. That did not happen until 30 years later, with the work of Thomas Young (1773–1829).[18] In his wave theory of light, Young used Euler's hypothesis to make initial calculations of the number of vibrations of each colour. This analysis gave rise, over the course of the 19th century, to a number of systems of equivalence between sound and colour, such as the ones proposed by Englishman George Field (1777–1854) (fig. 2). A chemist by training, who had opened a colour factory in Bristol in 1808, he published a series of treatises in which he presented not only a classification of colours but also a measuring system – the 'chromometer' or 'metrochrome', which enabled him to establish what he called 'chromatic equivalents' (the harmonious proportions of each of the three primary colours needed to produce white light), on which he based, a few years before Michel-Eugène Chevreul (1786–1889), a system of the harmonisation of colours. His seminal work, *Outlines of Analogical Philosophy* (1839),[19] was read by artists. The name John Constable features among the list of subscribers to the first edition.

Many paragraphs of the *Outlines* are devoted to these "correspondences" between sounds and colours that, due to their holistic nature, intrigued artists of the Romantic period. Seeking to consolidate the scientific principle of this rule, Field proposed a 'numerical' reading, aiming to determine the weight of each colour (primary, secondary and tertiary) in the production of white. He set out a numerical sequence that corresponds to the musical scale and that was partially adopted by David Ramsay Hay (1798–1866) in *The Laws of Harmonious Colouring* (1828) (fig. 3).[20] Hay substituted Field's dominant triad with a seven-element division, inherited from Newton (the seven notes of the musical scale, the seven fundamental colours of the spectrum – red, orange, yellow, green, blue, purple and grey – and the seven fundamental plane figures – circle, oblong, triangle, rhomboid, rectangle, ellipse and polygon). This enabled him to establish harmonic laws of perception on a universal principle linking forms and colours, just as, a century earlier, with Castel's cassolettes, fragrances had joined this analogical symphony. George William Septimus Piesse (1820–1882), author of a "theory of odours", built on the work of George Field[21] to measure 'scales of concordances' (volatility strength, weight according to temperature, refractive indices, etc.) using a series of thresholds that enable the construction of a range of olfactory sensations for perfumes, modelled on the spectrum of sound frequencies.

Scents, like sounds, appear to influence the olfactory nerve in certain definite degrees. There is, as it were, an octave of odours like an octave in music; certain odours coincide, like the keys of an instrument.[22]

It was on this principle that he established a "gamut of odours": purple is in "D in the treble or G clef", orange flower is in "G in the treble or G clef", acacia in "E in the G clef", syringa in "G in the G clef", jasmine in "C in the G clef". As with Castel and Poncelet, the instrument followed, reaching its culmination in Symbolist culture with the multisensory *Cantique des cantiques* in 1891, conceived by Paul-Napoléon Roinard (1856–1930) as a total work of art that featured projections of scents from the theatre balconies, in coordination with the song of colours, voices and instruments.[23] Later, Italian Futurists (fig. 4), who themselves were powerfully influenced by *fin-de-siècle* culture, despite their calls for a clean slate, went so far as to lay claim in their manifestos to a global pan-sensory orgy combining sounds, colours and tastes. Carlo Carrà, for example, in his manifesto *The Painting of Sounds, Noises and Smells* (1913), proposed his own chart of synaesthetic equivalences, where the ambient circulation of smells becomes an "environment-force", constructing, in a communal sensory immersion, "a pure plastic whole": "It is indisputably true that (1) silence is static and sounds, noises and smells are dynamic; (2) sounds, noises and smells are nothing but different forms and intensities of vibration; and (3) any succession of sounds, noises and smells impresses on the mind an arabesque of form and color. We must measure this intensity and perceive these arabesques".[24]

But this shifting geometry of correspondences was already casting doubt on its objective value. Perhaps it was just a case of changing the parameters? In *De la corrélation des sons et des couleurs en art* (1897),[25] Frenchman Albert Cozanet (1870–1938), known by his pseudonym of Jean d'Udine, recognised that "the notes of the scale (or degrees on the musical scale) cannot be likened to the colours of the spectrum, which differ in hue and not in chromatic degree, but that these melodic degrees are on the contrary, in music, essentially correlative to shades in the plastic arts".[26] So it is, rather, to the texture of the sound, notably through the modern notion of 'musical timbre', that he attributes the link with the spectrum of colours. Pioneers of abstract painting, in particular Wassily Kandinsky, followed him in this respect. In his painting *Impression III (Concert)* (1911, fig. 5), Kandinsky endeavoured to give life to this musical seed, this atmospheric extension of sound vibration: the musical "impression" is interpreted here through

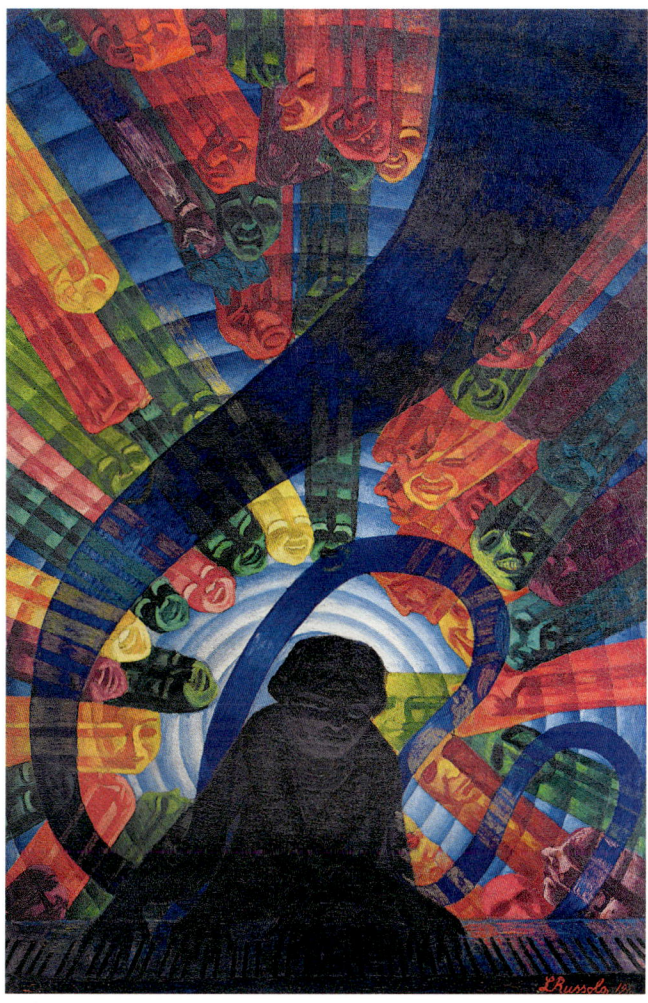

Fig. 4 Luigi Russolo
Music, 1911, oil on canvas,
224 × 145 cm
Estorick Collection of Modern
Italian Art, London

the spatial diffusion of yellow, which absorbs the entire pictorial space. We can still distinguish, in the black mark, the concert's grand piano and a few silhouettes of musicians and listeners, but it is undoubtedly the atmospheric buildup of sound that is the subject of this painting. We find this phenomenon again in the paintings of his musician friend Arnold Schoenberg, where figurative elements (notably the portrait) remain only in fragmentary form, bathed in a saturated colour that covers the image. So, in *Blue View* (1910, fig. 6), Schoenberg depicts, in the form of a kind of molecular movement, the impact of the breath and sound emitted by a face in profile on the surrounding air. It is clearly the exploration of timbre as a spatial dimension of music that fascinated Schoenberg here, at a time when he was giving thought to the writing of a *Theory of Harmony*, which was published

in December 1911.[27] Kandinsky, meanwhile, was developing the equivalent in painting: *On the Spiritual in Art*, published at around the same time, with a central chapter on "The Language of Form and Colour", whose opening line from Shakespeare, "Mark the music", is an invitation to discern in the emotional power of sound a model for harmony of colour. Of course, viewers need to be able to perceive and enjoy these harmonic correspondences. For that to happen, they must be able to translate these associations within their own sensory and cognitive framework. In the mid-19th century, this was given the scientific name of 'synaesthesia'.[28]

A multitude of contradictory explanations were given for these phenomena of sensory associations in the development of the physiology of perception and

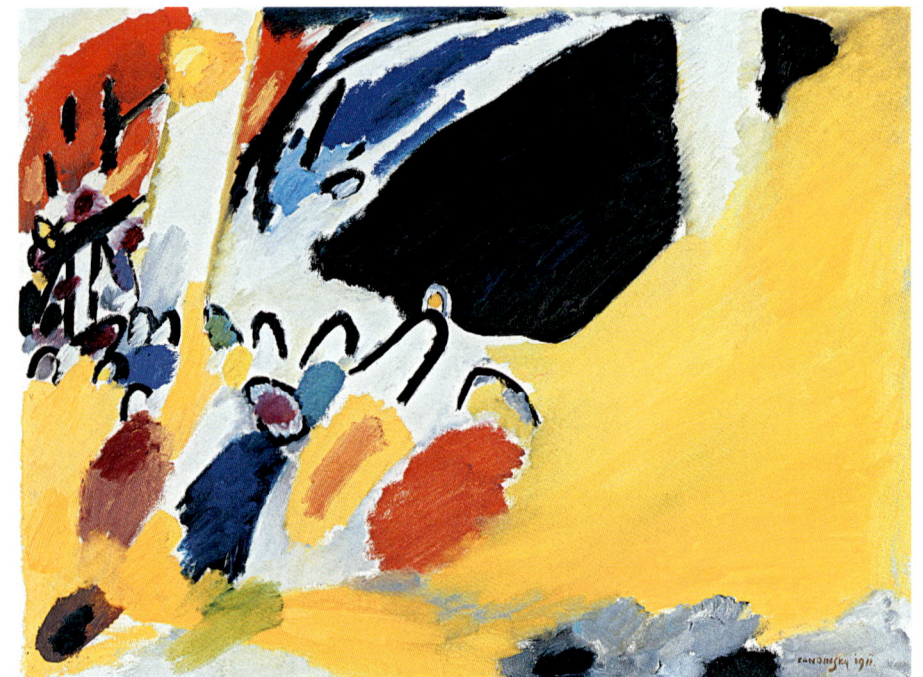

5

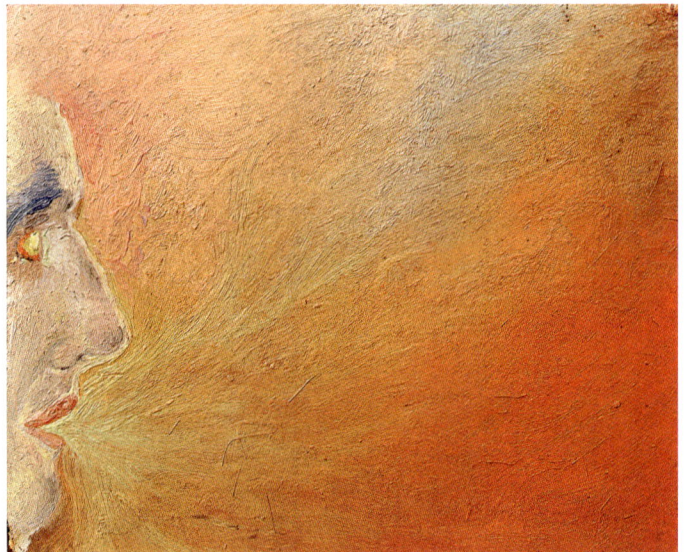

6

Fig. 5 Wassily Kandinsky
Impression III (Concert),
1911, oil on canvas,
78.4 cm × 100.6 cm × 2 cm
Städtische Galerie im Lenbachhaus
und Kunstbau München, Munich
Gift from the Gabriele Münter
Fund, 1957. GMS 78

Fig. 6 Arnold Schoenberg
Blue Gaze, 1910, oil on
cardboard, 20 × 23 cm
Lawrence Schoenberg Collection,
Los Angeles

226

experimental psychology.[29] This quest for a "unity of impression" denotes a very romantic nostalgia for lost unity[30] that was reflected, as the century progressed, in the evolution of the methods of 'colour music' (Louis Favre, Bainbridge Bishop, Alexander Wallace Rimington).[31] Colour music, which found expression in the language of abstract cinema around 1912–13 (notably with the Corradini brothers in Italy and Léopold Survage in France, fig. 7), came to be seen as the new model of a painting in action, *in statu nascendi* – "brought forth, as it were, before our eyes", as Wagner said of Beethoven's "pure symphonies", in a curious return to modernist self-reflexivity, where we least expect it, prefiguring the developments of action painting. This was the project of Oskar Fischinger, a key figure in interwar colour music, in his legendary film *Motion Painting no. 1* (1947). A bravura piece of work, this eleven-minute abstract film records the long process of the development of a painting created over a period of more than five months of painstaking labour. After each brushstroke, Fischinger captured a frame with his camera, set up in front of the canvas, which over time was overlaid with multiple sheets of Plexiglas to create subtle effects of superimposition and shifting styles. A feat of chromatic pyrotechnics, this 'filmed painting' with symphonic accompaniment relates Fischinger's obsessive relationship with 'musical form', but also his total abandonment to the gestural rhythm of painting. Art, then, becomes the ability to experience life itself, in the creative activity of a body energised by sound vibration, like the famous drip paintings by Jackson Pollock, another great fan of 'colour music'. But in the 1960s, painting was no longer the dominant medium; new media were already present, including the 'expanded cinema' and videosphere of Gene Youngblood.[32]

For Youngblood, new screen technologies propelled the view into an "oceanic consciousness … in which we feel our individual existence lost in mystic union with the universe".[33] This panpsychic audiovisual extravaganza, enhanced with saturated colours and strobe lights – not forgetting, once again, the addition of the olfactory dimension, with the diffusion of perfumes and aromas and even cinema's own Odorama solution: 'scratch and sniff' cards with micro-encapsulated scents – spread like wildfire through the alternative circles of hippie culture, ranging from *Infinity Projector* by Richard Aldcroft (1966) to Jordan Belson's *Vortex Concerts* (1957–59), the *Theater of Light* by Jackie Cassen and Rudi Stern (1969), *Lumia, Theatre of Light* by Christian Sidenius (1962) and the Merry Pranksters' installations in the legendary Trips Festival (1966). Taking an inventory of these chromokinetic means, Youngblood presents the intermedia mix of contemporary electronic arts as

a response to the expanded consciousness of the new computer algebras, auguring the imminent realisation of a cyber-age synaesthesia,[34] which Oliver Reiser later called "the language of world unity", "psychedelic electronic" Esperanto: "All such experiments, by way of psychedelic electronic synaesthesia, will certainly open up new forms and levels of consciousness expansion. But just how the kinds of 'total experience' we are here envisioning might be enhanced through the utilization of global communication satellites […] remains for the future to reveal … So … make way for TOMORROW'S TEMPLE OF THE PSYCHOSPHERE!"[35]

The artist Nicolas Schöffer (fig. 8), a pioneer of cybernetic art, had already taken note. His luminodynamic research followed in the wake of early experiments in abstract cinema, which he regarded as a preliminary stage in the development of "spatiodynamism".[36] With *Musiscope* (1960), he reactivated Castel's utopia in spatio-temporal anamorphoses projected on screens of varying sizes – from the television screen (the *Teleluminoscope*, in 1961) to the monumental version of a theatrical screen (*Mur-Lumière*, installed in 1962 at the Musée des Arts Décoratifs de Paris) – in a hypnotic vortex of abstract images that are in constant flux, drawing the viewer more deeply into the cognitive experience of "new dimensionalities".[37] When Nicolas Schöffer thought of "the art of the future", it was from the angle of new faculties developed by the cyber-connection of the senses: "Surrounded by audiovisual programmes (and olfactory and tactile ones) that will immerse them in a hyper-aestheticised environment, consumers will be able to adjust, recombine and reprogramme the various elements of this aesthetic immersion at will, allowing them to enjoy the experience, become aware, concentrate and express themselves in an increasingly absolute way".[38] It is no surprise that these chromo-mentalist devices are increasingly being used today in artificial intelligence and virtual reality tools, inviting Generation 2.0 to experience the perceptual euphoria of interactive chromatic environments in an 'augmented' way. Like the immersive screens of psychedelia, they are taking up the fluid, enveloping aesthetic of Castel's ocular harpsichord, but with far more effective technological means. Besides their hallucinatory power achieved through digital computation, they help to amplify an emotional ecstasy, the virtue of which lies in encouraging a unanimous communion between individuals, all the more elusive given the current fragmentation of society. All in all, nothing has changed. The dream of a global concordance of the senses still strives to breach the wall of reality to attain a utopian harmony among individuals – as precarious as fleeting impressions – with the colour spectrum as the most visual metaphor for this fragile alliance.

1
Maurice Denis, "Définition du néo-traditionalisme", *Art et critique*, 30 August 1890.

2
Kevin Tyler Dann, *Bright Colors Falsely Seen: Synaesthesia and the Search for Transcendental Knowledge* (New Haven: Yale University Press, 1998).

3
Isaac Newton, *Opticks: or, A Treatise of the Reflections, Refractions, Inflexions and Colours of Light* (London: S. Smith and B. Walford, 1704).

4
Alan E. Shapiro (ed.), *The Optical Papers of Isaac Newton, Vol. 1: The Optical Lectures 1670–1672* (Cambridge: Cambridge University Press, 1984), p. 543.

5
Ibid., p. 34.

6
Michel Blay, "Castel critique de la théorie newtonienne des couleurs", in Roland Mortier, Hervé Hasquin (ed.), *Études sur le XVIIIᵉ siècle. Autour du Père Castel et du clavecin oculaire*, vol. 23 (Brussels: Éditions de l'Université de Bruxelles, 1995), pp. 43–58.

7
Louis-Bertrand Castel, *L'Optique des couleurs, fondée sur les simples observations, et tournée surtout à la pratique de la peinture, de la teinture et des autres arts coloristes* (Paris: Briasson, 1740), pp. 73–74.

8
Quoted by Pierre Guillot, *Les Jésuites et la musique*, (Liège: Mardaga, 1991), p. 121.

9
Louis-Bertrand Castel, "Clavecin pour les yeux avec l'art de peindre les sons et toutes sortes de pièces de musique", *Mercure de France* (November 1725), pp. 2552–77.

10
Georg Philipp Telemann, "Description de l'orgue ou clavecin oculaire du P. Castel", in Louis-Bertrand Castel, *L'Optique des couleurs*, op. cit., p. 482.

11
Louis-Bertrand Castel, "Nouvelles expériences d'optique et d'acoustique, adressées à M. le président de Montesquieu", *Journal de Trévoux* (August 1735), p. 1451.

12
Ibid., October 1735, p. 2027.

13
Ibid., December 1735, p. 2692.

14
Ibid., p. 2693.

15
Louis-Bertrand Castel, "Difficultés sur le clavecin oculaire, avec leurs réponses", *Mercure de France* (March 1726), p. 151.

16
Polycarpe Poncelet, *Chimie du goût et de l'odorat ou principes pour composer facilement, et à peu de frais, les liqueurs à boire, et les eaux de senteurs. Avec figures* (Paris: Le Mercier, 1755) pp. 17–20 and 25. On this harpsichord of the senses, see Peter Szendy, "Toucher à soi (C., ou le clavecin des sens)", *Les Cahiers du Musée National d'Art Moderne*, no. 71 (Winter 2000), p. 54.

17
Leonhard Euler, "Lettre du 9 juin 1761", in Andreas Speiser (ed.), *Lettres à une princesse d'Allemagne* (Basel: Birkhäuser, 1960), p. 6, quoted by Georges Roque, "Ce grand monde de vibrations qui est à la base de l'univers", in *Aux origines de l'abstraction. 1800-1914*, exh. cat., Paris, Musée d'Orsay, 3 November 2003 – 22 February 2004 (Paris: Réunion des Musées Nationaux, 2003), pp. 52–53.

18
Thomas Young, "On the Theory of Light and Colours", *Philosophical Transactions*, vol. 92 (1802), pp. 12–48.

19
George Field, *Outlines of Analogical Philosophy, Being a Primary View of the Principles, Relations and Purposes of Nature, Science and Art* (London: Charles Tilt, 1839).

20
David Ramsay Hay, *The Laws of Harmonious Colouring Adapted to Interior Decorations* (Edinburgh: William Blackwood, 1847 [1828]), pp. 44–45.

21
"… the primary Odours assimilate to those of sapor, in the Roseate or sweet scent, the Lemonine or acid scent, and the Amygdaline or bitter scent; and so on to their secondaries and compounds. Ill-suited scents and ill-accorded flavours may be regarded as coincident with discords in music; and Pungent and Faint, or active and passive odours, as similar to the acute and grave of sounds, or light and shade in colours, &c." George Field, *Outlines of Analogical Philosophy*, op. cit., p. 191.

22
George William Septimus Piesse, *The Art of Perfumery and the Methods of Obtaining the Odours of Plants* (London: Longman, Green, Longman and Roberts, 1862), p. 25.

23
Pascal Rousseau, "Le spectacle des sens. La synesthésie sur la scène symboliste du Théâtre d'Art", in Isabelle Moindrot et al., *Le Spectaculaire dans les arts de la scène du romantisme à la Belle Époque* (Paris: CNRS Éditions, Arts du spectacle, 2006), pp. 157–65.

24
Carlo Carrà, "The Painting of Sounds, Noises and Smells". Available online at https://www.unknown.nu/futurism/paintsound.html1913 (accessed 7 May 2025).

25
Jean d'Udine, *De la corrélation des sons et des couleurs en art* (Paris: Fischbacher, 1897), p. 8.

26
Ibid., p. 18.

27
Arnold Schoenberg, *Theory of Harmony*, trans. Roy E. Carter (Berkeley and Los Angeles: University of California Press, 1978 [1911]).

28
"Synaesthesia refers to the association of several sensations of different kinds, only one of which is objective in origin. At the same time as they sense a given impression, subjects who possess this faculty will involuntarily associate it with a sensation that pertains to another sense, a sensation that, most of the time, has no affinity, or at least no apparent affinity, with the primary perception". Henry Laurès, *Les Synesthésies* (Paris: Bloud, 1908), p. 1.

29
Pascal Rousseau, "Confusion des sens : le débat évolutionniste sur la synesthésie dans les débuts de l'abstraction en France", *Les Cahiers du Musée National d'Art Moderne*, no. 74 (Winter 2000/2001), pp. 3–33.

30
Philippe Junod, "Synesthésies, correspondances et convergence des arts : la nostalgie de l'unité perdue", in *Contrepoints. Dialogues entre musique et peinture* (Geneva: Contrechamps, 2006), pp. 49–57.

31
Kenneth Peacock, "Instruments to Perform Color-Music: Two Centuries of Technological Experimentation, *Leonardo*, vol. 21, no. 4 (1988), pp. 397–406.

32
Gene Youngblood, *Expanded Cinema* (New York: Dutton, 1970).

33
Ibid., p. 92.

34
Pascal Rousseau, "Concordances : synesthésie et conscience cosmique dans la *Color Music*", in Sophie Duplaix and Marcella Lista (ed.), *Sons & lumières. Une histoire du son dans l'art du XXᵉ siècle*, exh. cat., Paris, Centre Pompidou, 22 September 2004 – 3 January 2005 (Paris: Éditions du Centre Pompidou, 2004), pp. 29–38.

35
Oliver Reiser, *Cosmic Humanism and World Unity* (New York: Gordon and Breach, 1975 [1966]) p. 227.

36
Nicolas Schöffer, *La Ville cybernétique* (Paris: Tchou, 1969), p. 74.

37
"The role of art is precisely to transcend these three dimensions and to create new dimensionalities". Ibid., p. 83.

38
Ibid., p. 83.

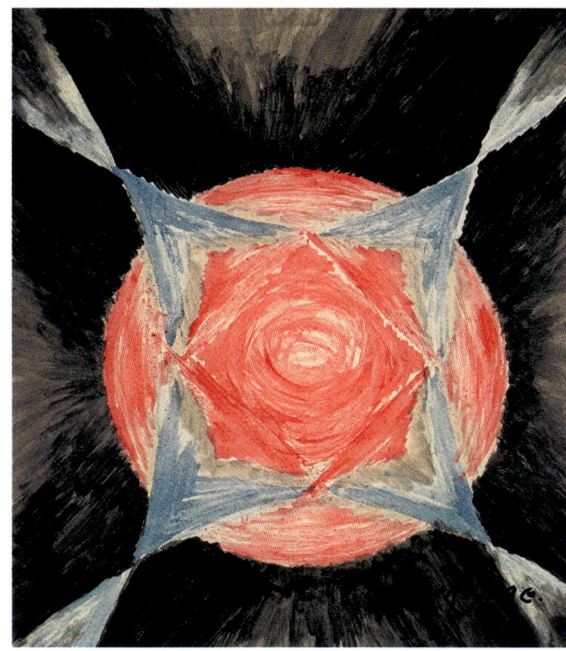

7

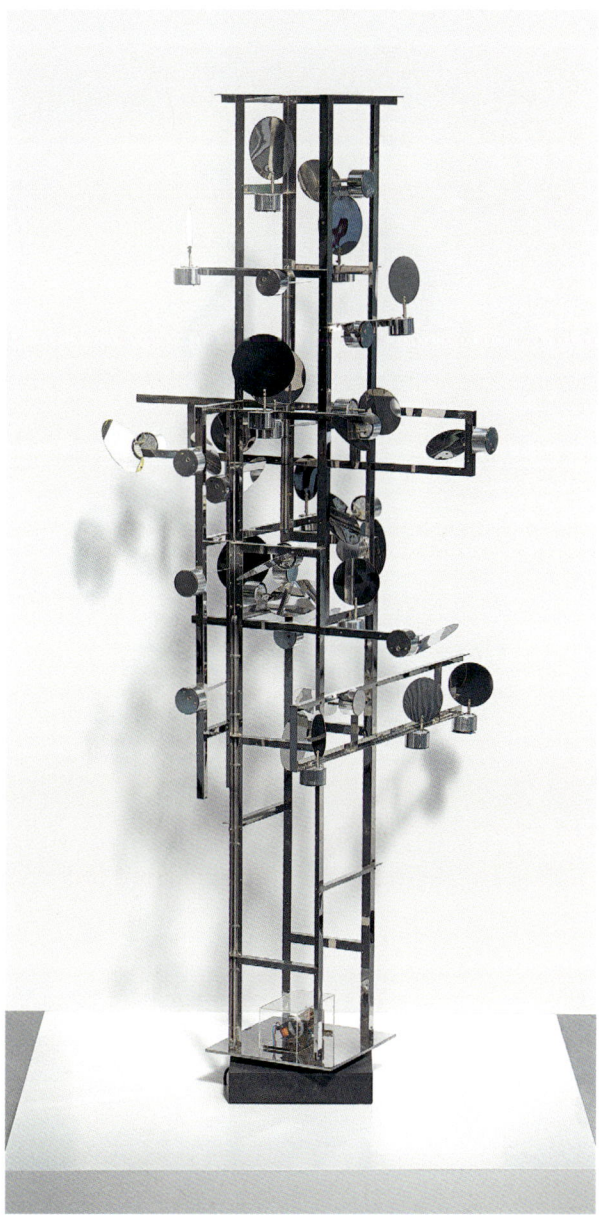

8

Fig. 7   Léopold Survage
Rythme coloré
[*Coloured Rhythm*], 1912,
graphite pencil and ink
on paper, fully mounted on
cardboard, 30.2 × 26.1 cm
Centre Pompidou – Musée
National d'Art Moderne –
Centre de Création Industrielle
Dation, 1979. AM 1979-13

Fig. 8   Nicolas Schöffer
Chronos 8, 1967, stainless
steel, mirrors, motors,
combiners, turntable, electrical
circuit, 308 × 125 × 130 cm
Centre Pompidou – Musée
National d'Art Moderne – Centre
de Création Industrielle, Paris
Purchase, 1979. AM 1979-351

THE SOUND OF COLOURS

Roque Rivas

For the exhibition "Colours! Masterpieces from the Centre Pompidou", I have created, with IRCAM (Institute for Research and Coordination in Acoustics/Music), an immersive sound design that represents certain properties of the seven colours featured in the exhibition.

The search for correlations between sounds and colours goes back a long way – we find it in the writings of Greek philosophers – but it was not until the 17th century that synaesthesia was recognised by science as a subject for study. This neurological phenomenon refers to the stimulation of one sense by another, provoking a response: a sound stimulus (note, chord or timbre) can thus be associated with an image or a colour. Despite the number of studies (and cases among artists), there is still no unanimity on the correlation between colours and sounds. Each manifestation of this phenomenon is unique and thus changes from one person to another. Added to this are the wide variations in how colours and sounds are perceived in different cultures.

A few years ago, IRCAM developed a collaborative working methodology that enables us to transcribe the terminology of a given field (design, fashion, oenology, automotive, etc.) into a sound lexicon. This tool is linked to audio software that illustrates the principal properties of a sound through different examples.

In collaboration with the exhibition designers, the characteristics of each of the colours were described in a subjective and emotional way. These descriptions were then translated into sound attributes.

For the seven colours, we obtained the following results:

BLUE

Contemplative, serene and gentle in character. Its sound is continuous, distant and round, with long, drawn-out notes.

RED

It is described as carnal, sensual, voluptuous, aggressive and martial, with a strong presence. Its sound is powerful and warm, with sharp and pulsating attacks.

"As the long echoes, shadowy, profound,
Heard from afar, blend in a unity,
Vast as the night, as sunlight's clarity,
So perfumes, colours, sounds may correspond".

Charles Baudelaire, *Correspondances*, translated by James McGowan

WHITE

White represents the crystalline, transparency, restraint and simplicity. Its sound is tonal, continuous, long, distant and muted, like a faint residual noise or a murmur.

BLACK

This colour symbolises the cosmos, infinity. Its sound is deep, muffled, gravelly, long, dissonant and distorted. Its kinematic quality is that of a black hole, a hurricane that absorbs matter.

GREEN

Organic in character – natural, fresh, invigorating, proliferating. Its sound is loud and harmonic, in a fairly high-pitched register. In terms of form, it moves from the simple to the complex.

YELLOW

Carnivalesque, yellow embodies joy. Its sound is penetrating, bright, somewhat shrill, dissonant, resonant, fast and dynamic.

PINK

Pink is described as childlike, irreverent, a bit kitsch. Its sound is round, close, synthetic and in a moderately high register. Formally, the image is of balloons that inflate and deflate.

The different sounds that have been produced at IRCAM use a variety of sound sources, including synthesised sounds, instrumental samples and sounds from nature. They have been assembled and mixed using a multichannel audio broadcasting system.

The seven exhibition galleries have been designed as isolated and multisensory spaces. The spectator is totally immersed in the sound, smell and colour, as they would be in certain spatial installations by James Turrell or Olafur Eiliasson. The speakers are located on the walls and ceiling of each room, which enables the sound to be diffused throughout the space, increasing the sense of immersion.

COLOUR NOTES

Alexis Dadier

In his poem *Correspondances*, Charles Baudelaire wrote "So perfumes, colours, sounds may correspond", illustrating the world of the senses and the synaesthesia that links them. I composed these fragrances to match the spatiality of the colour and the sound. Since each fragrance needed to evoke a specific colour unambiguously for as many people as possible, the challenge was to overcome the problem of the inherently subjective nature of the sense of smell. This is the creative journey I took in developing these seven fragrances.

WHITE

To create this white scent, I recalled atmospheres such as the clinical white of a medical environment, the sanctuary of a bathroom with its white cosmetic creams and a landscape of soft snow where sounds are muffled. It embodies the cold, impersonal quality of these places, but also their reassuring aspect – a kind of soft, cocooning gentleness. The shivering notes of menthol blended with accords of cotton wool and white cream and mousse translate these worlds.

BLACK

Like the glimmering and textured brushstrokes of Pierre Soulages, the expanse of asphalt on the road, wet and steaming after a storm, concentrates the vapours of black, earthy matter composed of greasy automotive grime and heated bitumen sullied by oil stains. This rather disturbing black is expressed through a combination of angelica root, mandarin petit-grain, cistus, frankincense, styrax and Java vetiver.

GREEN

All the greens of nature are conveyed in this composition, from the soft green of spring meadows to the dark green of dense woods covered in humus, and the green of damp, newly mown grass. The greenery is sometimes fresh, light and gorged with sap, at other times rooty, coarse and leafy. Galbanum, musk mallow, fig and patchouli transcribe these fifty shades of green.

RED

Red is a fascinating colour, synonymous with passions, desires and violence. To reveal the ambivalence of this colour, in this fragrance I blended the regressive pleasures and blood-red notes of juicy berries (raspberry, blackberry and blackcurrant) with metallic tones. The radiance of geranium, with its powerful floral and aromatic notes, evoking a thorny, passionate red rose, conveys the complex duality of love and hate, mirroring the depth of human emotions.

YELLOW

Yellow is the colour of the sun. From an early age, children spontaneously draw the sun using this colour. It was while dreaming of the Côte d'Azur and its sunshine that I imagined this yellow perfume, composed of sunny citrus scents (bergamot, lemon and grapefruit), mimosa flower (the winter sun) and saffron.

PINK

Rose is a flower, a colour and a fragrance. The queen of flowers in Grasse perfumery was at the heart of my inspiration for this soliflore fragrance composed of rose absolute, to which a few delicate, pearlescent notes of lychee add their playful sweetness.

BLUE

Blue instantly evokes a seascape blending with the infinite expanse of the sky. Between the sea foam and the deep blue, the dark abysses and the clear sky, the Big Blue takes on fresh and ethereal lavender notes with accents of salty sea air and ambergris, like a cerulean breeze, in this olfactory allegory.

COLOUR
AND HISTORY

Marguerite Leroy

> "To say that colour has once again become expressive is to write its history".
>
> Henri Matisse

"To say that colour has once again become expressive is to write its history",[1] declared Henri Matisse in 1945, suggesting that before its "rehabilitation"[2] by modern artists, it had suffered from a long eclipse, rendered mute by its submission to drawing. In these few remarks, Matisse offers up a concrete and evolutive 'history' of colour, but is it limited to "the restitution of its emotive power"?[3]

The "problems of colour",[4] whether ontological, material or phenomenological in nature, have been considered from philosophical and scientific viewpoints since before the time of Socrates. They have not only influenced the status of art – and of painting, in particular – but also triggered debates and controversies and caused artists to reflect deeply on their practice. Considering colour in the history of Western painting inevitably leads to a paradoxical observation: despite debates surrounding the status of colour and that enjoined artists to use it sparingly or to control its application, artists continued to buy pigments and to create and use colours. The laws of colour, which set different poles in tension (variegation and harmony, monochrome and polychrome, paint-colour and dye-colour), continued, right up to the modern era, to oppose artistic practice and narratives on colour, which remained the preserve of theologians, scientists and philosophers. Nevertheless, by distancing itself from philosophical and scientific arguments, art has managed to create its own 'history' of colour. The *Journal* of Eugène Delacroix (1798–1863), whose interest in Michel-Eugène Chevreul's theories is frequently mentioned, is evidence of the attention the painter paid to the "science of colour" developed by his predecessors – Paolo Veronese, Peter Paul Rubens and Anthony van Dyck – and reveals the extent to which their works influenced his own use of colour.[5] This introduction therefore places itself at the crossroads of the major theories of colour that have shaped the history of Western thought and artists' thinking. Without claiming to provide an exhaustive account of the complexity and multiplicity of these connections, which have been extensively researched by others,[6] it attempts to understand how works of art themselves became the focus for reflecting on colour, where artists have interpreted scientific theories through their studio practice, technical experimentation and observation of works.

THE AGE OF SUSPICION

Since Antiquity, the relationship between theories on the origin of colours and art criticism has thrown suspicion on colour and its use. In Book X of Plato's *Republic*, where Socrates states that "imitative art, then, is far removed from the truth" (598 b), the criticism of mimesis led to the rejection of representation and image as misleading and false. This widespread suspicion surrounding images was compounded by specific doubts about the nature and origin of colour: In *Timaeus*, Plato saw colour as a reaction born of the encounter between the fire in the eye and the emanation of objects, in keeping with atomist philosophers (68 d). Aristotle, meanwhile, considered it as "the proper object of sight"[7] in *De Anima*, and established two primaries, black and white, from which, when mixed, all other colours are made. Aristotle also countered Platonic criticism of imitation, claiming that mimesis supports knowledge and is a source of pleasure. He formulated an analogy between painting and tragedy, in which drawing was seen as the action, the "soul of the tragedy" (*Poetics VI*, 1450 b) and colours, the characters, "the second place". However, colour is only one of the "other means"[8] of mimesis and Aristotle asserted the primacy of drawing over colour: "The most beautiful colours, laid on confusedly, will not give as much pleasure as the chalk outline of a portrait" (*Poetics* VI, 1450 b). In Latin literature, criticism of the diversity of colours and their extravagant use is found in Pliny, whose *Natural History* offers, in addition to a classification of the different colours, a reflection on the origin of painting and its decadence, through a eulogy of the tetrachromy practised by Greek painters, first among whom was Apelles. Pliny deplored the use of *colores floridi* by the painters of his day and viewed colour as a show of luxury and wealth rather than as a primary quality of the works:

> It was with four colours only that Apelles, Echion, Melanthius, and Nicomachus, those most illustrious painters, executed their immortal works; melinum for the white, Attic sil for the yellow, Pontic sinopis for the red, and atramentum for the black; and yet a single picture of theirs has sold before now for the treasures of whole cities. But at the present day, when purple is employed for colouring walls even, and when India sends us to the slime of her rivers, and the corrupt blood of her dragons and her elephants, there is no such thing as a picture of high quality produced. (*Natural History*, XXXV, 50)

During the Middle Ages, discourses on colour were largely inherited from theories prevalent in Antiquity about the nature and perception of colours, particularly so from the 13th century, following the rediscovery of Aristotle's writings.[9] The dubious conditions surrounding the material creation of colour, which involved a range of recipes and chemical processes (although mixing was prohibited),[10] led to those involved being treated with hostility. According to Jacques Le Goff, dyeing was an "illicit trade",[11] and dyers were feared because they altered matter, disrupted the physical world and polluted the air and water.[12] While these perceptions are now seen in a more nuanced light,[13] the devaluation of colour and the suspicion it aroused is evident in one of the etymologies of the word "colour", which links it to the Latin *celare*, to hide.[14] Dyeing was also considered to be an art related to medicine: on the basis of the therapeutic properties attributed to certain mineral pigments, medieval manuscripts often combined treatises on painting and illuminated manuscripts with those on pharmacy and medicine. This association was also based on a factual reality: producing colours required the use of medicinal weights and painters would acquire their supplies of pigments from apothecaries.[15] Yet, although colours were used by artists in the largely polychrome Middle Ages,[16]

theoretical reflection on their use and association was generally limited to technical considerations relating to their manufacture and durability.

As Michel Pastoureau highlights in his books about colour and its symbolic interpretation,[17] the abundance of texts on light stands in sharp contrast to the relative paucity of sources dealing specifically with colour and its nature, despite the interest that many medieval scholars showed in colour phenomena such as the rainbow.[18] The "truth" of colour oscillated between its close association with light, in keeping with the logical order of Aristotelian thinking, which arranged the different tones along a scale from white to black, and a materialist interpretation of colour as a physical layer applied to objects and beings. In a Christian society in which the Church dominated artistic creation and its productions, the theoretical opposition between two "physical states" of colour led to a number of moral conclusions: on the one hand, a love of colour that saw colour–light as the radiance of divine glory; on the other, an aversion for colour–matter, viewed as a vile luxury that was unnecessary in the practice of true religion. These two poles were embodied in an exemplary way by the canonical opposition in the 12th century between Suger, Abbot of Saint-Denis, and Bernard of Clairvaux, proponent of the Cistercian order.[19] For Suger, colour not only provided revelation of divine light when the sun shone through stained-glass windows but also suggested the remanent presence of God in matter such as precious stones, for example the *materia saphirorum* that Suger used in the windows of Saint-Denis when the basilica was rebuilt from 1135 onwards. Georges Duby translated one of Suger's reflections in the *De Consecratione* as follows: "Transposing that which is material into that which is immaterial, multicoloured gemstones possess a beauty that has led me to reflect on the diversity of sacred virtues".[20]

However, it was precisely this *varietas colorarum* that Bernard of Clairvaux excoriated in Cluniac art,[21] and in opposition to which he advocated for the austerity of monasteries, favouring monochrome script in the scriptorium of Cîteaux Abbey.[22] Thus, in an organisation of colours that had moved away from scientific theory and whose use was presided over by religious authority, artists were constrained in their use of colours both by the symbolism attributed to them[23] and by the contracts governing the use and distribution of coloured materials.[24] Pigments, notably natural ultramarine (lapis lazuli),[25] were not always easy to obtain. The debate on colours was, effectively, both theological and economic. Moreover, colour, particularly when it was used by laymen, was associated with the deception of the faithful and the duplicity of representation: "They are shown the very fine form of this or that saint, and the more colourful they are, the saintlier they find them. They rush to kiss them, are invited to give, and admire their beauty more than they venerate sanctity"[26], wrote Bernard of Clairvaux. Saint Bernard's attack was part of a broader condemnation of religious imagery, which bordered on a rejection of sacred representation and was exacerbated by polychromy and the association of colour with morally suspect frivolity.

These two conflicting positions cannot subsume the complex reality of colour in the Middle Ages: far from being chromophobic, medieval art was bursting with colour, and textiles, indisputably a major industry of the period, displayed an impressive variety of colours. Heraldry was a colourful world: a large part of scriptural technique relied on colour (illumination, headings), and medieval illuminated manuscripts are rich in chromatic nuances, as evidenced by the enduring practice of colour annotations.[27] Meanwhile dyers, while their trade certainly caused pollution, were often organised into guilds that sometimes wielded considerable political power, particularly in Italy.[28] So we can see that there was a distinction between, on the one hand, the practical use of colour and its material reality and, on the other, the reflections on colour that punctuate the history of medieval thought.

DRAWING AND COLOUR

With the Renaissance and the rise of the artist's *inventio*, drawing, in writings about art, asserted its dominance over colour. Rooted in studio practice, Cennino Cennini's *Libro dell'Arte*, written between 1390 and 1437, addressed the practical aspects of painting. It offers less a theory of colours than a theory of the art of colouring: working with colour is closely linked to shading and, consequently, to the portrayal of light.[29] Cennini indicated where to acquire and how to produce a certain number of pigments, notably the famous sienna. Leon Battista Alberti, in his *De Pictura*, affirmed the supremacy of *disegno* and its link with the painter's intellect, but he emphasised that the "copiousness and variety of colours greatly add to the pleasure and fame of a painting".[30] He did not treat colour as an independent subject and was much more interested in its role in the rendering of form and in achieving harmony between colours, which he saw as essential to the effective representation of 'history', than in the intrinsic value of colours themselves. The painter's objective, according to Alberti, was to depict the relief of his figures. The role of colour was important but remained secondary: "I should like the [highest level of attainment] in industry and art to rest, as the learned maintain, on knowing how to use black and white. It is worth all your study and diligence to know how to use these two well".[31]

The establishment of a tension between colour and drawing, which began in the Renaissance, continued during the Classical era in France in the *Querelle du coloris*, a debate that raged at the Académie Royale des Beaux-arts during the late 17th century, in which the supremacy of drawing, defended by Charles Le Brun, among others, was pitted against that of colour, championed by Roger de Piles. The latter was elected to the Academy in 1699. The opposition between line and colour was not new, and its various movements form "one of the 'great narratives' of European cultural history".[32]

Roger de Piles' *Dialogue sur le coloris* [*Dialogue upon Colouring*], published in 1673,[33] lays out the main arguments in favour of the colourists: proposing to "leave aside philosophers' disputes" over the nature of colour, Pamphile, named after the Greek painter and master of Apelles, takes up the role of defender of colour. He resumed the Italian distinction between colour, "the Materials which Painters make use of"[34] to imitate nature, and colouring, "a part of Painting by which the Painter knows how to imitate the Colour of all natural Objects".[35] These definitions, which Pamphile gave "like a painter",[36] turned the traditional attacks against painting on their head, recognising colour for the mimetic attributes and the artifice it embodies: in using colours, the artist not only imitates nature but embellishes it. Colour became the essential attribute of painting, differentiating it from other arts, "as Reason, which is the Difference of Man, is what makes Man."[37] It would appear, then, that Roger de Piles was overthrowing antique theories of colour in art: the mimetic power of painting, and by extension of colour, was no longer a threat but had become, in a significant way, comparable with human reason, while Renaissance thinking made *disegno* (in French *dessein*, meaning both "intention", "design" and "drawing") the materialisation of thought, set 'outside' the painter's mind (painting as *cosa mentale*), and intrinsically linked drawing and geometric rationality. When Damon, champion of Nicolas Poussin and Raphael, asked Pamphile how painters' mastery of colours and colouring differed from that of dyers, the latter replied that painters, unlike dyers, have "the understanding of these same colours".[38] Thanks to this "understanding" of colours, which only a few painters possess (Pamphile numbers them at only six "since Painting was reviv'd"[39] in the 14th century),

> The Beauty of Colouring does not consist in a multiplicity of different Colours, but in their just distribution, so that the painted Objects have the same Colour as the true [...] that they altogether make an agreeable Union throughout the whole Piece.[40]

The reference to a "multiplicity" of colours both recalls and contradicts Aristotle's "wide variety of colours": the harmony of colours and the interplay of complementary and contrasting tones, even in the absence of established rules of colour use, thus fully contributes to the painter's design,[41] and are no longer seen as the superfluous and licentious artifices of an art of seduction that were denounced by Platonian philosophy for their deceptive nature and by Aristotle's aesthetics for their secondary nature.

OBJECTIFYING COLOUR

The controversy surrounding colour, one of the principal aesthetic debates of the late 17th century, was fuelled by a duality that extended, in various forms, until the modern era: in the 19th century, for example, Jean-Auguste-Dominique Ingres and Eugène Delacroix were opposed by critics in the same terms. The dispute also mirrored a scientific revolution that changed how colours were defined and had a significant impact throughout the 18th century: Isaac Newton's experiments with colour and their presentation to the Royal Academy in London. These were carried out between 1666 and 1672, then summarised in a treatise, *Opticks*, published in 1704. Although Newton's work was contradicted and revised from the time it was presented to the Royal Academy,[42] it marked a turning point in the history of the understanding of colours and their symbolic status. Freed from their "indecorous materiality",[43] to quote art historian Charlotte Guichard, colours became measurable entities, able to be systematised within a rational, physically demonstrable theory. Newton proved the composite nature of sunlight and proposed a theory of a spectrum made up of seven colours, corresponding to the seven musical intervals, adding to the harmony of sounds that of colour.[44] This correlation could not be measured physically, however; it arose from Newton's spiritual and philosophical intent to affirm the symbolic importance of the number 7.

During the 18th century, Newton's theories circulated throughout Europe: in France, his treatise was translated in the early 1720s, and in 1738, Voltaire published his *Elements of the Philosophy of Newton*, which popularised the physicist's theories. Half a century after the publication of *Opticks*, the article "Colour" in *Encyclopédie*, was a sign of the global acceptance and diffusion of Newton's theories of the "colour spectrum".[45] In it, D'Alembert mentions seven colours that, together, produce white: "The proportional range of these seven intervals of colour corresponds fairly closely to the proportional range of the seven tones of music".[46] Interest in the questions raised by colour and coloration was wider and related to both their material aspects, given the many innovations related to pigments that were made during the Age of Enlightenment, and to colour theories and the "operational reflection"[47] of painters who were incorporating them in their works. For example, in 1753, Jean-Baptiste Oudry presented his *Canard blanc* [*White Duck*] to the Salon – "a pictorial reflection on the tonal value of colours [...] [with] educational and demonstrative status"[48] – in which the painter depicted a white duck and various objects of the same colour on a white background.

After Newton, colour moved away from the materiality of the pigment in an intellectual context that recognised the value of painting as an art of illusion. When Denis Diderot praised Jean Siméon Chardin's paintings exhibited at the Salon in 1763, he expressed his admiration for the distinction between the pigment and the painter's masterful use of colour in the following famous salutation: "Oh Chardin, it is not white, red or black that you mix on your palette; it is the very substance of things; it is air and light that you take up on the tip of your brush and apply to the canvas".[49]

It was the mimetic power of colour that inspired admiration in Diderot, who considered Chardin to be superior to Apelles. The artistry of the painter, his ability to combine on the canvas different states of colour – at times vaporous, at times luminous – is a form of illusionism: "This magic defies understanding. [...] Come closer, and everything blurs, flattens and disappears; step back, and it all takes shape again and reemerges".[50] The rendering of volume and the painting's ability to generate forms no longer relied solely on drawing and chiaroscuro, but on the balanced arrangement of colour.

One of the main oppositions to Newton's theories was made in the early 19th century, when Johann Wolfgang von Goethe published his *Theory of Colours* in 1810.[51] The German philosopher, poet and scientist violently attacked Newton's experiments, which he described as having been made with "juvenile haste",[52] and countered them with a theory of colours that contradicted Newton's refraction of the prism and colour spectrum: "With this conviction we look upon the mistake that has been committed in the investigation of this subject to be a very serious one, inasmuch as a secondary phenomenon has been thus placed higher in order – the primordial phenomenon has been degraded to an inferior place; nay, the secondary phenomenon has been placed at the head, a compound effect has been treated as simple, a simple appearance as compound ... ".[53] Goethe refuted Newton's additive synthesis with observations made by "artisans and dyers", who, he claimed, "were the first to notice the deficiency of Newton's idea",[54] because pigment mixing is subtractive and combining different coloured pigments does not produce white, but black. According to Goethe, colours result from the limitation of light by darkness,[55] suggesting the polarity between shade and light as well as their mutual influences. Goethe did not offer a definitive theory of colour but rather made a series of empirical observations that form a symbolic conception of colours, divided between yellow poles (light overshadowed by darkness) and blue (darkness weakened by light). The German scholar's colour wheel, composed of six colours and diametrically opposing "those which reciprocally evoke each other in the eye",[56] associates each one with a psychological value: "Experience teaches us that particular colours excite particular states of feeling",[57] he wrote.

The *Theory of Colours* argues that it is the eye that produces colours, basing this claim on the phenomenon of "physiological colours", which arise from the eyes themselves. For Goethe, "colour is in the eye of the beholder".[58] A new place is given to sensory apparatus and subjective perception, the spectator becoming "the active, autonomous producer",[59] the source of scientific knowledge. According to this proponent of *Naturphilosophie*, nothing should be sought "beyond phenomena, which are themselves the theory".[60]

Goethe's work was translated into English in 1840; three years later, the painter Joseph Mallord William Turner created *Light and Colour (Goethe's Theory) – The Morning after the Deluge – Moses Writing the Book of Genesis*, one of the titles of which is a direct allusion to the *Theory of Colours*, which the painter had read and annotated.[61] The role of the coloured brushstroke in Turner's work was fundamental for the Impressionists (Claude Monet and Camille Pissarro travelled to London in 1871), as Paul Signac emphasised in *D'Eugène Delacroix au néo-impressionnisme*:[62] fascinated by the luminosity of his paintings, the Impressionists attempted to recreate

> this simplification of the palette, [which,] restricting them to a very limited range of colours, inevitably led them to break down the colours and multiply the elements. They sought to reconstitute these colour effects through the optical blending of innumerable multicoloured strokes placed next to, over and through one another.[63]

The simplification of the Impressionists' palette was linked to a major innovation in the 19th century in the art of colour: with the arrival of the tube of paint, invented in 1841, paint became a ready-to-use product that enabled the Impressionists to work from nature. This completed the transformation of paint as a material. It had moved from being an artisanal blend

of pigments to a manufactured product, although the system of pigments and binders purchased from apothecaries and then ground by the artists themselves had largely evolved since the arrival and spread of colour merchants in Venice in the 15th century, chemical innovations – including the invention of Prussian blue[64] – in the 18th century and the establishment of certain colour merchants (Sennelier, Boursin) in the 19th century, some of whom, including Julien François Tanguy ('Père Tanguy') in Montmartre, became key figures in the art world. Paint colours were gradually categorised and grouped into a new colour system – colour charts, which developed in the 1880s.[65]

Goethe's insistence on physiological colours – although this idea constituted only one part of his treatise – as well as on the psychological effects of colours, was largely responsible for its reception by artists, particularly in the early 20th century: in fact, the echoes of his theory by philosopher Arthur Schopenhauer and theosophist Rudolf Steiner had a profound impact on Bauhaus painters, such as Wassily Kandinsky, Johannes Itten and Paul Klee, and on their metaphysical conceptions of colour.

In France, however, Goethe's theory of colours was less well known. Its "non-reception" in France, to use Jacques Le Rider's expression,[66] touched both the scientific world, which criticised the work's lack of rigour, stressing that its author "does not have the frame of mind of those who are honestly seeking the truth",[67] and the art world: Neither Charles Baudelaire nor Eugène Delacroix, both of whom were interested in the perception of colour and were familiar with the German philosopher's work, made mention of the *Theory of Colours*. This was no doubt due to the relative novelty of his theories: in fact, his developments on "physiological colours" evoked the observations made by Georges-Louis Leclerc, Comte de Buffon, concerning "accidental colours", "[which] only ever appear when the organ is overstimulated or excessively strained",[68] that had been presented to the Académie Royal des Sciences in 1743. In addition, the notion of the complementarity of colours had been present, albeit in a diffuse form, in the writings of several painters and colour theorists from the Renaissance onwards, articulated in terms of harmonious and discordant colours.

The physiological response to the perception of colour and the resulting contrasts and harmonies gave rise to a theory that had a much greater impact on French artists, that of chemist Michel-Eugène Chevreul, appointed as director of the Gobelins Manufactory in 1824. In the 1820s, Chevreul became interested in the juxtaposition of colours and the psycho-physiological effects that this produced.[69] The presentation of a paper on the subject to the Académie in 1828 and the biennial courses and lectures that he gave at the Gobelins Manufactory soon sparked interest among artists.[70] In 1839, Chevreul published a major work that became decisive for many artists during the latter half of the century – *The Laws of Contrast of Colour*[71] – in which he stated the law of simultaneous contrast: "When two contiguous colours are seen at the same time, they appear as dissimilar as possible, both with regard to their optical composition and their depth of tone",[72] and claimed that these effects are multiplied when the two colours juxtaposed are complementary ones.

This rationalisation of visual experience, which echoed the preoccupations of painters regarding colour harmony, along with many plates illustrating Chevreul's book, circulated rapidly: in 1842, the magazine *L'Artiste* popularised the chemist's theory and Charles Blanc expounded on it in his *Grammaire des arts et du dessin*, the complete edition of which was published in 1867.[73] In it, Blanc defines colour not as "a gift from heaven [...] an impenetrable arcanum to him who has not received its secret influence",[74] but as something that can be learnt, "which is under fixed laws [and can] be taught like music".[75]

Charles Blanc also proposed a logical association between Eugène Delacroix's reflections on colour and Chevreul's law. Although Delacroix never met the chemist, he acquired a notebook of notes taken during the lectures he gave at the Gobelins Manufactory. According to Blanc,

> From having known these laws, studied them profoundly, after having intuitively divined them, Eugene Delacroix became one of the greatest colorists of modern times, one might even say the greatest, for he surpassed all others, not only in the aesthetic language of his coloring, but in the prodigious variety of his motives and the orchestration of his colors.[76]

The association between Delacroix and Chevreul's theory of colours creates an image of the former as a meticulous observer of colour laws, at the same time setting him up as an example to follow: the reflections on colour in Delacroix's *Journal*, the many discussions on the subject he is known to have had with other artists and with his colour merchant, Étienne-François Haro, as well as his use of an increasingly divided brushstroke – a technique known as *flochetage* – constituted for critics and generations of artists that followed, and in particular the Post-Impressionists, a model of painting in which "painting thinks for itself, independently of the objects it adorns".[77] Here is how printmaker and friend of Delacroix Frédéric Villot described the painter's technique in 1865: "Instead of laying down bright and pure colour in its proper place, he alternates the tones, breaks them up and, treating the brush like a shuttle, seeks to weave a fabric of multicoloured threads that cross and interrupt each other at every turn".[78] The association with tapestry and the optic blending of the painting technique validate the link between Delacroix and Chevreul. However, it was by observing works, especially those of Rubens, that Delacroix honed his own techniques in the use of colour. In 1822, in *Dante et Virgile aux Enfers* [*Dante and Virgil in Hell*], Delacroix understood "the importance of reflections for enhancing colour"[79] and reinterpreted the colourful strokes used by Rubens in *The Arrival of Marie de Medici at Marseille*, a work he had studied.[80]

The genealogy that Paul Signac developed in his book, *D'Eugène Delacroix au néo-impressionnisme*, published in 1899, links the birth of Neo-Impressionism with the knowledge of a "science of colour, simple and accessible, that everyone should learn and that would save us from so many misguided judgments".[81] Signac notably advocated the division of the brushstroke and the banishing of a mix of pigments in favour of optical blending. References to Chevreul are numerous, suggesting that the work was a source that Signac, like other artists, drew from. However, as Georges Roque points out, the majority of painters who aligned themselves with Chevreul failed to grasp his laws:[82] Roque attributes this lack of understanding to, among other things, the circulation of Chevreul's colour plates, which, for educational purposes, presented an exaggerated view of colour contrast, a contrast that, in reality, could only be internal.[83] It would thus seem that the widespread adoption of Chevreul's ideas and their influence on artists, right up to Robert Delaunay, had more to do with the artists' desire to reflect on colour and think about its effects on the canvas than it did with an actual understanding and the rigorous application of the scientific laws of colour, which, moreover, were difficult to read. In the practice of painters, scientific theories and artistic approaches to colour merged. For many artists, this harmony was crucial. Vincent van Gogh wrote to his brother Theo as follows:

> I certainly intend to study theory seriously, I do not think it at all useless, and I believe that what one feels by instinct or by intuition often becomes definite and clear if one is guided in one's efforts by some really practical words.[84]

"PURE COLOUR! EVERYTHING MUST BE SACRIFICED TO IT"[85] (PAUL GAUGUIN)

Goethe's theories and Chevreul's ideas had an important influence on painters at the turn of the 20th century, partly because the emphasis they placed on subjective perception and the sensitive composition of colours, now seen as phenomena in their own right, combined with a reversal of the imitative relationship between art and nature. Van Gogh was aware of this shift: "one ends by calmly creating from one's palette, and nature agrees with it, and follows".[86]

This revolution also entailed a radical transformation in approaches to colour, which became an expression of the painter's intent rather than merely a vehicle for illusion. The truth of colour no longer lay in its ability to conform to physical or physiological laws but rather in the painter's own sensibility. Such was the case with the Nabi painters (and the advice that Paul Gauguin gave to Paul Sérusier, encouraging him to paint colours following not real-life tones but his subjective impressions of them), but the expressiveness of colour is particularly evident in the work of the Fauvists, who were inspired by the subjective approach and sublime colours of their predecessors, especially Van Gogh. It was in 1901, at a retrospective of Van Gogh's work held at the Galerie Bernheim-Jeune, that Henri Matisse met Maurice de Vlaminck: "I saw Derain in the company of an enormous young fellow who proclaimed his enthusiasm in a voice of authority. He said, 'You see, you've got to paint with pure cobalts, pure vermilions, pure veronese.' I think Derain was a bit afraid of him".[87]

"The orgy of pure colours"[88] converging on the canvas in large flat tints became one of the main characteristics of Fauvism. At the Salon of 1905, in addition to the now-famous remark made by Louis Vauxcelles that gave its name to the movement, the critic Camille Mauclair spoke of "gaudy daubs [...] devoid of meaning".[89] For all that, the Fauvists were not guided by any intentional colour theory or rational approach to colour, except that of their own sensibility: despite being influenced by Chevreul's theories and Impressionism early in his career, Matisse criticised the mechanical aspect of the colour theories, stating, in 1908:

> The choice of my colours does not rest on any scientific theory; it is based on observation, on feeling, on the experience of my sensibility.[90]

Colour theories, which had led to Divisionism and a growing interest in optical blending at the end of the previous century, complementary colours and the division of the brushstroke were swept aside by a new generation of artists, who, following Cézanne's lead, were advocating a "colourful logic" that was not limited by the "logic of the brain".[91] Colour no longer sought to imitate real life but became, whether as coloured matter or a sensory and expressive substance, the very life of the work of art. In the wake of the investigations made by Cézanne and

the Impressionists, artists became interested in colour for its own sake. Among them was Henri Matisse: the painter's career was marked by a progressive emancipation of colour, from the translation of the sense of light in *Luxe, calme et volupté* [*Luxury, Calm and Pleasure*], with its juxtaposed dots of paint, to the paper cut-outs of the 1940s and 1950s, in which Matisse sought to "cut directly into colour".[92] For him, it was about translating a pictorial sensation, an expressiveness inherent to colour, onto the canvas, without regard for its mimetic function. This colour-as-sensation became a veritable chromatic system in his work: "The various symbols I use need to be balanced in such a way that they don't destroy each other",[93] he said.

Whether artists were refusing to measure the effects of colour scientifically, as was the case for Matisse; seeking, on the contrary, to rationalise it to the full, as in Neo-Plasticism; or whether they were playing with its materiality and chromatic codes, the narrative of colour became above all artistic. Scientific theories of the 19th century were drawn upon in a new way; the exploration of colour became an end in itself. Such was the case with Robert Delaunay's 'Windows' series. He wrote:

> Toward 1912–1913 I had the idea of a kind of painting which, technically, would rely only on color, on contrasts; of color, but these developing in time and making themselves perceived simultaneously, at one go. I used Chevreul's scientific term: simultaneous contrasts. [...] color acting, this time, almost independently, through contrasts.[94]

As Georges Roque notes, Delaunay cites Chevreul's "scientific term" but did not apply his laws,[95] and, with Orphism, developed an art of colour that was individual and shaped by his own reflections on the expressiveness of colour.

This reuse of scientific literature on colour as an inspiration for modern art was also found in the fortunes of Goethe's theory among the artists of the Weimar Bauhaus, where those holding a dynamic and symbolic view of colour (Paul Klee, Johannes Itten and Wassily Kandinsky) were countered by those in favour of the quantitative harmony of colours developed by chemist Wilhelm Ostwald in *The Color Primer* (1916), whose principles were adopted by the De Stijl group and reduced the contrasts between colours to an interaction between measurable pigments.[96] In 1920, Klee noted in his journal: "we are neither a paint industry nor a chemical dye house",[97] making clear his opposition to a rational and systematic approach to colour, which he viewed, moreover, as tied up with commercialism. In essence, this attack was reviving the age-old opposition between colour as used by artists and colour used for dyeing. Kandinsky and Itten, both teachers at the Bauhaus, also expressed the spirituality of their comprehensive theories of colour in their courses. Late 1911 saw the publication of Kandinsky's seminal work, *On the Spiritual in Art*, in which the painter advocated for the advent of an abstract art that would consider the image and its symbolic value in terms not of their representative capacity but of their intrinsic spiritual power: form and colour should be combined in compositions so that they "rest only on the principle of the corresponding vibration of the human soul",[98] and produce an abstract image that immediately resonates with the viewer's interiority. Seeing a painting "is not about perceiving a red object, nor even the colour red as such, but rather recognising the impression it makes on us."[99] In contrast to the Expressionist or Fauvist painters, this expressiveness of colour did not lie in its correspondence with human emotions, but in its very spirituality, its "innermost necessity":[100] colour became a purely pictorial medium.[101]

Kandinsky's investigations were contemporaneous with Constructivist research into the principles of the creation and appearance of monochrome paintings in modern art. Malevich's famous 'Squares' (the most of which was exhibited at the "0.10" exhibition in 1915) and Alexander Rodchenko's triptych *Pure Red, Pure Yellow, Pure Blue* (1921) were painted surfaces that aspired neither to mimetic representation nor to sensory expressivity but rather examined "the relationship between painting – rather than the subject of the painting – and meaning".[102] Colour became the very subject of painting, a surface onto which the artist projected their intentions. Colour assumed this role as a means of painting and, in so doing, became the instrument of its own criticism: as Clement Greenberg noted in a seminal article published in 1961, "Modernism criticizes from the inside, through the procedures themselves of that which is being criticized".[103]

The 'arc of the monochrome' that spanned 20th-century Western painting and reached the peak of its expression in the colour field painting of the 1940s and 1950s – which was informed by metaphysical reflection on the power and vibration of the pigment as it interacts with the space of the canvas (for example in the work of Ad Reinhardt and Mark Rothko) – was pushed to the limits in the painting of Yves Klein, dubbed 'Yves the Monochrome'. Exploration of monochrome, which he began in the late 1940s, led Klein logically to the most complete form of abstraction: "To sense the soul without explaining it, without vocabulary,

and to depict this sensation … is, I believe, one of the reasons that led me to monochromy!"[104]

This quest for a colourful transcendence was reflected in his choice of blue as total colour: "All colors bring forth associations of concrete, material, and tangible ideas, while blue evokes all the more the sea and the sky, which are what is most abstract in tangible and visible nature".[105] A blue was patented by the artist in the late 1950s under the name 'International Klein Blue'. This patent also touched on another aspect of the aesthetics of colour within modern artistic practice, with which it is linked. While Yves Klein sought the "dematerialisation of blue",[106] he rooted his practice in the physical materiality of painting, and protected his IKB from appropriation: "For a long time, I searched for a binding medium that would allow me to fix the grains of pigment, which, when they are still loose powder in the drawers of colour merchants, form an incandescent mass. It was disheartening to see this same pigment, once ground into oil, for example, lose all its brilliance, all life of its own."[107] In fact, colour, manufactured and distributed in a standardised way, had seen its status change at the turn of the century. The industrial production of tubes, aerosol cans and tins of paint had led, as Ann Temkin emphasised, to a new understanding of colour that was no longer based on scientific theory or the spiritual resonance of colours, and instead reinvented the colour wheel as a colour chart, in which colours are arranged arbitrarily.[108] From pigment, colour has become the painting itself: Frank Stella declared in 1954 that he wanted "to keep the paint as good as it is in the can".[109] Colours exist, radically, 'outside of' both the person who uses them and any attempt at rationalisation. This shift proved to be a potent source of creative energy for contemporary artists, transcending questions of aesthetic affinity: it enabled the exploration of new combinatory logics, as in the work of Ellsworth Kelly and Gerhard Richter, and the interrogation of the role of the artists in the creative process, as in François Morellet's "Répartitions aléatoires" ["Random Distributions"]. Here, colour is one of the components of the artist's protocol. For example, he used the sequence of even and odd numbers from the telephone directory to assign colour to the grids of the paintings in the 'Random Distribution of 40,000 Squares' series (1961). Colour was arbitrarily assigned to an area of the painting that corresponded to the even or odd number of a directory opened at random. In 1970, Robert Rauschenberg stated that he used surplus paint to create his works for economic reasons: in line with Jackson Pollock and Frank Stella, he emphasised the material expressivity of the paint itself.

"BUT THEN WHAT IS COLOUR REALLY? WHEN ONE SAYS RED OR GREEN, ONE SAYS NOTHING"[110] (GEORGES BRAQUE)

A blond-haired child, wearing a dark blue floral dress, holds a book with a red cover in her hands, struggling to make out the words. *Remarks on Color*, a video work by artist Gary Hill, made in 1994, shows his daughter Anastasia, aged eight, reading the first part of Ludwig Wittgenstein's *Bemerkungen über die Farben* [*Remarks on Colour*], published in 1951. The complexity of the philosopher's propositions, amplified by the artist's decision to replace all the scientific terms and proper nouns with phonetic transcriptions, is reflected in the difficulty the young reader has in pronouncing the author's first eighty-eight remarks clearly and distinctly. While Hill's work echoes the questions surrounding the meaning of words and the language games central to Wittgenstein's thought, it also illustrates the staggering gap between the complexity of philosophical and scientific reflections on colour and the disarming immediacy of coloured phenomena, for the chromatic games at play throughout the video also allude to the three primary colours: the yellow of the young girl's hair, the blue of her dress and the red of the book. This work, which incidentally was made in Spanish, German and French, opens a window onto the way artists have appropriated colour theories, grounding them in art practice, and offers a telling and far from isolated example of the connections that exist between fields of knowledge and artistic creation. It also forms part of a longer history of colour, for while it is an explicit quotation from Wittgenstein, the philosopher's *Remarks on Colour* were themselves a response to Johann Wolfgang von Goethe's *Theory of Colours*. Colour theories, whose forbidding complexity Hill brings into focus, have thus provided artists with both a "reservoir of images and ideas"[111] and a means through which to shape and reflect on their own practice. The many tensions between the scientific and physical rationalisation of colours, its philosophical interpretation and the field of art were perfectly summarised by artist František Kupka, who, in 1912, created his *Disques de Newton* [*Disks of Newton*], a reference to the system of colours that the English physicist established in 1666. However, in handwritten notes entitled "Colour and Light" and preserved in the Bibliothèque Kandinsky,[112] he writes that the observations on colour drawn from the painter's practice – intuitive and inspired by his own imagination – were:

lessons far more fruitful than all the colour theories that earnest physicists demonstrate in schematic diagrams. Painters are not ungrateful – most of them boast of having studied these colour theories. But what can they learn from such basic teaching?[113]

1
Jack D. Flam (ed.), *Matisse on Art* (New York: Phaidon, 1973), p 99. "To say that colour has once again become expressive is to write its history. For a long time colour was only the complement of drawing. Raphael, Mantegna, or Dürer, like all Renaissance painters, constructed with drawing first and then added colour".

2
Ibid.

3
Ibid.

4
Ignace Meyerson (ed.), *Problèmes de la couleur, exposés et discussions du colloque du Centre de recherches de psychologie comparative*, Paris, 18–20 May 1954, Paris, S.E.P.V.E.N., Bibliothèque Générale de l'École Pratique des Hautes Études, 1957. Quoted in "Introduction. Approches interdisciplinaires de la couleur", Michel Menu, Jean-Marie Schaeffer and Romain Thomas (ed.), *La Couleur en questions. Approches interdisciplinaires de la couleur* (Paris: Hermann, 2023), p.6.

5
Eugène Delacroix, Paul Flat, René Piot (ed.), *Journal*, entry of 14 May 1830 (Paris: Librairie Plon, 1926), pp.142–44.

6
Among the abundance of literature, we should mention, in particular: Jacques Aumont, *Introduction à la couleur. Des discours aux images* (Paris: Armand Colin, 2020 [1994]); Philip Ball, *Bright Earth: The Invention of Colour* (London: Viking, 2001); John Gage, *Colour and Culture: Practice and Meaning from Antiquity to Abstraction* (London: Thames & Hudson, 2024 [1993]); Aurélia Gaillard, *L'Invention de la couleur par les Lumières* (Paris: Les Belles Lettres, 2024); Michel Pastoureau and Dominique Simonnet, *Le Petit Livre des couleurs* (Paris: Seuil, 2014); Claude Romano, *De la couleur* (Paris: Gallimard, Folio essais, 2021); Georges Roque, *Art et science de la couleur. Chevreul et les peintres, de Delacroix à l'abstraction* (Nîmes: Jacqueline Chambon, 1997).

7
Anne Zagdoun, *L'Esthétique d'Aristote* (Paris: CNRS Éditions, 2011), p.29.

8
Ibid., p.28.

9
Alberto Virdis, "Color in Suger's Saint-Denis. Matter and Light", *Convivium*, vol.8, no.2 (2021), pp.78–95 (pp.82–84).

10
Michel Pastoureau, "Le tabou des mélanges", *Une histoire symbolique du Moyen Âge occidental* (Paris: Seuil, 2004), pp.177–80.

11
Jacques Le Goff, "Métiers licites et métiers illicites dans l'Occident médiéval", in Jacques Le Goff, *Un autre Moyen Âge* (Paris: Gallimard, 1999), pp.89–103.

12
Michel Pastoureau, "Du bleu au noir. Éthiques et pratiques des couleurs à la fin du Moyen Âge", *Médiévales*, no.14 (1988), pp.9–21 (p.12).

13
Mathieu Harsch, *La Teinture et les Matières tinctoriales à la fin du Moyen Âge: Florence, Toscane, Méditerranée*, doctoral thesis (Paris: Université Paris-Cité and Padua: Università degli Studi di Padova, 2021), pp.139–60.

14
Annie Mollard-Desfour, "La couleur garde-t-elle son secret ?", *Sigila*, no.47, Paris, Gris-France (Spring/Summer 2021), pp.25–31, §2.

15
Charles Cailhol, "Pigments et pharmacie", *Revue d'histoire de la pharmacie*, no.167 (1960), pp.453–58.

16
Anne-Solenn Le Hô and Sandrine Pagès-Camagna, "La polychromie de la sculpture médiévale française, xiie–xve siècles. Bilan des examens et analyses entrepris au C2RMF", *Technè*, no.39 (2014), pp.34–41.

17
Michel Pastoureau, *Une histoire symbolique du Moyen Âge occidental*, op.cit.

18
John Gage, "Unweaving the Rainbow", *Color and Culture: Practice and Meaning from Antiquity to Abstraction* (Los Angeles: University of California Press, 1999), pp.93–116.

19
Michel Pastoureau, *Une histoire symbolique du Moyen Âge occidental*, op.cit.

20
Transcribed in Georges Duby, *L'Europe des cathédrales 1140-1280* (Geneva: Albert Skira, 1966), p.16.

21
Georges Duby, *Saint Bernard. L'Art cistercien* (Paris, Flammarion, 1999 [1976]), p.93.

22
André Moisan, "Suger de Saint-Denis, Bernard de Clairvaux et la question de l'art sacré", *Le Beau et le Laid au Moyen Âge* (Aix-en-Provence: Presses universitaires de Provence, 2000), pp.383–99, §8.

23
Michel Pastoureau, *Les Couleurs au Moyen Âge. Dictionnaire encyclopédique* (Paris: Le léopard d'or, 2022).

24
Michael Baxandall, *L'Œil du Quattrocento. L'usage de la peinture dans l'Italie de la Renaissance* (Paris: Gallimard, 1985), pp.31–35.

25
See the chapter devoted to it in François Delamare, *Bleus en poudres. De l'Art à l'Industrie, 5000 ans d'innovations* (Paris: Presses de l'École des Mines de Paris, 2007), pp.123–47.

26
Bernard de Clairvaux, *Apologie à Guillaume de Saint-Thierry* (Paris: Librairie de Louis Vivè, ed., 1866), quoted by Marie-Anne Polo de Beaulieu in "Usages et mésusages des images selon les prédicateurs du Moyen Âge (xiiie–xve siècles)", in Jean-Philippe Genet (ed.), *Vecteurs de l'idéel et mutation des sociétés politiques* (Paris: Éditions de la Sorbonne and Rome: École française de Rome, 2021), pp.371–400, §46.

27
Marie-Thérèse Grousset and Patricia Stirnemann, "Indications de couleur dans les manuscrits médiévaux", in Institut de recherche et d'histoire des textes, Centre de recherche sur les collections and Équipe Étude des pigments, histoire et archéologie, *Pigments et colorants de l'Antiquité et du Moyen Âge* (Paris: CNRS Éditions, 2002), pp.189–98 (p.189).

28
Mathieu Harsch, *La Teinture et les Matières tinctoriales à la fin du Moyen Âge: Florence, Toscane, Méditerranée*, op.cit.

29
Yves Hersant, "La couleur de l'ombre", in Jackie Pigeaud (ed.), *La Couleur, les couleurs* (Rennes: Presses Universitaires de Rennes, 2007), pp.169–277, §5.

30
Leon Battista Alberti, *On Painting* (New Haven: Yale University Press, 1966 [1435]), p.82.

31
Ibid.

32
Jacques Le Rider, "Ligne et couleur : histoire d'un différend", *Revue Germanique Internationale*, no.10 (1998), pp.173–84, § 11. For history of the opposition in 16th-century Italy, see Isabelle Bouvrande, *Le Coloris vénitien à la Renaissance. Autour de Titien* (Paris: Classiques Garnier, 2015).

33
Roger de Piles, *Dialogue upon Colouring*, trans. Mr Ozell, 1711 [1699]. Translated from Roger de Piles, *Dialogue sur le coloris* (Paris: Nicolas Langlois, 1699).

34
Ibid., p.5.

35
Ibid.

36
Ibid.

37
Ibid., p.28.

38
Ibid., p.18.

39
Ibid., p.28.

40
Ibid., p.9.

41
Jacqueline Lichtenstein, *La Couleur éloquente* (Paris: Flammarion, 1999 [1989]), p.152 ff.

42
Bernard Maitte, "Les couleurs en physique au xviiie siècle. Débats autour du renversement de leur statut par Newton", *Dix-Huitième siècle*, vol.1, no.51 (2019), pp.93–109 (103 ff).

43
Charlotte Guichard, "Palettes et tableaux. Des laboratoires de la couleur ?", *Dix-Huitième siècle*, vol.1, no.51 (2019), pp.187–204 (p.195).

44
Jacob Lachat and Julien Zanetta, "De la couleur en critique", *Nouvelle revue d'esthétique*, vol.1, no.27 (2021), pp.77–86, § 5.

45
Bernard Maitte, "Les couleurs en physique au xviiie siècle. Débats autour du renversement de leur statut par Newton", op.cit., p.95.

46
Jean Le Rond d'Alembert, "Couleur", in *Encyclopédie*, vol.4, p.327 b, quoted by Bernard Maitte in "Les couleurs en physique au xviiie siècle. Débats autour du renversement de leur statut par Newton", op.cit., p.95.

47
Michael Baxandall, *Shadows and Enlightenment* (New Haven: Yale University Press, 1995), p.137.

48
Charlotte Guichard, "Palettes et tableaux. Des laboratoires de la couleur ?", op.cit., p.192.

49
Denis Diderot, "Salon de 1763", in Jules Assézat (ed.), *Œuvres complètes*, vol.10 (Paris: Garnier, 1875), p.195.

50
Ibid.

51
Johann Wolfgang von Goethe, *Theory of Colours*, trans. Charles Lock Eastlake (Cambridge: MIT Press, 1970).

52
Quoted in Hervé Fischer, "8. Goethe et Schopenhauer : la couleur est dans l'œil", *Mythanalyse de la couleur* (Paris: Gallimard, Bibliothèque des Sciences Humaines, 2023), pp.175–200, §8.

53
Johann Wolfgang von Goethe, *Theory of Colours*, op.cit., p.73.

54
John Gage, *Colour in Turner: Poetry and Truth* (London: Studio Vista, 1969), p.93.

55
Claude Romano, "De l'objectivisme au subjectivisme", *De la couleur*, op.cit., pp.81–128, §3.

56
Johann Wolfgang von Goethe, *Theory of Colours*, op.cit., p.21.

57
Ibid., p.305.

58
Hervé Fischer, "8. Goethe et Schopenhauer : la couleur est dans l'œil", op.cit.

59
Jonathan Crary, *Techniques of the Observer: On Vision and Modernity in the Nineteenth Century* (Cambridge: MIT Press, 1990), p.69.

60
Johann Wolfgang von Goethe, *Maximen und Reflexionen*, Hamburger Ausgabe (Munich: Beck), t.XII: *Kunst und Literatur* (1981), p.432, quoted in Claude Romano, *De la couleur*, op.cit., §4.

61
For the link between Turner and Goethe's theory of colours, see John Gage, *Colour in Turner*, op.cit.

62
Paul Signac, *D'Eugène Delacroix au néo-impressionnisme* (Paris: Henri Floury, 1921 [1899]).

63
Ibid., p.50.

64
Charlotte Guichard, "Palettes et tableaux. Des laboratoires de la couleur ?", op.cit., p.197 ff.

65
Ann Temkin, "Color Shift", in *Color Chart: Reinventing Color, 1950 to Today*, exh. cat., 2 March – 12 May 2008 (New York: Museum of Modern Art, 2008), p.16.

66
Jacques Le Rider, "La non-réception française de la 'Théorie des couleurs' de Goethe", *Revue germanique internationale*, vol.13 (2000), pp.169–86.

67
Chemist Jean-Henri Hassenfratz, quoted in Fernand Baldensperger, Goethe en France. *Étude de littérature comparée* (Paris: Hachette, 1920 [1904]), p.196 ff., quoted by Jacques Le Rider, "La non-réception française de la 'Théorie des couleurs' de Goethe", op.cit., §13.

68
Georges-Louis Leclerc, Comte de Buffon, Jean-Louis de Lanessan, *Œuvres complètes*, 1884 t.II, 2 (Paris: Abel Pilon, 1004), p.414.

69
Georges Roque, *Art et science de la couleur. Chevreul et les peintres, de Delacroix à l'abstraction*, op.cit.

70
John Gage, "Chevreul between Classicism and Romanticism", in John Gage, *Colour and Meaning: Art, Science and Symbolism* (London: Thames & Hudson, 1999), pp.196–200.

71
Michel-Eugène Chevreul, *The Laws of Contrast of Colour and Their Application to the Arts*, trans. John Spanton (London: Routledge, Warne, and Routledge, 1861 [1839]).

72
Ibid., p.9.

73
Charles Blanc, *The Grammar of Painting and Engraving*, trans. Kate N. Doggett (New York: Hurd and Houghton, 1974 [1867]).

74
Ibid., p.146.

75
Ibid.

76
Ibid., p.156.

77
Charles Baudelaire, *Curiosités esthétiques. Œuvres complètes de Charles Baudelaire*, vol.2 (Paris: Michel Lévy frères, 1868), p.241.

78
Frédéric Villot, *Catalogue de tableaux, aquarelles, dessins, croquis, études, planches gravées à l'eau forte par Eugène Delacroix, provenant du cabinet de M. F. V., vente du 11 février 1865*, Hôtel des commissaires-priseurs, 5, rue Drouot, "Introduction", p.6, quoted in Étienne Moreau-Nélaton, *Eugène Delacroix raconté par lui-même*, t.I (Paris: Henri Laurens, 1916), p.182.

79
Sébastien Allard, *Dante et Virgile aux Enfers d'Eugène Delacroix*, exh. cat., Musée du Louvre, 9 April – 5 July 2004 (Paris: Réunion des Musées Nationaux, 2004), p.90.

80
Here, the analysis followed is that proposed by curator Sébastien Allard in Sébastien Allard, *Dante et Virgile aux Enfers d'Eugène Delacroix*, op.cit., p.84 ff. Thanks are due to Charlotte Guichard, professor of modern art history at the École Normale Supérieure, for this reference and her valuable advice during the writing of this text.

81
Paul Signac, *D'Eugène Delacroix au néo-impressionnisme*, op.cit., p.100.

82
Georges Roque, "La réception de Chevreul par les peintres", in Georges Roque et al. (ed.), *Michel-Eugène Chevreul* (Paris: Publications scientifiques du Muséum, 1997), p.247-261, §9.

83
Ibid., §11 ff.

84
Vincent van Gogh, *The Complete Letters of Vincent van Gogh: with Reproductions of all the Drawings in the Correspondence*, vol.2 (London, Boston and New York: Little, Brown, 2000), p.297.

85
Charles Morice, *Paul Gauguin* (Paris: Henri Floury, 1920), p.246.

86
Letter to Theodore van Gogh, October–November 1885 [429], Vincent van Gogh, *Complete Letters of Vincent van Gogh*, op.cit., p.429.

87
Henri Matisse, quoted in J. Elderfield, *The Wild Beasts: Fauvism and its Affinities*, exh. cat., 26 March – 1 June 1976, Museum of Modern Art, New York (New York: MoMA, 1976), p.30.

88
Louis Vauxcelles, "Le Salon d'Automne", *Gil Blas* (17 October 1905), p.1.

89
Camille Mauclair, "La peinture et la sculpture au Salon d'Automne", *L'Art décoratif. Revue internationale d'art industriel et de décoration*, 7th year, 2nd semester 1905, p.225.

90
Henri Matisse, quoted in Jacques Aumont, "L'expressivité colorée: la peinture", *Introduction à la couleur. Des discours aux images*, op.cit., pp.109–39, §46.

91
Joachim Gasquet, *Cézanne – a Memoir with Conversations* (London: Thames & Hudson, 1991), p.161.

92
Henri Matisse, *Écrits et propos sur l'art* (Paris: Hermann, 1972), p.247.

93
Quoted in Philippe Dagen (ed), *Le Fauvisme. Textes de peintres, d'écrivains et de journalistes* (Paris: Somogy, 1994), p.177.

94
Quoted in Dora Vallier, *Abstract Art*, trans. Jonathan Griffin (New York: Orion Press, 1970 [1967]), pp.198–99.

95
Georges Roque, "La réception de Chevreul par les peintres", in Georges Roque et al. (ed.), *Michel-Eugène Chevreul*, op.cit., p.219.

96
Damien Ehrhardt, Hélène Fleury, *Luminosité de la couleur goethéenne et dialogue des arts au Bauhaus*. Paper presented at *Lumière et Musique : appropriations, métaphores, analogies*, Nicolas Dufetel; Katia-Sofia Hakim, Nov 2018, Paris, Fondation Singer-Polignac, France, p.3.

97
Jürg Spiller (ed.), *Paul Klee: The Thinking Eye: The Notebooks of Paul Klee*, trans. Ralph Manheim (New York: George Wittenborn and London: Lund Humpries, 1961 [1956]), p.521.

98
Wassily Kandinsky, *On the Spiritual in Art* (New York: Guggenheim Foundation, 1946, [1911]), p.43.

99
Michel Henry, *Voir l'invisible. Sur Kandinsky* (Paris: PUF, 2004), p.131, quoted in Ioulia Podoroga, "Abstraction et iconoclasme. Les cas Kandinsky et Malevitch", *Ligeia, dossiers sur l'art*, nos.157–60 (2017), pp.55–65 (p.60).

100
Wassily Kandinsky, *On the Spiritual in Art*, op.cit.

101
Ioulia Podoroga, "Abstraction et iconoclasme: les cas Kandinsky et Malevitch", op.cit., p.56.

102
Denys Riout, *La Peinture monochrome* (Paris: Gallimard, Folio essais, 2006), p.15.

103
Clement Greenberg, "Modernist Painting", *Arts Yearbook 4*, New York (1961), pp.101–08 (p.101).

104
Yves Klein, "L'aventure monochrome: l'épopée monochrome", in Yves Klein, Marie-Anne Sichère and Didier Semin (ed.), *Le Dépassement de la problématique de l'art et autres écrits* (Paris: École Nationale Supérieure des Beaux-Arts, 2003), pp.223–68 (p.228).

105
Yves Klein, "L'évolution de l'art vers l'immatériel, conférence à la Sorbonne" (lecture given on 3 June 1959 in the Sorbonne Grand Amphitheatre in Paris), in Yves Klein, *Le Dépassement de la problématique de l'art et autres écrits*, op.cit., pp.118–53 (p.138).

106
Yves Klein, "Ainsi, le Bleu tangible et visible sera dehors, à l'extérieur, dans la rue, et, à l'intérieur, ce sera l'immatérialisation du Bleu" in "Préparation et présentation de l'exposition du 28 avril 1958 chez Irio Clort, 3, rue des Beaux Arts, à Paris, 'La spécialisation de la sensibilité à l'état matière première en sensibilité picturale stabilisée'. Époque pneumatique".

107
Yves Klein, "L'évolution de l'art vers l'immatériel, conférence à la Sorbonne", op.cit., pp.145–46.

108
Ann Temkin, "Color Shift", in *Color Chart: Reinventing Color, 1950 to Today*, op.cit. p.17.

109
Ibid., p.16.

110
Dora Vallier, *L'Intérieur de l'art. Entretiens avec Braque, Léger, Villon, Miró, Brancusi (1954-1960)* (Paris: Seuil, 1982), p.49.

111
Georges Roque, "La réception de Chevreul par les peintres", op.cit., p.247.

112
František Kupka, "Couleur et lumière", n.p., n.d., Bibliothèque Kandinsky, Fonds František Kupka.

113
Ibid., p.8.

PHOTOGRAPHIC CREDITS

© Akg-images: p. 226 (fig. 6) / © bpk/Nationalgalerie, SMB, Verein der Freunde der Nationalgalerie / Jörg P. Anders: / © Ugo Carmeni. Courtesy of Jim Dine and Templon, Paris – Brussels – New York: p. 198 (fig. 3) / © Centre Pompidou, MNAM-CCI/Jacques Faujour/Dist. GrandPalaisRmn: pp. 12, 67, 174 (fig. 5) / © Centre Pompidou, MNAM-CCI/Jacqueline Hyde/Dist. GrandPalaisRmn: pp. 51, 168, 183 / © Centre Pompidou, MNAM-CCI/Audrey Laurans/Dist. GrandPalaisRmn: pp. 31, 32, 46, 82 (figs. 5–7), 105 (fig. 3), 106 (fig. 5), 115, 121, 139, 141, 148, 159, 162 / © Centre Pompidou, MNAM-CCI/Hélène Mauri/Dist. GrandPalaisRmn: pp. 47, 66, 86, 93, 133, 157, 180, 188, 190–91 / © Centre Pompidou, MNAM-CCI/Georges Meguerditchian/Dist. GrandPalaisRmn: pp. 24, 29, 48, 56, 64 (fig. 10), 167, 179, 182, 185, 192 / © Centre Pompidou, MNAM-CCI/Philippe Migeat/Dist. GrandPalaisRmn: pp. 33, 34–35, 36–37, 38, 49, 50, 53, 58, 64 (fig. 9), 71, 72, 75, 87, 88, 91, 95, 100, 112, 114, 118, 119, 122, 127 (fig. 3), 134, 137, 142–43, 144, 145, 147, 160–61, 163, 165, 176 (fig. 9), 186–87, 189, 193, 229 (fig. 8) / © Centre Pompidou, MNAM-CCI/Jean-Claude Planchet/Dist. RMN-GP: pp. 92, 117, 138, 176 (fig. 10) / © Centre Pompidou, MNAM-CCI/Bertrand Prévost/Dist. GrandPalaisRmn: pp. 10, 55, 68–69, 73, 74, 76, 97, 99, 111, 153 (fig. 1), 164 / © Centre Pompidou, MNAM-CCI/Adam Rzepka/Dist. RMN-GP: p. 52 / © Centre Pompidou, MNAM-CCI/Jean-François Tomasian/Dist. RMN-GP: p. 89 / © Centre Pompidou, MNAM-CCI/Service de la documentation photographique du MNAM/Dist. GrandPalaisRmn: pp. 28, 44 (fig. 7), 54, 57, 96, 108–109, 113, 127 (fig. 2), 135, 158, 174 (fig. 6), 181, 229 (fig. 7) / © Christie's Images/Bridgeman Images: pp. 18 (fig. 6), 43 (fig. 3) / © Collection Raphaël Gaillarde, Dist. GrandPalaisRmn / Raphaël Gaillarde: p. 201 (fig. 6) / Photo © Giorgio Colombo, Milan: p. 82 (fig. 8)

Courtesy Gagosian, photograph Mike Bruce: p. 130 (fig. 10)
Courtesy of the artist and Perrotin: p. 202 (fig. 7)
Courtesy Perrotin, photograph Pierre Antoine: p. 43 (fig. 5)
Courtesy of the George Eastman Museum, Rochester, New York: p. 153 (fig. 3)
Courtesy National Gallery of Art, Washington: p. 106 (fig. 6)
Courtesy Venus Over Manhattan, New York: p. 84 (fig. 10)
Courtesy Walker Art Center, Minneapolis: p. 44 (fig. 10)
Courtesy Yale University Art Gallery, New Haven: p. 17 (fig. 5)
Courtesy David Zwirner: p. 18 (fig. 8)
Courtesy of David Zwirner Gallery, New York: p. 63 (fig. 5)
Courtesy of David Zwirner Gallery, New York: p. 128 (fig. 7)

© Detroit Institute of Arts/Bridgeman images: p. 173 (fig. 4) / © 2025 Digital image, The Museum of Modern Art, New York/Scala: pp. 18 (fig. 7), 43 (fig. 4), 44 (fig. 9), 64 (fig. 8), 106 (fig. 4), 125 (fig. 1), 154 (fig. 4), 174 (fig. 7) / © Droits réservés/LaM/Lille Métropole Musée d'art moderne, d'art contemporain et d'art brut, Villeneuve d'Ascq: p. 198 (fig. 4) / © Estorick Collection / Bridgeman Images: p. 225 (fig. 4) / © Établissement public du Palais de la Porte-Dorée / Collection du Musée national de l'histoire de l'immigration: p. 128 (fig. 6) / © Philippe Fuzeau: p. 154 (fig. 5) / Glenstone Museum. Photo: Ron Amstutz: p. 105 (fig. 2) / © GrandPalaisRmn (Musée national Picasso-Paris)/Adrien Didierjean: p. 17 (fig. 2) / © GrandPalaisRmn (musée d'Orsay)/Hervé Lewandowski: p. 63 (fig. 4) / © GrandPalaisRmn (musée d'Orsay)/Patrice Schmidt: p. 64 (figs. 6–7) / © GrandPalaisRmn/image GrandPalaisRmn: p. 173 (fig. 1) / © Ville de Grenoble/ Musée de Grenoble-J.L. Lacroix: p. 127 (fig. 5) / © Guerrilla Girls. Courtesy guerrillagirls.com, Photo © courtesy of the artist: p. 153 (fig. 2) / © Paul Hester. Courtesy of the Rothko Chapel: p. 201 (fig. 5) / © 2025 Image copyright The Metropolitan Museum of Art/Art Resource/Scala, Florence: pp. 81 (fig. 3), 127 (fig. 4), 222 (fig. 3) / Kunstmuseum Den Haag, The Hague: p. 17 (fig. 3) / Kunstmuseum Den Haag, The Hague – bequest Salomon B. Slijper: p. 17 (fig. 4) / © François Lagarde / opale.photo : p. 197 (figs. 1–2) / © Mayor Gallery, London / Bridgeman Images: p. 20 (fig. 9) / © Mike Lundgren: p. 130 (fig. 9) / © 2010 MIT. Harold E. Edgerton. Courtesy MIT Museum: p. 44 (fig. 8) / Photograph © 2025 Museum of Fine Arts, Boston: p. 81 (fig. 4) / © MM Studio: pp. 206–207, 208–209, 210–11, 212–13, 214–15, 216–17, 218–19 / © National Galleries of Scotland – Antonia Reeve: p. 63 (fig. 2) / © Gerhard Richter 2025 (19022025): p. 21 (fig. 10) / Photo © Don Ross: p. 43 (fig. 6) / © Royal Academy of Arts, London: p. 222 (fig. 2) / © Ed Ruscha. Courtesy of the artist and Gagosian: p. 84 (fig. 9) / © Sotheby's/ Akg-images: p. 105 (fig. 1) / « Source BnF »: p. 41 (fig. 1), p. 173 (fig. 3) / The Picture Art Collection/Alamy banque d'images: p. 173 (fig. 2) / Van Gogh Museum, Amsterdam (Vincent van Gogh Foundation): pp. 63 (fig. 3), 79 (fig. 1), 176 (fig. 8) / © Waddesdon Image Library: p. 221 (fig. 1)

COPYRIGHTS

© ADAGP, Paris, 2025 for the works of Jean Arp (p. 52, 88), Martin Barré (p. 46), Joseph Beuys (p. 63 [fig. 2]), Vincent Bioulès (p. 67), Georges Braque (p. 189), Pierre Buraglio (p. 96), Enrico Castellani (p. 56), Auguste Chabaud (p. 114), Marc Chagall (pp. 47, 134, 145), Giorgio De Chirico (p. 138), Jim Dine (p. 198 [fig. 3]), Otto Dix (p. 105 [fig. 3]), Piero Dorazio (p. 58 [detail], 75), Jean Dubuffet (p. 182), Dan Flavin (p. 63 [fig. 5], p. 128 [fig. 7]), Nathalie Goncharova (pp. 48, 72), Raymond Hains (p. 10), František Kupka (pp. 66, 73, 91, 106 [fig. 5], 117, 157), Mikhail Fiodorowitsch Larionov (p. 86), Fernand Léger (p. 12), Richard-Paul Lohse (p. 33), Heinz Mack (p. 43 [fig. 5]), René Magritte (p. 95), Piero Manzoni (pp. 49, 50), Brice Marden (p. 130 [fig. 10]), François Morellet (p. 64 [fig. 10]), Louise Nevelson (p. 168 [detail], 183), Michel Parmentier (p. 113), Otto Piene (p. 55), Martial Raysse (p. 137), Ad Reinhardt (p. 174 [fig. 6]), Nicolas Schöffer (p. 229 [fig. 8]), Frank Stella (p. 174 [fig. 7]), Léopold Survage (p. 229 [fig. 7]), Niele Toroni (p. 87), Raoul Ubac (p. 100 [detail], 119), Günther Uecker (p. 38 [detail], 53), Henry Valensi (p. 164), Bernar Venet (p. 193), Claude Viallat (p. 64 [fig. 9]), Maurice de Vlaminck (p. 112) / © The Josef and Anni Albers Foundation/ADAGP, Paris, 2025: p. 127 (fig. 4) / © The Estate of Francis Bacon/All rights reserved/ADAGP, Paris and DACS, London / 2025: pp. 111, 133 / © All rights reserved for Marcelle Cahn: p. 57 / © 2025 Calder Foundation, New York/ADAGP, Paris: p. 192 / © Salvador Dalí, Fundació Gala-Salvador Dalí/ADAGP, Paris 2025: pp. 190–91 / © DB-ADAGP, Paris 2025: p. 201 (fig. 6) / © Thomas Demand/ADAGP, Paris 2025: p. 76 (detail), 97 / © The Easton Foundation/ ADAGP, Paris, 2025 Glenstone Museum: p. 105 (fig. 2) / © Estate of Robert Filliou. Courtesy the Estate of Robert Filliou & Peter Freeman, Inc. New York / Paris: p. 167 / © Fondazione Lucio Fontana, Milan/by SIAE/ADAGP, Paris, 2025: p. 148 (detail), 159, 162 / © Llyn Foulkes: p. 158 / © 2022 Helen Frankenthaler Foundation, Inc./ADAGP, Paris, 2025: p. 130 (fig. 9) / © Succession Alberto Giacometti/ADAGP, Paris 2025: p. 54 / © Jasper Johns/ADAGP, Paris, 2025: p. 20 (fig. 9), 185 / Donald Judd Art © Judd Foundation/ADAGP, Paris, 2025: p. 18 (fig. 8) / © Ellsworth Kelly Foundation: pp. 34–35 / © Succession Yves Klein c/o ADAGP, Paris, 2025: pp. 93, 135 / © The Willem de Kooning Foundation/ADAGP, Paris 2025: p. 181 / © Tamara de Lempicka Estate, LLC/ADAGP, Paris, 2025: p. 18 (fig. 7) / © Successió Miró/ADAGP, Paris, 2025: pp. 82 (figs. 5–7), 89 / © Olivier Mosset: p. 165 / © 2025 The Barnett Newman Foundation/ADAGP, Paris: pp. 15 (fig. 1), 18 (fig. 6) / © 2023 The Pollock-Krasner Foundation/Artists Rights Society (ARS), New York: pp. 17 (fig. 5), 44 (fig. 9), 176 (fig. 9), 179 / © Robert Rauschenberg Foundation/ADAGP, Paris, 2025: p. 43 (fig. 6) / © 2000 Kate Rothko Prizel & Christopher Rothko/ADAGP, Paris, 2025: p. 81 (fig. 2) / © 1998 Kate Rothko Prizel & Christopher Rothko/ADAGP, Paris, 2025: pp. 106 (fig. 6), 201 (fig. 5) / © 2025 Robert Ryman/ADAGP, Paris: p. 44 (fig. 7) / © Succession Sanejouand: p. 144 / © Richard Tuttle: p. 139 / © Christophe Vigouroux, 2025: pp. 122 (detail), 142–143 / © The Andy Warhol Foundation for the Visual Arts, Inc./Licensed by ADAGP, Paris, 2025: pp. 108–109, 154 (fig. 4) / © Tarsila do Amaral Licenciamiento e Empreendimentos S.A./Cnap: p. 127 (fig. 5) / © Estate of Jean-Michel Basquiat Licensed by Artestar, New York: pp. 186–87 / © Georg Baselitz 2025: pp. 68–69 / © General Idea 1994: p. 128 (fig. 8) / © 2025 The Estate of Jack Goldstein: p. 84 (fig. 10) / © The Estate of Philip Guston: pp. 160–61 / © Guerrilla Girls. Courtesy guerrillagirls.com, Photo © courtesy of the artist: p. 153 (fig. 2) / © 2010 MIT. Harold E. Edgerton. Courtesy of the MIT Museum: p. 44 (fig. 8) / © 2025 Mondrian/ Holtzman Trust: p. 17 (figs. 3–4) / © 1991 Hans Namuth Estate. Courtesy Center for Creative Photography, University of Arizona: p. 176 (fig. 9) / © Succession Picasso 2025: pp. 17 (fig. 2), 81 (fig. 3), 92, 141 / © Pracusa SA: p. 31 / © Arnulf Rainer: p. 176 (fig. 10) / © Gerhard Richter 2025 (19022025): p. 21 (fig. 10) / © Gerhard Richter 2024 (27112024): cover pages, pp. 36–37 / © Ed Ruscha. Courtesy of the artist and Gagosian: p. 84 (fig. 9) / © Claude Rutault: p. 202 (fig. 7) / © Chéri Samba. Courtesy Galerie MAGNIN-A: p. 128 (fig. 6) / © Cindy Sherman. Courtesy the artist/Cnap: p. 154 (fig. 5) / Mark Tansey © copyright retained by the artist: p. 44 (fig. 10) / © James Turrell: p. 82 (fig. 8) / Courtesy Archivio Eredi Nanda Vigo: p. 42 (fig. 2) / © Carrie Mae Weems. Courtesy of the artist, Gladstone, New York, Fraenkel Gallery, San Francisco, Galerie Barbara Thumm, Berlin, and the George Eastman Museum, Rochester: p. 153 (fig. 3) / Van Gogh Museum, Amsterdam (Vincent van Gogh Foundation): pp. 63 (fig. 3), 79 (fig. 1) / Van Gogh Museum, Amsterdam (purchased with support from the VriendenLoterij and the members of the Yellow House Circle): p. 176 (fig. 8)

Public domain for the works by:

Alphonse Allais: p. 41 (fig. 1) / Pierre Bonnard: p. 74 / Robert Delaunay: pp. 24 (detail), 28, 29 / André Derain: p. 125 (fig. 1) / George Field: p. 222 (fig. 2) / Paul Gauguin: p. 64 (fig. 6) / Francisco de Goya: p. 173 (fig. 3) / Arshile Gorky: p. 71 / Juan Gris: p. 127 (fig. 3) / Winslow Homer: p. 81 (fig. 4) / Wassily Kandinsky: pp. 99, 127 (fig. 2), 226 (fig. 5) / Paul Klee: p. 188 / Kazimir Malevich: pp. 43 (fig. 4), 174 (fig. 5), 180 / Édouard Manet: p. 63 (fig. 4) / Henri Matisse: p. 64 (fig. 8), 106 (fig. 4), 121, 147, 163 / Amedeo Modigliani: p. 115 / Piet Mondrian: p. 17 / Claude Monet: p. 43 (fig. 3), 173 (fig. 1) / David Ramsay Hay: p. 222 (fig. 3) / Luigi Russolo: p. 225 (fig. 4) / Charles-Germain de Saint-Aubin: p. 221 (fig. 1) / Egon Schiele: p. 105 (fig. 1) / Arnold Schönberg: p. 226 (fig. 6) / Paul Sérusier: p. 64 (fig. 7) / Paul Signac: p. 173 (fig. 2) / Chaïm Soutine: p. 118 / Félix Vallotton: p. 176 (fig. 8) / Theo Van Doesburg: p. 32 / Vincent van Gogh: pp. 63 (fig. 3), 79 (fig. 1) / Johannes Vermeer: p. 61 (fig. 1) / Gerda Wegener: p. 153 (fig. 1) / James Abbott McNeill Whistler: p. 173 (fig. 4)

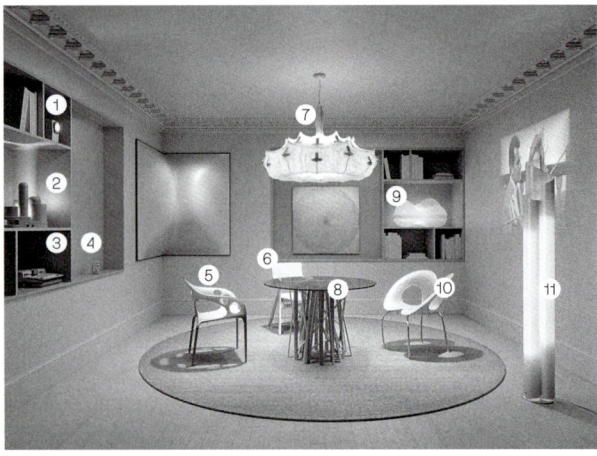

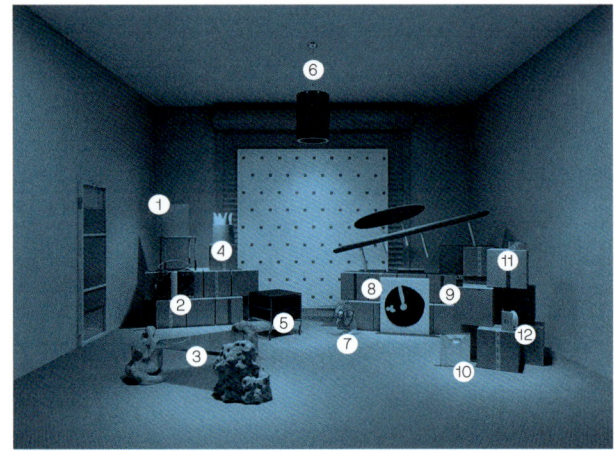

Pages 206–07 – *White for a Library*

Pages 208–09 – *Blue for a Garage*

1   Dieter Rams
    D6 slide projector, 1963
    Plastic and metal
    18 × 20 × 10 cm
    Manufactured by Braun AG,
    Frankfurt am Main (Germany)
    Gift of Braun in 1992
    AM 1993-1-578
    © Dieter Rams

2   Gae Aulenti
    Rimorchiatore table lamp, 1967
    Cast iron, lacquered aluminium sheet
    37 × 32 × 16 cm
    Commissioned by
    Pontana Arte (Italy)
    Purchase in 2009
    AM 2009-1-35
    © Gae Aulenti

3   Richard Sapper
    IBM-PC Convertible, 1986
    Plastic case, metal handle
    54 × 31 × 35 cm
    Manufactured by IBM,
    New York (USA)
    Gift of IBM in 1992
    AM 1993-1-267
    © Richard Sapper

4   Luigi Colani
    Lady concept camera, 1982
    Prototype
    13 × 8 × 4 cm
    Manufactured by Canon France,
    La Garenne-Colombes (France)
    Gift of Strafor in 1992
    AM 1992-1-416
    © Luigi Colani

5   Ross Lovegrove
    Supernatural chair, 2005–2008
    Polypropylene monocoque
    79 × 64 × 56 cm
    Gift of Moroso in 2017
    AM 2017-1-73 (1)
    © Ross Lovegrove

6   Antonio Citterio
    Dolly chair, 1995
    Structure and seat in high-strength
    polypropylene, fibreglass filler
    additive, solid colouring
    81 × 52 × 55 cm
    Commissioned by Kartell,
    Noviglio (Italy)
    Gift of Kartell in 2000
    AM 2000-1-60
    © All rights reserved

7   Marcel Wanders
    Zeppelin, 2005
    Cocoon resin, crystal, PMMA, steel
    Height: 74 cm
    Diameter: 110 cm
    Gift of FLOS SpA in 2016
    AM 2016-1-53
    © Marcel Wanders

8   Patrick Jouin
    Table Solid T1 [*Solid T1 table*], 2004
    3D printing (epoxy resin,
    stereolithography [SLA])
    Height: 73 cm
    Diameter: 110 cm
    Commissioned and manufactured
    by MGX by Materialise,
    Leuven (Belgium)
    Purchase in 2010
    AM 2010-1-64
    © Studio Patrick Jouin iD

9   Ross Lovegrove
    Cosmic Landscape lamp, 2009–11
    Polymer
    44 × 48 × 80 cm
    Gift of Artemide in 2017
    AM 2017-1-67
    © Ross Lovegrove

10 Ron Arad
    Ripple chair, 2005–2006
    Moulded polypropylene shell,
    varnished steel base
    80 × 68 × 59 cm
    Commissioned by Moroso,
    Udine (Italy)
    Gift of Moroso in 2009
    AM 2009-1-99
    © Ron Arad & Associates Ltd

11 Vico Magistretti
    Chimera lamp, 1969
    Polymethyl methacrylate
    (PMMA), metal
    180 × 22 cm
    Commissioned by Artemide,
    Pregnana Milanese (Italy)
    AM 2013-1-28
    Inventory listing in 2013
    © Vico Magistretti

1   George James Sowden
    Prototype chair, 1981
    Structure in painted metal
    and painted wood
    90 × 40 × 46 cm
    Gift of the Amis du Centre
    Pompidou, Groupe d'Acquisition
    pour le Design in 2019
    AM 2019-1-88
    © George James Sowden

2   Philippe Starck
    Bouteille Vittel [*Vittel bottle*], 1984
    Plastic material
    50 × 48 cm
    Manufactured by Vittel,
    Vélizy-Villacoublay (France)
    Gift of the artist in 2005
    AM 2005-1-64
    © Philippe Starck

3   Garouste & Bonetti
    Table basse Rocher [*Rocher
    low table*], 1983
    Sheet steel, enamel paint, stone
    40 × 105 × 105 cm
    Commissioned by Galerie Neotu,
    Paris (France)
    Purchase in 1993
    AM 1993-1-465
    © ADAGP, Paris, 2025

4   Philippe Starck
    Tabouret Bubu 1er
    [*Bubu 1er stool*], 1989
    Injected polypropylene,
    opaque blue colouring
    Height: 43.5 cm
    Diameter: 33 cm
    Commissioned by XO, Servon (France)
    Gift of XO in 2007
    AM 2007-1-120, © Philippe Starck

5   Antonio Citterio
    Mobil container, 1995
    Chrome-plated tubular frame,
    drawers in acrylonitrile butadiene
    styrene (ABS)
    48 × 52 × 48 cm
    Commissioned by Kartell,
    Noviglio (Italy) (with the
    collaboration of Glen Oliver Löw)
    Gift of Kartell in 1999
    AM 1999-1-170, © All rights reserved

6   Carlotta de Bevilacqua
    TET suspension lamp, 2005
    Varnished metal, 90°
    and 45° light beam
    Height: 48 cm
    Diameter: 35 cm
    Manufactured by Danese Milano,
    Milan (Italy)
    Gift of Danese Milano in 2006
    AM 2006-1-21, © Carlotta
    de Bevilacqua and Danese

7   Calor
    Fan no. 977, c. 1950
    Plastic and steel
    40 × 34 × 25 cm
    Manufactured by Calor, Lyon (France)
    Gift of Mr. Christian Dechaux in 2009
    AM 2009-1-128
    © Calor

8   Itsuko Hasegawa
    Armchair, n.d.
    Textile and lacquered steel
    Gift of the artist in 2011
    AM 2012-1-104
    © Itsuko Hasegawa

9   Antoine Cahen
    Lampe SL [*SL lamp*], 1993
    Plastic material
    9 × 6.5 × 2.5 cm
    Manufactured by Leclanché (France)
    Gift of Prohelvetia, Centre culturel
    suisse in 2006
    AM 2006-1-41 (1)
    © Antoine Cahen

10 Raymond Loewy
    Bathroom scales, 1952
    Lacquered metal and chrome
    6 × 26 × 30 cm
    Manufacturer: Borg-Erickson
    Corp., Chicago (USA)
    Gift of the Société des Amis
    du Musée National d'Art
    Moderne in 2001
    AM 2000-1-93, Courtesy
    of Raymond Loewy Estate

11 Paul Rand
    IBM Tech III ribbon packaging,
    1974–90
    Printed and folded cardboard
    15.7 × 7.5 × 2.6 cm
    Manufactured by IBM,
    New York (USA)
    Gift of IBM in 1992
    AM 1993-1-151, © All rights reserved

12 matali crasset
    Soundsation, 1996–98
    FM clock radio
    Acrylonitrile butadiene styrene
    (ABS) plastic and rubber
    16 × 9 × 11.2 cm
    Artistic direction: Philippe Starck
    Commisioned by Lexon Design
    Concept, Argenteuil (France)
    in partnership with Thomson
    Multimedia
    Gift of Lexon Design Concept
    in 2000
    AM 2000-1-108 (2)
    matali crasset © ADAGP,
    Paris, 2025

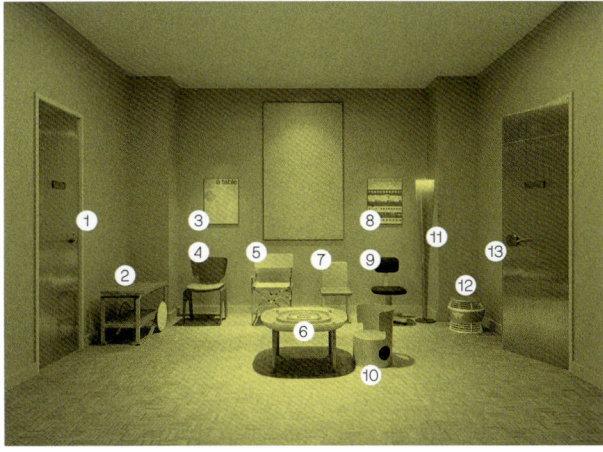

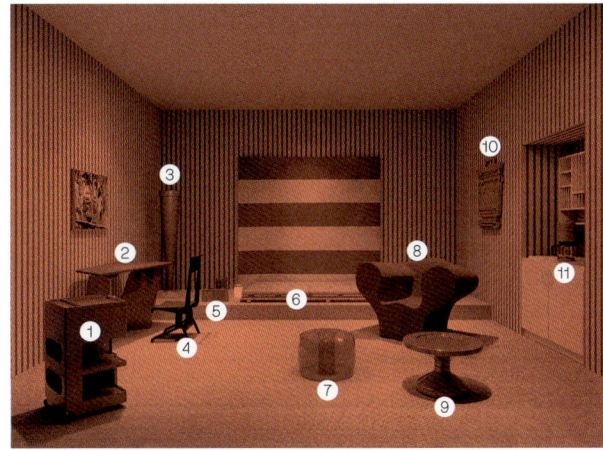

Pages 210–11 – *Yellow for a Waiting Room*

Pages 212–13 – *Red for a Student's Room*

1 Philippe Starck
Poignée de porte [*Door handle*], n.d.
Stainless steel
8 × 13 cm
Commissioned by Kleis
Gift of the artist in 2005
AM 2005-1-137, © Philippe Starck

2 Alvar Aalto
Table no. 98, 1936
Solid birch, curved glulam, plywood
56 × 46 × 90 cm
Manufactured by Oy Huonekalu-ja
rakennustyötehdas, Helsinki (Finland);
Commissioned by Artek, Helsinki
(Finland), after 1936
Purchase in 1993, AM 1993-1-613
© Alvar Aalto Foundation

3 Jean Widmer
Poster 'à table', 1970
Fluorescent print and black ink
on paper pasted on feather board
64.6 × 48.2 cm
Inventory listing in 1992
AM 1993-1-298, © ADAGP, Paris, 2025

4 Kenzo Tange
Chair, 1957
Beech plywood, textile and metal,
with removable cushion
79 × 48 × 57 cm
Gift of Galerie Downtown in 2013
AM 2014-1-3, © All rights reserved

5 Gae Aulenti
April folding chair, 2008
Stainless steel, Vela fabric
86 × 51 × 55 cm
Commissioned by Zanotta, Nova
Milanese (Italy)
Gift of Zanotta in 2009
AM 2009-1-109, © Gae Aulenti

6 Radi Designers
Table basse [*Low table*], 2001
Tray in PETG thermoformed using
the twin sheet process,
legs in solid wood
44 × 75 × 75 cm
Prototype created by Ufacto
(David Toppani) in collaboration
with Durotherm
Donation by the V.I.A./Industries
françaises de l'ameublement, 2010
Support for creation in 2001
AM 2010-1-99, © Radi Designers

7 George James Sowden
Prototype chair, 1999
Painted wood and metal tubes
75 × 40 × 40 cm
Gift of the Amis du Centre
Pompidou, Groupe d'Acquisition pour
le Design in 2019, AM 2019-1-74
© George James Sowden

8 Jean Widmer
Poster 'modèles réduits', 1973
Yellow background, silkscreen
on paper
65 × 49.9 cm
Inventory listing in 1992
AM 1993-1-322
© ADAGP, Paris, 2025

9 Ettore Sottsass
Z9R office chair, 1968–73
Cast aluminium, acrylonitrile
butadiene styrene (ABS), steel,
rubber, synthetic textile,
polyurethane foam
82 × 43 × 56 cm
Manufactured by Olivetti S.p.A,
Ivrea (Italy)
Gift of The Gallery Mourmans
in 2003, AM 2003-1-323
©erede Ettore Sottsass,
ADAGP, Paris, 2025

10 Jean-Louis Avril
Siège enfant « Elephant »
[*Elephant child's seat*], 1967
Lacquered celloderm cardboard
Height: 50 cm
Width between armrests: 38 cm
Seat diameter: 35.3 cm
Commissioned by Marty-L.A.C.
(Établissements Les Applications
du Carton)
Gift of the Utopie Gallery in 2014
AM 2014-1-62, © Jean-Louis Avril

11 Marc Sadler
Mite lamp, 2001
Brushed steel stand, glass fabric
with Kevlar thread
185 × 21 × 21 cm
Commissioned by Foscarini
Murano, Marcon (Italy)
Gift of Foscarini Murano in 2003
AM 2002-1-25, © Marc Sadler

12 Calor
Cooling fan no. 955, 1952
Belt and top in lacquered metal,
plastic grilles
Height: 37 cm
Diameter: 44 cm
Manufactured by Calor, Lyon (France)
Gift of Calor in 1992
AM 1992-1-425, © Calor

13 Philippe Starck
Poignée de porte [*Door handle*], n.d.
Stainless cast aluminium
Height: 44.5 cm
Diameter: 13 cm
Commissioned by Kleis
Gift of the artist in 2005
AM 2005-1-136, © Philippe Starck

1 Joe Colombo
Boby trolley, 1970
Acrylonitrile butadiene styrene (ABS),
injection moulding
74 × 43 × 43 cm
Commissioned by B Line, Grisignano
di Zocco (Italy)
Gift of Strafor in 1997
AM 1997-1-103
© Ignazia Favata, Studio Joe
Colombo

2 Bernard Cache, Patrick Beaucé
Table Objectile [*Objectile table*],
2003–2005
Medium
73 × 152 × 75 cm
Purchase in 2006
AM 2006-1-4
© Bernard Cache, © Patrick Beaucé

3 Philippe Starck
Vase Popopo [*Popopo vase*], 1991
Polyester resin and aluminium
Height: 158 cm
Diameter: 40 cm
Commissioned by XO, Servon
(France)
Gift of XO in 2007
AM 2007-1-140
© Philippe Starck

4 Jean Prouvé
Chaise inclinable
[*Reclining chair*], 1929
Lacquered sheet steel, canvas
95 × 45 × 52 cm
Gift of Famille Prouvé in 1993
AM 1993-1-757
© ADAGP, Paris, 2025

5 Achille Castiglioni
FD 1101 radio, 1967
Acrylonitrile butadiene styrene (ABS),
rubber, electronic components
17.5 × 35 × 9 cm
Manufactured by Brionvega,
Lissone (Italy)
Purchase in 1992
AM 1992-1-240
© Fondazione Achille Castiglioni

6 matali crasset
Quand Simon monte à Paris, 1995–98
Hospitality column with bed,
lamp and alarm clock
190 × 118 × 11.5 cm
Commissioned by Domeau & Pérès,
La Garenne-Colombes (France)
Gift of the Société des Amis du
Musée National d'Art Moderne, 1999
AM 1999-1-173 and AM 1999-1-174
matali crasset © ADAGP, Paris, 2025

7 Anonymous
Pouf, 1968–70
Polyvinyl chloride (PVC)
Height: 32 cm
Diameter: 45 cm
Purchase in 2007
AM 2007-1-19

8 Ron Arad
Big Soft Easy armchair, 1990
Upholstered in polyurethane and
wood structure, covered in 100%
brushed wool warp and weft fabric
in bright red, bevelled armrest foam
92 × 125 × 93 cm
Commissioned by Moroso,
Udine (Italy)
Purchase in 1992
AM 1992-1-252
© Ron Arad & Associates Ltd

9 Achille Castiglioni,
Pier Giacomo Castiglioni
KS 4901 table, 1968
Red lacquered acrylonitrile butadiene
styrene (ABS), injection moulding
Height: 38 cm
Diameter: 60 cm
Base diameter: 40 cm
Commissioned by Kartell,
Noviglio (Italy)
Gift of Kartell in 2001
AM 2001-1-158
© Fondazione Achille Castiglioni
© Pier Giacomo Castiglioni

10 Ettore Sottsass
Valentine poster, 1969
Impact polystyrene (SB)
Thermoforming for the typewriter
advertising campaign
76.5 × 62 × 2 cm
Manufactured by Olivetti S.p.A,
Ivrea (Italy)
Gift of the Société des Amis
du Musée National d'Art Moderne
in 1999
AM 1998-1-17
©erede Ettore Sottsass,
ADAGP, Paris, 2025

11 Florian Seiffert
KF 20 coffee-maker, 1972
Acrylonitrile butadiene styrene (ABS)
Height: 39 cm
Diameter: 21 cm
Manufactured by Braun AG,
Frankfurt am Main (Germany)
Gift of Braun in 1992
AM 1993-1-514
© Braun Gmbh

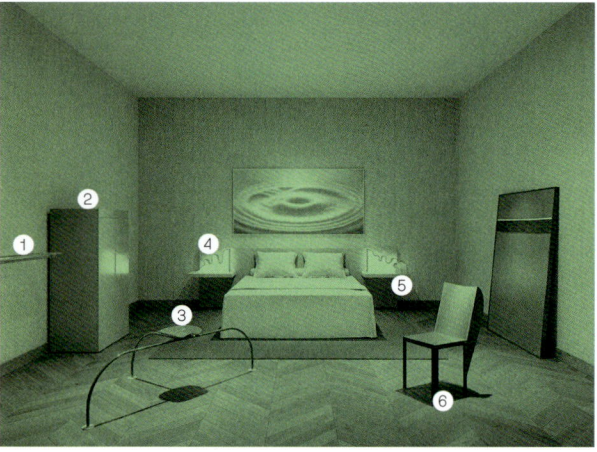

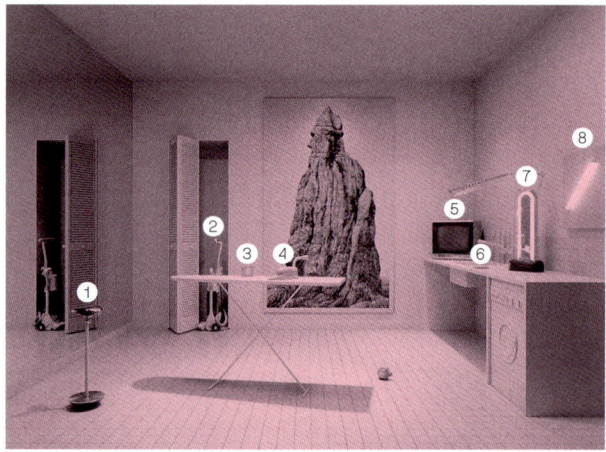

Pages 214–15 – *Green for a Bedroom*

Pages 216–17 – *Pink for a Laundry Room*

1 Radi Designers
Étagère murale [*Wall shelf*], 2001
Glycolised polyethylene
terephthalate (PETG) thermoformed
using the twin sheet process
41 × 100 × 30 cm
Donation by the V.I.A./Industries
françaises de l'ameublement, 2010
Support for creation in 2001
AM 2010-1-97
© Radi Designers

2 Michel Cadestin
Armoire [*Cabinet*], 1978
Lacquered metal, adjustable feet
140 × 83 × 47 cm
Commissioned by Strafor (France)
Inventory listing in 2002
AM 2002-1-38
© Design Michel Cadestin

3 Achille Castiglioni,
Pier Giacomo Castiglioni
Allunaggio seat, 1965–80
Frame in enamelled tubular steel,
seat in cast aluminium
47 × 152 × 74 cm
Commissioned by Zanotta,
Nova Milanese (Italy)
Gift of Zanotta in 1999
AM 1999-1-167
© Fondazione Achille Castiglioni,
© Pier Giacomo Castiglioni

4 Superstudio
Onda Italiana lamp, 1966
Prototype, Perspex
34 × 50 × 10 cm
Purchase in 2001
AM 2001-1-161
© Superstudio

5 Ettore Sottsass
Basilico teapot, 1972
Indian Memory Collection
Lacquered wood
17 × 20 cm
Gift of the artist in 1999
AM 1999-1-80
©erede Ettore Sottsass,
ADAGP, Paris, 2025

6 Philippe Starck
Chaise Milch [*Milch chair*], 1988
Sheet steel
79 × 33 × 51 cm
Commissioned by Idée (Japan)
Gift of the artist in 2005
AM 2005-1-68
© Philippe Starck

1 Achille Castiglioni,
Pier Giacomo Castiglioni
Sella seat, 1957
Lacquered steel, stainless steel,
cast iron, bicycle saddle (leather)
70 × 30 × 28 cm
Commissioned by Zanotta, Nova
Milanese (Italy)
Gift of Zanotta in 1999
AM 1999-1-166
© Fondazione Achille Castiglioni
© Pier Giacomo Castiglioni

2 James Dyson
G-Force vacuum cleaner, 1986
Body in acrylonitrile butadiene
styrene (ABS) and polycarbonate,
telescopic tube
Dual cyclone technology
118 × 31 × 37 cm
Gift of Dyson in 2001
AM 2001-1-85
© Dyson

3 Marc Berthier
Réveil Tykho Ana
[*Tykho Ana alarm clock*], 1997
One-piece silicone rubber
8.5 × 8 × 4.5 cm
Commissioned by Lexon Design
Concept, Argenteuil (France)
Gift of Lexon Design Concept
in 2000
AM 2000-1-104 (4)
© Elise Berthier, 2025

4 Michele De Lucchi
Iron, 1979
Model, painted wood
18 × 38 × 12 cm
Gift of the artist in 2004
AM 2003-1-372
© Michele De Lucchi

5 Brionvega
Helios VR 20 television, 1970
Enclosure in acrylonitrile
butadiene styrene (ABS),
painted plywood, glass, metal
47 × 48 × 34 cm
Manufacturer: Brionvega,
Lissone (Italy)
Purchase in 1992
AM 1992-1-234
© All rights reserved

6 Marc Berthier
Calculatrice Tykho Euro
[*Tykho Euro calculator*], 1995
One-piece silicone rubber
1 × 11.5 × 11.5 cm
Commissioned by Lexon Design
Concept, Argenteuil (France)
Gift of Lexon Design Concept
in 2000
AM 2000-1-105 (3)
© Elise Berthier, 2025

7 Ettore Sottsass
Astéroïde lamp, 1968
Plexiglas, lacquered metal
73 × 27 × 15 cm
Commissioned by Poltronova,
Florence (Italy)
Purchase in 2005
AM 2005-1-154
©erede Ettore Sottsass,
ADAGP, Paris, 2025

8 Martine Bedin
Applique Negresco
[*Negresco wall lamp*], 1981
Laminate, fluorescent tube
13 × 60 × 60 cm
Commissioned by Memphis,
Pregnana Milanese (Italy)
Purchase in 2004
AM 2004-1-1
© ADAGP, Paris, 2025

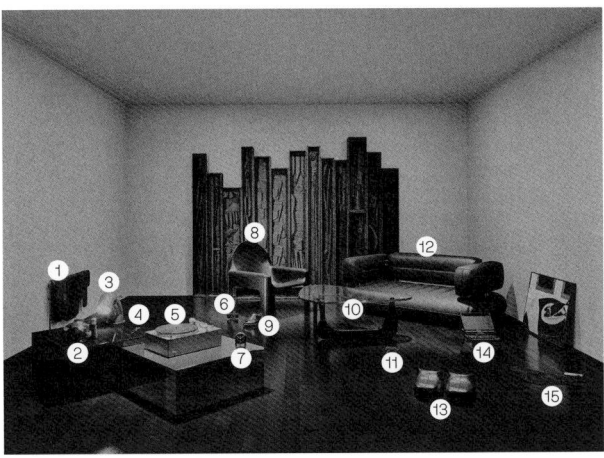

Pages 218–19 – *Black for a Bachelor Flat*

1 Studio GGSV
Radiateur Trou noir
[*Trou Noir radiator*], 2011
Heating project based on
asbestos recycling
Cofalit, copper
56 × 88 × 6 cm
Purchase of the Amis du Centre
Pompidou, Groupe d'Acquisition
pour le Design in 2016
AM 2018-1-94
© All rights reserved

2 Luigi Colani
CB 10 camera, 1982
Painted wood
14 × 18 × 20 cm
Experimental study for Canon
Manufacturer: Canon France,
La Garenne-Colombes (France)
Gift of Strafor in 1992
AM 1992-1-415
© Luigi Colani

3 Cini Boeri
602 lamp, 1968
Polyvinyl chloride (PVC), metal
Height: 27 cm
Depth: 35 cm
Dimension base: 15.5 cm
Commissioned by Arteluce,
Milan (Italy)
Purchase in 2008
AM 2008-1-123
© Cini Boeri

4 Roger Tallon
Montre Led [*LED watch*], 1973–74
Rubber strap, LED
(Light Emitting Diode) display
4.5 × 24 cm
Manufactured by Lip,
Besançon (France)
Purchase in 1995
AM 1995-1-11
© ADAGP, Paris, 2025

5 Dieter Rams
PS 1000 Turntable, 1965
Plastic and metal
43 × 17 × 32 cm
Manufactured by Braun AG,
Frankfurt am Main (Germany)
Gift of Braun in 1993
AM 1993-1-539
© Dieter Rams

6 Leica Camera AG
Série 0 camera, 2000
Die-cast aluminium case covered
in artificial leather, stamped
brass interior
6.5 × 13.3 × 3.9 cm
Manufactured by Leica Camera,
Gennevilliers (France)
Gift of Leica Camera in 2003
AM 2003-1-324
© Leica Camera AG

7 Dieter Rams, Jürgen Greubel
AB 2 alarm clock, 1984
Acrylonitrile butadiene styrene (ABS)
9 × 7.5 × 4 cm
Manufacturer: Braun AG,
Frankfurt am Main (Germany)
Gift of Braun in 1992
AM 1993-1-492
© Dieter Rams, © Braun Gmbh

8 Gae Aulenti
4794 armchair, 1972
Rigid lacquered expanded
polyurethane, reaction moulding (RIM)
77 × 73 × 45 cm
Commissioned by Kartell,
Noviglio (Italy)
Gift of Kartell in 2000
AM 2000-1-43
© Gae Aulenti

9 Philippe Starck
Chaussure [*Shoe*], 2004
Prototype of a low shoe,
leather and rubber
31 × 11.5 cm
Size 44
Manufactured by Heschung,
Steinbourg (France)
Gift of the artist in 2007
AM 2007-1-166
© Philippe Starck

10 Isamu Noguchi
Low table, 1944–47
Base in lacquered birch, glass top
40 × 128 × 92 cm
Commissioned by Herman Miller Inc.,
Zeeland (USA)
Gift of M. Alexander von Vegesack
in 1993
AM 1993-1-654
© All rights reserved

11 Anonymous
Glasses, 1800–1900
Metal, glass
Inventory listing in 1993
AM 1993-1-889

12 Quasar (Nguyen Manh Khan'h, called)
Chesterfield sofa, 1968
Polyvinyl chloride (PVC)
65 × 185 × 98 cm
Commissioned
by Quasar (France)
Purchase in 2007
AM 2007-1-6
© All rights reserved

13 Gaetano Pesce
Shoe, 1975
Polyurethane foam
16 × 41 × 19 cm
Manufactured by Cassina,
Meda (Italy)
Inventory listing in 1996
AM 1996-1-25
© 2025 Gaetano Pesce.
All rights reserved

14 Richard Sapper
*IBM PS/55 Notebook computer
(model)*, 1991
Painted wood
6 × 29 × 33 cm
Made for IBM (USA)
Gift of IBM in 1992
AM 1993-1-256
© Richard Sapper

15 Philippe Starck
Vêtement Starck Naked Puma
[*Starck Naked Puma briefs*], 2004
Men's Lycra briefs
Commissioned by Puma France,
Illkirch-Graffenstaden (France)
Gift of the artist in 2007
AM 2007-1-163
© Philippe Starck

ACKNOWLEDGEMENTS

The curator and Éditions Skira would like to thank all those
who supported this exhibition and its catalogue with unwavering
enthusiasm, as well as the entire team at the Grimaldi Forum
for their availability and professionalism.

Sincere thanks to the "accomplices" who made the exhibition's
"synaesthetic" spaces possible: Agnès Webster and Éric Fabre
from Maison Fragonard, Philippe Maubert from the
Robertet Group, Alexis Dadier, creator of the "coloured"
perfumes, Roque Rivas, designer of the "coloured" sounds,
and Emmanuelle Zoll from IRCAM.

Gratitude is also extended to Marion Mailaender and her team,
who created the "domestic" spaces and their installations
from the Centre Pompidou's design collections.

Éditions Skira warmly thank the authors for their invaluable
contributions to the publication, as well as all the institutions
that made this catalogue possible.

ISBN: 978-2-37074-283-4
© 2025 Grimaldi Forum Monaco
© Éditions du Centre Pompidou, Paris, 2025
© Éditions Skira, 2025

All rights reserved.
No part of this publication may be reproduced, stored in a retrieval system
or transmitted, in any form or by any means, electronic, mechanical, photocopying,
recording or otherwise, without the prior permission of the publisher.

This book has been printed on FSC-certified paper, and all stages
of its manufacture have complied with this certification, which supports
the environmentally appropriate, socially beneficial and economically
viable management of the world's forests, using materials from well-managed
forests, recycled materials and other controlled sources. www.fsc.org

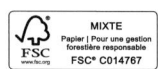

Printed in May 2025 by Graphius, Ghent, Belgium.
Legal deposit June 2025.